A CRITICAL POLITICAL ECONOMY OF THE MIDDLE EAST AND NORTH AFRICA

Stanford Studies *in* Middle Eastern
and Islamic Societies *and* Cultures

A Critical Political Economy of the Middle East and North Africa

Edited by
Joel Beinin, Bassam Haddad,
and Sherene Seikaly

STANFORD UNIVERSITY PRESS
Stanford, California

STANFORD UNIVERSITY PRESS
Stanford, California

Printed in the United States of America on acid-free, archival-quality paper

Library of Congress Cataloging-in-Publication Data
Names: Beinin, Joel, 1948– editor. | Haddad, Bassam, editor. | Seikaly, Sherene, 1971– editor.
Title: A critical political economy of the Middle East and North Africa / Joel Beinin, Bassam Haddad, and Sherene Seikaly.
Other titles: Stanford studies in Middle Eastern and Islamic societies and cultures.
Description: Stanford, California : Stanford University Press, 2021. | Series: Stanford studies in Middle Eastern and Islamic societies and cultures | Includes bibliographical references and index.
Identifiers: LCCN 2020025580 (print) | LCCN 2020025581 (ebook) | ISBN 9781503613836 (cloth) | ISBN 9781503614475 (paperback) | ISBN 9781503614482 (epub)
Subjects: LCSH: Middle East—Economic conditions. | Africa, North—Economic conditions. | Middle East—Economic policy. | Africa, North—Economic policy.
Classification: LCC HC415.15 .C756 2021 (print) | LCC HC415.15 (ebook) | DDC 330.956—dc23
LC record available at https://lccn.loc.gov/2020025580
LC ebook record available at https://lccn.loc.gov/2020025581

Cover design: Christian Fuenfhausen

Typeset by Newgen in 10.5/14.4 Brill

Contents

List of Contributors vii

Introduction 1
Joel Beinin

PART 1. CATEGORIES OF ANALYSIS

1 Landed Property, Capital Accumulation, and Polymorphous Capitalism: Egypt and the Levant 25
Kristen Alff

2 State, Market, and Class: Egypt, Syria, and Tunisia 46
Max Ajl, Bassam Haddad, and *Zeinab Abul-Magd*

3 Ten Propositions on Oil 68
Timothy Mitchell

4 Regional Militaries and the Global Military-Industrial Complex 85
Shana Marshall

PART 2. COUNTRY/REGIONAL STUDIES

5 Rethinking Class and State in the Gulf Cooperation Council 105
Adam Hanieh

6 Capitalism in Egypt, Not Egyptian Capitalism 123
Aaron Jakes and Ahmad Shokr

7 State, Oil, and War in the Formation of Iraq 143
Nida Alahmad

8 Colonial Capitalism and Imperial Myth in French North Africa 161
Muriam Haleh Davis

9 Lebanon Beyond Exceptionalism 179
Ziad M. Abu-Rish

10 The US-Israeli Alliance 196
Joel Beinin

11 Repercussions of Colonialism in the Occupied Palestinian Territories 215
Samia Al-Botmeh

Notes 237
Selected Readings 305
Index 321

Contributors

JOEL BEININ is the Donald J. McLachlan Professor of History and professor of Middle East history, Emeritus, at Stanford University. He has written and coedited twelve books, most recently, *Workers and Thieves: Labor Movements and Popular Uprisings in Tunisia and Egypt*. In 2001-2 he served as president of the Middle East Studies Association of North America (MESA).

BASSAM HADDAD is the director of the Middle East and Islamic Studies Program and an associate professor at the Schar School of Policy and Government at George Mason University. He is the author of *Business Networks in Syria: The Political Economy of Authoritarian Resilience*, and coeditor/founder of *Jadaliyya* e-zine. Bassam received MESA's Jere L. Bacharach Service Award in 2017 for his service to the profession and as executive director of the Arab Studies Institute. He is the founder of the Middle East Studies Pedagogy Project, MESPI.org.

SHERENE SEIKALY is an associate professor of history at the University of California, Santa Barbara. Seikaly's *Men of Capital: Scarcity and Economy in Mandate Palestine* explores how Palestinian capitalists and British colonial officials used economy to shape territory, nationalism, the home, and the body. Her next book project, *From Baltimore to Beirut: On the Question of Palestine*, follows the trajectory of a peripatetic medical doctor to place Palestine in a global history of race, capital, slavery, and dispossession. She is the coeditor of *Journal of Palestine Studies* and cofounder and coeditor of *Jadaliyya* e-zine.

ZEINAB ABUL-MAGD is a professor of Middle Eastern history at Oberlin College. She is the author of *Militarizing the Nation: The Army, Business, and Revolution in Egypt* and *Imagined Empires: A History of Revolt in Egypt*. She earned her PhD in economic history at Georgetown University and BA in political science at Cairo University.

ZIAD ABU-RISH is Co-Director of the MA Program in Human Rights and the Arts and Visiting Associate Professor of Human Rights at Bard College. In 2020–21 he was the American Druze Foundation Fellow in the Center for Contemporary Arab Studies at Georgetown University. He serves as Co-Editor of *Arab Studies Journal* and *Jadaliyya*.

MAX AJL is a post-doctoral researcher at Wageningen University and an associated researcher with the Tunisian Observatory for Food Sovereignty and the Environment. His articles have appeared in the *Journal of Peasant Studies* and *Review of African Political Economy*. He writes on national liberation and postcolonial development in the Arab region.

NIDA ALAHMAD is a lecturer at the University of Edinburgh's Politics and International Relations department. She is currently completing a book manuscript with the tentative title *State Matters: Theorizing the State and Its Experts through the Iraqi Experience*.

KRISTEN ALFF is an assistant professor of history and international studies at North Carolina State University. Her work focuses on business history, the history of capitalism, gender, and agrarian history of the Levant between the late Ottoman and early Mandate periods. Kristen's book manuscript in progress is a global history of capital and property in Palestine.

SAMIA AL-BOTMEH is an assistant professor of economics at Birzeit University. Her areas of interest include gender economics and political economy of development with a special focus on Palestine.

MURIAM HALEH DAVIS is an assistant professor of history at the University of California, Santa Cruz. Her current book project investigates how colonial ideas of Islam underpinned the construction of economic planning initiatives in Algeria, from the liberal capitalist system envisioned by French planners to the socialist policies introduced by the independent Algerian state. She has articles in *Journal of Modern History* and *Journal of European Integration*, and she recently coedited an edited volume entitled *North Africa and the Making of Europe: Governance, Institutions and Culture.*

ADAM HANIEH is a reader in development studies at SOAS, University of London. His research focuses on the political economy of class and state formation, with a geographical emphasis on the Middle East. He is the author of three books, most recently *Money, Markets, and Monarchies: The Gulf Cooperation Council and Political Economy of the Contemporary Middle East*, which was awarded the 2019 International Political Economy Group (IPEG) Book Prize of the British International Studies Association and the 2019 Middle East Political Economy Project Book Prize by the Arab Studies Institute.

AARON G. JAKES is an assistant professor of history at the New School, where he teaches on the modern Middle East and South Asia, comparative studies of colonialism and imperialism, global environmental history, and the historical geography of capitalism. He is the author of *Egypt's Occupation: Colonial Economism and the Crises of Capitalism.*

SHANA MARSHALL is the associate director of the Institute for Middle East Studies at George Washington University. She earned her PhD in international relations and comparative politics of the Middle East at the University of Maryland–College Park in 2012. Her research focuses on the political economy of militaries in Egypt, Jordan, and the UAE, and has appeared in *Middle East Report* (*MERIP*), *International Journal of Middle East Studies*, *Jadaliyya*, and the Carnegie Middle East Center.

TIMOTHY MITCHELL is the Ransford Professor of Middle Eastern Studies at Columbia University. He teaches and writes about the politics of the Arab world, the making of economic ideas and other forms of expert knowledge, and the history and politics of energy. His books include *Colonising Egypt*; *Rule of Experts: Egypt, Technopolitics, Modernity*; and *Carbon Democracy: Political Power in the Age of Oil.*

AHMAD SHOKR is an assistant professor of history at Swarthmore. His writings on historical and contemporary political issues have appeared in *Arab Studies Journal*, *Middle East Report*, *Jadaliyya*, *Critical Historical Studies*, and *Economic and Political Weekly*. He is also a contributor to several volumes, including *Dispatches from the Arab Spring: Understanding the New Middle East* and *The Journey to Tahrir: Revolution, Protest, and Social Change in Egypt.*

INTRODUCTION

Joel Beinin

THIS VOLUME SEEKS TO STIMULATE A BROAD DISCUSSION ON studying the Middle East and North Africa (MENA) using the methods of political economy. Political economy addresses the mutual and historical constitution of states, markets, and classes. Traditionally, class analysis—the historical origins and trajectories of classes, the relations among them, the articulation of local classes with regional and global markets, states and empires, and the institutional, legal, and cultural forms that sustain and situate them in complex social formations—has been the most distinctive form of political economy. Class analysis emphasizes understanding social life through the relations between the producers and expropriators of wealth. It has historically been associated with an ethical/political commitment to radical material equality.

While class has often been the conceptual entry point of political economy, we propose a more expansive understanding of political economy influenced by the concept of overdetermination. In this perspective, causes are simultaneously effects; all events are situated in a relational matrix; all social hierarchies are subject to contestation.[1] Analytical categories are neither objective facts nor merely discursive constructions; they may be reconfigured by debates over their meanings and social struggle.

Class is a social relation; one class implies the existence of at least one other class. Capital is a social relation based on the extraction of value from the direct producers of commodities, which capital then sells to realize a profit. In volume 1 of *Capital*, Karl Marx elaborated an abstract analysis of the dynamics of capitalism. But historical social formations in which capitalist relations of productions predominate are always more complex than this abstraction, as Marx himself acknowledged. Class analysis alone cannot explain everything about social formations; neither can they be adequately understood without it.

The historical development of social formations dominated by capital is inextricably intertwined with genocides, slavery and other forms of unfree labor, racialization, patriarchy, national oppression, and empire. For example, the history of the nineteenth-century English textile industry is organically connected to slavery in the American South, the transformation of large parts of Egypt into zones of cotton monocropping where large landlords dominated peasant sharecroppers or seasonal day laborers, and the soil degradation caused by intensive cotton cultivation. Construction of the two Aswan Dams was partly motivated by the desire to expand cotton cultivation. Those dams wrought ecological damage, the proliferation of schistosomiasis and malaria, the inundation of Nubia, and the migration of Nubians to Cairo and Lower Egypt, where they often became workers in racialized occupational categories.[2]

The establishment of the Misr Spinning and Weaving Company in al-Mahalla al-Kubra, Egypt, in 1927 entailed not only the transformation of peasants into a new class of mechanized textile production workers and the repositioning of hand loom weavers in the textile industry. Many of these new "workers" still owned or rented agricultural lands. For a generation, at least until the massive strike of 1947, their social identities remained shaped by their villages of origin. Capital also formed ambiguous class fractions like shop floor foremen. As Hanan Hammad's *Industrial Sexuality: Gender, Urbanization, and Social Transformation in Egypt* demonstrates, new class and gender relations were co-constituted in both the workplace and wider urban space. Women worked in the factory while entrepreneurial *Mahallawiyyat* (female city natives) rented rooms to male factory workers who migrated from surrounding villages. Factory life shaped new cultural conceptions of masculinity and forms of urban violence, sexual harassment, child labor, child molestation, and prostitution, and sometimes made homosexuality more visible.[3]

These examples suggest that merely seeking to revise Marx's abstract definition of capitalism—a mode of production based on private ownership of the means of production (capital) to produce commodities for exchange in markets and profits derived from exploitation of free wage labor—is unlikely to enhance our understanding of the social world. Capital accumulation by individuals, partnerships, and even contemporary corporations can occur through exploiting many different forms of labor as well as cheap nature. Apple is the largest corporation in the world with a market valuation of some US$1 trillion. Foxconn, the largest employer in China, assembles most of Apple's iPhones in factories in Shenzhen and other Chinese cities.[4] There are good reasons to doubt that Foxconn's workers are free in the commonly understood sense of the term. But they undoubtedly form a key class in the contemporary capitalist mode of production.

The ambit of political economy also includes the legal, political, and cultural forms of the regulation of regimes of capital accumulation; relations among local, national, and global forms of capital, class, and culture; the social structure of reproduction; the construction of forms of knowledge and hegemony; technopolitics; the environment as both a resource and field of contestation; the role of war in the constitution of states and classes; and practices and cultures of domination and resistance.

Circuits of production, finance, and commodities are often imbedded in ethnic or sectarian networks and intertwined with imperial and patriarchal structures. The confluence of class, sect, and political orientation informed the 1975–90 Lebanese civil war. Classes may emerge from or alongside status groups like tribal shaykhs, sayyids (descendants of the Prophet Muhammad), 'ulama' (scholars of Islamic learning), or the effendiyya (those educated in a Western style and employed in professions and modern-style businesses). A status group can become a class.[5] In contemporary Lebanon and the Gulf Arab states, domestic workers are commonly migrant Filipinas or South Asians. Their positions as wage workers, as vulnerable women exposed to sexual and other forms of abuse, and as noncitizens are inseparable.

Political economy is not simply the intersection of previously existing disciplinary boundaries (politics and economics). It seeks to critically examine disciplinary, geographic, ethnic, and sectarian boundaries. Those boundaries, many of them constructed from the late nineteenth through the mid-twentieth centuries, obscure social hierarchies, society as a wholistic object of investigation, and the contradictions of the capitalist mode of production. They divide the world into units conducive to imperial rule, encourage construction of romanticized national and communal histories, and establish standards of common sense and normality that criminalize or marginalize ideas, identities, and behaviors that challenge the existing order.

These broad strokes do not prescribe a single "correct" analytical method. We understand political economy as a family of intellectual orientations and research methods and eschew ideological claims that it is "scientific" or "objective." Its intellectual genealogy includes, but is not limited to Adam Smith, Karl Marx, Rosa Luxemburg, Antonio Gramsci, John Maynard Keynes, Karl Polanyi, the *Monthly Review* school, Dependency and World-Systems Theory, Black Marxist traditions, the socialist current of second wave feminism, and neo-Marxian currents including the "Regulation School," "Social Structures of Accumulation," "Social Reproduction Theory," ecosocialism, and studies of technopolitics. The authors of this volume embrace the methodological pluralism this genealogy implies.

CRITIQUE

The best known political economy overviews of the MENA region in English are *A Political Economy of the Middle East* (henceforth, *PEME*), originally by Alan Richards and John Waterbury, now in its fourth edition with the addition of Melanie Cammet and Ishac Diwan to the authorial team since the third edition, and *Globalization and the Politics of Development in the Middle East* (henceforth, *GPDME*) by Clement M. Henry and Robert Springborg.

PEME originally sought to apply a unified analytical framework to the MENA region based on the mutual interactions among economic growth, state structure and policy, and social classes. Despite some caveats, the authors adopt a positivist stance toward these categories and the statistical data deployed to measure them—regarding them as self-evident rather than subjecting them to critical analysis. All four editions of *PEME* acknowledge the problems of using GDP as an indicator of economic and social development. They do so nonetheless, arguing that it provides "the most comprehensive available set of statistics on national income" (4th ed., 36–37). The authors offer a cursory and pro forma critique of the notion that per capita GDP is "a crude indicator of average social welfare" (4th ed., 36). But they offer no critique of the concept of "average social welfare," which has little social meaning. People do not live in average, but rather in highly stratified and unequal, circumstances. Any value derived from referencing widely used statistical categories is undermined by their obscuring much of importance. Moreover, the international financial institutions (IFIs—primarily the International Monetary Fund and the World Bank) that compile this data rely on national statistics, which may be unreliable or even falsified.

For example, an independent "country assistance evaluation" commissioned by the World Bank claimed that Tunisia's poverty rate declined from 40 percent in 1970 to 4 percent in 2000.[6] For comparison, in 2016 the Census Bureau estimated that the poverty rate in the United States was 12.7 percent. So, this claim should have prompted intense scrutiny. A 2010 World Bank *Country Brief for Tunisia* revised the poverty figure upward and claimed, "Tunisia has made remarkable progress on equitable growth, fighting poverty and achieving good social indicators . . . underscored by a poverty level of 7 percent that is amongst the lowest in the region."[7] In 2015 the World Bank published revised figures indicating that Tunisia's poverty level was 32.4 percent in 2000 (more than eight times the independent estimate), 23.5 percent in 2005, and 15.5 percent in 2010 (over twice as high as the *Country Brief* for that year claimed). The poverty figures the World Bank published before 2015 were not simply worthless; they were offered as "evidence" to support economic policies that were not producing the advertised results. A modicum of critical thinking and on-the-ground familiarity with Tunisia could easily have led to this conclusion.

The UN Development Program's Human Development Index, which was designed "to emphasize that people and their capabilities should be the ultimate criteria for assessing the development of a country, not economic growth alone," is a better measure than GDP of health, education, and standards of living.[8] Since 2002 the UNDP has sponsored six *Arab Human Development Reports* whose principal contributors are scholars based in the Arab region. The 2003 *Arab Human Development Report* concluded that poverty in the Arab region is higher than usually reported in the statistics compiled by the IFIs.[9] Neither the Human Development Index nor the *Arab Human Development Report* appear in the first three editions of *PEME*. The fourth edition briefly mentions health and education indicators based on the Human Development Index (63, 162). These indicators suggest that following the IFI's policy prescriptions reduced social welfare from 1990 to 2010. The *Arab Human Development Reports*, which develop that argument in detail, remain unmentioned.

Uncritical reliance on their statistical data is one expression of *PEME*'s friendly stance toward the policy preferences of the IFIs, despite their manifest failure in all but exceptional cases (Turkey, for a time, in our region). It is more assertively indicated by the replacement of "class" with "social actors" as a category beginning with the second edition. The first volume promisingly defines class in "relational terms" and by "differential property rights" whose "core is . . . access to the means of production" (1st ed., 40), but this terminology is not consistently deployed throughout the text. The elimination of class in the subsequent editions reflects both a deference to the world outlook of the IFIs and perhaps a too hasty conclusion about the irrelevance of Marxian analytical categories in the post–Cold War world. The fourth edition of *PEME* contains some significant revisions to account for the Arab popular uprisings of 2010–11. But there is no critique of the earlier editions' failure to spotlight what Cammet and Diwan consider the causes of the uprisings (4th ed., 1–6). And there is no suggestion that the uprisings are an expression of a fundamental structural crisis in the regional modes of capital accumulation and governance.

One strength of Henry and Springborg's *GPDME* is its acknowledgment of the lasting impact of colonialism on the MENA region (8–10). It too offers a comprehensive analytical perspective, proposing that "politics drives economic development and that the principal obstacles to development in the region have been political rather than economic or cultural in nature" (15). While this critique of culturalism is commendable, it compartmentalizes politics and economics in precisely the way that we seek to overcome and directs attention to the state and state-centered politics.

The late Nazih Ayubi, an influential theorist of the Arab state, argued that Arab states have weak extractive capacity, institutional strength, and ideological appeal. Therefore, they rule primarily through coercion.[10] By the 1990s, this was empirically correct, as the popular uprisings of 2011 (Tunisia, Egypt, Libya, Morocco, Bahrain, Syria, Yemen) and 2019 (Sudan, Algeria, Lebanon, Iraq) highlighted. However, Ayubi's formulation of the problem as the failure of state hegemony tends to reify the state and extract it from both its domestic social context and the global political economy. It gives insufficient attention to the historical processes through which tribal formations, ethnic groups, military officers, dependent state bourgeoisies, and national liberation movements, which were originally not consolidated as class formations, came to power and either did or did not establish something resembling Antonio Gramsci's notion of hegemony, or rule by consent. It elides the transition from authoritarian populist regimes—which, even if they deployed coercion against their domestic oppositions (typically Marxists or Islamists) and therefore did not fully consolidate their hegemony, enjoyed considerable popular support and pursued developmentalist economic policies with a significant redistributionist element to more nakedly authoritarian regimes that retreated from redistributionist approaches to national economic development: Egypt from Nasser to Sadat, Mubarak, and Sisi; Syria from the Ba'th of the 1960s to As'ad family rule; Tunisia from the first postindependence years to the more intense authoritarianism of the later Bourguiba and Ben Ali eras; and Algeria from Ben Bella to the rule of the shadowy "pouvoir" (power).

Some scholars of the MENA region regard rentier state theory (RST) as an important contribution of scholarship on "their" region to the discipline of political science. RST argues that oil- or mineral-rich states are autocratic because they have no need to tax their citizens to obtain revenue.[11] RST also reifies states and detaches them from their local, regional, and international social contexts. The chapters in this volume that address petroleum and petroleum-rich states—Timothy Mitchell on oil (3), Adam Hanieh on the Gulf Cooperation Council countries (5), and Nida Alahmad on Iraq (7)—explicitly reject RST.

One useful point of departure for situating states in rather than in opposition to society is Bertell Ollman's observation that the state is "the set of institutional forms through which a ruling class expresses its political nature . . . [it] is an essential feature of the class itself."[12] This volume does not propose a unified theory of "the Arab state," which is not a very promising project. The chapters on the GCC countries and Iraq noted above and by Max Ajl, Bassam Haddad, and Zeinab Abul-Magd on Egypt, Tunisia, and Syria (2), Aaron Jakes and Ahmad Shokr on Egypt (6), Muriam Davis on French North Africa (8), and Ziad M. Abu-Rish on Lebanon (9) differ in their level of abstraction and the balance they propose among global, regional, and local forces. But all are committed to understanding the regional states as inextricably intertwined with local and global markets and classes. They do not suggest that states simply reflect social relations. But neither do they detach the states they examine from the local and transnational social relations that brought them into being and sustain them.

Several chapters of this volume address what appear to be exceptional cases, which the tools of political economy render less exceptional. Shana Marshall's chapter (4) examines how a particular repressive state apparatus, the military, becomes embedded in the local and global political economy, and in the case of Egypt, comes to be the dominant fraction of the ruling coalition. Joel Beinin's chapter on the United States and Israel (10) argues that cultural affinity, the power of the Zionist lobby, and a military aid relationship grew into a powerful transnational structure of capital investment, production, and technological development linking the military and homeland security-surveillance industrial complexes and the closely related hi-tech sectors of the two countries. Samia Botmeh's chapter on Palestine (9) demonstrates how the paradigm of development promoted by the World Bank undermined the projects of state construction and national independence.

GPDME is explicitly framed by the paradigm of "development," which tends to assume that regions of the global South, if correct policies were adopted, could and should replicate the trajectories of the developed capitalist world. Proponents of development tend to consider it a neutral, technical process that can be successfully realized by any country, regardless of its situation in the global political economy, by applying scientifically established methods. *PEME* offers mild reservations about this version of development without suggesting an alternative (69).

The development paradigm draws on the liberal political tradition and its linear view of progress and the reform projects initiated in response to the crisis of British and French imperialism in the interwar period. After World War II, development became a discourse—a comprehensive political-economic-ideological program for managing the global South deploying intertwined forms of knowledge, institutions, social practices, and power. In his 1949 Inaugural Address, President Truman denounced "the old imperialism" of Europe and proposed an American-led "program of development" to overcome "underdevelopment," a term popularized by this speech.[13] The promise of development was a central ideological claim valorizing the US empire during the Cold War, as announced in the title of W. W. Rostow's influential *The Stages of Economic Growth: A Non-Communist Manifesto.*

In its crudest form, development is coterminous with modernization theory, whose classic expression in Middle East studies is Daniel Lerner's *The Passing of Traditional Society: Modernizing the Middle East.* Like Rostow, Lerner adopted a teleological conception of history exemplified by his claim, "What America is . . . the modernizing Middle East seeks to become."[14] Social scientists like Rostow and Lerner, even when they did not directly shape policy, articulated the "common sense" motivating USAID, the Peace Corps, and the facile explanations for the "backwardness" of the MENA region that still appear regularly in the "serious" Anglo-American media. However, the global South was never a passive recipient of development. Development projects required considerable local participation, which inevitably altered the terms of their implementation.[15] Until the 1970s, both advocates and critics of development orthodoxy envisioned active roles for states in the process. Since the 1980s, the meaning of development has shifted. It is now associated with the neoliberal market fundamentalism promoted by the IFIs.

Despite their regional perspective, ultimately *GPDME* and *PEME* deploy a Weberian methodological nationalism that explains the behavior of states in terms of typologies particular to the region. As the chapters by Timothy Mitchell (3) and Adam Hanieh (5) demonstrate, methodological nationalism is particularly unhelpful in understanding the petroleum industry. It diverts attention from the structural relationships among control of the lion's share of MENA crude oil production by US multinational firms until the 1970s, post–World War II US hegemony over the noncommunist world, and monarchical rule in the oil-producing states of the Gulf, first and foremost Saudi Arabia. GPDME devotes a few bland sentences to Aramco; *PEME* mentions Aramco only in passing and treats petroleum primarily in terms of its price. Neither book questions the conventional wisdom regarding the origins and impact of the 1973 oil crisis, as Timothy Mitchell's chapter in this volume (3) and other substantial works do.[16] Nor do they discuss the circulation of post-1973 petrodollars as a lubricant in the transition to the financialized global economy, which they largely accept as a given. They ignore the pioneering work of Fred Halliday and Joe Stork, which, along with more recent books by Robert Vitalis, Adam Hanieh, and Toby Jones that appeared after the publication of *GDPME* and the first two editions of *PEME*, offer much more incisive understandings of the political economy of Saudi Arabia and the Gulf and the technopolitics of oil.[17] *PEME* and *GPDME* understate the transregional connections that would contextualize and challenge the uniqueness of late twentieth- to early twenty-first-century globalization.

ALTERNATIVES TO WESTERN EXCEPTIONALISM

Janet Abu-Lughod's *Before European Hegemony: The World System A.D. 1250–1350* poses a powerful alternative to still influential triumphalist accounts of the "European Miracle" as a universal history culminating in Western victory in the Cold War, globalization, and the "end of history."[18] She argues that during the thirteenth to fourteenth centuries, vast regions of Eurasia were integrated by an "archipelago of cities." The MENA region was the fulcrum of this system, in which no single power exercised hegemony. Commercial and cultural exchanges proliferated and wealth accumulated. China and the Middle East were then economically far stronger than Europe, and China was a more likely candidate for future global hegemony. The archipelago of cities was also the vector for the progress of the Black Death of 1346–53, a major factor in the decline of this system along with the collapse of the Pax Mongolica.

Kenneth Pomeranz's *The Great Divergence: China, Europe, and the Making of the Modern World Economy* argues that until 1750–1800, the wealthiest regions of Northwest Europe (England) and China (the lower Yangzi Delta) enjoyed comparable agricultural productivity, consumption, wages, fertility rates, life expectancy, and product and factor markets, and experienced similar shortages of land-intensive products and environmental degradation.[19] Plentiful coal deposits located near cities and convenient to water transport and conquest of the Western Hemisphere—not internally generated cultural, institutional, or economic advantages—allowed England and Northwest Europe to transfer their surplus populations and secure access to sugar, timber, cotton, and tobacco that uniquely enabled them to escape the ecological cul-de-sac that previously limited all of Eurasia.

Abu-Lughod and Pomeranz's work, although not beyond criticism, should caution us against considering the ultimate incorporation of the MENA region into the world capitalist market on a subordinate basis as determined or as a case of delayed development along the trajectory pioneered by Europe. Nonetheless, however much we seek to provincialize Europe and reject its claims to universalism, we must ultimately contend with the two institutions—the capitalist market and the nation-state—which it has largely succeeded in imposing on the rest of humanity, although certainly not in a homogenized or even functionally "successful" manner.

THE OTTOMAN ROAD TO THE WORLD CAPITALIST MARKET

The Ottoman Empire and Europe embarked on extensive territorial expansion about the same time—symbolized by the conquest of Constantinople (1453) and the invasion of the Americas in 1492. By the mid-sixteenth century the Ottoman Empire ruled over Greater Syria, Egypt, Iraq, most of coastal North Africa, the Balkans, and Hungary. But the influx of New World silver weakened the Ottoman currency, and Vasco da Gama's circumnavigation of Africa broke Muslim dominance of the maritime trade with India.

Nonetheless, Ottoman rule in the MENA region was not a period of cultural or economic stagnation. In inland regions like Jabal Nablus and Mosul, vibrant commercial and market relations flourished independently of Europe.[20] Hala Fattah argues that the economies and societies of Iraq, the Arabian Peninsula, and the Gulf "operated on a dynamic that was peculiarly their own, and for a long time held the forces of an expansionist Europe at bay."[21] Even the Mediterranean coastal regions did not passively submit to the emerging world capitalist market. As Kristen Alff's chapter (1) demonstrates, Beiruti joint-stock companies actively shaped trans-Mediterranean trade while remaining embedded in local social relations and forms of capital accumulation.

The MENA region did succumb to military conquest. The Napoleonic expedition to Egypt (1798), the French invasion of Algeria (1830) and imposition of a protectorate over Tunisia (1881), and the British occupation of Egypt (1882) and imposition of protectorates in the Gulf (1820–92) inaugurated the imperial interventions that gradually reorganized the Ottoman Empire and its environs into polities that became nation-states. European rule relied on local allies, typically large landowners, merchants, or minorities. The profound influence of those relationships on the class structures and political economies of the states that eventually emerged in the twentieth century persists today.

CLASS, GENDER, EMPIRE

The debate over women wearing the niqab (face veil) in late-nineteenth to early-twentieth-century Egypt illustrates well the intersection of class, gender, and empire. The vast majority of Egyptian women were peasants who could not wear a niqab while working in the fields. The practice was restricted to women of the urban elite. The middle-class pioneers of the Egyptian women's movement focused their efforts on education and marriage rights, not the niqab. Nabawiyya Musa, the first Egyptian woman to graduate from high school and later the first woman school headmistress, appears in a widely circulated photo without a niqab. But she did not advocate making the niqab a central issue. Malak Hifni Nasif, another prominent women's educator, opposed unveiling and argued that many of the wealthier women who did so were motivated by attraction to European fashion.

Nonetheless, Qasim Amin's attack on the niqab in *The Liberation of Women* (1899) became the centerpiece of the debate—an expression of gender hierarchy and class privilege that persists in many contemporary discussions of this issue. Amin, a French-educated lawyer and the son of an aristocratic Turkish father, accepted much of the colonial-Orientalist characterization of Egyptian women as backward compared to European women. His arguments appear to be primarily motivated by the belief that moderately educated women were the most appropriate companionate marriage partners for "modern" middle-class and elite men and mothers for future nationalist sons.

Amin frequented the intellectual circle around Muhammad 'Abduh, the modernist chief mufti of Egypt who may even have written the section of *The Liberation of Women* that argues that shari'a requires that women wear a hijab (headscarf), but not a niqab. Lord Cromer, the British proconsul in Egypt, supported 'Abduh's appointment as chief mufti in 1899, considered him a friend, and regarded 'Abduh and his circle as "the natural allies of the European reformer."[22] But while Cromer apparently supported Qasim Amin's limited conception of women's "liberation," he was unequivocally a male supremacist at home. In 1909, after returning to Britain under the cloud of the Dinshaway Incident, Cromer became the founding president of the Men's League for Opposing Woman Suffrage and its successor organization, the National League for Opposing Woman Suffrage.

Huda Sha'arawi, who was raised in a harem as a member of a wealthy family, is *the* icon of Egyptian feminism. In 1923, returning from the International Woman Suffrage Alliance Congress in Rome, she and her young protégée, Ceza Nabarawi, disembarked at Cairo Station without their niqabs. Sha'arawi's authority, due to her class position and nationalist credentials, quickly and organically made the niqab unfashionable.

Empire and its aftermath remain gendered today. Following the 2001 US assault on Afghanistan, then first lady Laura Bush asserted, "Because of our recent military gains in much of Afghanistan, women are no longer imprisoned in their homes. They can listen to music and teach their daughters without fear of punishment. . . . The fight against terrorism is also a fight for the rights and dignity of women."[23] Contemporary French politics and culture are obsessed with veiled Muslim women. Former president François Hollande opined, if France "can offer the conditions for [a Muslim woman's] self-fulfillment, she will free herself from her veil and become a French woman, whilst remaining religious, if she wants to be, capable of having an ideal."[24] These are updated versions of imperial feminism—what Gayatri Chakravorty Spivak termed "white men . . . saving brown women from brown men."[25]

GLOBAL CAPITALISM SINCE WORLD WAR II

By mid-1942, prominent US businessmen and their media mouthpieces understood that the United States would "emerge as the strongest single power in the postwar world" with the unique capacity to shape the global political economy. Based on that premise, the editors of *Fortune*, *Time*, and *Life* copublished "An American Proposal" advocating "a new American 'imperialism'" to "complete the work the British started."[26] They disparaged Europe's territorial, colonial empires as passé. Instead they advocated a resumption, under US leadership, of the globalizing dynamic inherent in capitalism, which the protectionism and competitive currency devaluations of the 1930s and World War II had halted.

In July 1944 the United Nations Monetary and Financial Conference convened at Bretton Woods, New Hampshire, and began the process of institutionalizing a version of this "American Proposal." The regime of capital accumulation established at Bretton Woods was managed by institutions, norms, and expectations that the Regulation School of political economy terms Fordism-Keynesianism.[27] *Fordism* (after Henry Ford, pioneer of the moveable assembly line) signifies domestically oriented mass production using Taylorist "scientific" management techniques and mass consumption. *Keynesianism* refers to John Maynard Keynes's advocacy of government spending to stimulate employment and sustain aggregate demand when capitalist markets fail.

Fordism-Keynesianism was politically secured by the New Deal and European social democracy. This implicit compromise between labor and capital delivered high levels of growth, wages, productivity, and profits in Western Europe and North America from about 1948 to 1971. The success of Fordism-Keynesianism depended on US military power, economic supremacy, and leadership in shaping the economic and political reconstruction of Europe and Japan.

The United States insisted that the Bretton Woods system of international monetary management be based on both gold and the US dollar; it was in a position to do so because it controlled two thirds of the world's gold, and the dollar was the only currency that enjoyed international confidence. The value of the dollar was fixed at $35 = 1 oz. of gold. Except for the Soviet Union, the conference attendees agreed to align their foreign exchange rates on this basis, thus establishing the dollar as the international reserve currency and the United States as manager of the capitalist monetary system.

The Bretton Woods conference also established the International Monetary Fund to promote stability of exchange rates and financial flows and the World Bank (initially known as the International Bank for Reconstruction and Development) to promote economic development. During the "golden age" of Fordism-Keynesianism, these IFIs along, with the US government, supported state-led, developmentalist economic policies in the global South: moderate land reform, import-substitution industrialization, modest protective tariffs, and a substantial safety net for urban workers and government employees. Chapter 2 discusses the trajectory of these policies in Egypt, Syria, and Tunisia, while Chapter 6 focuses more closely on Egypt.

An important element of the Marshall Plan, by which the United States financed the recovery of Western Europe with economic aid totaling over $13 billion (nearly $110 billion in 2016 US dollars) was shifting Europe from a coal-based to a petroleum-based energy regime. Oil as a proportion of Western European energy consumption increased from 10 percent in 1948 to 15 percent in 1951 to 32.3 percent in 1960. Over 10 percent of all Marshall Plan aid from 1948 to 1951 financed imports of dollar-denominated oil. As early as 1947 American-owned transnational companies supplied about half of all Europe's oil, mostly from Middle Eastern sources. To meet this demand, Aramco's production in Saudi Arabia increased from 89.8 million barrels in 1947 to 277.9 million barrels in 1951.[28]

The Bretton Woods system began to unravel in the late 1960s, its demise symbolized by President Nixon's 1971 announcement that dollars would no longer be freely convertible to gold. A decade of low growth and high inflation (stagflation) in the Western economies ensued, punctuated by the oil price shocks of 1973 and 1979. These price increases did not undo the Bretton Woods system. The more fundamental causes—declining profit rates and the accumulation of US trade and budget deficits due to competitive manufactures from fully recovered Europe and Japan, the Vietnam War, and President Johnson's Great Society programs—preceded them by several years.[29]

During the 1970s the US government established a functional arrangement with Saudi Arabia: all oil would be priced in dollars and the United States would guarantee the security of the Saudi regime. The huge influx of petrodollars to Saudi Arabia, Iran, and the other Arab oil-producing states was mostly recycled to the United States and Britain through investments in US Treasury bonds and the New York and London stock exchanges, and the purchase of weapons and other commodities. The recycling of petrodollars and the Volcker Shock of 1979–81, which ended stagflation with a crippling recession brought on by raising the federal funds rate to over 20 percent, eased the way to the gradual consolidation of a new regime of capital accumulation in the 1980s termed "Flexible Accumulation" by the Regulation School, also known as financialization, neoliberalism, or simply globalization.

In the global North, Margaret Thatcher's election as prime minister of the United Kingdom in 1979 and Ronald Reagan's inauguration as president of the United States in 1981 symbolized the transition. They broke the power of trade unions and aggressively promoted dismantling the welfare state that had undergirded Fordism-Keynesianism.

In the global South, the IFIs proclaimed developmentalism a failure due to its insufficient levels of economic growth. However, the evidence on growth rates is inconclusive; in the MENA region, factors like the 1967 and 1973 wars and the oil boom and bust make direct comparison difficult.[30] The "third world debt crisis" of the early 1980s allowed the IMF to impose "conditionalities" on loans to countries that experienced foreign exchange shortages or large budget deficits. John Williamson codified those terms as the "Ten Commandments" of the Washington Consensus, which he avidly promoted:

(1) Reduce government budget deficits to less than 2 percent of GDP.
(2) Prioritize primary health, education, and infrastructure (practically impossible under an austerity regime).
(3) Broaden the tax base and cut tax rates.
(4) Unify interest rates.
(5) Unify currency exchange rates at low enough levels to encourage exports.
(6) Remove trade restrictions and reduce tariffs.
(7) Encourage foreign direct investment.
(8) Privatize public enterprises.
(9) Abolish restrictions on establishing new businesses.
(10) Secure private property rights.[31]

Since the 1970s, the IFIs have advocated export-led growth and business-friendly policies to attract foreign direct investment, which they claim lead to higher levels of growth. Williamson acknowledged that in the 1980s Washington "was essentially contemptuous of equity concerns."[32] Disregard for equity provoked 146 "IMF food riots" throughout the global South from 1976 to 1992.[33] The January 1977 Egyptian "bread intifada" was among the first.

POLITICAL ECONOMY CHALLENGES TO ORIENTALISM AND MODERNIZATION THEORY IN MIDDLE EAST STUDIES

Two anglophone institutions and their publications fostered the development of political economy as an alternative to the Orientalist and modernization theory approaches that dominated Middle East studies through the 1970s. One was the seminar that convened at the University of Hull (UK) in 1974 and published the *Review of Middle East Studies* (*ROMES*) edited by Talal Asad and the late Roger Owen. *ROMES* sought "to encourage the production of theoretically relevant work informed by a critical appreciation of the Middle East and its history."[34] After three issues, *ROMES* ceased publication, though it was twice briefly revived. The Middle East Research and Information Project (MERIP) was established in 1971. Its flagship publication, now the online *Middle East Report*, initially focused on current events and addressed an audience of alternative media and activists. By the late 1970s, it adopted a more scholarly tone and gained broad influence due to its well-informed analysis of the Lebanese Civil War and the 1979 Iranian Revolution, both of which contradicted modernization theory expectations.

Early efforts in political economy challenged the canons of Orientalism and modernization theory along four axes: (1) refuting the narrative of Ottoman decline and stagnation since the sixteenth century; (2) valorizing class analysis; (3) demonstrating that Ottoman land tenure practices were not a barrier to commercial agriculture, the commodification of property, and capital accumulation; (4) and what was then called "restoring women to history."

From 1950 on, Raúl Prebisch, executive director of the UN Economic Commission for Latin America, challenged the orthodox development paradigm based on the empirical observation that North Atlantic–style capitalism was not developing in Latin America. Prebisch influenced the Dependency and World-Systems theories advanced by André Gunder Frank and Immanuel Wallerstein. Frank, Wallerstein, and their followers emphasized the global character of capitalism and situated its origins in the sixteenth century, not the Industrial Revolution of the late-eighteenth -early nineteenth centuries.[35] They argued that the historic processes of genocide, enslavement, plantation monocropping of sugar, tobacco, cotton, palm oil, rubber, and so on for export, and the extraction of gold and silver and other minerals to be worked into manufactures by colonial or neocolonial powers, aided by local accomplices denigrated as a comprador bourgeoisie, had relegated most of the global South to the periphery or semiperiphery of the world capitalist market. In contrast, traditional Marxists believed that proper capitalist development in the Third World could only occur by supporting a "national bourgeoisie." Samir Amin critiqued both dependency theory and traditional Marxism, arguing that only "delinking"—establishing a modulated relationship with the world capitalist market and local control over its terms—would allow the global South to develop.[36]

Using the framework of World-Systems theory and Marx's notion of an Asiatic Mode of Production, Huri Islamoğlu-İnan and Çağlar Keyder proposed an ambitious "Agenda for Ottoman History." They advocated redirecting inquiry from the traditional and often ahistorical studies of political, military, and cultural institutions to the processes of the incorporation of Ottoman territories into the world capitalist market on a subordinate basis. Islamoğlu-İnan republished the article a decade later with an autocritique rejecting World-Systems theory as economistic and attributing too much agency to Europe. She concluded that attempting to remedy the ahistorical character of the

Asiatic Mode of Production concept by defining the Ottoman state as the surplus-receiving class nonetheless entailed a form of class reductionism.[37] Islamoğlu-İnan proposed that attention to the specific local histories and class relations and the politico-juridical structures that legitimated the Ottoman state would establish that the global South could not be understood simply as a periphery of Europe.

Arab nationalists and Marxists pioneered efforts at class analysis in the region.[38] There was also a school of Soviet Marxist scholarship.[39] Among anglophone scholars, Hanna Batatu's *The Old Social Classes and the Revolutionary Movements of Iraq*, Eric Davis's *Challenging Colonialism*, and Ervand Abrahamian's *Iran Between Two Revolutions* were the first scholarly works to demonstrate that class analysis illuminated important aspects of the modern Middle East obscured by Orientalism and modernization theory. They inspired Joel Beinin and Zachary Lockman to apply a version of this method in *Workers on the Nile*.[40] The imprint of Princeton University Press on these books helped to validate the methods of political economy.

Egyptian nationalist historiography considers Bank Misr, founded in 1920 amid Egypt's 1919 nationalist uprising, an exemplary Middle Eastern national bourgeoisie. The bank leveraged its capital to promote many industrial and other enterprises, most famously the giant Misr Spinning and Weaving complex in Mahalla al-Kubra. Bank Misr's leading founder, Tal'at Harb, effectively advertised its enterprises as essential to Egypt's national economic revival and persuaded the state to provide critical support to the Misr group after it secured tariff autonomy in 1930. Davis frames Bank Misr's project as "challenging colonialism," which seems to endorse the image Harb cultivated of himself and the Misr group as an emergent national bourgeoisie. But Davis acknowledges that Misr enterprises collaborated with Europeans as early as the 1920s and, by the 1930s, even with British textile firms seeking to circumvent Egypt's tariffs. Robert Vitalis's study of Misr's rival, Ahmad 'Abbud, argues that Bank Misr could not have adopted any other strategy, as Europe was the only available source of technical expertise and capital. Demonstrating that there was no fundamental difference between the practices of Tal'at Harb and Ahmad 'Abbud, Vitalis shows that the distinction between a "national" and a "comprador" bourgeoisie is invalid.[41] Aaron Jakes and Ahmad Shokr make a similar argument in their chapter (6). Beyond any other consideration, capital seeks profit or, if it can manipulate states and markets in its favor, rent.

An alternative approach is proposed by Sherene Seikaly's study of the aspiring Palestinian Arab business class. She rejects the common view that these "men of capital," as they termed themselves, were indifferent or traitors to the national cause.[42] They envisioned their business projects and related intellectual/cultural activities as essential to building a future Palestinian national economy. That project was thwarted by limitations imposed by the British Mandate, the Zionist settler colonial project, and the British-Zionist repression of the 1936–39 Arab revolt. The contrast between Egypt and Palestine highlights the importance of local specificities, such as the inability of the British Empire to intervene militarily in Egypt by the 1930s, in contrast to its massive intervention in Palestine.

Peasant histories are much more elusive than those of workers. Peasants are largely illiterate, rarely leave a paper trail, and operate primarily on a local scale before the advent of modern nationalism. Ted Swedenburg concluded that the best strategy to account for Palestinian peasants' participation in the 1936–39 Arab Revolt was to study peasant memories of the events.[43] But ethnographic and archival research on rural populations has also yielded substantial results.[44]

Kenneth Cuno's *The Pasha's Peasants* demonstrates that farmers in the Nile Delta sold, mortgaged, and bequeathed their usufruct rights to land at least as early as the mid-eighteenth century and very likely before. Beshara Doumani's study of Jabal Nablus and its olive oil and soap production demonstrates the rapid commodification of land, the commercialization of agriculture, and preindustrial manufacturing for a regional market. Kristen Alff's chapter (1) in this book and her doctoral dissertation demonstrate that Beirut-based joint-stock companies accumulated substantial capital by trans-Mediterranean trade in agricultural products while relying on the local practices of land tenure.[45] Thus, there were no institutional barriers to capital accumulation in important agricultural regions of the Ottoman Empire.

Judith Tucker's *Women in Nineteenth-Century Egypt*, which employs a Marxist-feminist analysis, was the first history of women in the modern Middle East and one of the early efforts to use shari'a court records as a source for social history, which subsequently became a popular methodology.[46] Tucker's book appeared before the publication of Joan Scott's influential essay, "Gender: A Useful Category of Historical Analysis."[47] Since then Scott's basic argument, if not necessarily her poststructuralist theoretical commitments, has revised understandings of gender in the MENA region. A second wave of MENA women's and gender studies reoriented attention to the historical construction of gender relations, introducing terms like "the patriarchal bargain" (coined by Deniz Kandiyoti) or "state feminism" (coined by Mervat Hatem) or addressing the role of the colonial state in reinforcing patriarchy in Syria-Lebanon or the agency of women in reshaping gender relations in Lebanon.[48]

WHAT NOW?

After a hiatus due to the ascendency of discourse analysis, poststructuralist theory, and the "end of history" moment in the 1990s, political economy reemerged in the 2000s.[49] The 2007–8 financial crash stimulated new interest in global histories of capitalism, including the emergence of a new center of capital in the Gulf Arab states. In the MENA region, the Arab popular uprisings of 2011 spotlighted the failure of Washington Consensus policies in Egypt and Tunisia (as Chapter 2 argues), as well as Morocco, Jordan, and ultimately even Turkey—the principal sites of the attentions of the IFIs.[50] Chapter 2 also demonstrates that in Syria, where there was no formal connection with the IFIs, independent adoption of their preferred policies produced similar failures.[51]

Several directions in political economy analysis have emerged from the conjuncture of these events. First is the confluence of political autocracy, oil, and the emergence of a regional center of capital (*khaleeji* capital) in the Gulf Arab states, as Adam Hanieh argues in his chapter in this volume (5) and other recent work. Hanieh argues for a more global approach to petroleum and Gulf capital formation. But oil can also be analyzed at the micro level as a factor sustaining Kurdish separatism.[52] Second is the gendering of labor relations, both before and during the era of Flexible Accumulation.[53] Third is the Gulf Arab states as major importers and abusers of migrant labor.[54] Fourth is the study of specific commodities, infrastructures, and services and their places in the structure of capitalism and class power, such as Shana Marshall's chapter (4) in this volume.[55] Fifth is the institutions of security, surveillance, and counterinsurgency.[56] Sixth is the studies of the role of social movements of workers, farmers, and other subalterns before and after the 2011 uprisings, which have challenged facile punditry about "Facebook revolutions" and the like.[57] And finally are the efforts to revisit the most canonical topics in political economy: the processes of capital accumulation and the origins of capitalism in the MENA region, such as Kristen Alff's chapter in this volume (1).[58] So, critical approaches to political economy are flourishing. Their intellectual agenda is expansive and can accommodate a broad range of topics.

Part 1

CATEGORIES OF ANALYSIS

Chapter 1

LANDED PROPERTY, CAPITAL ACCUMULATION, AND POLYMORPHOUS CAPITALISM

Egypt and the Levant

Kristen Alff

FOR OVER HALF A CENTURY, SCHOLARS OF THE MIDDLE EAST HAVE debated the origins of modern capitalism in Egypt and the Levant. Two seminal works on this question, Maxime Rodinson's *Islam and Capitalism* and Peter Gran's *The Islamic Roots of Capitalism*, argue that an indigenous capitalist sector existed in Islamic merchant societies.[1] More recent scholarship begins the timeline later, in the nineteenth century. Kenneth Cuno and Beshara Doumani, for instance, show how forms of capitalism emerged in Egypt and Palestine, building on local scaffolds of agricultural and manufacturing institutions formed in the eighteenth century or earlier.[2]

The foundational scholarship of Rodinson and Gran usefully posed challenges to Eurocentric definitions of capitalism rooted in narrow readings of Marx. Rodinson recognized that Marxist definitions were compatible with the trajectory of capitalism in the global South only if taken as an "ideological ensemble" rather than the dogmatic Marxism of many of his contemporaries.[3] Gran recommended avoiding "scientific" models based on the case of industrial capitalism in England and instead looking for moments of capital accumulation in local Egyptian and Mediterranean contexts.[4] But his cultural history is inadequate for the task.[5] Despite efforts of these pioneering scholars to challenge English ideal-types, we still do not have a history of capitalism in Middle East contexts that shows how capitalism built upon mercantile activities that first S. D. Goitein and later Rodinson described, yet is differentiated from the expansion of enterprise in the early modern period.[6] Furthermore, too many scholars of the Middle East have continued to privilege an abstract "scientific" model—a list of strict expectations for relations of production—that, perhaps unintentionally, replicates modernization theory narratives centered on the English factory. The task is to find empirical evidence for how capitalism actually emerged and evolved as global without losing sight of the historical specificity of place and time. Acknowledging its global character, I focus here on regional expressions that are part and parcel of the ongoing global process of capitalism itself. In the Middle East, expressions and productions of capitalism in the nineteenth and early twentieth centuries were imbricated with local and global forms of handicraft and industrial production, historical formations like slavery and the contested category of setter-colonialism, as well as local understandings about individuals' relationship to labor, property, and capital.

I argue that capitalist practices became widespread in parts of the Levant and Egypt in the nineteenth century as part of the global circulation of goods, capital, and ideas. But their local substance was slightly different than what Cuno and Doumani suggest. Based on examples from existing literature and my own research on Eastern Mediterranean companies, I contend that global capitalism produced and was produced by polymorphous practices in the Middle East. Bringing the global South into conversation with American- or European-centric new histories of capitalism, I define capitalism here as the simultaneously global and regionally specific forms of creation of surplus value through an ongoing and incomplete process of primitive accumulation, relentless capital accumulation, and the depersonalization and abstraction of social relations, including the abstraction of labor power. In many parts of the Levant and Egypt, the latter required immense physical and epistemic violence, which reached a climax during World War I.

CAPITAL AND CAPITALISM IN THE LEVANT AND EGYPT

Ethnic-based merchant networks and rulers accumulated wealth and capital in the Middle East both before the formation of the Ottoman Empire and in the Ottoman era. Jewish merchants based in Cairo devised business strategies to dominate Mediterranean and Indian Ocean trade from the mid-tenth to the mid-thirteenth centuries.[7] New Julfan Armenians employed deep interpersonal connections and dependent relationships to forge trade routes and expand commercial exchange in the Mediterranean and Indian Ocean between the sixteenth and eighteenth centuries.[8] Merchants and Mamluk rulers in Egypt energetically acquired money and capital to sustain their military corps and purchase luxury goods from Europe.[9]

Because these merchants engaged in long-distance trade and reinvested their returns, Rodinson and others refer to their wealth as capital and their investments as part of the "capitalist sector."[10] Gran uses the terms *wealth* and *capital* interchangeably.[11] But, accumulating wealth is insufficient as a definition of capital or capitalism. Merchants in the early modern period sometimes invested funds with the explicit objective of employing human labor power to add value in the Smithian-Marxian sense, yet often they did not. While they could accumulate great wealth, their practices did not necessarily promote large-scale capital accumulation through the creation of surplus value, a process fundamental to modern capitalism. Capital accumulation entails the satisfaction of the logic of capital over human necessities, leading to the overproduction of commodities and greater pressure to curtail the rights and needs of labor.

However, these classical elements of the definition of capitalism alone are also insufficient to understand the character of mid-nineteenth-century capitalism in the Middle East and the global South more broadly (and even England, for that matter). One distinctive aspect of nineteenth-century Middle Eastern capitalism was that surplus value was created from specific local forms of ongoing primitive accumulation, building on variable social conditions, local legal regimes, and attendant relations of production. Gershon Shafir and Roger Owen understand sharecropping and corvée as vestiges of an earlier epoch that would eventually require overturning in order for the region to fulfill capitalism's global historical mandate.[12] Cuno and Doumani valuably look for local conditions of private ownership and production for regional and global markets to show how Egyptian and Palestinian institutions were not incompatible with the experience of European industrial models. Alternatively, I argue that the absence of criteria like freehold private property, "free" wage labor, or tenant contracts is *not* an appropriate marker of the nonexistence of capitalism. Instead, they are integral to specific expressions of capitalism that emerged in regions of Egypt and the Levant in the nineteenth century as part of the global system of circulation of capital, commodities, people, and culture. Surplus value was created on legally state-owned land through forms of corvée labor in Egypt, sharecropping in parts of the Levant, and something approximating freehold property in Palestine in the nineteenth century. Social relations akin to freehold in the Levant and Egypt coexisted with sharecropping, small peasant plots, and other regimes of labor control, even on the same pieces of land. Capitalists intentionally created surplus value through the combination of all of these as well as in their major investments in manufacturing companies across the Mediterranean.

The comingling of labor relations in the service of capital accumulation is not unique to the Middle East. The same variety of labor-capital relations and attendant cultural and moral norms also make up the local histories of capitalism across the globe. Walter Johnson contends that the transatlantic slave trade and, specifically conceptions of race, gave industrial capitalism its shape.[13] Isabelle Guérin suggests that bonded labor in India is not a residue of tradition that vanished with the modernization of production, but rather integral to the emergence and endurance of capitalism itself.[14] Family-owned and operated farms (as opposed to "free" wage labor) existed, and sometimes even increased in Europe and the United States well into the era of industrial capitalism.[15] Local labor relations in the Levant and Egypt initiated and sustained the expressions of capitalism there. Regionally specific forms of primitive accumulation intermingled with changing familial and patriarchal structures to serve the needs of capital and society.

A second, associated part of the process of capitalism in the Levant and Egypt that distinguished it from earlier mercantile activities was that it was built upon a transformation from interpersonal connections to "impersonal and 'thing-like' relations."[16] The dappled advent of capitalism did not necessarily destroy guilds, unincorporated companies, slavery, or sharecropping. Instead, it performed a form of epistemic violence against what Michael Löwy terms in his reading of Marx, "all qualitative values: use values, ethical values, human relations, human feelings."[17] The case of the Levant illustrates that the criteria for capitalism are also historically cultural. In the nineteenth century, members of a new patriarchal capitalist class began to operate on the basis of dualisms whose underlying ontologies had become mechanical: capital was separated from labor power; share owners were distinct from their companies; and society was removed from the physical environment. Labor power, companies, and nature became abstract objects that Levantine capitalists acted upon, displacing more personalized relations of interdependence that they had previously fostered.

LANDED PROPERTY IN THE LATE OTTOMAN EMPIRE

The agricultural property regime of the Ottoman Empire and local legal institutions of the Levant and Egypt in great measure account for the distinctiveness of local models of labor-capital relations and the particular ways that labor power and the company model became abstractions. Theoretically, the two most prominent categories of land ownership under Ottoman law were *miri* and *mulk* (Tr. *mülk*) land. *Miri* was agricultural property under the eminent domain of the state. *Mulk* resembled freehold ownership and encompassed urban property, olive trees, vineyards, forests, buildings, and other structures on agricultural land.[18] In the case of the former category, and often even in the latter, the concept of proprietorship did not provide the owner a singular or absolute claim over the land itself. Instead, under the Ottoman legal system, rights of ownership on landed property was multitiered and dispersed.

Rights on a piece of land—for purposes of usufruct or revenue extraction—were types of ownership not equivalent to ownership of the object itself.[19] An individual could own rights to the products of an olive grove for one season. He or she could own rights to water use for two days. These individuals sometimes promptly sold all or parts of these rights to others, ensuring a profit or simply shielding themselves from complete loss. These multiple forms of ownership all came with specific entitlements as well as obligations and spaces for negotiation. They also changed in law and practice as cultural norms evolved, and as struggles between individuals with influence over law, *kadis* (judges, *qadis*, Ar.), and local peasants altered the meanings and definitions of these legal categories to fit changing political, economic, and social situations.[20]

EARLY MODERN FOUNDATIONS OVER THE LONG EIGHTEENTH CENTURY (1695–1820)

Political and economic changes in the Levant and Egypt between the introduction of the *malikâne* system in 1695 and the beginnings of the cultivation of long-staple cotton in Egypt in 1820 did not necessarily signal the emergence of indigenous capitalist practices that approximated those of the British industrial model. Instead, they served as the foundation for nonlinear processes of surplus value creation fundamental to capitalism specific to these regions.

In the seventeenth century, military defeat and economic decline of the Ottoman central treasury strengthened the bargaining positions of urban notable families in Greater Syria and regimental officers and beys in Egypt.[21] One consequence of the disastrous war of 1683–99 was the shift from the *timar* system to a tax-farming (*iltizām*) system in the Levant and Egypt. As an aspiring tax farmer (*multazim*), a grandee would bid at auction for the right to collect taxes on a village or district at a price reflecting how much tax he expected to collect as well as his potential profit. The total number of tax *multazims* in Egypt increased 250 percent between the mid-1600s and 1797.[22] Moreover, the Porte extended even more rights to tax farmers, who increasingly came from a growing group of provincial notables. To increase the stability of revenue, in 1695 the Ottoman government introduced the *malikâne*. In contrast to the earlier annual *iltizām* contracts for revenue rights, holders of *malikânes* considered their tenure life-long and often even hereditary.[23]

Mamluk households and Cairene merchants participated independently in commodity production of cash crops by serving as tax farmers themselves or dealing directly with *multazims* in the countryside.[24] Likewise, as the specialization in export crops grew in places like southern Syria in the late seventeenth and early eighteenth century, *malikânes* concentrated wealth into the hands of families connected to Istanbul.[25]

In the latter half of the eighteenth century, prominent families in the Levant began to accumulate wealth and capital from their investments in the production of raw materials from large villages. Following a second defeat in the Russo-Turkish War (1768–74), the Ottoman state introduced the *esham* system. It allowed individuals with capital to buy shares of the annual land tax in cash for a lump-sum payment.[26] The Ottoman state lent its coercive power and prestige to support the investments of Muslim and non-Muslim tax farmers and moneylenders.[27] Prominent Greek Orthodox, Maronite, and Druze families and rich peasants found legal support for their control over plots in fertile coastal regions of Syria. The Maronite Khazin and Hubaysh families partnered with the Sursuq family to acquire wealth by overseeing expansive plots in the Kisrawan, Batrun, and Jubayl districts of Mount Lebanon. The Junblats controlled *miri* land in the Biqa'.[28]

Concomitant with the rise of notable tax-farming families in the Levant was a downturn in agricultural productivity in late-eighteenth-century Egypt, brought on by political instability and a series of natural disasters, including drought and disease.[29] The monopoly system and other state-centralizing systems that the duumvirs Ibrahim Bey and Murad Bey (1775–98) established as a result of the downturn further distanced tax farmers from peasants in the countryside.[30] The 1798 Napoleonic expedition's response to political and economic instability in Egypt was to seize land, consolidate holdings, and form a central bureaucracy to control irrigation and taxes. This built on earlier attempts of Ibrahim Bey and Murad Bey to break free from the Ottoman yoke by forming a centralized local administration.[31]

To be clear, the fact that a rural class of notables possessed new agricultural investments in the eighteenth century does not mean that they owned the land outright or that, conversely, the rights of notables and peasants were respectively limited to tax farming or use. In practice, peasants and tax farmers struggled over the meaning of land tenure well before capitalism became a significant category. Generally, Ottoman peasants cultivated land under sharecropping (*sharika* or *muzara'a*) arrangements in which they continued to hold their right to use *miri* land, or usufruct, which they treated as a form of effective ownership.[32] Ottoman officials, local *kadis*, *multazim*s, and Mamluks often placed conditions on planting. At the same time, peasants also possessed a wide space to negotiate what they grew on their plots.[33] Village leaders (*mukhtar*s) signed contracts with tax farmers pledging a percentage of the agricultural product as a tax and a percentage as repayment for tools, seeds, and other materials. In other regions, existing social relations, the location of the land, and powerful business interests pointed to other circumstances. On Mount Lebanon, for instance, tax farmers held land in a manner similar to freehold. They permitted peasants to plant crops between mulberry trees and granted peasants some land in exchange for tending to the trees.[34] In parts of Egypt, certain urban Mamluk households relied on unpaid corvée labor to preserve the highest percentage of their earnings from cash crops, such as sugar.[35]

The political economies of specific regions of the Levant and Egypt informed their future trajectory in domestic and global markets. Over the course of the long eighteenth century, landlords and merchants integrated the existing scaffolding of local and foreign trade and commodity production established by peasants and upheld by state institutions to participate in the global market for commodities. Their role in the global market was primarily, but not exclusively, the export of raw materials and manufactured products to other parts of the Ottoman Empire, to the Ottoman state apparatus, and to England. Merchants and peasants in Jabal Nablus, for instance, traded in cotton and textiles and produced soap and olive oil for the global market.[36] Local dynamics, such as the transformation of property relations, the extension of credit to producers, and merchants and peasants use of *salam* contracts—which put the moral onus on the seller to deliver a product at a later date—contributed to the shape of later forms of surplus value creation.[37]

Land tenure relations and their meanings were certainly changing in the eighteenth century and differed in more-centralized Egypt from the locally dominated Levant. In Egypt, some notables, merchants, and state bureaucrats viewed labor in abstract terms by this time or earlier. Ömer Lüfti Barkan has documented examples of the logic of enumerating and categorizing work and workers in the Ottoman state records on the buildings of the Süleymaniye Mosque in Istanbul from the mid-sixteenth century.[38] Even so, social relations in the long eighteenth century were still distinct from the kinds of depersonalization of labor that peasants experienced in the nineteenth century. In Egypt, depersonalization began in small and isolated ways during the period of Murad and Ibrahim. But it only became pronounced with Mehmet Ali's introduction of long-staple cotton in 1820 and even more so under the *'izba* system in which peasants were either tenants who lived on the land or were brought in as *anfar* (daily wage workers). In Greater Syria, the scarcity of labor and the more diffuse nodes of political and economic power made the creation of the abstract worker a more obscure process compared to Egypt. The continuation of sharecropping in regions producing nearly exclusively for the market led to an alienation of a different type, one prompted by a rush of foreign and local capital in land and urban industry following a period of decreased European demand during and immediately after the Napoleonic Wars (1803–15).[39]

The construction of a centralized regime of resource management in Egypt and the strengthening and crystallization of a class of state-backed urban tax farmers, creditors, and factory owners in the Levant laid the foundations for the transformation of peasants into abstract labor power. The different political and economic circumstances in the late eighteenth century Levant and Egypt produced similar ends in this regard. In both regions, a new class of entrepreneurs and financiers became more culturally dislocated from labor power in the countryside. Beirut became, in Albert Hourani's words, "a new kind of city, a new kind of urban society with a new kind of relationship with the rural hinterland."[40] The Sursuqs' migration from Jubayl to the developing commercial port of Beirut in the eighteenth century expressed this change.[41] Other Greek Orthodox families—the Abella, Bustrus, Trad, Fayyad, Jubayli, Tueni, and Tabat families—also migrated to the urban center to oversee trade and supply credit.[42] From the Gemmayzeh district of the city, the merchant families continued to exert control over the hinterlands through their local mangers. But this dissolved many interpersonal connections to peasant sharecroppers. In Egypt, the new centralized government that began to emerge in the eighteenth century created strong institutions based in Cairo, including specific institutions for capital accumulation.[43]

From their absentee space in Beirut, merchants in the Levant began to make money for money's sake, that is, they transformed the accumulated cash they acquired from collecting taxes in agricultural regions into capital. The renewal of the French Capitulations with the Ottoman Porte and the establishment of the *berat* system (which permitted foreign states to extend commercial privileges and legal protection to non-Muslim subjects) in 1740 promoted cotton exports from Palestine in the era of Zahir al-'Umar (1730s–1775) and ultimately silk exports from Mount Lebanon. In the early nineteenth century merchants switched from sailboats to steamboats, which reduced the travel time between Beirut and Marseille. The journey that normally took three months suddenly took only two weeks.[44] Levantine families established small workshops in Beirut and silk-reeling factories in Mount Lebanon, following the French Portalis Brothers, who had built the first of these factories in 1841. At the same time the French invested in six new steamships that stopped in Beirut.[45] While running their factories, the Levantine families continued to exert increased control over the wheat harvests in Jubayl from afar. In the early nineteenth century, they invested in silk production in Kisrawan, the Shuf, and elsewhere on Mount Lebanon to supply their growing number of factories.[46] Also at this time, some of these Lebanese Christian merchant families migrated to Egypt, building upon an already robust trade network of trade, which also included Marseille and Livorno.[47]

THE COMMODITY ECONOMY AND CAPITAL ACCUMULATION, 1820–1920

Between the early nineteenth century and the end of World War I, capitalism became widespread in the Eastern Mediterranean. It was marked by variegated and historically grounded processes separating producers from the means of production through a specific form of primitive accumulation, as well as the general abstraction of labor power and the company. Military commanders and urban merchants in Egypt and Greater Syria continued to enrich themselves by participating in markets in Beirut, Damascus, and Alexandria. They also forged more robust ties to the local and central state apparatuses and began to systematically reinvest their capital into the production of agricultural goods in the Levant and Egypt for the global market.

The formation of joint-stock companies was a new feature of the period. The Sursuq family formed their companies as early as the 1830s.[48] Around the same time, two brothers of the Sunni Beyhum family formed Beyhum & Company.[49] Other prominent families did the same. Jews, Greeks, Armenians, and Syrian Christians developed their own firms in Egypt. They grew their businesses in the trade, financing, and production of fruit, tobacco, cotton, silk, and cloth.[50] These businesses paid monthly sums to their shareholders, including the women in the family. Although male heads of the family often took control of the household finances, women, particularly widows in family companies, could purchase, sell, mortgage, and rent their shares without any outside approval. They also made business decisions and negotiated with European buyers for silk and cotton produced on the villages where they held shares.[51]

In cotton-producing regions of Egypt, the shape of the new economy depended largely on state policies of its provincial governor (*wali*) and self-titled khedive, Mehmet Ali Pasha. After coming to power in 1805, Mehmet Ali built upon the commercial activities of peasants and land consolidation techniques of his predecessors to embark on a strategy for state-led agricultural development for international markets. His plan was to forge industrial projects, such as a naval arsenal, other weapons production, and mechanized spinning and weaving production, to supply the growing Egyptian army. The pasha's cotton exports, in turn, paid for the modernization and expansion of the army. Mehmet Ali began by fully abolishing *iltizāms* whose tax payments were in arrears in favor of a monopoly system. In so doing, he further strengthened the reach of the state into the countryside.[52] From the 1820s on, the pasha expanded the production of long-staple cotton through land reclamation in the Nile Delta. Richards regards Mehmet Ali's murder of the Mamluks and seizure of their properties, the abolition of the *iltizam*, and the establishment of a monopoly on agricultural products as a form of primitive accumulation of capital—akin to what David Harvey calls "accumulation by dispossession" for another era.[53] In the Eastern Mediterranean, this form of primitive accumulation was unique to Egypt.

In the mid-nineteenth century, merchant landholders in many parts of Greater Syria called on the Ottoman government to protect their newly acquired agricultural investments. The production of commodities in this region became particularly salient after the 1838 Anglo-Ottoman Convention (Treaty of Balta Limanı) opened up markets to British merchants and promised to tax British and Ottoman merchants equally. It came into force in Egypt in 1841 but only had a minor impact on Egypt's already European-oriented trade. Prominent Beiruti companies controlled the planting and harvesting of cash crops by hiring local merchants to manage production in Jaffa.[54] In Mount Lebanon, silk production and exports skyrocketed at the same time as cotton in Egypt. Between the early parts of the nineteenth century and World War I, the number of mulberry trees in the region of Mount Lebanon increased tenfold.[55] The price and total volume of silk exports rose after the Maronite-Druze Civil War of 1860. In 1857 silk accounted for approximately 25 percent of the total value of exports from Beirut. By 1873, it accounted for 82.5 percent of the total.[56] At the other end of the class spectrum from the women in Beiruti family companies, young women became the majority of the workers in Mount Lebanon's silk-reeling factories by the late nineteenth century.[57]

The growing urban business class who produced for European markets and entered into partnerships with European companies affected local legal decisions regarding commerce and trade. In Egypt, the royal family's need for investment in the Suez Canal and loans for foreign debt repayments strengthened political positions of Egyptian companies with capital. Members of the

Sursuq family company, for instance, negotiated with British and French creditors and invested in the Canal themselves. Isma'il Pasha rewarded them by giving them additional shares in the Canal project from the pasha's own portfolio in addition to granting them large tracts of cotton-producing land.[58] In 1839 the Ottoman government established the Agricultural and Manufacturing Council under the Ministry of Trade. In 1843 it was reorganized and combined with the major reform council Meclis-ı Vala-yı Ahkam-ı Adliye with the objective of improving transportation, credit, and the reassessment of taxation in the countryside. Urban elites populated these councils as well as other administrative councils and commercial courts. They used these institutions to influence commercial decisions, the application of land laws, and the development of transportation infrastructure along eighteenth-century land routes from the rain-fed fertile plains and irrigated regions to major ports on the Eastern Mediterranean coast.[59]

Local capital accumulation expanded with the influx of European capital in the late nineteenth century. Upon Europe's recovery from the great depression (1873–96) new industrializers, Germany and Italy, began to compete with France and Britain for wheat, grains, dura, cotton, and metals emanating from the Eastern Mediterranean. Consistent with Rosa Luxemburg's theory of imperialism, European companies turned to Egypt and the Levant as "commodity frontiers," as new firms exploited perceived shortages in raw materials entering Manchester ports.[60] From the late nineteenth century on, European companies deluged local companies with offers to invest in large-scale production of cash crops for the European market. At the same time, local companies welcomed foreign investments. French investments in the production of agricultural commodities in the Levant totaled at least 20,000,000 francs (£25,000,000) in the years leading up to 1914.[61] In Palestine, Zionists and German Templers offered large sums to buy landed property outright. Zionist land purchasing agents—the Jewish Colonization Association and Jewish National Fund—offered forty times the market value of the land.[62] Eventually, companies based in the Levant and Egypt began to vertically integrate their businesses by working with foreign companies locally and buying up stocks in manufacturing companies in Europe.

During World War I, the local Eastern Mediterranean companies' capacity to create capital for the sake of reinvestment was further augmented as they made superprofits by monopolizing wheat and grain markets and transportation. Companies of the Beyhum, Sursuq, Tabet, and Trad families strengthened their political and economic alliances with the Committee of Union and Progress (CUP)—the governing regime during the war led by the triumvirate, Enver Pasha, Talaat Pasha, and Jamal Pasha.[63] Building on these alliances and others forged with local and European companies in the leadup to the war, the new business class sold and resold thousands of pounds of wheat, barley, and corn from their agricultural estates. This contributed to a multifold increase in prices of foodstuffs and other basic necessities, which the war profiteers reinvested in new production in the countryside and other local economic institutions.[64] In Palestine and the Levant, well-established local companies reaped superprofits from selling lands to the Zionists and Templers, sometimes based on dubious claims that they held it as freehold, and engaged in rampant war profiteering.

In Egypt under British rule an urban business class including Greeks, Jews, and Syrians, as well as Muslims and Copts, came into its own, augmenting the older Levantine elements, during World War I.[65] Their experiences during World War I were, however, different from the Levantine urban companies.[66] Even though British officials told Egyptians in the countryside that they would not have to contribute to the war effort, these same officials commandeered farm animals, cotton, food, and eventually young conscripts for the auxiliary Egyptian Labor Corps. Thus, local *'umdas*, or heads of villages, were in a position to profit from the war, and large landlords profited from high cotton prices. But unlike their counterparts in the Levant, urban businessmen in Egypt did not benefit economically. Their economic losses due to British policies between 1914 and 1919 were a primary reason why Muslim Egyptian entrepreneurs like Tal'at Harb supported the 1919 revolution.

LAND AND LABOR IN THE LEVANT AND EGYPT

When accumulating capital in the growing commodity economy, firms in the Levant and Egypt encountered different strategies in European and other contexts. However, the local capitalists did not simply import these techniques from the West, as much of the literature on capitalism in the Middle East maintains. Nor does their capitalist quality derive from their proximity to the putative qualities of the British industrial model. Instead, capital accumulation relied on land and labor configurations connected to the specific historical circumstances of these regions. That is, whether they liked to or not, new generations of business leaders in the Levant and Egypt worked within and sought to influence the political and economic realities that they inherited. In many instances, these conditions were the most efficient forms of capital accumulation. At other times and places, structural constraints on land and labor relations frustrated companies' business objectives and local political economies permitted small cultivators to retain their usufruct and other property rights.

From the early nineteenth century, Mehmet Ali's policies led to Egyptian peasants' loss of usufruct and further consolidation of large agricultural estates under increasingly powerful urban landholding businessmen and companies. Through the 1829 Regulation of Peasant Agriculture, which codified a centralized system for growing, planting, and marketing long-staple cotton, peasants lost much of their remaining autonomy. In the 1820s, capital accumulation entailed the increase of corvée labor to 467,000 persons annually, with some peasants forced to work outside of their own village community for little or no pay.[67] While peasants fought for some of their own necessarily fractured visions of land tenure, Mehmet Ali curtailed their rights even further when he abolished the monopoly system during the global economic crisis of 1836–37. He made large land grants to military elites, urban notables, and his family members. The number of these estates increased as Khedive Isma'il (1863–79) raised taxes to repay foreign debt incurred when the cotton boom created by Northern blockades of Southern ports during the American Civil War suddenly ended. Peasants in large regions dedicated to cash crops increasingly lost their right of usufruct for failure to pay taxes. Small shareholdings were still common. But by 1900, large landowners, including some Syrians, owned the majority of the most fertile regions in Egypt, much of it acquired by appropriation, over which they increasingly asserted freehold property claims.[68]

As local companies in the Levant and Egypt began to integrate their businesses vertically, they expected that land purchases would help them accumulate even more capital by "avoid[ing] the cost of intermediaries" for production and distribution.[69] From the early nineteenth century, companies began to grow more capital-intensive, high-value crops for the global market, first in Egypt and then in Syria. As a result, they further invested in transportation and manufacturing, and added value through a series of guarantor and rental contracts. They sought further jurisdiction over the land and its products. Many of these companies began to buy up more land outside of the growing ports of Alexandria, Haifa, and Mersin, as raw goods from these regions fetched high prices for long- and short-staple cotton, silk, wheat, metals, petroleum products, and other raw materials on the global market in the mid-nineteenth century.[70] By 1913, roughly 60 percent of cultivated land in Syria was in plots of 100 hectares or more.[71] Companies confiscated land from peasants as debt repayments. The owners often added value by mortgaging this land to guarantors, who paid a fixed sum and an agreed amount for expenses and received a share of the agricultural surplus in return.

During this period, certain businessmen took an active part in influencing the designation of landed property connected to domestic and foreign capital. The Mardam-Beg, Quwwatli, and other elite Damascene families established themselves as important intermediary merchant companies in the Damascus market. They provisioned the pilgrimage route by selling their agricultural products from the oasis region of Ghuta.[72] Since owners of the cash-crop-growing plots had invested capital in building irrigation systems and were personally responsible for the tax, these new owners sought ways to secure their investments.[73] Notable families in Damascus petitioned local courts for the land in Ghuta to be designated as *mulk*. These moves often guaranteed that the lands of this new business class were heritable, protected from state seizure, and taxed on a portion of the viable harvest, not a fixed annual sum. Peasants on this land then became wage workers. Similarly, the plain of Akkar outside of Mount Lebanon consisted almost entirely of large tracts owned by wealthy landlords.[74]

In the 1860s, particularly after the civil war, similar processes were underway in dry-farming regions like the Hawran, just south of the Ghuta oasis. The effects of a greater degree of the Ottoman government's central control over the region and the intensifying economic interests of English and French entrepreneurs led to the diversion of wheat from the pilgrimage route to the coast for export. Attracted by the high prices on the global market for wheat, large landlords took control over parts of the Hawran in the 1870s. Local Hawranis fought against the commercial interests of the Ottoman central government and rising domestic and European business elements in the region.[75]

In Egypt, Turco-Egyptian elites, urban businessmen, and foreigners continued to take measures to control production, attenuating peasant ownership rights on medium-sized irrigated cotton-growing estates in the Delta in the process. In the mid-1860s, the Egyptian government increased taxes by 70 percent to combat the looming threat of bankruptcy.[76] Many peasants could not pay the higher taxes, which resulted in the loss of their usufruct rights. This trend intensified after the government enacted the Muqabala Loan Law of 1871, which benefitted large entrepreneurs, who were the only group that could pay the six years of taxes in advance required to gain the legal designation of private property.[77] The British occupation of 1882 and the British commitment to laissez-faire policies further encouraged institutions recognizing freehold private property. By World War I, only about 20–25 percent of peasants held land as small family farms in Egypt and in Syria.[78]

In parts of the Levant, changes in land and labor relations differed from the turn to widespread wage labor and private property in Egypt. From the 1830s, merchants purchased title deeds for the most fertile land in the Levant. Some of them were most likely influenced by the political and economic changes in Egypt. They acquired some of their lands by auction after the Ottoman government began to conduct land surveys and register title deed holders in the 1860s in order to identify whom to tax. The new title deed holders began to think of their rights to large agricultural estates as a form of property ownership, even referring to their property in Egypt and the Levant by the same designation, "private property" (*mulk khass*). Moreover, the Ottoman state recognized its limits on titleholders' control over the land during this period.[79] By the beginning of the twentieth century, members of parliament determined that the state could not dictate terms of cultivation, mortgage, credit, and so forth on *miri* land, which was already the site of major capital investment by politically connected companies in the provinces.

Although companies were gaining more political, economic, and social power, the Ottoman government and the landholders themselves were cognizant of the fact that title holders did not own the rights to the land itself in the Levant. For the most part, peasants continued to hold legally defensible rights as one holder among the multiplicity of rights holders on agricultural land. In contrast to Egypt, the Levant was a coastal region with multiple and changing administrative districts. It did not have the same degree of administrative centralization as Egypt, even before Mehmet Ali. Nor did it produce a product comparable in value to long-staple cotton or as likely to promote industrialization for a large and (after 1930) protected market. Silk could not sustain investment in industrial development once East Asia undersold silk from Mount Lebanon. Prices in the Levant fluctuated throughout the late nineteenth century as French factories began to import cheaper, better quality silk from Japan and China in escalating quantities. As a result, companies did not have the sustained inflow of capital necessary to continue to invest in modernizing their equipment to compete with East Asia and European manufactures. They could not combat the high operational costs necessary to produce silk and thus they were left with no other option but to produce low-quality silk by superexploitation of workers, often young women from peasant families. The fall in prices in the 1870s and 1880s continued until the silk industry could not recover.[80] Lebanon largely abandoned industrial development (except for tobacco) and Beirut became a major mercantile and financial center for the import of manufactures and export of raw materials, whereas Alexandria hosted Egypt's first mechanized textile factories and other industrial establishments prior to World War I.

Ties to European capital in the Levant were not historically as robust as those of Alexandria. Moreover, companies in the Levant faced the real possibility of labor shortages. In the Anatolian district of Mersin-Adana, companies relied on the security of new tenant-contracts with attenuated peasants' rights to land on plots where labor was otherwise scarce. During the labor-intensive, cotton growing season, they supplemented existing cultivators with paid seasonal help.[81] In interior regions around Nazareth, the companies signed rental contracts with peasants, who continued to hold titles.[82] In regions like 'Ajlun, the southernmost district of the Hawran, a downturn in international grain prices in the 1870s made large landlords less willing to exhaust their political capital to combat opposition to their control over tracts of land.[83]

Consequently, by the turn of the century, capital accumulation processes in the Levant and Egypt were on distinct trajectories. Because of the shortage of labor, local companies convinced European firms that sharecropping was the most efficient form of capital accumulation in the cotton regions outside of Mersin. But in Egypt, the legacy of Mehmet Ali's distribution of large landholdings allowed elements of the Levantine business class to join forces with European investors to establish real estate and land speculation companies for the "purchase, development, and subsequent leasing or re-sale of agricultural and building land," and "lending money, on mortgage."[84] Firms of this type included the Kafr al-Zayyat Cotton Company Ltd. in 1894[85] and United Egyptian Lands Limited, established by Negib Joseph Sursuq (Sursuq and Bros.) in partnership with Alexander Sidney Henton Carver (of Carver Bros.) and others. Behind the doors of their Cairo meeting rooms, the investors concluded that their interests would be best served by taking advantage of the "steady rise in the value of property" in Egypt.[86]

In Palestine, the presence of settlers contributed to shaping labor-capital relations. The above-market prices for the most fertile regions of Palestine offered by the German Templers and Zionist purchasing agents compelled the title holders to attempt to make the land appear as freehold in order to be suitable for purchase by these high-paying buyers. The Jewish Colonization Association and the Jewish National Fund altered the landscape of peasant-landholder relations in fertile regions tied to European centers of capital. Even as the offers rolled in, Levantine companies remained hesitant to alter sharecropping arrangements on the lands they held. They correctly suspected that, as in the region of Mersin, labor shortages would limit their ability to employ enough wage-laborers to accumulate the same amount of capital as they did under tenant contracts should the sales not go through as planned.[87]

THE VIOLENCE OF CAPITALISM: ABSTRACTION OF LABOR POWER

Throughout the nineteenth century a crystalizing class of urban businessmen continued efforts to accumulate capital for reinvestment. They did so by building on the scaffolding of trade, property relations, and investments over the long eighteenth century. Both peasant labor and companies underwent a process of abstraction. That is, they became "thing-like" objects to act upon, rather than humans, albeit in dependent relationships.

During World War I, rapid changes in gender dynamics and labor-capital relations were concurrent with violent manifestations of extreme disassociations between labor and capital and shareholder and company that had been underway for nearly a century. Both labor and the firm lost their interpersonal character, as exemplified by violence against peasants and women. Furthermore, as Alan Mikhail suggests, peasants and workers became "hollow lifeless castings of men, laboring machines to be used to carry out a task."[88] This abstraction only became more pronounced as disenfranchised peasants in Egypt moved to cities for industrial or other work.

Despite the objectification of labor and company, until World War I peasants still formally retained some of their rights as sharecroppers in many parts of the Levant. Joint-stock companies accumulated capital by attenuating peasants' rights from the safety of their shareholders' urban residences. Unlike earlier land tenure regimes, company partners disassociated themselves from these peasants by treating them as machines for the objective of making money. Still, peasants possessed a limited space for petition and negotiation with the state to influence the terms of land tenure and labor. In the mid-nineteenth century, some peasants successfully won back land titles from Levantine companies. With the support of local Ottoman officials, they prevented many land sales between these companies and Zionist purchasing agents in Palestine. Similarly, widows of company shareholders negotiated with their families' patriarchs. Through local shari'a courts, they fought for the continuation of income that they regularly received from agricultural surpluses through sharecropping contracts.[89] In Egypt workers had gained experience with labor organizing before the war. Urban industrial labor also provided access to collective spaces and formal organizations. At the initiative of the cigarette workers, Egyptian workers began to revive their labor unions, and the labor movement grew rapidly after World War I.

By the start of World War I, and in some cases because of it, the process of abstraction permitted companies to privilege capital over social relations, and even human life, in both Egypt and the Levant. In Egypt this violent disassociation had already become common at the end of the long eighteenth century, with the expansion of the Ottoman bureaucracy and the dislocation of peasants from their villages to work on massive irrigation projects. In Palestine, Jewish settlers and Arab companies hired armed guards to police labor. Between 1916 and 1918, Levantine companies used the exigencies of war to justify taking 100 percent of the seasonal crop, leaving peasants to starve. Many cultivators died of starvation while the companies held elaborate dinner parties for Ottoman officials in their palace gardens. Observers from that era recount stories of such extreme desperation that starving families sold their daughters for food.[90] Villages that comprised Ottoman communications hubs, like ʿAfula, were raided multiple times by the RAF. A general strengthening of patriarchal norms also permitted the male heads of family companies to disenfranchise their female siblings through coercive use of power of attorney. As a result, they created companies that were legally sheltered from individual whims and interpersonal kinship relations.

The evolution of global forms of capitalism with all its local iterations, as I have recounted it here, was thus a polymorphous process. It constantly changed in form and substance. The wartime violence permitted companies in the Levant to make land sales to Zionists and other European buyers in Palestine immediately following the war. The companies used the chaos of war and their leveraged political positions as elements loyal to the CUP to consolidate their shares on *miri* land. Often, they also went a step further to formally disenfranchise peasants in the Ottoman register and extend the boundaries of their properties beyond what they were legally entitled to, both in actuality and in the written record. The policies of Khedive Ismaʿil, the consequences of World War I in the Levant, and later the arrival of the British in Egypt simply eliminated or minimized the power of Ottoman state, whose social formation had frequently upheld the multiple rights of peasants.

At the end of the war, the companies could present their claims to land rights, managerial practices, and goals in terms legible to classically liberal-minded officials of the British and French governments. The local companies began to employ foreign military officers in the place of local overseers, an example of the immense physical and cultural distance between capital and labor in the new commodity economy. In the 1920s, the British and French governments brought different versions of property and labor relations to the Levant and Egypt, and attendant policies and legal institutions. They included diverse forms of sharecropping, subsistence farming, and various other forms of labor that were all part and parcel of local capitalism and its place in the global and highly contingent system of capitalism. Yet, even on the lands in Palestine, which companies sold to the Jewish National Fund as freehold private property, regimes of sharecropping and tenant contracts continued to coexist in a bundle of rights on large estates, such as Nuris and Maʿlul, in the 1920s and 1930s.[91] Local companies, as well as workers, peasants, and women, did not cease to influence the shape of this capitalism.

The historical record of capitalism in the Levant and Egypt is necessarily different and locally variegated due to its agricultural basis and Ottoman social and legal context than the European factory. But this is not a history of absences. The history related here is one of a capitalism that actually existed, involving the emergence of a new urban business class and how they perceived their techniques and objectives for capital accumulation and the social and cultural and global capitalist relationships that changed in tandem with them.

Chapter 2

STATE, MARKET, AND CLASS

Egypt, Syria, and Tunisia

Max Ajl, Bassam Haddad, and Zeinab Abul-Magd

COLONIAL RULE AND CAPITALIST PENETRATION IN EGYPT, SYRIA, and Tunisia (re)shaped the state and, in turn, remolded class structures rooted in the Ottoman period. But the particularities of colonial capitalism structured these countries' place in the world capitalist market, the forms and class compositions of their national movements, and their capacities for postcolonial planning and redistribution. These authoritarian populist republics with only modest petroleum reserves exemplify the rise and fall of developmentalism in the Middle East and North Africa. Israel's defeat of the Arab armies in the 1967 war, for which the United States gave a green light (alternatively, a yellow light that President Johnson knew Israel would ignore), fatally destabilized their developmentalist projects. But their transition to state-assisted private accumulation, beginning in the 1970s and eventually regulated by Washington Consensus neoliberal policies, was not solely due to external pressures from Israel, the international financial institutions (IFIs), Washington, and Europe. Nor was it determined primarily by Cold War allegiances. Prior histories and internal configurations of class forces informed their trajectories. The tensions and contradictions of state-managed-and-softened capitalism of the 1950s/1960s and the limits of the versions of *infitah* (economic open door, or liberalization) adopted in the 1970s—a decade later in Syria—combined with external shocks and delegitimization, including the global ideological discrediting of socialism and developmentalism, led to the redeployment of the states in relation to their class structures in the 1980s and 1990s. These policies hollowed out large sectors of what remained of socially embedded capitalisms, creating widespread discontent, expressed in the 2010–2011 popular uprisings.

After more than eight decades of increasing Franco-British competition and European economic penetration of Egypt, British troops invaded in 1882, setting the terms of Egyptian politics until their evacuation was secured after the 1956 Suez War. Egypt's globally prized long-staple cotton and the Suez Canal, which became the main route from London to Bombay and, in the twentieth century, the most important global corridor for petroleum shipping, allowed capitalism to dig deepest into its social formation. Egypt's large population, its pioneering experiments in military and administrative modernization under Mehmed Ali Pasha (r. 1805–1848), the intellectual ferment around the protonationalist 'Urabi revolt of 1879, and its role as a refuge for Levantine journalists and intellectuals seeking freedom of expression during the despotism of Ottoman Sultan Abdülhamid II (r. 1876–1909) made Egypt a regional center of gravity. From the mid-nineteenth century until recently, it exerted a powerful influence on politics and culture in the Arab world and beyond.

Geographical Syria (*bilad al-sham*) was long connected to Europe through trade. But its borders and the terms of its local identity remained contested into the mid-twentieth century. French ambitions shaped Syria as a modern nation-state—a non-Christian majority strategic rear to Lebanon. France imposed its colonial rule gradually, in the form of a League of Nations Mandate from 1920 to 1923. French colonial divide-and-rule fractured the population in ways encouraging military rule. Consequently, although postindependence Syria adopted the most radical planning measures and the largest leveling of internal inequalities in the Arab world, its ruling coalition could not sustain that project. Its Arab Socialist Ba'th Party, established in 1947 by Michel Aflaq, Salah al-Din al-Bitar, Akram al-Hawrani, and Zaki al-Arsuzi, was a model, ally—and competitor—for Egypt's Gamal Abdel Nasser, who relied more on charisma than ideological consistency.

Tunisia's substantial Italian and French settler population, though fewer and less politically significant than in Algeria, informed a distinct form of colonial capitalism and the nationalist movement's agrarian demands. Partly in response to British designs in Egypt, partly to defend its own capitalists, France occupied and declared a protectorate over Tunisia in 1881. French capital developed Tunisia's most important industrial sector, the phosphate industry, and colonial authorities sought to coopt the Sahel's large olive growers. Tunisia's workforce, eventually organized under the powerful UGTT (Union Générale Tunisienne du Travail), was unique in the region. Tunisia's principal nationalist leader, the Francophile Habib Bourguiba who headed the Neo-Destour, warily deployed the armed struggle required to dislodge settler supremacy. After independence, he turned his pro-Western orientation into state policy. Nonetheless, the Tunisian regime and the international agencies that supplied it with grants and loans carried out their policies subject to pressures from neighboring states professing Arab Nationalism, Arab Socialism, and Cold War nonalignment.

FROM COLONIAL CAPITALISM TO INDEPENDENCE

The application of the 1838 Anglo-Ottoman trade convention (Treaty of Balta Limanı) imposed an "imperialism of free trade" on Egypt.[1] Egypt's midcentury rulers, Sa'id Pasha (1854–63) and Isma'il (1863–79), who took the title of khedive, welcomed foreign capital, most fatefully the Paris-based Universal Maritime Suez Canal Company and the first European bank loan to the government during Sa'id's reign. Under their rule, Egypt was integrated into the capitalist world economy dominated by Europe, climaxing in a state bankruptcy in 1878 that provided a pretext for British occupation.[2]

Following the occupation, European capital invested more intensively in banks, industrial enterprises, and service companies. The colonial administration coopted local agrarian capitalists who expanded cotton farming in the Nile Delta for the British textile industry.[3] Upper Egypt was marginalized. But colonial capitalism still penetrated it through the sugar industry. Peasants in the Delta and Upper Egypt were indebted to European creditors and faced dispossession.[4]

During World War I the British drafted laborers to serve in battles abroad, especially from Upper Egypt. The economic dislocation of the peasantry and a nascent labor movement provided a mass base for the Wafd-led 1919 nationalist uprising and its chief, Sa'd Zaghlul. Workers and peasants participated prominently in the 1919 nationalist uprising through strikes, occupations of landlords' properties, and attacks on railroad and telegraph lines and government buildings.

The establishment of Bank Misr in 1920, which proclaimed itself "an Egyptian bank for Egyptians only," amid the nationalist uprising, embodied the version of economic nationalism its founder, Tal'at Harb, and its Muslim, Christian, and Jewish shareholders advanced. Bank Misr created pioneering enterprises in several sectors, although, as Aaron Jakes and Ahmad Shokr discuss in their chapter in this book, there is debate about how much Harb sought to challenge colonial capitalism. While touting the bank's nationalist aims, Harb and his colleagues on Misr's board of directors kept their distance from the nationalist movement's popular elements, while Zaghlul proudly called himself "a son of the rabble."[5] Nonetheless, the Wafd adopted socially conservative policies to accommodate its most influential constituency, large landowners.

The nationalist uprising achieved an attenuated independence. From 1922 to 1952 Egypt's ruling bloc contained (1) a newly established autocratic constitutional monarchy; (2) the British occupiers, who retained supremacy over four "reserved" areas (defense, the Suez Canal, Sudan, "protection" of minorities); (3) large landholders; and (4) by the 1930s, an emergent industrialist class including the Misr group and its rivals. The Wafd and the nationalist movement subordinated workers' and peasants' demands to what they considered the larger "national" cause.

The Anglo-Egyptian Treaty of 1936 reduced British power in the country. But it failed to secure the demand for "total evacuation," radicalizing Egypt's political and social movements. Workers organized many major strikes. One of the largest, the 1937 strike at the Misr Spinning and Weaving Company, marked a departure in working-class consciousness, if not yet organization. Trade unions were not legalized until 1942, though federations remained illegal.[6] Trade unions subsequently became involved in a more organized manner in national struggles.[7] The nationalist movement mostly ignored peasants' interests, but small farmers and agricultural seasonal laborers engaged in daily acts of resistance against large landowners and the colonial administration. During the interwar period, women began to move beyond traditional occupations into the capitalist job market as factory laborers, salespeople on the floors of luxury department stores, and less "respectably" in the eyes of some, renters of housing to male industrial workers, singers, and prostitutes.[8]

§

In Syria during French Mandatory rule (1922–46), the relationship between capitalist penetration, the growth of dominant classes—landed notables, commercial landowners, merchant entrepreneurs, and industrialists[9]—and the lure of state power governed the country's development. The leadership of the National Bloc and the nationalist movement was drawn mainly from the anticolonial landed notables, absentee landowners, traders, and professionals, representing dozens of Syria's most prosperous families. Unlike Egypt and Tunisia, no single cash crop dominated Syria's economy, nor did it have a substantial extractive sector like Tunisia or large industrial enterprises like Egypt. The limited flow of capital investment favoring merchants contributed to deeper radicalization within the marginalized and partly determined the conflict between Syria's landowner-bureaucrats and merchants/manufacturers.[10] They vied for power as they expanded, in alliance with the colonial regime. These patterns prior to and just after independence set the stage for five decades of Ba'thist rule.[11]

Unsuccessful in wresting Syria away from the appeal of Arab Nationalism or the ascendant professional urban classes allied with poor peasants, the old social classes resorted to coups and countercoups in the late 1940s.[12] They introduced reformist accommodations with a growing segment of politicized and marginalized social groups and classes who began to play a political role. These measures did not forestall mass dissatisfaction and mobilization against the poor political, military, and economic performance of the ruling classes. Populist politics, affirming the state's redistributive commitments, overtook all previously warring ruling class factions.[13]

The ascendant Egyptian and Syrian political leadership, owing to more class-oriented and emergent Arab Socialist and Arab Nationalist ideologies, shared similar responses to traditional classes and attempted socialist transformation. Pan-Arab Nationalist appeals, more intrusive forms of capitalist penetration, and fear of communism by the new ruling social strata enabled Egypt and Syria's brief unification (1958–61) as the United Arab Republic (UAR) when developmentalist states were proliferating throughout the global South. In contrast, Bourguiba sought to "indigenize" Tunisia rather than fundamentally transform the colonial order.

The UAR's few successes and abundant failures were foundational for the two sectors that dominated Syria after its dissolution. The first comprised the old social classes, an amalgam of reconstituted landowners, industrialists, merchants, and associated bureaucrats and army generals. The second was an ascendant rural social group, including long-marginalized minority communities (among them, 'Alawis and Druze), poorer Sunnis, and well-placed individuals in the military, which, as in Egypt, was among the most significant routes for social advancement. In September 1961 these forces backed a short-lived coup that dissolved the UAR.

From 1961 to 1963, Syria's "liberal" social forces capitalized on Egypt's insistence on dominating the UAR. Subsequently, the historically marginalized bloc resurrected the UAR's ideology and redistributive policies, while maintaining a rivalry with Egypt (and Iraq).[14] This largely rural-minoritarian coalition, rooted in lower- and middle-level farmers bent on instituting a redistributive state role, captured the helm from 1963 until the present.[15] Their path was characterized by enormous changes in the character of the ruling elites and zig-zagging between the dominance of public and private sectors, governed by the intersection between the evolving interests and exigencies of the ruling classes and changes in the global political economy.

§

In Tunisia, formal colonial rule began in 1881. However, already by 1860 France, Britain, and Italy controlled 92 percent of Tunisia's foreign and domestic trade, in the aftermath of reforms engineered to facilitate European engorgement of Tunisian wealth.[16] European lenders extended ever more credit, which the Regency could not repay. By 1869, it was bankrupt. Tunisia lost control of its economy through the imposition of a European-helmed International Financial Commission to take over Tunisia's finances—de facto nonterritorial colonialism. Formal French rule sought to protect large French capitalist interests and preempt British designs.[17] The motives for the French occupation of Tunisia were similar to those of the British in Egypt. But Egyptian colonial-capitalism was based on mercantile or financial value-drain, while Tunisia became a settler-capitalist project. It came to center on land ownership, alongside substantial extractive industry, primarily phosphates. The Gafsa Phosphate and Railway Company was one of French colonial-capitalism's prizes, towering over the world phosphate market until 1930, totaling 20 percent or more of Tunisia's exports from 1910 to 1930, and creating a substantial proletariat, the base for industrial unionism.[18] Colonialism's violent dawn accelerated social differentiation. Absentee *baldi* (city dwelling) Tunisian landowners sold littoral and northern lands to European capitalist farmers. Swathes of collective land were doled out to private Tunisian landowners to ensure a stable workforce near the colonial-capitalist farms and created a collaborator class aligned with France.[19] By the 1930s, a substantial Tunisian landholding class was born, mimicking French capital-intensive and labor-light methods. Meanwhile, dispossession, semiproletarianization, and penury pulverized the people of the countryside and created a mass constituency for the nationalists, but the nationalist movement was led primarily by a well-educated elite.[20]

In 1934, mainly younger cades led by Habib Bourguiba split the Destour Party and established the Neo-Destour at a congress in Ksar Hellal.[21] The Neo-Destour initially sought to take over the state apparatus and arrange for partial sovereignty with the French. Direct control over production was central to the transfer of value from Tunisia to France. France had also created a settler social base for continued colonial control. Tunisian decolonization occurred only in response to an armed struggle fought by the *fellaga*, landless and nearly landless rural fighters, alongside the Neo-Destour and the UGTT. In 1955, some of the same fighters and their ally, Salah Ben Youssef, balked at France's offer of partial independence and launched a second insurrection (1955–56).[22] They compelled more complete independence. But because they represented a socially more radical force than Bourguiba's Francophile wing of the Neo-Destour, oriented toward Arab Nationalism and Muslim culture, French and Bourguibist violence destroyed them, one of many acts that excluded them from the developmentalist pact.[23]

INDEPENDENCE, STATE PLANNING, AND "SOCIALISMS"

After independence from British and French colonialism, Egypt, Syria, and Tunisia embarked on ambitious projects of state planning. In Egypt and Syria, this was dubbed "Arab Socialism." Tunisia in the 1960s embarked on a more limited "socialist experiment." However, the three social formations each had mixed economies in the 1950s and 1960s, maintaining remnants of colonial capitalism while establishing a limited number of state-owned enterprises—Tunisia later than the other two countries. In the 1960s, they transitioned to more centralized planning and adopted developmentalist state capitalism and import-substitution industrialization (ISI), alongside shifts in land ownership. These policies promoted the formation of new classes who managed postcolonial economics and politics. Urban and rural standards of living improved in Egypt and Syria, whereas austerity combined with improved social services for Tunisians. But narrow internal markets, insufficient access to capital, technological dependency, and delegitimization because of the 1967 war limited ISI's success.

In Egypt, the Free Officers under Nasser (r. 1954–1970) undertook a military coup in 1952 and overthrew the monarch. The new regime forced the final withdrawal of British colonial power after the 1956 Suez War. The coup quickly became a social "revolution from above," as the new military regime carried out an agrarian reform aimed at undermining the large landholders who had dominated Egyptian politics since the mid-nineteenth century. The properties of the royal family were confiscated. Owners of large cotton and sugar plantations were allowed to sell holdings above the permitted limit (initially 200, eventually 50 feddans; 1 feddan = 1.04 acres). Middle and rich peasants (owning 5 to 50 feddans), not the landless or agricultural seasonal laborers, were its main beneficiaries. Most poor peasants had to rent land to support their families and benefitted primarily from rent controls instituted with land reform.[24] The regime later established rural cooperatives, which were fully under the control of the one ruling party—the Arab Socialist Union (ASU).

At first, the ruling officers lacked a coherent stance toward private capital, partly because they came from varying socioeconomic and political backgrounds. Most, like Nasser, were from the lower-middle classes. Some were from the pre-1952 elite, some close to the Muslim Brotherhood, others close to Marxist parties. Throughout the 1950s, they applied a mixture of economic planning and pro-private-enterprise measures with some attention to social justice. They encouraged local and foreign capital through reforms in business legislation, while establishing state-owned enterprises. The Free Officers were anticommunist and initially sought good relations with the United States. However, their unwillingness to accept the Manichaean terms of international relations promoted by the Dulles brothers during the Eisenhower presidency preceding the Suez War of 1956 drew them closer to the USSR. Egypt accepted Soviet arms and financial and technical assistance to construct the largest state-led project of the era, the Aswan High Dam.[25]

From 1958 to 1961, the era of the UAR, Egypt governed Syria as a province. The Ba'th had a more elaborated version of Arab Socialism and Arab Nationalism and expected to become Nasser's political tutor. Nasser's unwillingness to accept this role alienated his strongest potential allies in Syria. In 1960, with the nationalization of Bank Misr, the Egyptian state took more control over economic activity and adopted more extensive redistributive measures. The Syrian business class and elements of the army rebelled and dissolved the UAR when Nasser tried to impose the nationalization of major private enterprises on Syria.

Nasser deployed his charismatic persona to take bold political initiatives—participating in the 1955 Bandung Conference of Asian and African states and the nonaligned movement that emerged from it. An arms purchase agreement from Czechoslovakia that year broke the Western monopoly on arms sales to the region. Egypt's nationalization of the Suez Canal in 1956 prompted the tripartite aggression of Israel, Britain, and France. Despite Egypt's military defeat in the Suez War, British forces evacuated Egypt, and Nasser became a symbol of anti-imperialism throughout the global South.

Building on his expanding popularity, in 1960–62 Nasser nationalized all Egyptian private enterprise. The 1962 National Charter proclaimed the regime's official ideology as Arab Socialism and established the ASU as its sole party. Subsequently, the regime embarked on an ambitious industrialization scheme with centralized planning. Industrial investment went into previously marginalized Upper Egypt. Textile spinning and weaving enterprises were scattered throughout the Nile Delta to provide jobs and educational uplift for the peasantry. Workers in public sector enterprises benefitted from a living wage, job security, public housing, subsidized food, and health care. Boys and girls from peasant and working-class backgrounds had access to free public education through university. Women benefitted from "state-feminism," which sought to give them equal access to education and public employment without challenging the patriarchal family.[26] The state encouraged good socialist families to practice birth control. Many urban working and middle-class women and most university students stopped wearing the headscarf.[27]

Despite gaining important economic rights, workers and women lost political freedoms under Nasser. The ASU assimilated their unions and associations.[28] Peasants were never fully liberated from the oppression of the old landowning classes.[29] The construction of the Aswan Dam to generate electricity for factories and regulate the flow of the Nile for farming displaced numerous Nubian villages. Nubians were resettled in urban areas and assimilated into the educational and employment systems of the state, as their ethnic culture and native language were marginalized by Arab nationalist ideology. Army officers appointed themselves managers of government enterprises and grew into a new elite. Additionally, a new social group of middle- and upper-middle-class bureaucrats grew in the public sector and enjoyed financial advantages and top positions within the ASU.

§

The drive to restore Syria's capitalist order after the UAR's dissolution cemented the ruralization and radicalization of the Ba'th party. Based among the minority 'Alawi and Druze populations and other poor rural elements, the Ba'th set Syria on a path of development more radical and more repressive than Egypt's due to the precarious rule of formerly subjugated populations who had not yet become the dominant social forces. Between the 1963 coup that brought the military committee of the Syrian Regional Branch of the Ba'th to power and 1966, its rural-minoritarian leadership struggled to free Syria from the legacy of domination by Sunni large landlords and urban notables.

A second coup brought Salah Jadid and the Ba'thist military committee to power from 1966 to 1970. Under his direction, Syrian Arab Socialism adopted its most radical form. ISI accelerated in an effort to achieve economic independence and nurture domestic industry. The state nationalized even more industry, eliminated middlemen in the rural sector, and put in place a more far-reaching agrarian transformation than in Egypt and certainly Tunisia.[30] In theory, aspirations for socialist transformation might have united the victims of land-owning classes, but Jadid's team was unable to maintain the unity of the Ba'th party.

The anti-imperialist rhetoric and relatively radical economic policies of the post-1966 radical Ba'th led to its domestic, regional, and international isolation. Within a few years, it alienated some of its natural allies on the left, including ousted fellow Ba'thists and nearly all communists, as well as reactionary Arab states like Saudi Arabia. Relations with Egypt were strained since the dissolution of the UAR. Neighboring Arab states rightly feared that Syria's support for the armed actions of Fatah would destabilize the region. Fatah's attacks from January 1965 were a factor in Israel's decision to launch a preemptive strike in the 1967 war that hit at the heart of the regime. The consequences of the war, augmented by the lack of capital, overly coercive rule, and weak planning capacity established the limits of socialist transformation in the 1966–70 period. The precarious regime was ripe for another coup.[31]

Hafiz al-Asad, then defense minister, supported socialist reform but prioritized national unity and augmenting the state's coercive apparatuses over socialist transformation. He regarded the remains of the regime's social base, the middling classes in rural Syria, as crucial to achieving domestic security. For Asad, their interests established a red line that land reforms could not cross, a principal point of contention between him and Jadid. A reconstituted loyal base within the military and intelligence services served as Asad's vehicle to blocking further socialist reforms. In 1970, Asad launched the so-called Corrective Movement—a coup that left all his opponents languishing in prison and established the contours of the Syrian regime, which endured in one form or another until 2011 and beyond. This "change within continuity" approach contrasts with the more resolute and explicit rupture in political-economic direction in post-Nasser Egypt.

§

As in Egypt and Syria, during the immediate postcolonial period Tunisia's leadership demurred from extensive planning or immediate nationalizations. The UGTT was allied to but somewhat autonomous from the Neo-Destour. It had an advanced workerist ideology, a wage-workers' analogue to Hawrani's peasant-based (pre-Ba'th) Arab Socialist Party in Syria. But Bourguiba's wing of the party, which took power with independence in 1956, was pro-Western, Francophile, liberal, and anti-Arab Nationalist. It focused on state formation and political consolidation and bet on an entente with private capital. The ruling bloc included the UGTT, which was strongest among state functionaries and workers, weakest among the rural proletariat, and by far the most combative in the mines.[32] After Bourguiba quashed the union's stirrings toward independent political activity and Ahmed Ben Salah's ambition for a party-union fusion, it became the Neo-Destour's junior partner under the more compliant leadership of Ahmed Tlili. The UGTT lacked the social strength in the countryside to force through its agrarian program—an equivocal commitment to agrarian reform, and a massive investment fund for the center and the south—and was unable to penetrate and organize the rural regions adequately, in part because the Neo-Destour continually preempted such attempts.[33]

From 1956 to 1959 Tunisia experienced massive capital flight. While private capital was terrified of what independent Tunisia might do to its wealth and refused to invest in industry, the United States, and to a lesser extent France, were terrified of what might happen to the entire system of domestic capitalism if the state failed to promote economic development. In the rural sector, low-intensity absentee farming prevailed over labor-intensive cultivation, leading to crises of rural employment and low levels of production. Unemployment was rampant in the cities.

Bourguiba did not personally favor the kind of land reform, economic planning, and nationalization of private enterprises adopted by Egypt and Syria. But, by 1962 the regional and global moment of *dirigisme* (state-led development), which Egyptian and Syrian policies had helped to constitute, pushed him to adopt these policies. By 1964, Tunisia toyed with Destourian Socialism, a limited degree of developmentalism without radical redistribution that would threaten the interests of large olive growers of the Sahel or the larger cereal farmers of Tunisia's north. The socialist experiment became an ideological terrain over which planners, trade unionists, and politicians struggled to determine the role of private capitalism in Tunisia.[34]

As in Egypt, US Public Law 480 permitted the sale of American grains to Tunisia, paid for in soft local currency. This food aid simultaneously subsidized American farmers, contained radical pressures in Tunisia, and held open the political space for the government to carry out a substantially externally oriented planning regime, relying on massive external capital infusions and technological imports. Tunisia became one of the world's largest per capita recipients of food aid.

From 1962 to 1969, planning rested on several policies: (1) a cooperative movement, (2) massive state investment in ISI, (3) infrastructural development, (4) liquidating commercial channels to entice capitalist investment in productive and job-creating enterprises, and (5) wage austerity.[35] As in Egypt and Syria, ISI established a massive, state-owned industrial base.[36] By the late 1960s, the large portions of private capital invested in a state-assisted tourism industry became a substantial base for capitalist accumulation. However, unlike Egypt and Syria, there was no serious agrarian reform. The cooperatives provoked cross-class unease, since they radically changed the living and labor environments of the smaller farmers while threatening the wealth of the larger ones. But they managed to absorb much of the smaller peasantry and some of the medium peasantry, especially in the north, and gave decent jobs to the landless. Landholders were less happy, as the smaller farmers in effect became a rural proletariat, working for the state. In the final phases of the cooperatives, the smallest farmers sold off their working capital, especially animals, in effect foreclosing the possibility of a return to private farming. Meanwhile, the landed bourgeoisie substantially increased its holdings throughout the country from 1956 to 1969, through a variety of methods: purchase of land from smallholders and departing French and Italian settlers, or somehow grabbing ahold of former settler land that passed into state possession during the 1956–1964 period of agrarian decolonization. Meanwhile, private accumulation continued apace, leading to concentration of wealth within the Tunisian ruling class.[37]

Throughout this period, in line with the regime's Francophilism and its alliance with US imperialism, Bourguiba's policies on the Palestine question were even to the right of the Gulf Arab states. This led to conflict with Nasser and other avatars of Arab Nationalism and anticolonialism. Ultimately, the regime's open support for the US regional agenda undermined the state's capacity to act as the guarantor and architect of the framework for private accumulation, as events in Vietnam and Palestine activated domestic social unrest.

THE ROLLBACK OF DEVELOPMENTALISM, PLANNING, AND IMPORT-SUBSTITUTION INDUSTRIALIZATION

Israel's massive defeat of Egypt and Syria in 1967 delegitimized their official ideologies of Arab Nationalism and Arab Socialism and exacerbated prewar economic crises. The March 30, 1968, Program indicated Nasser's intention to reorganize Egypt's political economy. But the War of Attrition and his death deferred the task to his successor Anwar al-Sadat (r. 1970–1981). Tunisia abandoned its socialist experiment in 1969. Syria took another decade to follow this trend.

Sadat signaled a radical policy shift with the May 15, 1971, "corrective revolution" and the arrest of leading Nasserists. But no substantial changes occurred until after Sadat established his competence and legitimacy by Egypt's partial victory in the 1973 Arab-Israeli War. His 1974 "October Working Paper" announced an *infitah*—an "open door" to domestic and foreign private investment. Recognizing that his envisioned economic reorientation required capital only available from the West, Sadat switched Cold War camps from the Soviet Union to the United States and, in 1979, signed a peace treaty with Israel. In exchange, since 1978 Egypt has received over $50 billion in military aid, making it the second largest non-NATO recipient of US military aid after Israel, and nearly $30 billion in economic aid.[38] Sadat invited the return of exiled local capitalists, including wealthy Muslim Brothers who accumulated capital in oil-producing Gulf states, and foreign investors. Saudi Arabia and other Gulf Arab states invested heavily in Egypt until relations were frozen for nearly a decade by the peace treaty with Israel. On the advice of an IMF delegation, in January 1977 the government announced a sharp cut in consumer subsidies. The response was a "bread uprising," which came close to toppling the regime, compelling it to walk back the cuts and to proceed more slowly to reverse Nasserist policies than both it and the IFIs desired.

The same technocrats who managed the public sector enterprises welcomed the transition to the new model as long as it did not undermine the public sector sufficiently to diminish their power. Alongside them, pre-Nasser capitalists who returned to Egypt and those associated with new money made in Libya or the Gulf (many of them, Islamists) benefited from the new business opportunities.[39] *Infitah* inaugurated an era of new consumer goods, crony capitalism, and corruption, as ascendant capitalists deepened business and familial ties with the regime. Those with old and new money were no longer embarrassed to display it lavishly. Consequently, they were commonly viewed as a "parasitical" capitalist class that thrived on patron-client relations with corrupt state officials, similar to Syria's experience.[40]

§

Syria proceeded more cautiously than Egypt in rolling back Arab Socialism because the regime feared full-scale incorporation into the global market might threaten its power. The regime also needed to retain some mass support while it plunged into a more aggressive regional role. Furthermore, to make its actions reversible and unchecked, Syrian liberalization was informal and avoided the putative benefits and constraints of dealing with IFIs.[41] Like Egypt, Syria sought rapprochement with conservative domestic social forces as well as with Arab states it had previously deemed reactionary. Until the late 1980s,

Asad opted for a more incremental, informal, and limited approach to liberalization,[42] while jailing or containing the Ba'th's left and communist critics.

Asad introduced a mixed economy combining public sector dominance with broadened space for select private business/public sector partnerships. He expanded the regime's social base by building a new class of entrepreneurs and informal economic networks whose fate and success were beholden to the regime's security. The allegiance of important business sectors stabilized the regime and allowed it gradually to shed socialist claims and its labor-peasant social base, but without ever restoring lost public sector jobs. Workers lost many rights and gains of the 1960s as well.[43] The regime's legitimacy among the working classes eroded even faster than public sector productivity rates.

§

In Tunisia, the block that led the country to independence and ruled it since 1956 was shattered by 1969 due to austerity and dissatisfaction with the government. Cooperatives were perceived as top-down and had little support from former small farmers, who disliked what had been done to their lives. The threat to expand them nationally alarmed large farmers, who worked back channels, while the World Bank refused to fund cooperative expansion to the Sahelian olive groves. Protests erupted in 1967/1968 at Bourguiba's pro-US foreign policy, silence on Palestine, hosting of Hubert Humphrey amid US aggression against Vietnam, and the austerity and command-and-control rural policies.[44] At the end of 1969, amid wildcat strikes in crucial primary-extractive industries, unrest in the student and labor sectors, and unease among the landed elite, with its sub rosa relationship to the ruling party, since 1964 renamed the Socialist Destourian Party (PSD), the cooperative experiment collapsed.

By 1972 the state shifted gears, moving to state-guided capitalism. Various private sectors benefited, enjoying the fruits of the 1960s' social infrastructure investments.[45] A mini oil boom, remittances from migrants in Libya and France, and phosphate exports underpinned massive hydraulic investments, setting the stage for an agro-export boom. The agrarian bourgeoisie benefited from state support for input subsidies, mechanization, input-intensive crop varieties, and a Green Revolution—all oriented to northern large-scale capitalist cereal growers, who accelerated previously sluggish moves to intensify production.[46] The subsidy system encouraged the growth of medium-scale farms using family labor. Floor prices for olive oil, but not olives, allowed oil producers but not olive growers to concentrate profits. Olive oil production remained crucial for capital accumulation, particularly around the southern port of Sfax.

Much like Syria's controlled opening to foreign capital, a 1972 law established a virtual "off-shore" platform in Tunisia, stimulating a boom in ready-to-wear clothing assembly. The textile factories were primarily turn-key. The cloth was imported, and the final products were marketed in Europe. Consequently, clothing assembly had fewer backwards and forwards linkages and was less socially embedded than the metallurgical and primary-processing industrial plants created during the 1960s. In the services sector, tourism became a central vector for accumulation. Oil partly enabled a subsidy system that compressed the costs of social reproduction, by reducing the prices of basic consumer food items like pasta and bread, and thus allowing for lower wages. Meanwhile, in the 1970s, the UGTT broke through its corporatist bridles, initiating a decade-long strike wave. Fearing the UGTT was once again out of control, the state bloodied it severely following a January 1978 general strike, hoping to contain wages.

OIL BOOM, OIL BUST, DEBT CRISIS

Between rising internal debt and the oil bust of 1986 that reduced export revenues and remittance incomes, two pincers closed on the Arab developmentalist states. Those with large-scale debts were suddenly faced with an offensive from the IFIs to restructure their economies and make them ever more open to foreign capital while diminishing state regulation and social protections. The IFIs deployed loan conditionalities and an ideological assault on the legitimacy of developmentalism. Tunisia buckled and restructured its economy in the mid-1980s. Egypt resisted until the 1991 invasion of Iraq created the political space to undertake economic restructuring. Syria was prepared to follow a similar path, as it served the class interests of the leadership and its networks, but would not succumb to IFIs conditionalities nor to a formal relationship so as to preserve nationalist credentials.

Egypt's fourth military president, Hosni Mubarak (r. 1981–2011), maintained *infitah* policies. But fearing a repeat of the January 1977 bread uprising, he resisted US-IMF pressure to fully liberalize the economy. At the time of the 1991 Gulf War, Egypt had nearly US$50 billion in foreign debt. As a reward for supporting the US-led military campaign to oust the Iraqi occupation of Kuwait, Egypt's Western creditors cancelled half this debt. This political intervention made it possible for Egypt to conclude an Economic Reform and Structural Adjustment Program agreement with the IMF and World Bank and to begin to privatize the public sector in earnest.

An important symbol of the reversal of Nasserist policies was the abrogation of controls on agricultural rents established when land reform was instituted in 1952 along with a new rural property code. Hundreds of thousands of peasants were evicted from lands on which they could no longer afford rent or that the state returned to the elite families of the pre-1952 era. Police violently backed the returning agrarian capitalists against evicted farmers.[47]

Another emblem of the transition to Washington Consensus policies and the close entanglement of the state and private enterprise was the installation of the "government of businessmen" headed by Ahmad Nazif in 2004. Gamal Mubarak, the president's younger son, took over the ruling National Democratic Party by forming a Policies Committee composed of his coterie of business cronies who profited from the accelerated privatization of public assets and the removal of agrarian rent controls. A former banker and a true believer in the policies promoted by the IFIs, Gamal was groomed to succeed his father. His allies dominated the parliaments of 2005 and 2010. Large-scale capital could not do business in Egypt without connections to Gamal's cronies, the various state security apparatuses, or the NDP.[48]

During the mid-2000s Egypt received substantial foreign direct investment, and GDP grew at about 7 percent annually. Gulf capital flooded the market with investments in commercial agriculture, beach resorts, and luxury housing. Cairo's upper-class suburbs, initiated in the Sadat era, grew rapidly. Gated communities catered to an expanding, globalized new bourgeoisie.

As part of his efforts to attract capital investment and promote a counterweight to the Nasserist forces, in 1972 Sadat invited members of the Muslim Brotherhood who had escaped the Nasser regime and become wealthy while living in exile in oil-producing states to return to Egypt. From the 1980s to the 2000s, the regime allowed the Muslim Brothers to win parliamentary seats and establish lucrative businesses but periodically repressed them when they exceeded the regime's vague political and economic limits. For example, Mubarak mostly welcomed Islamic enterprise but broke up Islamic investment companies and jailed some of their owners in 1988 when he believed they posed a political threat.[49]

Beginning in the early 1990s, Mubarak allowed the army to create profitable business enterprises with legal and financial privileges not enjoyed by the public and the private sectors. Military entrepreneurs collaborated with foreign capital, especially from the Arab Gulf states, to expand investments in heavy industries such as manufacturing cement, steel, and vehicles. They ventured into land reclamation for commercial agriculture activities and dominated the public construction sector.[50]

The security apparatus generally supported the business elite against discontented peasants and workers who lost out in liberalization. Private capital created new jobs, but mostly at inferior conditions than the public sector, which dismissed hundreds of thousands of workers or compelled them to take early retirement. A wave of strikes erupted in the 2000s.[51] The labor movement did not directly cause the 2011 popular uprising, but did popularize a politics and culture of protest, delegitimizing the regime.

§

The tipping point for Syria's more aggressive departure from developmentalism was the severe balance of payments crisis in 1986.[52] The regime saw no other option, especially given the embourgeoisification of the political class.[53] As state officials and their partners in the "private"[54] sector accumulated capital, their structural power in Syria grew. By the early to mid-1990s the private sector started to rival the state's economic power, making it another anchor of power for the state and select social strata, including the "state bourgeoisie"—state officials who enriched themselves through corrupt business practices.[55]

After the late 1980s the gradual unraveling of the central command economy and the expanding liberalization produced a transformed Syrian ruling class and severe social polarization. Popular classes suffered as state social safety nets frayed, dramatically decreasing social welfare and public sector employment. Regime officials' and private actors' alignment in capital accumulation was originally underwritten by the former's dirigisme and the latter's search for lucrative and guaranteed investments. Until the mid-1990s, the development of informal economic networks with their attendant shadow institutions suited both state strongmen and enterprising business actors without having to answer publicly to the growing contradictions between the regime's "socialist" discourse and the drift toward neoliberal-like policies.

After the mid-1990s Syria began to resemble Egypt and Tunisia: only state-approved business interests, in many cases in partnership with leading state personnel, could flourish beyond a certain threshold of capital accumulation. The regime shaped the market; policies served particular business interests, mediated by the government's Guidance Committee and Higher Investment Council. By then, the structural power of capital had developed sufficiently so that the state was no longer the only means to achieve wealth, power, and status.

In 2005 Hafez al-Asad's successor and son, Bashar, adopted a Social Market Economy model to guide Syria's "modernization," which eventually sounded the death knell of the pre-2011 social order. Three major factors produced unprecedented discontent and social polarization from 2005 to 2011. Neoliberal policies dried up the last vestiges of redistributive policies at a time of high unemployment and an expanding labor market. In contrast, the state provided ample support to the private sector—including various networks close to or dominated by regime social circles—by establishing a new private banking system, high-end commercial and communications ventures, and holding companies. Finally, there was the near decimation of the agricultural sector, due to decades of neglect and poor management and debilitating waves of unprecedented drought, causing the migration of more than 400,000 families to urban areas already overburdened by underemployment and poor living conditions.[56] On the heels of the devastation in Iraq and neoconservative drumming to bomb Syria, 2005–2011 saw no appetite for public protest. Nonetheless, discontent reached the highest and broadest level in Syria in almost three decades, encompassing, for the first time, the dwindling middle classes, who could not benefit from the glittery new cities or the new commerce-based job market requiring mostly unskilled or semiskilled labor. This discontent, aided by the Egyptian and Tunisian examples, erupted into protest in 2011.

§

In the mid-1980s, Tunisia moved to a carefully modulated neoliberalization. Due to the social power of the UGTT and entrenched familial-business networks, breaking direct state control of the economy was more complex and contested than in than Egypt or Syria. So Tunisia's transition was earlier but lighter. Nevertheless, by the early 1980s, the exploding costs of commodity subsidies stressed the current accounts balance, which no longer became manageable with the collapse of oil prices in 1986 and the decline in migrant worker remittances.

Tunisia adopted a structural adjustment package meant to "open" the economy, shrink subsidies, and force agriculture to compete with global production. The opening was partial, with mafia-type sectors securing substantial slices of national wealth.[57] This partial *infitah* included "industrial upgrading": select firms gained access to state assistance in modernizing production processes. Substantial capitalist sectors operated informally to evade restrictions and bribes. Ultimately those close to the Ben Ali dictatorship controlled much of the economy, especially the Trabelsi clan, the family of Ben Ali's second wife, Leila.[58]

Women laborers spread from previous concentration in textiles to call centers and the rural sector.[59] Preferential investment codes for capital-holders set the stage for a renaissance of agricultural capitalism.[60] A burgeoning rural bourgeoisie profited from the late 1970s to 2010, especially intensive olive producers.[61] Because capitalism is inherently polarizing, it also rested on widespread land alienation for smallholders.[62] In the phosphate mining regions corruption in job allocations led to serial social explosions. A six-month-long riot/uprising erupted in the Gafsa mining basin in 2008, as people revolted against poverty and lack of opportunity, amid unemployment rates dwarfing the national average. Among the participants were the unorganized unemployed dissident UGTT members. The rebellion roiled the country, a foretaste of the 2010–2011 uprising that directly targeted political authoritarianism.[63]

UPRISINGS AND AFTER

The self-immolation of Mohammed Bouazizi in Tunisia was the spark that set the region ablaze in 2010–11. Uprisings of various size, pacing, and penetration and manipulation by outside forces cascaded across the region.[64] In most cases, discontent was partially due to neoliberalism. Commodity subsidies declined, wages stagnated, and poverty rates increased region-wide. While the uprisings swept the political order in the three countries around the same time, the state-capital relationship in Egypt has taken a new turn, setting it apart from the war economy in Syria or continued neoliberalism in Tunisia.

Since former general Abdel Fattah al-Sisi assumed the presidency of Egypt in 2014, military entrepreneurs have replaced private capital as the leading force in the government and the market. The state apparatus is increasingly constituted of retired officers who also occupy top government positions controlling the economy. They foster the military institution's monopolies in sectors of civilian production and services. As the new military regime pursues drastic neoliberal measures, the old business elite is reduced to either subcontracting for military business or being sidelined completely.[65]

As in Egypt and Syria, relationships of exclusion gave birth to a substantial dispossessed sector in Tunisia. It partook in a revolution, spreading from poorer and drier regions and only later arriving to the coast. Recalling that generally the working class has propelled political democracy, the 2011 uprising fits the pattern of classic bourgeois revolutions.[66] Subsequently, democracy has been an instrument for the further integration of Tunisia into global capitalism, amid pervasive "counter-terrorist" militarization.[67]

The state has absorbed the political effects of mass immiseration, distributing subsidies to popular classes to absorb social unease. Its primary role has been to contain the discontent by the carrot of subsidies and the stick of state violence while serving as a mechanism for increasing integration of Tunisia into the international division of labor: by increasing subjugation to the global law of value through currency devaluation, deepening trade agreements with the EU, and opening agriculture for foreign investment.[68] Unrest has intensified. The government has become almost entirely a mechanism for ever-continuing accumulation.[69]

Unlike Egypt's and Tunisia's uprisings, Syria's was, from early on, deeply penetrated by regional and international allies and foes, shattering national social reproduction and accumulation, and reconstituting state/market/class relationships. Less than two years after the Syrian uprising exploded, new opportunities for capital accumulation and class re-formation, such as oil; smuggling; trade in archeological, military equipment, and other commodities; idiosyncratic taxation; and racketeering emerged, increasing the power of new business actors: warlords in rebel-held areas and various entrepreneurial interlocutors in regime and Kurdish-controlled territories. They are emerging as the strongest prop of the new "business community" and quickly overtaking their pre-uprising predecessors. There are, of course, notable remnants of the pre-uprising order such as the president's business mogul cousin, Rami Makhlouf.

With the Syrian regime deserving ultimate responsibility, an embryonic new Syria, damaged and disfigured, has begun to take shape. The evolving relationship forged after 2013 among the state, market, and the class of new "entrepreneurs," let alone neighboring and faraway states, prolonged the conflict and obstructed peace and reconciliation. For all the main players—the regime, the opposition, ISIS, neighboring states—the war economy was simply too lucrative to dissolve. The formation and consolidation of new groups of capitalists across political and territorial divides is in progress among the residual mayhem. The extent to which these might find common cause in any future political configuration is unclear. The new capitalists are unlikely to yield illicit wealth flows as the embattled regime recovers territory and resources. These new "entrepreneurs" may become a social anchor facilitating medium-term stability, amid growing resentment, destitution, repression, and the return of refugees.

Despite efforts of remnants of Tunisia's old regime to stifle class politics and return to Washington Consensus economic policies, the existence of the UGTT has put some limits on its freedom of maneuver. Military totalitarianism and the continuing repression of public politics has delayed the reemergence of class politics in Egypt in Syria. But the popular uprisings in Sudan, Algeria, Lebanon, and Iraq in 2018–20 and Morocco's Hirak Rif of 2016–17 demonstrate that the structural crisis of the regional form of capital accumulation and governance manifested in the popular uprisings of 2010–11 has not been resolved.

Chapter 3

TEN PROPOSITIONS ON OIL

Timothy Mitchell

THE IMPORTANCE OF OIL TO HOW WE LIVE APPEARS TO DICTATE the terms in which we think about it. Vital to industrial society and world trade and a source of extraordinary government, corporate, and private wealth, oil often seems to overwhelm our attempts to understand it. Since the organizing of industrial life has come to depend on the supply of petroleum, those supplies, we assume, have to be continually secured. This vulnerability of supply brings repeated risks of conflict and war, especially in the Middle East, the region with the world's largest reserves of hydrocarbons. Oil has determined much of the political economy of the Middle East, it follows from such ways of thinking, and shaped the forms of its states.

This energy determinism is not helpful. On the one hand, it grants too much power to oil: such power had to be built and shaped, taking some paths and not others. On the other hand, it often says little about oil itself—how it is pumped, refined, shipped, sold, used, and by whom. It does not consider the alternatives to a world built on energy from oil, alternatives that we must rapidly adopt if the world is to remain hospitable to human flourishing. Something considered "vital" to our way of life turns out to be a threat to life's very continuation.

This chapter develops ten propositions for the study of oil in the Middle East, illustrated with a variety of events from the history and politics of the region. The ten points are not intended as a comprehensive account; they highlight issues of debate or where common understandings might be questioned or reconsidered.

The first three arguments address the arrangements that governed oil production in the Middle East in the first half of the twentieth century, when a handful of Western oil companies controlled the industry. The fourth and fifth consider how these monopoly arrangements were challenged in the second half of the twentieth century, first by those who worked in the industry and then by the states formed to govern the producing regions and to police challenges from labor. These states succeeded in taking control of oil production. Four further arguments cover the political economy of oil in the decades following the widespread nationalizations of the 1970s. The final proposition addresses how to write a historical political economy of oil in the face of catastrophic climate change. It poses this as a question not of how history shapes our understanding of oil, but how oil has shaped our understanding of history.

1. THE PROBLEM OF OIL IS NOT THE VULNERABILITY OF ITS SUPPLY, BUT THAT IT MIGHT FLOW TOO EASILY.

To understand the political economy of oil, we should not start from the assumption that oil is a source of vulnerability—that it is so vital to our way of life that its supply is constantly endangered or at risk. On the contrary, a more important factor shaping the political economy of oil is that, throughout most decades of the last century, there has been too much of it. Examples include East Texas in the early 1930s, the Organization of Petroleum Exporting Countries (OPEC) period in 1970s and 1980s, and recent efforts to limit production. The normal threat, especially to those controlling the oil fields of the Middle East, was not that its supply might be interrupted, but that it might flow too freely. The problem of surplus reflects not the needs of industrial society, which were relatively easy to meet, but the opportunities for capital.

Oil has a special place in the study of political economy. Over the course of the twentieth century, industrial life came to depend on the supply of oil, as a source of energy and an essential raw material for making plastics, chemicals, and agricultural fertilizers. It became the largest commodity in world trade, the only one whose price and supply featured regularly on the front pages of newspapers, just as it is the only commodity that seems to merit its own chapter in a book such as this. Since the world's largest reserves of petroleum are found in the Middle East, the region came to be identified with struggles to control and protect the global supply of oil. The need to secure those supplies, and their vulnerability to disruption, seemed to place the Middle East at the center of international economic and political contestation.

The dependence on oil made human populations liable, not so much to threats of sudden, unauthorized interruption in supply, but to the steady, authorized power of those who developed ways to limit or slow the rate of production. By restricting the supply, it was possible to raise the price at which crude oil was traded, allowing the capture of extraordinary levels of surplus (or profit). The scale of this surplus can be seen today from the example of Iraq, which has experimented with different methods of auctioning contracts for oil production. The contracts signed in 2018 estimate the average cost of production, covering both capital expenditure and operating costs and including some of the more difficult fields, at US$6 per barrel. With oil then selling at prices more than ten times that rate, the surplus captured by the government of Iraq was estimated at 95 percent.[1] The political economy of oil is the study of this extraordinary apparatus of surplus: how it was constructed and the subsequent struggles to capture, extend, and protect it.

The ability to limit the supply of oil is often associated with the rise of the producer cartel, OPEC. Starting in the 1970s, the major exporting countries attempted to set production quotas to regulate and limit the supply, although in subsequent decades a series of wars and sanction regimes provided more effective limits. From 2016 Saudi Arabia, in collaboration with other OPEC members and with Russia, worked to reestablish production quotas, in order to restrict supply and raise the level of surplus revenue. However, organizing the restriction of supply and the capturing of an enormous surplus was not something invented in the 1970s. It shaped the beginnings of the corporate-run petroleum industry nearly a century before OPEC became a factor in the Middle East oil production regime.

Oil production first developed on an industrial scale in the United States. Since oil was available in relatively few locations, it was possible for just one firm, the Rockefeller-controlled Standard Oil, to dominate production and establish a near monopoly over much of the world's supply. As oil was discovered in new regions, including the Middle East, and as the main use of oil changed from making kerosene for lighting to producing fuel for transportation, a handful of large companies emerged and gained control. These firms collaborated to limit the supply of oil and maintain monopoly prices.[2]

The origins of the oil industry in the Middle East are usually dated to 1901, when the Persian government granted exclusive rights to prospect for oil across the entire southern half of Iran to a British firm. The firm subsequently known as the Anglo-Persian (later Anglo-Iranian) Oil Company discovered its first oil field in 1908. Negotiations were under way in the same period for exclusive rights to all the oil reserves of the Ottoman Empire, which were granted to a group of London-based investors on the eve of the World War I. However, these arrangements were motivated as much by the aim of restricting the production of oil as the development of new reserves.

In the case of Iraq, for example, after World War I a consortium of Western oil companies gained a monopoly of the country's oil. The consortium restricted exploration to a few areas, and slowed the development of oil, sometimes deliberately drilling shallow wells or plugging those that struck oil so as restrict production.[3] In Saudi Arabia, an American consortium acquired exclusive rights in 1933 and discovered oil in commercial quantities five years later. But the expansion of oil production was halted during World War II, and large-scale production began only a decade after its discovery.[4] Such delays allowed the United States, where restrictions were harder to impose, to dominate world oil production.

2. THE NEED FOR OIL IS NOT A NECESSARY FEATURE OF INDUSTRIAL LIFE BUT THE RESULT OF TAKING DELIBERATE PATHS TOWARDS CARBON-HEAVY WAYS OF LIVING.

Oil was important to the organization of industrial society in the twentieth century, especially with the introduction of the internal combustion engine and the building of societies in the West based on the mass ownership of automobiles. However, the importance of oil was not simply an inevitable consequence of the growth of industrial life.[5] Oil companies and related businesses—banking and real estate, petrochemicals and agriculture, automobile and construction firms—manufactured the need for oil, through the building and promotion of carbon-heavy ways of living. Creating suburbia at the expense of sustaining viable cities, defunding public transport in favor of subsidized highways for private cars, replacing reusable materials with plastic goods whose price did not include their environmental cost, promoting chemical- and fuel-intensive agriculture organized around meat production instead of sustainable alternatives: these and other policies placed the demand for oil at the center of a mode of life characteristic of the group of industrialized countries that historically accounted for most of the world's oil consumption. They were especially pronounced in the United States, which used oil at more than double the rate per capita of other industrialized countries. As a result, in the 1950s the United States alone consumed 60 percent of all oil produced and as recently as 2005 accounted for more than a quarter of annual world consumption.[6] The wastage of a nonrenewable resource was heavily promoted by the oil industry itself.[7] At the same time, as large US oil companies accumulated evidence of the catastrophic impact of burning fossil fuels on the earth's ecological balance, they systematically misled the public about the facts of climate change, to avert this threat to increased consumption.[8]

In recent decades, some of the highest levels of oil consumption per capita have spread among oil-exporting countries, such as Saudi Arabia and other Gulf states. As their domestic consumption rapidly increased, such countries had proportionately less oil to export. More seriously, over the next three to five decades, as the world follows a path toward the elimination of fossil fuels, those countries (along with the United States) will be doubly affected. They will face larger costs in switching away from the use of oil compared to countries with much lower per capita consumption at the same time as their income from oil production is likely to rapidly decline and then disappear.

The dependence on oil had a strange consequence: what mattered was not the free flow of cheap oil, but the ability to restrict its flow and reap extraordinary profits. In other words, it was not simply the demand for energy that shaped the politics of oil, a demand that varied enormously with the building of different energy regimes, but the opportunities for capital.

3. THE MULTINATIONAL FIRM EMERGED NOT TO MEET THE NEEDS OF OIL PRODUCTION BUT TO ORGANIZE THE POSSIBILITY OF LIMITING SUPPLY AND REALIZING EXTRAORDINARY PROFITS.

To understand oil's relation to capital, one can compare it with other extractive industries on which industrial society depends. For example, the mining of sand and gravel, materials used to make concrete, has been basic to building cities and transportation. Found in most countries on earth, those materials are both abundant and ubiquitous. In comparison, oil is abundant but uncommon, found in extraordinary quantities but restricted to relatively few locations around the world. The limited geographical availability of oil, especially in the early and middle decades of the last century, made it possible for a handful of firms to attempt to monopolize production across the globe. By controlling and limiting supply, these firms could produce superprofits—earnings that vastly exceeded the cost of production. Superprofits were always vulnerable to the arrival of new supplies that might undermine monopoly prices, hence the continual threat of abundance.

We can explain in these terms the rise of a distinctive agent of twentieth-century politics, the multinational oil firm. The giant Western oil firms (the so-called seven sisters of the post–World War II period, consolidated into four today—ExxonMobil, Shell, BP, and Chevron)—are often thought to owe their size to the technical complexities of a new industry operating on a global scale, or the quantities of capital it required.[9] It would be better to see this the other way around: the scale of profits offered by oil production could be secured only by simplifying production into a handful of firms.

There is a further connection between the nature of oil production and the extraordinary size of the multinational firms that came to dominate it. The production of oil was notable not only for the scale of the earnings it generated, but also for their duration. Large oil fields, especially those of the Middle East, were stores of energy so abundant that they could be expected to generate revenue not for years but for decades. The control of an oil field constituted a source of earnings stretching far into the future. The oil corporation, organized as a joint-stock company, became a means of profiting from this future in the present. The company offered investors the opportunity to buy and trade its shares, which represented claims on the value of its future revenue. Until the rise of internet technology companies in the early twenty-first century, oil corporations were by far the world's largest publicly traded companies measured not only by current earnings but by market capitalization—meaning the present value of future earnings.

The oil corporation was a particular kind of financial machine, one that could claim and profit from a durable future. The durability of future revenue depended partly on the longevity of the flow of hydrocarbons from the giant oilfields of the Middle East. It also depended on the reliability of the labor force, the pipelines, the distribution arrangements, and the political control that assured this long-term future. The mechanism of its capture was political as much as financial. The oil company was not just a business firm that grew very big to cope with the technical demands of oil production. It was a distinctive apparatus organized to capture surplus from both the scale and durability of the production of oil.

4. IF COAL ENABLED WORKERS TO CREATE MASS DEMOCRACY, OIL HELPED TO SET ITS LIMITS.

The monopoly arrangements that developed to control Middle Eastern oil in the first half of the twentieth century faced two threats of increasing significance in the second half. One was from those who worked in the industry, the other from the states that had emerged to govern the producing regions.

Like industrial workers in other parts of the word, oil workers in the Middle East found themselves subject to poor and sometimes dangerous working conditions and few or no social and political rights. Employment and housing were typically segregated along racial lines, with the local Arab or Iranian workforce usually restricted to the lowest paid jobs and forced to endure the most rudimentary living conditions. Protests against these arrangements began in the early decades of the industry. In the period after World War II, workers in most oil-producing countries began to organize and demand improvements. The labor strikes that often followed sought better working and living conditions, as well as the right to unionize and a claim to wider political rights.

Since the production of energy was made central to the organizing of industrialized societies, energy workers have often shaped the course of political and social struggles. It is instructive to compare the fate of the demands made by oil workers in the Middle East to similar demands made by European workers earlier in the twentieth century—where the labor movement was also especially strong among those involved in energy production. In Europe, the production of coal rather than oil provided the mechanism for advancing demands for worker rights and for wider political freedoms. In Britain, France, and other European states, coal workers, together with those who ran the railways and the docks—which were choke points in the movement of carbon energy—were able to use their country's dependence on coal to achieve an unusual political power. By organizing strikes at the nodes of the networks along which coal was carried, they could shut down a country's main source of energy. This power, or the threat of using it, enabled working classes in the West to win critical democratic and social rights.

In the case of oil-producing states, the situation was different. In part, this reflected differences between coal and oil. Unlike coal, oil is a fluid that comes out of the earth under its own pressure. Therefore, workers are not sent underground to extract it, but remain on the surface, in smaller numbers compared to coal production and under the closer supervision of managers. This reduced the autonomy of workforces and made labor organizing more difficult. As a fluid, oil can be moved by pipeline, which also requires fewer workers than the railways typically used to move coal and is more difficult than rail transport to disrupt. Lastly, oil can be easily moved by tankers across oceans, making it easier for the firms shipping oil to evade or defeat the threat of labor protests. As oil from the Middle East was mostly shipped to regions that had industrialized earlier using coal, especially to Europe, the production of energy was now separated by a great distance from the sites where it was consumed, making it difficult for the workers producing oil to form alliances with workers at the sites of consumption. From this perspective, the West was able to outsource the production of energy (to regions where labor was easier to police) long before it began to outsource manufacturing production. For all these reasons, oil workers in the Middle East found it much more difficult than other energy workers to engineer out of the production of carbon energy a machinery for making effective political demands.[10]

5. THE ABILITY TO CHALLENGE THE POWER OF INTERNATIONAL OIL COMPANIES WAS EVENTUALLY ACQUIRED BY GOVERNMENTS BECOMING RESISTANT TO COUPS RATHER THAN BY WORKERS.

The other threat to Western corporate monopoly came from the sovereign governments that came to control the producing regions. The emergence of these centralized powers out of earlier patterns of empire, urban government, and rural authority was the outcome of longer-term processes. But the political order in the main oil-exporting countries—Iran, Iraq, Saudi Arabia, and the smaller Gulf nations, along with two North African producers, Libya and Algeria—was shaped by their developing oil industries. From the start, powers of government were defined in struggles over the terms of oil concessions. This framed emergent national politics as an anti-imperial struggle. Consequently, governments were able to transpose labor disputes and wider working-class politics into battles against the terms of oil concessions and the foreign control of oil, as in Iran in 1951–53 and at other moments in Iraq, Libya, Algeria, and other oil-exporting countries.[11]

At first, Britain and the United States met these threats by assisting in undermining and overthrowing nationalist governments. Decisive confrontations unfolded in Iran and Iraq—two populous and productive oil producers with the strongest labor and social movements. In Iran in 1953, the United States and Britain organized a military coup to overthrow the nationalist government led by Muhammad Mosaddeq. This government had challenged both the rights of the British-owned Anglo-Iranian Oil Company (later BP) and the autocratic power of the shah. In Iraq, the revolution of 1958 overthrew the British-backed monarchy and brought to power ‘Abd al-Karim Qasim, whose government embarked on a program of social and economic reform and took steps to create a national oil industry and reduce the control of the international oil companies. The companies responded by limiting oil production to weaken Qasim, whose government was overthrown in 1963 by a new military regime, welcomed and probably assisted to power by the United States.[12] In a number of other cases, Britain or the United States used political influence and covert operations in an attempt to forestall efforts to establish a greater national control over oil production.

The attempts to prevent Middle Eastern states from taking control of local oil production were successful only through the 1960s. After that, regimes either built security apparatuses that made them immune to US-supported military coups or were willing to accommodate US interests while pursuing greater government control. Smaller producers like Syria, Algeria, and Libya were the first to nationalize production, working with independent foreign oil companies that were challenging the monopoly of the oil majors. The decisive step was taken by Iraq. By 1970, also working with independent oil companies, Baghdad had developed the ability to produce and market its own oil outside the control of the majors. In 1972, Iraq nationalized the foreign-owned Iraq

Petroleum Company.[13] By the following year, Iran and Saudi Arabia had forced the international oil firms to accept national ownership and control of the oil industry, a transformation that was completed throughout the region within a decade.

Across the world, efforts to limit large corporations' power to capture the surplus from large-scale industrial processes were a key battle of twentieth-century political life. Workers in every country played a role in those battles. But in the case of the international oil industry, it was emergent national governments rather than labor organizations that acquired the decisive ability to challenge corporate control. From this confrontation there emerged a new kind of power in the Middle East, the petro-state.

6. THE CONCEPT OF THE "RENTIER STATE" IS NOW OF LIMITED USE.

Establishing national control of their resources transformed the oil-producing countries of the Middle East. But the political economy of petro-states did not conform to an expected pattern. Until the 1960s, it was commonly thought that the main obstacle to successful economic development by countries in the global South was lack of capital for investment. By the mid-1960s, oil-producing countries like Iran were acquiring significant revenues from oil rents—the payments they received from the international oil firms. Yet despite this access to abundant capital, they were failing to industrialize extensively or achieve more rapid growth in economic production. In 1970, the Iranian economist Hossein Mahdavy began to examine this problem of what he termed the "rentier state."[14] He proposed that oil exporters produced a particular form of developmental state. The oil industry created an industrial sector that was oriented to export, dependent on imports, and consequently unable to produce linkages with other productive activities, whether in agriculture or manufacturing, or to stimulate more intense interindustry relationships. For these reasons, development did not follow the pattern of successful late industrializers, such as Japan, where the lack of natural resource rents had pushed the country down the path of industrialization.

Subsequent discussions of the rentier state problem often diluted Mahdavy's insights, transforming the issue into a general problem of states with large surplus revenues rather than a set of arrangements specifically tied to the enclave nature of oil production and its connection with other productive sectors. As producer states took control of revenues and invested them, the enclaves were transformed into hubs of prosperity organized in specific ways, with the surplus often recycled into speculative real estate and military spending. As Adam Hanieh notes in his chapter in this book and elsewhere, the revenue from oil was not monopolized by the state but led to the emergence of a distinctive class of entrepreneurs who established large conglomerates in construction, the import and distribution of consumer goods, banking, and other fields.[15]

The idea of the rentier state then morphed into an argument about oil and democracy. Scholars used the term to explain patterns of political, not economic, development. Oil-exporting states were able to avoid the pressure to increase political freedoms, they argued, due to the way oil production channeled revenue into the hands of the government. Regimes could use these resources either to purchase support, to build an unusually repressive state, or to avoid the need to tax the population and grant political rights in return.[16]

These arguments often rest on liberal assumptions about the sources of democracy that ignore both the specific struggles that produced mass democracy elsewhere and the role of outsourcing energy production to oil regions in the weakening of democratic politics even in the West.[17] By considering the material and technical differences between the earlier history of coal and the growth of oil production in the Middle East, one can better address the question of oil and democracy. Every account of oil and democracy rests not only on arguments about "the Middle Eastern state" but on a set of assumptions about the origins and sources of democratic politics elsewhere.

7. THE "MARKET" FOR OIL AND ITS "PRICE" ARE COMPARATIVELY RECENT DEVELOPMENTS.

In the period governed by the monopolization of oil by a handful of major corporations, there was no international "oil market" and no "price" of crude oil that consumers or governments might know. Prices and markets were not a necessary feature of energy production, but the outcome of a struggle over the control of oil revenues in the 1970s.

From the mid-1960s, the threat of nationalization, and its gradual accomplishment, allowed the producer states to acquire a larger share of oil revenues. But this came not from reducing the revenues taken by Western oil firms, which continued to grow, but by shifting the cost to oil consumers. The main reorganization of costs occurred through the events known as the "oil crisis" of 1973–74. Those events, which led to a sudden shortage of petroleum supplies at gas stations in the United States and other countries and an abrupt quadrupling of its price, changed the way consumers and their governments thought about the problem of energy. They continue to shape discussions today. But exactly what happened is usually misunderstood.

The crisis is often misleadingly referred to as the OPEC price increase. In popular accounts, it is said that the OPEC states, seeking to raise the price of oil, cut off supplies to the West. This is wrong for three reasons. First, the actions of OPEC, spread over several years, were concerned not with the price of oil but the use of taxes to redistribute its revenues. Second, the rapid price increase of 1973–74 was a response not to decisions by OPEC but to actions taken by US allies, in particular Saudi Arabia, in a dispute over US obstruction of a settlement to the question of Palestine. Third, the shortage of supplies at gas stations was caused by other factors, unconnected with the actions of OPEC or Saudi Arabia. Standard accounts of the "OPEC price increase" confuse the question of claims on revenue with the question of price, conflate the dispute with OPEC and the conflict over Palestine, and ignore the role of the US government's petroleum policies in making the country vulnerable to a threatened dip in supplies.[18]

The confusion between the price of oil and the distribution of its revenues was possible because, before the mid-1970s, there was no way to know the actual price of oil. Unlike other major commodities, oil had no mercantile exchange where traders bought and sold supplies. In place of an international market, oil was exchanged largely within and among the multinational corporations that controlled its supply, at prices that were fixed internally and/or subject to long-term supply agreements. One advantage of this arrangement for the oil companies was that when producer states in regions like the Middle East tried to increase the tax on corporate revenues, they had no way of knowing the price of a barrel of oil and thus the actual revenue liable to taxation. Instead, the tax was based on a fixed benchmark, known as the "posted price." From the later 1960s, as rapid inflation eroded the value of the US dollar, producer states sought to maintain or increase their share of oil revenues by raising the level of taxation. Their negotiations with the major oil companies took the form of requesting an increase in the benchmark, or posted price. Since the discussions appeared to refer to the level of a "price" rather than a "tax," the oil companies and the media were able to portray this as a dispute over the price of oil, not the distribution of its revenues. Rather than suffer an increased tax on the extraordinary profits earned from Middle East oil, the companies were able to convert the tax into increased prices for oil products.

As the dispute over the distribution of oil revenues unfolded, it proved useful to have a "crisis" that served to explain the transfer of increased prices to consumers. This was provided by the October 1973 Arab-Israeli war. However, the embargo on oil supplies to the United States announced by Saudi Arabia in response to US intransigence on the Palestine question was not the cause of the subsequent shortages at US gas stations. These were due to, among other factors, a lack of investment in US refinery capacity and President Nixon's imposition of price controls.[19]

Following the crisis, economists for the first time began to develop models to "explain" the price of oil; and, with oil majors no longer able to monopolize the global supply, there emerged a commodity market in which oil contracts were exchanged and where financiers and oil companies were able to speculate in the movement of oil prices. This world of prices, markets, and speculators was not an essential feature of energy use, but a new arrangement created after more than a century of oil production—one that would govern the second, and presumably final, century of the widespread use of oil.

8. MILITARY SPENDING OPERATES PRIMARILY NOT TO PROTECT THE FLOW OF OIL BUT TO ENABLE THE CIRCULATION OF OIL REVENUES AND THE PRODUCTION OF CREDIT MONEY.

The relationship between oil, militarism, and security can best be approached in these terms—rather than in terms of putative "threats" to the security of supply, initially ascribed to Soviet ambitions and later to the "rogue states" of Iran and Iraq.

If the Soviet Union was a problem in the Cold War decades, it was not as a threat to the oil market. Rather, if it were to find a way to support oil production outside the control of the major oil corporations, the USSR threatened to *create* an oil market. It attempted to do this partly by searching for ways to export its own oil and gas to the West, something the United States continually tried to block, and partly by aiding the efforts of certain producer states like Iraq to develop an oil industry free from the technical and financial control of Western oil companies. Later, once Iraq and Iran had acquired this technical independence, these two countries posed a similar threat—the ability to supply large amounts of oil outside the arrangements managed by the international oil companies.

The purported "threat" of the Soviet Union to the supply of oil was useful in a different way. It appeared to lend a justification for the extraordinary levels of military spending by the main oil-producing states.

Oil revenues can be linked to militarism in the Middle East in terms of the particular usefulness of arms spending to the problem of capital. This works in two time frames. First, as the producer states began to acquire a much greater share of oil revenues, the opportunity arose for extraordinary levels of purchases from the West, offering channels for firms, brokers, suppliers, and officials to turn oil income into fees and payments. Some of the new revenue went into building civilian infrastructure and real estate and the importing of consumer goods, creating private fortunes for many of the individuals and businesses involved. But such investment can quickly reach its limit, especially where populations are small and incomes are unequally distributed. Military spending addresses this limit. Compared even to luxury consumer purchases and real estate, the cost of military equipment is astronomical. A relatively small item like a fighter jet can cost US$100 million. In addition, unlike most consumer goods, justifying the purchase of military equipment does not require having any practical use for it. So compared to, say, luxury cars or apartments, military goods provide a vastly more effective means of organizing the flow of expenditures and the opportunity for fees and payments.

Second, the incomes of oil-producing states represented not just a surplus in the present but a future revenue against which Western financial firms had opportunities to create new levels of credit. The oil revenues of producer states represent an unusually secure and long-term source of payments. The West had devised a system of finance in which private firms—the large, international banks—had the power to create money on a large scale by extending credit, from which the bank profits through interest payments and fees. But the creation of credit money requires an apparatus for capturing revenues that promises reliable repayment. The reliability of future oil revenues, combined with the scale of financing to which arms expenditures gave rise, were especially suited to provide this mechanism.

The recycling of surplus Middle East oil revenues into military spending was one part of a broader reorganization of international finance made possible by the changes in the control of oil in the 1970s. The expanded oil revenues of the Gulf, referred to as *petrodollars*, were deposited in New York and London banks, causing a rapid expansion in private financial markets that overwhelmed the postwar system of control over international capital movements by central banks. The new liquidity of finance, tied to the movements of another liquid, petroleum, ushered in the forms of deregulation, financialization, and assaults on the protection of living standards that came to be known as neoliberalism.[20]

9: OIL IS NOT THE CAUSE OF WAR, BUT PROVIDES A RATIONALE THAT ENABLES IT.

In the fifty years from 1918 to 1968, Western oil firms took control of the oil reserves of the Middle East and relied on the United States and its allies to maintain its power over those resources and help suppress or overthrow local threats to that power. The United States provided this support without the need for military bases, major wars, or losing soldiers in battle.[21] In the fifty years after 1968, the United States supported a series of invasions and occupations, launched wars of its own in Afghanistan and Iraq, and found ways to prolong and intensify others. It built a string of military bases across the region and through the early decades of the twenty-first century remained engaged in war in at least half a dozen countries of the Middle East. The violence cost hundreds of thousands of lives.

Was oil the cause of this intensifying violence? That argument would be too simple. As US firms from the late 1960s lost direct control over the production and supply of oil, the US government began to form closer alliances with forces in the region that had their own agendas: the Zionism of Israel, the Wahhabism of Saudi Arabia, and many others. At the same time, unable to sustain its own hegemony directly, the United States substituted in its place the support for wars of attrition and prolonged conflict, to weaken regional powers like Iran and Iraq that would not accept its authority. These conflicts did not protect the supply of oil; if anything, they helped indirectly to deal with the problem of oversupply by debilitating two of the three largest oil producers in the region. But the scale of the region's oil reserves and the repeated assertion that this put US security at risk provided a rationale for almost endless violence.

10. THE CLIMATE CRISIS CHALLENGES THE VERY IDEA OF POLITICAL ECONOMY.

It can be useful to understand oil historically, to see how the current political economy of oil developed. But the world produced by the accelerating consumption of oil over the last century challenges the very conceptions of history and political economy as fields of concern. We have usually written history as the study of how human agents, individual or collective, make and remake the world, slowly conquering nature, developing resources, and building increasingly complex and technically capable societies. But the combustion of carbon energy on which these processes relied has caused the warming of the earth's climate system, setting in motion changes in the earth's atmosphere and oceans that can be slowed but not reversed by human action. Together with the mass extinction of species brought by the carbon-fueled trampling of the earth, these changes threaten not just the feasibility of human societies but the collapse of the thin envelope of biogeochemical processes—the fragile, porous skin connecting the lower atmosphere to the subsoil and its parent rocks—in which the exchanges occur that allow forms of life to thrive.[22] We can no longer speak of nature as something apart from society, resources as merely materials to be developed, politics as the organizing of an increasing technical competence, or our collective future as the continued development of human potential.

The future is now different: to have a chance of at least mitigating the catastrophic consequences that the earth faces, the world must largely decarbonize by 2050. This was the goal implied by the 2015 Paris climate agreement, to limit the increase in global average temperature to 1.5°C above preindustrial levels, and spelled out in 2018 by the Intergovernmental Panel on Climate Change.[23] If this target is to be approached, within a generation the Middle East will undergo a radical reorganization of its political and economic life. Some of the changes are already under way: despite an increase of almost 50 percent in production, the region exports no more oil today than it did forty years ago. In many of the smaller producing countries of the region, oil production has hit a plateau or is declining. The largest producer, Saudi Arabia, has been forced to limit production, in part due to the long decline in oil consumption in OECD countries.

But even if decarbonization were achieved, catastrophic consequences may be inevitable. Since 1998, the region has been experiencing a drought, due in part to global warming, that has seen the lowest levels of rainfall, not in recent memory, but in at least nine hundred years.[24] In Syria and Yemen, the drought is a direct cause of social collapse and conflict; in Iran, it is a serious threat to livelihoods. By the end of the twenty-first century, drought combined with the diversion of remaining waters into reservoirs may cause the rivers that form the Fertile Crescent to disappear. In Iraq, the activist campaign "Iraq without Rivers" reports that even today, due to the loss of water in the rivers and the increasing levels of salts in what is left, 25 percent of the country's irrigated area no longer supports cultivation.[25] Rising global sea levels combined with the effect of upstream reservoirs are having a similar effect on the agricultural plain of the Nile Delta.[26] In the longer term, rising sea levels imperil all the coastal cities and hinterlands of the region. Future humidity levels threaten to make areas of the Gulf too hot for human habitation.

This raises the question of how to approach the political economy of oil in the face of catastrophic climate change. It poses this as a problem not of how history shapes our understanding of oil, but how oil has shaped our understanding of history. We inhabit a historical mode of being, seeing ourselves as the products of unfolding historical processes driven by human social and political action. That mode of being was made possible by the extraordinary forces unlocked during the brief era of almost limitless access to fossil fuels. The viability of a future in which humans still have a place now depends on ending that era, reducing the global production of oil and gas almost to zero by 2050, a point now much closer in time than, say, the great expansion of the Middle East oil-producing states in the early 1980s. This entails not just finding new approaches to the political economy of oil but, starting from the vantage point of the Middle East and North Africa, recognizing the limits of our ordinary conceptions of the economic and the political.

Chapter 4

REGIONAL MILITARIES AND THE GLOBAL MILITARY-INDUSTRIAL COMPLEX

Shana Marshall

ARMED FORCES AND MILITARY ESTABLISHMENTS HAVE PLAYED an enormous role in shaping the political economy of the contemporary Middle East and North Africa. Not only is the region the world's largest importer of arms, but the ambitions of military officers have long had a dramatic impact on resource distribution and political dynamics. Many of the region's most fundamental transformations, including coups, state-building projects, and the assumption of ruinous debt loads were intertwined with the military and its institutional prerogatives. Access to the physical means of repression—weapons and related military technologies—remains central to the foreign policies of MENA states. Similarly, US and European foreign policy toward the region is most concretely expressed in militarized forms, including arms sales and technology transfers, defense pacts, military training exercises, and armed interventions. Because the region's militaries are important political actors and integral to the global arms market, leading civilians and serving officers in the arms industries and military establishments of the core capitalist countries of the United States and Europe have complex and often personal relationships with MENA military officers. Together they form an integrated network of corporate and political leaders working to expand militarization and legitimize military regimes.

The weapons industry is not merely a collection of national firms trading and selling finished products. Like other industries, arms production and associated technologies have been globalized. They are characterized by supply chains that span the globe with diffuse and overlapping patterns of transnational ownership and investment. Even if specific countries lack the technological or industrial resources to develop expensive weapons systems on their own, the globalization of the arms industry provides many opportunities to participate in the weapons industry. This is manifested in the resurgence of military industrial production in the Middle East through foreign partnerships, including establishing defense technology centers in regional universities, building military-industrial economic parks, and the growing number of arms fairs and weapons exhibitions in the region. International economic and financial policy that prioritizes investment in military over civilian projects are accelerating the militarization of the regional political economy.

Armies have been a central factor in the politics of the MENA region and much of the global South. In the 1940s–1960s social scientists identified armies as prime movers in independence struggles, revolutions, modernization, state building, and formation of national identity. The military remained central in the postindependence period of the 1950s–1970s, when coups and countercoups shaped regional political life, beginning with the three coups of 1949 in Syria (and several subsequently). Egypt's 1952 coup/revolution established and legitimized the military republic as a regional political model that, at least initially, enjoyed real popularity. The model was adopted in more or less stable forms in Syria, Iraq, Yemen, Algeria, Libya, Sudan, and Turkey.

When scholars and journalists puzzled over the endurance of unpopular authoritarian regimes from the 1980s through the early 2000s, the military was again highlighted, this time as an institutional pillar blocking popular calls for democratic change. Political scientists in particular focused on how regimes balanced material resources, political cooptation, and identity politics to satisfy the armed forces while also limiting their capacity to stage further coups.[1] Likewise, they frequently constructed regional regime typologies in terms of the military's role in the structure of government: military democracies (Turkey, Israel) where democratic institutions exist but powerful militaries exercise substantial influence; states where large militaries are counterbalanced by a powerful array of competing agencies allied with the leader, such as praetorian guards and intelligence agencies (Saddam Hussein's Iraq and Mu'ammar Qaddafi's Libya); regimes with a civilian autocrat with a military background and extensive perquisites for the armed forces (Hosni Mubarak's Egypt, Ali Abdallah Saleh's Yemen, and Abdelaziz Bouteflika's Algeria); and monarchies that rely heavily on mercenary forces and foreign advisors (Saudi Arabia, United Arab Emirates, Bahrain, Qatar, Kuwait).[2] In Jordan a military composed largely of Bedouin was historically the loyal social base of the Hashemite monarchy and a counterweight to the Palestinian majority of the population. Tunisia, and to a lesser extent Morocco, are the exceptional cases where the military has not been a central political actor.

THE FORMATION OF MODERN REGIONAL MILITARIES

The postcolonial states of the MENA region deployed the extensive military, police, and intelligence structures built by colonial authorities, first to enforce their own rule and later to organize the populations and economies in support of the Allied war effort in World War II. Writing on postindependence regimes in the Middle East in 1960, Hisham Sharabi observed that colonization and imperialism had destroyed many social and political structures but "the one institution that was preserved—and indeed invigorated . . . was the army."[3] In fact, many proponents of modernization theory believed that these large armies represented the most "progressive elements"[4] in newly independent states, because they were "hostile toward parochial enclaves"[5] and "focused on the acquiring of technical skills that are of particular value for economic development."[6] Writing in the postwar period, when state-led development and import-substitution industrialization (sometimes labeled *developmentalism* or *peripheral Keynesianism*; see the Introduction to this book) was the prevailing economic model, they envisioned the military as an engine of progress.

The MENA region's large armies did participate in public works projects, building dams, roads, seaports, schools, and hospitals.[7] The engineering and construction expertise required for such projects led many states to develop industrial policies that assigned to the military a key role in critical sectors like industrial manufacturing and provision of basic inputs like steel and cement. In addition, military officers were appointed alongside civilian technocrats to manage state-owned industries as well as newly nationalized conglomerates. This gave the military a foothold in the economy that would last decades.

Gamal Abdel Nasser's Egypt (1954–1970) was the pioneer and leading example of this, but it was adopted to varying extents in many of the region's authoritarian republics. As the armed forces expanded their ranks, with armies in Algeria, Egypt, Iraq, and Syria more than doubling in size from the 1960s to the late 1970s–early 1980s, they also expanded their efforts for self-provisioning in food, uniforms, and housing.[8]

Another factor in the expansion of the economic role of militaries was the imperative of ensuring a cheap domestic supply of basic commodities and consumer goods such as bread, infant formula, refined cooking oil, and household appliances. The availability and affordability of such goods was an important component of the "authoritarian bargain." States guaranteed a basic standard of living in exchange for popular support and severe limits on political expression.[9] The militaries' access to land, conscript labor, energy inputs, industrial goods, and public financing made them key to providing these basic necessities. In Egypt, the National Service Projects Organization, a military conglomerate created by President Anwar Sadat (1970–1981)[10] expanded the production of such goods. Hosni Mubarak's (1981–2011) defense minister, 'Abd al-Halim Abu Ghazala, further diversified the military's commercial activities by capitalizing on his relationships with the executives of major US companies, including General Motors.[11] During the 1980s in Syria, the Milihouse firm (short for Military Housing) became one of the country's two largest construction companies. Originally formed to construct military housing, it expanded into building roads, bridges, schools, irrigation systems, and hospitals.[12] Similarly, Iraqi military industries that had mobilized during the war with Iran (1980–88) expanded into civilian production. The Ministry of Industry and Military Industrialization oversaw more than forty separate state agencies tasked with dam construction, fertilizer and chemical production, and prefab housing construction.[13]

High growth levels, buoyed by oil prices and labor remittances from the Gulf, facilitated many of these projects. Multinational conglomerates and private investors also participated in military-led projects and incorporated military partners, especially when public financing and subsidized inputs were forthcoming.[14] But in the mid-1980s the economies of the largest Arab countries began to stagnate.[15] As oil prices dropped precipitously in 1986, so did aid and remittances from the Gulf states. Soviet assistance, which had financed the building of the Aswan Dam in addition to projects in Algeria, Iraq, Iran, Syria and Yemen, also began to dry up.[16] Already heavily indebted, countries across the MENA region could not compete in the global market with rising exports from the "Asian Tigers," where infrastructure built during the World War II–era Japanese occupation, cheap labor, and massive US subsidies to support anticommunist governments fueled dramatic growth.[17] The International Monetary Fund (IMF) used the opportunity of the 1980s debt crisis of the global South to impose Economic Reform and Structural Adjustment Programs and "conditionalities" that slashed state sponsorship of economic activity and investment in social services and public goods. To decrease debt levels and secure loans from the IMF and other international financial institutions and to finance imports and maintain subsidies on food and fuel, governments sold off key public sector industries to private interests—often to regime cronies at bargain basement prices.

Large armies engaged in public works are fundamentally incompatible with the Washington Consensus neoliberal doctrine of the IMF and other international financial institutions, which argues that a large public sector is inimical to economic growth. In many ways the military was an obstacle to the Washington Consensus program.[18] At the same time, military enterprises were increasingly operated as a vehicle for distributing perks to regime loyalists and retired high-ranking officers.[19] Economic efficiency, productivity, and technological innovation were rarely priorities. The military that had once been a state-building tool and an avenue for social mobility became ossified. It was no longer an effective fighting force, and its officer corps became primarily concerned with preserving its eroding privileges and maintaining its role as guarantor of regime stability.[20]

The neoliberal policies promoted by the international financial institutions and their local allies sought to depoliticize the military and remove it from the economy through institutional "professionalization." US policy emphasized international exchanges for officers, joint training, and equipment upgrades. Extensive and sophisticated security assistance programs like the International Military Education and Training, Excess Defense Articles, and Foreign Military Financing programs became new channels for networking and enhancing military power.[21] Despite the accompanying rhetoric of security sector reform, truly divesting militaries from the economy was politically problematic. Influential officers and extensive patron-client networks depended on the military's role in construction, contracting, manufacturing, and service provision. Thus, many enterprises remained in the hands of influential officers.

THE EVOLUTION OF MILITARY PRIVILEGE

Notwithstanding the shift from state-led development and peripheral Keynesianism to neoliberal Washington Consensus economic doctrine, the privileges of MENA region armed forces have been remarkably resilient. These include subsidized access to fuel and electricity, and industrial materials like steel and concrete; infrastructure such as factories, warehouses, and transportation systems; hard currency to purchase arms and capital equipment; land for housing and commercial development; and scarce social welfare goods for themselves and their families, such as access to hospitals and seats in public universities. Military-operated industries also have extraordinary regulatory privileges, avoiding tariffs, import restrictions, licensing requirements, and most forms of taxation. Conscription armies may also employ soldiers for extremely low (or no) wages. In both Egypt and Algeria, the last six months of a conscript's term is typically spent working in a military-owned enterprise.[22] Even where the state does not deploy the military as a major engineering or construction authority, they have worked to insinuate themselves into large projects as either a regulatory body (approving licenses and providing "security" waivers) or a supplier and subcontractor with privileged access in the bidding process. Armies are also frequently major land owners, and have used their property to build lucrative clubs, hotels, and resorts, all exempt from real estate taxes.

A major exception in the era of IMF-mandated structural adjustment programs and austerity regimes was continued high levels of spending on military equipment and personnel benefits, as well as support for firms owned or operated by the armed forces. The international financial institutions—the IMF, World Bank, regional development banks, and quasi-private actors like the US government's Overseas Private Investment Corporation—impose strict limits on public spending, but stop short of requiring cuts in military expenditures. In the aftermath of structural adjustment in Jordan, the state continued to subsidize the military, enacting an increase in retiree pensions and benefits as well as housing subsidies, while also maintaining existing benefits like health insurance, free higher education for family members, and subsidized co-ops—all while cutting services to nonmilitary populations.[23]

In Egypt, after the January 25 popular uprising, despite several currency crises and a new IMF loan agreement that imposed austerity measures and policies similar to those that had failed in the two decades before 2011, the pensions and salaries of the armed forces were repeatedly increased. Major arms exporters and their host governments were often at the forefront of efforts to pressure the international financial institutions to rescind demands for sharp reductions in defense spending.[24] Regional governments are allowed this continued support for the armed forces and their enterprises under the guise of respect for sovereignty. However, the military is also a critical pillar of regime security; sidelining it could threaten the political status quo while disrupting energy markets and lucrative Western defense contracts. A well-entrenched authoritarian regime in a volatile region is a reliable customer—sufficiently durable to sign large procurement contracts that are typically executed over many years, but sufficiently precarious in its legitimacy to require expensive tools for maintaining internal security and external defense.

The value of this strategy for the US government and military-industrial complex was confirmed when the Egyptian military intervened to remove Hosni Mubarak, whose legitimacy had been exhausted, and again when the military overthrew Mubarak's successor, Muslim Brother Muhammad Morsi, on July 3, 2013. Secretary of State John Kerry declined to call Morsi's ouster a coup. Had he done so, the Obama administration would have been obliged by law to suspend military aid, a measure that no American administration has seriously contemplated since Cairo made peace with Israel, regardless of the country's sham democratization, failed economic reforms, and egregious human rights violations. Egypt underwent two political upheavals in two and a half years, but the relationship between the US and Egyptian militaries remained close.

The privatization of large parts of the public sector, liberalization of trade, and growth in financial service firms that accompanied IMF-mandated Economic Reform and Structural Adjustment presented the militaries of the Middle East and North Africa with new obstacles and opportunities. Despite their association with state-led economic development and nationalization of private enterprises formerly owned by foreigners, minorities, and those dubbed compradors, few officers turned out to be principled adherents to protectionist policies. In Egypt, the military eagerly courted Gulf conglomerates, as well as Western and Asian multinationals, as partners in private enterprise.[25] Many of these projects had nothing to do with defense or provisioning for the army, but instead were aimed at generating revenues by selling consumer items like air conditioners and computers.[26] In Jordan, the military's primary industrial entity is the King Abdullah Design and Development Bureau, which, according to official promotional literature, has joint venture partnerships with at least twenty-six different foreign companies, producing everything from prepackaged field rations and boots to backpack-portable drones and armored vehicles.

This expansion of military activities into diversified foreign partnerships has made it much easier for individual officers to control significant productive assets and use them to build independent patron-client networks.[27] Maintaining existing networks and creating new ones has exploited and deepened these existing silos of influence. Arms manufacturers often cultivate relationships with specific individuals they identify as close to procurement decisions. In the United Arab Emirates (UAE), for instance, a specific member of the royal family is the preferred intermediary for Italian defense firms hoping to sign contracts with the government. Various industries, economic projects, and regulatory structures remain under the control of different elements of the armed forces, which often overlap with previously existing cleavages built around service branches, families with martial lineages (as in Algeria), alumni of particular military colleges or training programs (as in Egypt), and familial or tribal links to the ruling regime (as in Syria, Jordan, pre-2003 Iraq, and pre-2011 Libya). Semiautonomous control over existing projects and policies, combined with access to foreign investment and technologies, help reinforce these discrete patron-client networks.

Modernization theorists of the 1950s and 1960s overoptimistically predicted that cadres of professionally educated military officers could serve as an antidote to domestic political obstacles, including insufficiently entrepreneurial capitalists and reactionary large land owners who blocked rural development initiatives. Today, to varying degrees in Egypt, Syria, Turkey, Jordan, Algeria, and Iran, the regional militaries are corrupt grifters, dismantling public enterprises and exploiting liberalization policies to enrich themselves.[28] The

Syrian Tlass family, which includes a long-serving defense minister and many high-ranking military officers, is an archetypical example. After securing a large number of government contracts, their firm, MAS, went on to partner with multinationals like Orascom and Lafarge and became a sprawling conglomerate with interests in many sectors of the economy, making the family a symbol of corruption.[29] In Jordan the Majali family used their connections and access to branch out into the private sector. In the mid-1980s, ʻAbd al-Hadi al-Majali, who served as both army chief of staff and ambassador to the United States, founded one of Jordan's first private security ventures—the Middle East Defense and Security Agency (MEDSA).[30] ʻAbd al-Hadi's son Sahil al-Majali is the current head of MID Contracting, a major beneficiary of the postwar reconstruction boom in Iraq. His cousin Shadi Ramzi al-Majali is the former head of both the King Abdullah II Design and Development Bureau and its affiliated KADDB Investment Group.[31]

In terms of the degree of military influence on domestic politics and economics, the smaller Gulf states have followed a different trajectory. There, the abundance of oil and gas reserves, early British and American discouragement of industrialization and diversification, and relatively small populations limited both the emergence of a domestic military-industrial base and politically potent militaries. Historically much of the military establishment, from enlisted soldiers to engineers and technical advisors, has consisted of foreign personnel or militarized minority populations. Although the 1991 Gulf War scared the Kuwaiti regime off from hiring foreign mercenaries, they have been largely unnecessary because as late as 2014 there were 50,000 US troops stationed there.[32] For most of the twentieth century the primary driver of military spending and related industrial policy in the Gulf has been the cultivation of alliances with Western governments, primarily the United States, the United Kingdom, France, and Germany. The perception—true or not—that American military influence in the region is shrinking has led many Gulf states to institute varying forms of military conscription over the last five years. They are also sending larger numbers of officers to train at elite overseas academies such as the UK Royal Military Academy at Sandhurst.[33]

Although Saudi Arabia has a large population and could, in principle, build a powerful army and military-industrial complex, the monarchy has often taken steps to prevent this. As a strategy of regime preservation, the military has long been divided into the Royal Saudi Armed Forces, controlled by the Ministry of Defense, the Saudi Arabian National Guard, and the Royal Guard Regiment, which has a separate communications network and reports directly to the king.

In addition to the brief discussion in Timothy Mitchell's chapter in this book, there is a large literature on "petrodollar recycling" and the "oil-weapons" nexus.[34] Since the 1970s, the Gulf Arab regimes (and Iran before its 1979 revolution) have used the revenues generated by petroleum exports to acquire or invest in the development of expensive weapons systems from the United States, the United Kingdom, France, and Germany, all among the largest consumers of petroleum products. These weapons systems are often redundant, with similar (sometimes incompatible) equipment arriving from multiple foreign suppliers. As demonstrated by Kuwait's inability to defend itself from the 1990 Iraqi invasion and the failure of the Saudi-Emirati military coalition to restore their chosen presidential candidate through a vicious war in Yemen, expensive equipment and training contracts do not guarantee an effective military.

Saudi Arabia imports more arms than any other country in the world (the UAE is number two), and more than half this total comes from the United States.[35] In 2018 the Saudis signed orders to buy US$14.5 billion of weapons from the United States. Although this represents a small fraction of the total US GDP, export orders can be critical for individual firms. For example, in 2018 Lockheed Martin's annual report showed that 40 percent of its net sales were international.[36] The industry itself is central to capital flows into the United States: the military and aerospace industry is the second-largest gross exporter (petroleum is the largest) and has the largest positive trade balance of any manufactured goods sector,[37] making it a highly influential corporate actor.

There are many cases of direct oil-for-weapons agreements in the regional arms race. During the 1980–88 Iran-Iraq war both countries traded oil in exchange for military equipment from Japan, the USSR, Brazil, Pakistan, Taiwan, France, Korea, Italy, and India.[38] In 1983, when Iraq was unable to pump enough oil to meet its financial obligations to France (for arms purchases), Kuwait, Qatar, and Saudi Arabia provided additional oil to make up the difference on Baghdad's behalf. The 2003 US-led invasion of Iraq and sanctions against Iran led both countries to once again propose oil-for-weapons deals.

During Libya's long period under Western sanctions (1986–2003), it bartered oil for arms with other countries, including the former Yugoslavia and, after its breakup, Serbia.[39] In 2008 Russia wrote off US$4.5 billion of Libya's Cold War–era debt to the Soviet Union, much of it for military equipment, in exchange for new military and civilian contracts.[40] After Mu'ammar Qaddafi's overthrow in 2011, Libyan militias issued public statements requesting arms from anyone willing to take payment in oil.[41]

Such deals themselves can in turn produce *more* arms sales. For example, France, in recognition of its extraordinary efforts to deliver fighter jets to Iraq during the war with Iran (including taking partial payment in crude), was promptly awarded two major weapons deals with Kuwait and the UAE, who were backing Baghdad in the conflict.

The most significant case of oil-for-weapons is the US$50 billion al-Yamamah deal between Saudi Arabia and the London-based multinational giant BAE Systems. In order to beat out a competitive French bid, the United Kingdom agreed to take payment for its arms in roughly half a million barrels of oil, which Saudi Arabia transferred to the British firms British Petroleum and Royal Dutch Shell.[42] They collected a US$30 million commission for selling the oil on the international market, with the remaining profits turned over to BAE.[43] The deal had additional conditions that further capitalized on the symbiosis of the oil and weapons industries: the Saudis required BAE to recruit third-party British firms to partner with and invest in domestic Saudi ventures. Ultimately many of the firms BAE brought on board were European petroleum and petrochemical companies.[44]

The military-industrial sector is evolving and new patterns of trade and production are emerging. For example, Saudi companies are acquiring advanced manufacturing equipment in anticipation of assembling weapons systems, including Lockheed Martin's BlackHawk helicopters; they already produce components for BAE aircraft.[45] As Adam Hanieh's chapter in this volume shows, a regional (*khaleeji*) capitalist class has formed and is investing in several sectors beyond oil, gas, and related products.

THE DOMESTIC PURSUIT OF REGIONAL WEAPONS DEVELOPMENT

An advanced military-industrial establishment has always been a hallmark of global power and economic development. As early as the nineteenth century,

Egypt, Iran, Morocco, and the Ottoman central government sought to develop military industries as the core of state modernization projects and to defend themselves against Western imperial incursions. Egypt's rebellious Ottoman governor, Mehmed Ali Pasha (1805–1848), built the region's earliest military-industrial complex, consisting of factories and a shipyard to produce muskets, cannons, and warships, and spinning and weaving mills to manufacture military uniforms.[46] Mehmed Ali's army, supported by this industrial effort and European technical advisors, became the basis of the modern Egyptian state. However, the factories underwent a multifaceted crisis in the 1830s and ceased production after a European-Ottoman alliance drove Mehmed Ali out of Syria in 1840. Mehmed Ali's grandson, Khedive Ismail, attempted to replicate this effort by working with the US gun manufacturer Samuel Remington to construct a number of armament factories before they were shuttered by the British, who invaded and occupied Egypt in 1882.[47]

A century and a half later, Egypt again sought to make arms production central to its industrial strategy by establishing the Arab Organization for Industrialization in 1975. Originally meant to combine the industrial and labor resources of Egypt with the capital of the Arab Gulf states to construct a regional armament industry, President Sadat's 1979 peace treaty with Israel led the Gulf states to withdraw their support. Shortly thereafter, the latter redirected their investments to support Iraq's massive military-industrial buildup, fearing the appeal that a revolutionary Iran might have for their own repressed Shi'a populations.

Iraq's development, from a point of military weakness, barely able to produce ammunition in 1981, to producing ballistic missiles by 1989, involved free-flowing credit from the United States and Europe as well as substantial technology transfers.[48] Between 1985 and 1990 two out of every seven technology export licenses issued by the United States were for the Iraqi military.[49] Baghdad also contracted with the Lebanese-based Arab Projects and Development, a consulting firm founded by Anthony Zahlan (a physics professor at AUB) and financed by Hasib Sabbagh to help support Arab scientists and students, especially Palestinians, to launch a massive recruitment campaign to hire Arab scientists, engineers, and technicians.[50]

In Saudi Arabia, an attempt to foster an indigenous military industrial base in the mid-1980s with assistance from US companies stalled as the regime increasingly feared that supply chains would be infiltrated by saboteurs. After this failed effort, in 2017 Saudi Arabia established a new entity, Saudi Arabian Military Industries. This appears to be part of Crown Prince Muhammad Bin Salman's Vision 2030 plan, which includes a goal of increasing the domestically produced content going into the kingdom's weapons systems. Such local production currently provides only about 2 percent of these inputs.[51] As the Saudis already have a shortage of engineering and technological personnel despite a high unemployment rate, the kingdom will likely fail to achieve this goal.

Today the UAE appears to have the region's most sophisticated military-industrial base. In a relatively short time, it has built a sizeable public conglomerate by establishing new enterprises, buying up existing domestic firms, and acquiring foreign firms and relocating their production lines. They have also coordinated with other Arab states, such as Jordan and Algeria, in the production of armaments. Many states, including Jordan, the UAE, and Saudi Arabia, now have industrial parks and free-trade zones dedicated to military research and industrial production.[52] The renewed drive for domestic development with foreign partners is even impacting states with less integrated economies such as Algeria, which now has joint ventures with Russian, French, German, Italian, Serbian, and Emirati companies to produce armored vehicles, drones, helicopters, and heavy troop transport vehicles.[53] Many states have established specialized investment funds to promote military industrial activities; these are militarized sovereign wealth funds, with capital supplied by foreign weapons producers as well as oil revenues.[54]

THE MIDDLE EAST AS A CORNERSTONE OF THE GLOBAL ARMS INDUSTRY

It is not only strategic defense concerns or quotidian patronage politics that shape the way the global arms trade impacts the Middle East. Capitalism as a system requires constant growth. Firms (including weapons producers) must grow or die.[55] They must accumulate sufficient profits to maintain or expand their market share by reinvesting in new machinery or technology and augmenting efficiency. Cutting labor costs by wage reductions is another common mechanism for enhancing profits. This new capital formation subsequently allows for the accumulation of even greater profits.

Such continuous growth can only be achieved by breaking down barriers to capital accumulation. In the weapons industry these include: arms embargoes, export restrictions, slack demand for new weapons, shortages of hard currency to purchase expensive systems, norms against the use of certain weapons, and the absence of new markets. In the Middle East and North Africa, many of these barriers are easily and cheaply overcome. Because of its wars, oil wealth, arms races, and "exceptional" status as a zone where certain norms do not apply, arms manufacturers consistently see the region as a source of growth. Consequently, they devote significant resources to marketing military equipment and technologies to the region.[56]

Countries engaged in long-term hostilities are irresistible clients. During its war with Iran, Iraq hosted hundreds of Western companies who designed, built, equipped, and maintained military research and production facilities.[57] Iraq also attracted tens of thousands of highly skilled foreign scientists, engineers, and technicians who relocated to Baghdad for lavish salaries.[58] Other conflict dyads, such as Turkey and Greece, and Egypt and Israel, have experienced similarly high levels of foreign military sales and training. These four were the largest recipients of US foreign military aid for nearly two decades, obtaining over US$60 billion in grants and subsidized loans to purchase weapons between 1975 and 1994.[59]

Today Turkey, Greece, Egypt, and Israel all have significant domestic military industries. In the mid-1980s, Turkey launched an ambitious program to expand its military-industrial base through partnerships with foreign firms. It now generates nearly US$7 billion in turnover annually, including a recent multi-billion-dollar tank deal with Qatar.[60] Turkish governmental incentives have drawn many firms not initially engaged in arms production into the military sector, participating in the global trend of economic militarization.[61]

From 1991 to 2018, US legislation allowed Israel, unlike any other recipient of military aid, to spend 26.3 percent of aid funds on goods and services produced in Israel.[62] Historically, US military firms that established subsidiaries in Israel were able to profit both from exports to Israel and from the subcontracts granted to their Israeli subsidiaries.[63] The 2016 Memorandum of Understanding that committed US$38 billion in US military aid to Israel from fiscal year 2019 to 2028 introduced a gradual requirement that all future aid be spent in the United States. Consequently, Israeli arms firms are seeking US firms as partners to qualify as suppliers for both Israeli and US government contracts. For more on these arrangements, see Joel Beinin's chapter in this book. As in

Egypt and Jordan, retired Israeli military officers frequently own or manage the local subsidiaries and subcontractors that reap the biggest benefits from joint production and research and development agreements with US firms.[64]

Like wars, major diplomatic realignments create sizeable opportunities for arms manufacturers. Egypt's abandonment of its alliance with the Soviet Union after the 1973 war and its realignment with the United States became a new profit stream for US arms manufacturers. The independence of Oman (1951), Kuwait (1961), and the UAE (1971) allowed them to diversify their sources of armaments. After exclusively purchasing British materiel, they began to place orders with suppliers from the United States and other Western countries. Establishing new supply relationships can entail a massive overhaul of existing weapons arsenals and windfall profits for military exporters of the new suppliers.

Similarly, winding down sanctions regimes and Western-imposed isolation in Libya (in 2004) and Iraq (after the US invasion of 2003) created openings for Western arms producers. The financial liquidity and economic diversification strategies of the Gulf states have made them a focal point for military firms, many of which have established sizeable subsidiaries and regional headquarters in the Gulf. The UAE has even provided advance funding directly to these firms to drive the development of next-generation weapons systems. In the early 2000s the UAE funded development of the Al Hakim series of guided munitions built by GEC-Marconi as well as updates to Northrop Grumman's APG-68 Agile Beam Radar.[65] In 2004, the UAE gave US$3 billion to Lockheed Martin to finance the development of a modified F-16 that made it more advanced than those flown by the US Air Force.[66] These early export deals proliferate the most advanced technologies and incentivize host governments to finance further research and development for subsequent generations of weapons. This guaranteed and predictable demand has positioned weapons producers as among the world's most profitable entities and has also stoked arms races in the Middle East and far beyond.

Foreign and military policy intellectuals and lobbyists form an infrastructure interwoven with the global military-industrial complex and have dramatically affected regional politics; security justifications and the drive for profit are mutually reinforcing.[67] Most Washington-based policy institutes (think tanks) like the International Institute for Strategic Studies, the Brookings

Institution, the Center for Strategic and International Studies, and the Arab Gulf States Institute produce material that promotes an aggressive foreign policy. Twelve of the twenty-five most-cited US think tanks receive big money from weapons manufacturers.[68] The Gulf states spend large sums to influence political campaigns and are major donors to US think tanks, providing over US$85 million to nine such organizations between 2010 and 2017. Most of these funds were disbursed in 2015–17 to deflect criticism of the Saudi-UAE bombing campaign in Yemen and to undermine the Iran nuclear deal.[69] This financial support partly explains the limited opposition to the war on Yemen from establishment US foreign policy circles and Congress (at least until the Saudis murdered Jamal Khashoggi in October 2018), as well as the promotion of new weapons exports and defense programs. In 2016 the UAE paid US$250,000 for a policy paper at a major US think tank that argued for loosening the Missile Technology Control Regime that prohibited the export of sophisticated drones to the UAE. Two months after the paper was released, a bipartisan group of House members wrote to President Trump pressing him to approve the UAE drone sale, using the same arguments cited in the paper.[70] Other states, including Libya, Syria, Tunisia, and Egypt, retain highly paid lobbying firms to plant op-eds in American newspapers, secure private meetings with influential government officials, and fund friendly policy memos, often in anticipation of opposition to big defense deals, another way that government policy and spending patterns are shaped by the arms trade and military prerogatives.[71]

EMPOWERING ARMIES AND GROWING REGIONAL CONFLICT

The legacy of colonial military policy, foreign military intervention, arms races, repressive internal security, and growing economic militarization are central to the political configurations, economic challenges, and escalating interstate military interventions of the MENA region. Eight of the top fifteen military spenders, as a percentage of GDP, are in the Middle East.[72] Spending is accompanied by a rise in the token symbols of militarism, such as propaganda-style military parades in Saudi Arabia and expertly produced publicity campaigns for the UAE's various military branches. Increased military spending also heightens interaction between regional militaries through joint exercises and coordinated campaigns without explicit US sponsorship. The end of the US ability to dictate partnerships and regional outcomes has been a boon for

European and other foreign governments. Their firms are renewing projects with regional dictatorships after a hiatus due to the Arab uprisings that began in 2010. Net foreign direct investment in Egypt under the praetorian dictatorship of President Sisi has steadily increased, from US$2.8 billion in 2012 to US$7.4 billion in 2017.[73] Although four of the six largest investors are Western democracies, concerns about accountable governance and human rights have rarely seriously impeded arms sales.[74] Weapons contracts were also signed during President Mubarak's final weeks and during the interim rule of Supreme Council of the Armed Forces. This suggests that regime instability is not an obstacle to signing new contracts, especially since many of these are backed by export loan guarantees from the firms' host governments that ensure the firms get paid regardless of domestic political outcomes.[75] This support also pays dividends to regional armies. At its 2018 weapons exhibition, Egypt displayed an expanded range of locally available products (produced or assembled under license) including air defense systems, drones, armored vehicles, naval corvettes, training jets, rocket launchers and mine-clearance devices.[76] Similar inflows for postconflict reconstruction in Syria and Libya will no doubt contribute further to the region's military-industrial footprint. Unfortunately, the legacy of war and economic devastation is alive and thriving.

Part 2

COUNTRY/REGIONAL STUDIES

Chapter 5

RETHINKING CLASS AND STATE IN THE GULF COOPERATION COUNCIL

Adam Hanieh

RECENT CRITICAL RESEARCH ON THE GULF COOPERATION COUNcil (GCC) (Saudi Arabia, United Arab Emirates, Qatar, Bahrain, Kuwait, and Oman) has developed in new and exciting directions. Scholars from several disciplines have challenged traditional methodological approaches to the region that tended to exceptionalize the Gulf as distinct from other parts of the Middle East or wider global processes. This rethinking includes rejecting periodizations that posit a sharp break between the Gulf's "pre-" and "post-" oil eras, pointing instead to the enduring regional and global connections that have shaped flows of people, goods, and ideas in and through the Gulf from colonial times to the present.[1] This work has also sought to move beyond a simple focus on oil to explore other aspects to the Gulf's development, including the nature of ports, logistics, and infrastructure networks; the differentiated forms and histories of urbanism in the Gulf; and the diaspora, trade, and labor flows that connect the Gulf to the wider Indian Ocean space.[2] This sensitivity to issues of space and scale means that much of the new research on the Gulf carries insightful lessons for scholars working on other parts of the Middle East.

Figuring less prominently in writing on the Gulf, however, are the concerns of political economy: the relations among class, capital accumulation, and the nature of state power. Although "capitalism" in the Gulf is often named, it remains undertheorized, and scholarship on the Gulf still tends to emphasize regionally specific histories and geographies, speaking less frequently to debates in political economy. The notion of class, in particular, often disappears from view, or is loosely elided with anachronistic or imprecise labels such as "merchants" and "elites." Somewhat exceptionally in this regard, Rosie Bsheer has noted that "the authoritarian regimes of the [Arabian] peninsula were not formed outside class politics and global economic processes. On the contrary, class formation and dominant capitalist orientations were as instrumental to the production and maintenance of power in the peninsula as they were—and are—in states elsewhere."[3] The full implications of this critical point are yet to be adequately explored.

The lacuna around class and capitalism is perhaps the ongoing legacy of the standard political economy model of the Gulf, namely Rentier State Theory (RST). As the name suggests, RST focuses on the role of rents derived from the exports of hydrocarbons and other minerals, drawing causal relationships between this "free gift of nature"[4] and the political and economic structures found in places such as the Gulf. The theory has been described as "one of the major contributions of Middle East regional studies to political science"[5] and, since its initial formulation by Iranian economist Hossein Mahdavy in 1970, it has been subject to numerous elaborations that have found widespread resonance outside of the Middle East (for example, in studies of mineral-rich African states). Although there have been a number of critiques of RST, it remains the dominant framework for understanding the Gulf. Its basic assumptions, even if not explicitly articulated, continue to shape how many scholars understand political and economic power in the Gulf.

One of the central analytical claims of RST, and the core theoretical issue of this chapter, concerns the nature of state power and its relationship to wider social structures. In this respect, a consistent thread runs through all RST approaches: the availability of oil rents has fostered a pronounced *autonomy*—of the Gulf state (and hence ruling families) from society, allowing the state to dominate and shape all other social groups. According to this perspective, Gulf monarchies, freed by oil revenues from the constraints of taxation and the need to account for societal pressures, constitute an archetypal "strong state," with a particularly enhanced capacity "to penetrate—society, regulate social relationships, extract resources, and appropriate or use resources in determined ways."[6] Scholarship that relies on this rubric denies the salience of class as a conceptual category. It depicts private capital as weak and underdeveloped and it either dismisses the significance of labor or identifies it as a regulatory and policy challenge; in this respect, the analytical focus shifts to how ruling families and states wield their rents in the context of fluctuating global oil markets.

My goal in this chapter is to critically engage with these perspectives. In the first section, I present an alternative reading of state-class relations. I draw here upon Marxian and other critical political economy approaches, which foreground processes of class formation and capital accumulation as "internally related" to state power. By this, I mean that state and class do not exist as separate, discrete categories or ideal-types. Rather, the state is an institutional form that embodies the nature of class power in the Gulf. The relations between state and class are part of how both categories are constituted. We thus need to reject any dichotomous interpretation of state and class in the Gulf. The secret of the Gulf state's power is to be found in the *strength*—of its capitalist class, not its alleged weakness.

The second part of the chapter demonstrates these theoretical observations by mapping the Gulf's class structure. Obviously it is impossible here to comprehensively explore patterns of accumulation and the specificities of each of the GCC states. Therefore, I present a general outline of how the capitalist class and the control of capital is organized in the contemporary Gulf; the main sites of accumulation of this class; the relations among ruling families, private capital, and the state; and, finally, the growing propensity for Gulf capital's cross-border expansion. The third section turns to the other side of the Gulf's class structure, the question of labor. Standard accounts of the Gulf's political economy frequently omit or marginalize labor. However, any understanding of how capital and state are constituted in the Gulf must consider its overwhelming reliance on a noncitizen, migrant workforce. Finally, I offer some conclusions on what all this might mean for the Gulf's future.

FRAMING CLASS AND STATE

RST's essential argument is that predictable, long-term rents accruing to governments from the export of oil and other minerals causally shape political, economic, and social structures in a deleterious manner.[7] Such financial flows create distorted patterns of development because they allow governments to spend with little effective limits. Mahdavy characterized this situation as "fortuitous *étatisme*."[8] The scholarship identifies a long and varied list of possible negative effects. These include: a "rentier mentality" characterized by political passivity and a lack of entrepreneurial spirit among the citizen population; autocratic forms of government, enabled by the absence of taxation and the enhanced repressive capacities funded by rents; a tendency for governments to spend on consumption rather than pursue industrial diversification; and uncompetitive economies marked by weakly developed educational and occupational specification.[9]

Before turning to how these accounts depict categories such as class and state, it is important to note the conceptions of the "global" and the "national" implicit in the RST framework. RST approaches view the national as a "self-evident container of political, cultural, and economic relations"[10]—a discrete territorial unit that is spatially distinct from the global. Because the national is posited as a self-enclosed repository of social relations, RST approaches focus on the supposedly determinate factors operating inside national borders—that is, the presence of oil rents—that then shape patterns of social and economic development. While these rents may arise from the interaction between the national and the global, they do so in an externally imagined fashion. The global exists "out there," and its presence stops at the nation-state's borders. What this means conceptually is that the global is in effect disappeared from what happens inside the state. This is a profound weakness in standard accounts of RST: issues such as imperialism and war, the nature of capitalist accumulation at the global scale, and the rivalries and interdependencies between states are absolved of any explanatory relationship to the nature of the state in the Gulf and beyond.[11] Instead, the accidental geography of oil and its associated rents become the deus ex machina that determines forms of state and power. To give one significant example, is it possible to understand the autocratic character of the Saudi state today without reference to the country's longstanding relationship to US power as it has evolved through the postwar period, and the particular military and political alliances that have emerged around this?

At a more abstract level, such accounts implicitly adopt a form of "commodity fetishism," to employ Marx's productive concept.[12] This form explains patterns of social development through the presence (or absence) of a commodity-as-"thing" rather than the social relations in which that commodity is embedded.[13] Understanding the Gulf's relationship to the world market, for example, requires stepping beyond the question of oil as such to examine the underlying dynamics of global capitalism that have given meaning to oil as a commodity and made it so central to the reproduction of the system as a whole. This raises many issues such as the profound internationalization of production over the past few decades, the immense growth of financial markets, and the forms of democracy and state power that have emerged globally across the twentieth century.[14] All these factors intersect with the materiality of oil and shape oil politics at the global scale. In short, these immanent features of capitalism undergird the formation of the Gulf states and their hydrocarbon exports within the shifting configurations of the global political economy over the past century.

Beyond questions of the global and the national, how have standard accounts of RST conceptualized state-class relations in the Gulf? Despite variations among RST approaches, the underlying theoretical framework generally rests upon two basic analytical categories: the state and civil society (often abridged as "society") as they are conceived within Weberian sociology and political science. According to Weber's well-known definition, the state is defined by its monopoly over the "legitimate use of force" within a given territory[15] and is made up of the various political institutions that govern a country. Civil society, on the other hand, involves "institutions autonomous from the state which facilitate orderly economic, political and social activity."[16] These two ideal-types, the state and civil society, are depicted as mutually exclusive categories; the state stands as an autonomous body that holds a wide degree of freedom "as a public realm separate from the private realm of civil society."[17]

This methodological assumption of state "separation" (or autonomy) is foundational to RST approaches to the Gulf. Typically, in this framing, the notion of a capitalist class drops from view, either subsumed into an all-encompassing civil society or reduced to one of many different social actors (such as private business). Nonetheless, despite this disappearing of class as a category, implicit in RST accounts is a view of the state dominated by the ruling monarchies as a separate or dichotomous sphere that stands apart from capital—the latter is considered weak and ultimately powerless against the pervasive strength of the former.

It is revealing that the scholarly debate around RST has largely ignored any critical interrogation of these foundational assumptions concerning state and class. This gap persists despite the rich discussion around state theory in the wider political economy literature. Numerous scholars have argued against the dichotomization of state and class, instead viewing the state as a social form that emerges through the production and reproduction of society itself.[18] Thus, states are always "class-states," which act to preserve the existing structures of class power and mediate the conflicts that inevitably appear between and within classes.[19] Although the state may appear to us as an independent political institution, it is in fact a social relation, which, in the words of the philosopher Bertell Ollman, constitutes a "set of institutional forms through which a ruling class relates to the rest of society."[20] The relationship of the ruling class with the state is part of what constitutes it as a class; state and class are mutually reinforcing and co-constituted. Class provides the conditions of existence for the state.

This recognition of class and state as constituting each other redirects our attention to class and capitalism and helps us transcend binary oppositions between the political and the economic, the public and the private, the state and the market. For the Gulf, the key issue is tracing how and where capital accumulation takes place. This entails mapping patterns of ownership and control over capital, and their relationship to the state and ruling families. Most significantly, the analysis must squarely locate forms of labor within these accumulation patterns. The labor/capital relation remains essential to how accumulation takes place in all capitalist societies, including in the Gulf. Of course, this argument is not meant to deny the vital role of oil revenues in shaping the trajectories of Gulf capitalism. The point is to move away from drawing determinate and causal conclusions simply from the availability of oil rents as such and analyze how forms of class and state developed in the Gulf, as well as how institutions, such as the state, act as social forms that mediate relations of class power. This method avoids the commodity-fetishism typical of RST approaches and divests oil of a "mystical character" that inevitably arises when this commodity is severed from the social relations in which it is embedded.

CAPITALIST CLASS FORMATION IN THE GULF

What then, is the nature of the capitalist class in the Gulf, and how is the control of capital organized? Despite distinct trajectories of class formation in each of the GCC states, there is strong commonality to how capital is constituted. In the contemporary period, one useful way of mapping this is by examining three interconnected sites of capital accumulation in the Gulf: (1) industry, manufacturing, and transport; (2) the urban built environment; and (3) financial markets. These three sites comprise the main activities in which private Gulf capital is active as opposed to upstream hydrocarbon production. As we shall see, the state plays a critical role in supporting private firms throughout these moments of accumulation. These are not the only types of economic activities in the Gulf. But taken together they capture how various commodities are produced and circulate as well as the particular moments when accumulation takes place.

The first of these sites, industry, manufacturing, and transport, encompasses a range of different commodities. In manufacturing, four products are notably prominent: aluminum, steel, cement, and petrochemicals. Each of these commodities depends on the primary raw materials produced in the hydrocarbons sector, namely, chemical feedstocks and cheap energy. The availability of these raw materials has given the GCC a relative advantage at the global level. Joint investments between state-owned companies and smaller privately owned firms has been essential to supporting the growth of these industries. The development of the petrochemical and aluminum industries, in particular, has been closely connected to the Gulf's shifting location in the global economy, with exports of these products increasingly aimed at markets in China and East Asia.

In addition to these hydrocarbon-related commodities, another important industrial activity is agro-industry. Although the Gulf's primary agricultural sector is very small due to a lack of arable land and limited water resources, state support has once again been crucial to the growth of large agribusiness firms, particularly in Saudi Arabia and the UAE.[21] Large Gulf-based firms such as Savola, Al-Marai, Al-Dahra, and Americana produce agro-commodities and processed food items; in many cases, these firms have become deeply involved in agribusiness activities across the wider Middle East. GCC governments justify this cross-border expansion through the notion of "food security" and encourage land purchases and investments in other parts of the agricultural value chain through state-backed loans and agreements with foreign governments.

Transport and logistics have also become key components of Gulf economies.[22] The region's air and maritime ports, particularly in the emirate of Dubai, play a central role in the circulation of goods and people throughout the global economy. The Gulf now hosts the busiest airport in the world, Dubai International Airport, and Gulf-owned airlines have become major players in the global aviation market. In 2016, for instance, Dubai-based Emirates Airlines stood at number one globally in both international passenger and freight traffic, while Qatar Airways took sixth place for international passengers and third for freight traffic. In the maritime sector, Dubai's Jebel Ali Port is now the fourth-largest container port globally, forming a critical transshipment hub for goods moving across the Middle East and Africa as well as in wider East-West trade routes. Jebel Ali is operated by DP World, a firm owned by the Dubai government that now ranks as the third-largest container terminal operator in the world. Other Gulf states, notably Saudi Arabia and Oman, are developing maritime and airport capacities. In addition to this transport infrastructure, several very large Gulf logistics firms manage the circulation and movement of goods throughout the GCC and neighboring regions.

Many of the commodities produced in these industries circulate materially through a second major site of accumulation: the *urban built environment.* As widely noted in the literature, the urban scale has been fundamental to the development of Gulf capitalism in recent years. The striking prominence of new malls, towers, and residential blocks compete to exceed one another in size and extravagance.[23] State policies such as land grants, zoning regulations, and, perhaps most imaginatively, the reclamation of large swathes of the Gulf's waters have been essential to facilitating these developments.[24] These projects provide a constant stream of construction work, as well as reinforcing and bolstering retail and other commercial activities. In this respect, a long-standing element in the accumulation of Gulf capital has been the import and distribution of foreign commodities—automobiles, food, technology, basic consumer goods, and so forth—that are essential to the reproduction of social life in these urban spaces. This import trade is largely organized through an agency and franchise system, mediated by the state, which typically provides exclusive licensing rights to distribute consumer goods in the Gulf. In some cases, these rights extend to neighboring countries (such as the UAE conglomerate Majid Al-Futtaim, which holds exclusive rights to the Carrefour brand across the Middle East and Central Asia). In recent years, a further vital aspect to the urban built environment is the centrality of telecommunications and technology firms such as Etisalat (UAE), Ooredoo (Qatar), and Zain (Kuwait). These firms have taken a prominent role in the actual planning of urban spaces in the Gulf, perhaps best epitomized in the ubiquitous concept of "Smart Cities" now found in most Gulf urban planning strategies. Although these telecommunications firms are dominated by state ownership, they also tend to be partially listed on regional stock markets; through this route, private Gulf capital has become deeply integrated into their ownership structures.

A final site of accumulation is that of *financial markets* and their related institutions, which play a critical part in shifting capital surpluses within and between different corporate groups and economic activities. For both industry and the built environment, financial markets have been an essential site for Gulf firms to draw upon wider pools of surplus capital (through, for example, listing on equity markets), as well as borrowing money for further expansion (debt markets). Institutionally, domestically owned banks are dominant in the Gulf, and these typically display ownership structures that involve private Gulf-based individuals and firms as well as state funds and government representatives. Moreover, the last decade has seen the growing weight of new financial institutions such as private equity companies, Islamic finance, and other types of asset management firms. As with traditional banking structures, a mix of state and private Gulf capital dominates these new forms of finance capital.

What are the patterns of capital ownership and control that characterize these different moments of accumulation? Although tens of thousands of small firms and businesses may be involved in each of these sectors across the Gulf, a striking feature of every GCC state is the predominant weight of a handful of large diversified conglomerates that dominate all these economic activities. These conglomerates are characteristically structured as holding companies, with a complex network of subsidiaries and interlocking ownership structures that simultaneously span industrial and manufacturing activities, real estate, commerce, retail, finance, and so forth. They are usually controlled by influential families (often drawn from the older merchant class) or by members of the ruling families themselves. In some sectors, such as petrochemicals, transport infrastructure, real estate, and banking, state-owned firms may play a dominant role. Yet, even in such instances large, privately held conglomerates are usually represented on the boards of these state-owned firms, or are involved in joint ventures or subsidiary activities down the value chain. In all cases, state investment and various other forms of state support have been essential to the conglomerates' growth.

In this conglomerate structure, ruling families are deeply associated with the three sites of accumulation noted above, controlling major firms and holding groups through which they have come to constitute a core part of the capitalist class. In the case of Qatar, for example, 80 percent of all firms listed on the Qatar Stock Exchange have at least one member of the ruling Al-Thani family sitting on their boards (thirty-six of forty-five firms). The vast majority of these individuals occupy their board positions in a *private capacity*, not as representatives of state institutions.[25] Similarly, Dubai's ruler, Mohammed Bin Rashid Al Maktoum, privately owns a dizzying array of the largest firms in the emirate—including a 20 percent stake in du (Emirates Integrated Telecommunications Company), Dubai's major telecom. These patterns prevail throughout GCC states, even in the case of Kuwait, where the ruling family has historically been less involved in private business activities.[26]

Thus, Gulf ruling families, while clearly dominating state power, are *part* of the Gulf capitalist class itself, rather than simply the locus of political power. There is no strict division between capital and state in this regard. Many individuals from ruling families occupy positions in the state apparatus as well as operating their own private business interests. They simultaneously act in both "private" and "public" capacities. The Gulf is not an anomaly among capitalist states internationally. It is not the case that in the GCC a "weak" capitalist class is arrayed against a "strong, independent state." Rather, the Gulf state is an institutional form that articulates and intermediates the power and interests of a powerful capitalist class. This class is inclusive of but broader than the ruling families. The Gulf state is, as in all capitalist societies, a *class-state*, not a neutral or parasitic institution severed from the social relations of production and accumulation or one that "crowds out" the private sector.

THE INTERNATIONALIZATION OF GULF CAPITAL

Aside from these questions of ownership and control, another important feature of capital accumulation in the Gulf is the cross-border expansion of these diversified conglomerates over the past two decades. At one level, this internationalization of capital is apparent at the scale of the GCC itself, including pan-Gulf investments in areas such as petrochemicals, construction, and finance; the establishment of subsidiaries in neighboring Gulf states; cross-border share ownership on regional stock markets; and the incorporation of numerous Gulf states within a single conglomerate's agency rights. Such cross-border investments point to how circuits of capital in the Gulf are increasingly elaborated at a pan-GCC scale, with share-ownership and boards of directors tending to involve conglomerates from different Gulf states. Most advanced in this regard are private equity firms, where corporate structures are typically made up by a variety of different Gulf nationalities. This internationalization of Gulf capital within the GCC does not mean the attenuation of national rivalries in the Gulf. Indeed, it is a sharply hierarchical process largely dominated by a Saudi-UAE axis. However, internationalization does mean that the major Gulf conglomerates increasingly conceptualize accumulation beyond the borders of individual domestic markets.

Moreover, such internationalization processes are notable throughout the wider Middle East. This feature of the regional scale became strikingly clear during the 2000s. Capital flows from the Gulf began encompassing key economic sectors across other Arab countries, including real estate and urban development, agribusiness, telecommunications, retail, logistics, banking, and finance.[27] Critically, this regional expansion of Gulf capital was predicated upon the adoption of structural adjustment packages by many Arab countries during the 1980s, 1990s, and 2000s, and the subsequent liberalization and opening up to foreign direct investment flows. Gulf capital was a primary beneficiary of the neoliberal turn throughout the Middle East. It became intimately involved in the ownership and control of capital across the region.

The internationalization of Gulf capital raises important questions around neoliberal processes of capital accumulation and class formation in the rest of the Middle East. Precisely because of the way that Gulf capital groups are increasingly enmeshed in the class structures of other Arab states, including, most significantly, in the critically strategic sector of banking and finance, we must pay much more attention to how the political economy of the wider region is being shaped by the dynamics of accumulation in the Gulf. Moreover, concepts such as the "national bourgeoisie," which have been popular in certain traditions of political economy, also need to be rethought. Looking at Egypt, for example, it is important to consider how Gulf capital's interiorization in Egyptian class structures upsets any simple notion of an "Egyptian" bourgeoisie. There are many illustrations of this—more than one-fifth of real estate firms listed on the Egyptian stock market are connected to GCC capital;[28] nearly 60 percent of non-government-owned Egyptian banks are GCC-related;[29] and Gulf firms are a major factor in Egypt's agribusiness sector.[30] This is not to endorse an amorphous or deterritorialized concept of "transnational capital," or to deny the salience of national borders. It is imperative, however, to reflect more deeply on the implications that cross-border interpenetration and ownership has for our notions of class in the Middle East.

In the Gulf itself, these internationalization tendencies present a further challenge to standard RST approaches. Oil revenues clearly remain a core component of how Gulf states fund government budgets and determine levels of social spending. But the concept of "oil rent" does not fully capture the diverse overseas activities that generate financial flows to the Gulf—indeed, already by the late 1980s, Kuwait was earning more from its international investments than oil exports. For many of the largest GCC conglomerates, profits from overseas ventures, subsidiaries, and investments, both in the Middle East and traditional Western markets, now constitute a substantial component of their overall balance sheets. With private capital increasingly oriented toward accumulation in spaces outside of the domestic market, financial inflows are not necessarily captured by the state itself. The degree to which this is the case is an empirical question that may not be possible to answer in any straightforward manner because of data limitations, but it certainly qualifies the supposedly all-powerful capacity of the Gulf state "to penetrate—society [and] regulate social relationships."[31]

LABOR AND CITIZENSHIP IN THE GULF

An inseparable counterpart to the development of capital in the Gulf has been the unique ways that ongoing and massive flows of migration have constituted the labor force. Today, nonnationals in the Gulf account for a staggering 48 percent of its 49 million total population. This proportion is even higher for the labor force, ranging from between 56 and 82 percent of the employed population in Saudi Arabia, Oman, Bahrain, and Kuwait, to around 93–94 percent in Qatar and the UAE.[32] Throughout the entire Gulf, 70 percent of the total employed population is made up of nonnationals. This is the largest proportion of migrant workers in any country or region in the world. The overwhelming majority of these migrant workers, around 88 percent, are located in the Gulf's private sector. These figures give the Gulf a distinct position in global migration flows. Indeed, the GCC hosts more migrants than any other region in the global South, with the UAE and Saudi Arabia ranking as the second- and third-largest sources of remittances in the world, after the United States.[33]

The recruitment and management of Gulf migrant workers takes place through the infamous *kafala* system, a work visa arrangement that binds the migrant to a sponsor (known as a *kafil*). This system forbids workers from seeking alternative employment and prevents them from leaving the country without employer permission.[34] The *kafala* system provides a powerful tool of labor discipline and underpins the particular nature of citizenship in the Gulf. Because the *kafil* is granted the right to bring in workers by the state, and subsequently becomes responsible for monitoring and managing them, it creates a situation in which Gulf citizens and firms are drafted into the day-to-day control of the noncitizen workforce. In effect, the state subcontracts power over migrant labor to individual citizens and businesses.[35] This provides lucrative income streams for citizens through the sale of work permits and situates citizens as intrinsic to the containment and disciplining of labor.[36] This subcontracting increases the vulnerability of migrants to violence, abuse, and poor working conditions. It also diffuses and internalizes a securitizing logic throughout the citizenry; private citizens become an arm of state policy. Moreover, competition between citizens over access to *kafil* rights generates vertical social segmentation and encourages the profession of loyalty and allegiance to the ruling family.[37] In this manner, the institutional structures governing migration in the Gulf shape both the lived experience of migrants as well as the social integration of Gulf citizens themselves.

A large body of literature has compared these structures to bonded or "unfree" labor. Workers are tied to particular employers, denied mobility between jobs, frequently have their passports withheld, and are often trapped in structures of debt that purchasing work permits accrues. Migrant workers are also banned from forming unions, going on strike, or engaging in any kind of political activism.[38] Low-paid migrant workers are often segregated from urban populations in specially designed labor camps, with the movement to and from work organized through employer-provided transportation. Movement restrictions also arise from economic barriers and are highly racialized, with worker accommodations consciously located far away from citizen or tourist spaces. At times these restrictions are legally enforced. In 2011, for example, Qatari authorities prohibited male migrant workers (mostly South Asian and involved in construction) from living in established residential areas. Female domestic workers are particularly subject to restrictions of movement, as they typically live with their employer who may bar them from leaving the house and subject them to physical, psychological, and sexual abuse.

Through such mechanisms, employers hold significant power over living and working conditions. This is reflected in low wages, long hours, and hazardous, substandard conditions of work, particularly in economically significant sectors such as construction. There are no minimum wages in the private sector, where most migrants work. There are large wage differentials between citizen and noncitizen labor. These disparities are more pronounced if we include nonwage costs, such as access to education, health, and housing. In some sectors, notably domestic work, wages are linked to the national origin of the migrant. This exploitation is accompanied by a heavily racialized discourse that projects the various kinds of "threats"—security, demographic, cultural, or sexual—that migrants allegedly pose to Gulf societies.[39]

Much of the discussion around migration to the Gulf emphasizes human rights abuses and mistreatment of migrants. It locates the reasons for these in poor policy making, lack of awareness of international norms, actions of unregulated labor recruitment agencies, or weak legislative oversight. This discussion misses the essential *systemic* role that this labor structure plays in the reproduction of Gulf capitalism. This is true at several levels. First, any attempt at worker mobilization or political protest can be legally met with termination of employment and immediate deportation, producing a state of permanent precarity for the majority of the Gulf's working classes. This has directly underpinned the accumulation of the conglomerates described above, particularly in the construction and real estate sectors. From this perspective, the lofty towers and expansive real estate projects throughout the Gulf are the material embodiments of superexploitation. They are not simply the fortuitous outcomes of a "petrodollar" bonanza or the supposed far-sighted, modernist visions of Gulf rulers.

Second, the nature of migration to the Gulf provides these states with a unique means of dealing with moments of crisis and economic downturn. At such times, the corridors of migration and remittance can act as transmission belts for crises, allowing Gulf states to spatially displace their impact onto poorer zones of the world market. Saudi Arabia currently offers a clear example. Following the global oil price decline that began in mid-2014, it began a program of austerity and cutbacks to government expenditures on major infrastructure and construction projects. While these measures significantly affected the kingdom's economic growth, their major implications need to be viewed through the particular class structure outlined here. As Saudi firms shuttered construction projects, hundreds of thousands of migrant workers lost their jobs. Government-backed deportation campaigns began at the same time, with millions of migrant workers rounded up and expelled by police and security forces. By the end of 2015, the Interior Ministry claimed that more than 1.2 million workers had been removed from the country since the beginning of 2014.[40] In March 2017, the government announced a second deportation campaign that sought to expel a further 1 million migrant workers, around 10 percent of the official noncitizen workforce. By the end of July 2017, over 600,000 workers had left the country as part of the new campaign.[41] Should this trend continue, it could have profound implications for labor-exporting countries—particularly in South Asia, where remittances make up a significant proportion of GDP and overseas workers are overwhelmingly located in the Gulf.

Finally, and perhaps most importantly, this class structure has acted to impede the emergence of indigenous labor movements that could challenge the political power of Gulf monarchies. Indeed, this is a key reason the Gulf's labor structure developed as it did.[42] The majority of the labor force is composed of migrant workers who lack any collective organizing rights. There are sharp and highly racialized divisions between migrant workers and citizens. As a result, the contemporary development of trade unions or any other form of labor militancy has been largely blocked, unlike in neighboring countries such as Iraq and Iran. The one exception that proves the rule is in Bahrain,[43] where a marked degree of proletarianization among citizens created an active trade union movement and an organized Left. The suppression of such movements has been facilitated by a sectarian pattern of rule (a Sunni monarchy and large Shi'i population) consciously exacerbated by the country's leaders.

None of this means that there are not significant contradictions arising from the Gulf's reliance on migrant workers. Prominent among them are very high levels of citizen youth unemployment, particularly in Oman and Saudi Arabia, where 50.8 percent and 30.1 percent of youth respectively were out of work in 2016, according to ILO estimates.[44] To address this, all Gulf states have put in place so-called Gulfization programs, which set quotas for the private sector employment of nationals. The aim is to increase citizen employment while reducing the proportion of migrant workers in particular sectors. These policies, however, have largely failed. Citizens are unwilling to accept the poor wages and working conditions of migrants, and the private sector continues to depend almost exclusively on a low-paid foreign labor force. There is no legislative solution to this dilemma without a drastic transformation of the political order—it is difficult to conceive of any qualitative change to the status quo given the ongoing systemic need for a cheap and precarious workforce in the Gulf.

Such contradictions of high citizen unemployment levels, growing polarization of wealth, and the extreme concentration of power in the hands of ruling families were critical factors fueling the political protests that emerged across the GCC through 2011 and 2012, most notably in Oman and Bahrain. These movements have precursors in earlier struggles, and belie the claims of passive populations and the supposed political quiescence of Gulf societies. The violent repression of these struggles, backed by coordinated pan-GCC intervention, reminds us of the other side to the Gulf's political economy—a highly securitized state apparatus that is growing in reach and that involves close surveillance of populations (citizen and migrant alike) and the deployment of force when necessary.

CONCLUSION

A renewed attention to processes of class and state formation in the GCC foregrounds how capital, labor, and the state constitute each other. This perspective moves the focus away from the oil surpluses as such, and asks how these revenues have reinforced the development of powerful capitalist classes, always understood as inclusive of ruling families, whose activities encompass a variety of sectors cutting across different sites of accumulation. The enormous concentration of power and wealth in the Gulf is emblematic of the emergence of this class and its domestic and international expansion over the last two decades. Gulf states have played a critical role in fostering these conditions of capital accumulation, bolstering economic opportunities through joint investments and other forms of support. In this sense, the state is a midwife of capitalist class formation, and approaches that posit a "strong state" versus "weak capital" miss this essential relation.

Moreover, in these dynamics of capital accumulation, the specific character of migrant labor is a central factor. In contrast to standard narratives of the Gulf's political economy abstracted from relations of domination and exploitation, forms of labor are no less essential to constituting capital and state in the Gulf than the presence of petrodollar surpluses. Migrant working classes have directly produced the particular character of Gulf urban spaces over recent decades, underpinning the accumulation of the Gulf business conglomerates. Politically, the citizen/noncitizen divide mediates this reliance on migrant labor and is foundational to ruling-class power in the Gulf. It binds citizen allegiance to the region's leading families and state structures. At times of economic turmoil, the precarity of migrant work has been utilized by Gulf rulers and leading businesses as a means of affecting a spatial displacement of crisis. This shifts the burden of globally induced problems onto labor-exporting countries. For all these reasons, migrants in the Gulf constitute one of the most important and neglected components of the Middle East's working classes.

These arguments carry important implications for interpreting the decline in global oil prices since mid-2014 and its possible impact on future trajectories of the Gulf political economy. The oil price drop has presented major economic challenges for all GCC states, with low growth rates and significant current account deficits emerging from 2016 onward. In response, Gulf governments, led most conspicuously by Saudi Arabia, launched a series of "Vision" documents proclaiming a strategic diversification away from oil. At the time of writing these plans are still at an early stage, and it is uncertain where they may head politically or, indeed, what might be the future direction of oil prices. Despite this unpredictability, the core logic codified in the new economic strategies aims at extending the reach of the market. This includes an unprecedented push toward privatization and public-private partnerships (PPPs) in areas such as energy, education, health, transport, and logistics, as well as wide-ranging cuts to social spending.

While these strategic plans appear to be ostensibly "technocratic" responses to the economic downturn, they are, in fact, another expression of how the Gulf states continue to prioritize advancing the frontiers of capital accumulation. These plans may well destabilize elements of the Gulf's social model. They threaten to marginalize poorer citizens and migrant workers, who have already experienced a wave of deportations and a sharp deterioration in living conditions. These new economic strategies may also generate an increasing differentiation within the Gulf's capitalist classes. Early evidence from profit rates of firms listed on GCC stock markets confirms the growing dominance of the largest conglomerates and a simultaneous weakening of smaller scale capital.[45] Regardless of these uncertainties, the basic logic of these plans confirms that Gulf states are not autonomous political institutions, suspended over society through the bountiful windfall of petrodollars, but rather class-states that act to mediate and reproduce the power of capital.

Chapter 6

CAPITALISM IN EGYPT, NOT EGYPTIAN CAPITALISM

Aaron Jakes and Ahmad Shokr

HOW CAN A HISTORY OF CAPITALISM BE AT ONCE LOCAL AND global? How can we tell a story that is both faithful to distinctive experiences in a particular place and attentive to the larger patterns that make a category like "capitalism" meaningful? Our answers to these questions hinge upon a simple but significant distinction. This chapter offers a reinterpretation of the history of capitalism in Egypt, not "Egyptian capitalism."[1] That history is recognizably different from histories of capitalism in England, India, or the United States, but at no point have such histories unfolded neatly within the national borders that exist today. In tracing the profound transformations of the last two centuries, our chapter therefore advances two interrelated arguments.

First, people in Egypt, like people everywhere, live inside multiple spaces of power and accumulation at the same time. Those spaces and the interactions between them can and do change. How those spaces are produced should be an object of analytical inquiry rather than a presumed feature of any country's geography. Existing scholarship on Egypt commonly divides its history into distinct phases: defensive developmentalism, colonial capitalism, state capitalism, and neoliberalism. This periodization usefully connects what has happened in Egypt to broader global patterns, but it risks treating Egypt as a stable entity wherein historical change results from impulses originating elsewhere. Egypt, however, is not simply a site where preexisting crisis tendencies and accumulation strategies reenact themselves. Rather, a variety of social, political, economic, and ecological dynamics—some generated within the country, others outside—have interacted to produce unique configurations of political and economic power across multiple geographic scales. Those uneven configurations have always been embedded in transregional and transnational processes without being reducible to them. They depend on local arrangements that govern everyday life across Egypt as well as on flows of goods, people, capital, and ideas that bind the country to other regional and global centers.

Second, throughout Egypt's modern history, an array of actors has leveraged various political mechanisms to generate the funds necessary for successive regimes of accumulation. Capital accumulation through the production of commodities requires the prior existence of funds that can be put into motion as capital. Whether growing cotton or building factories, capitalists in Egypt have often required more capital than they possessed. To address the shortfall, they have relied on changing combinations of taxation, rent, debt, aid, and expropriation—in short, forms of accumulation that involve political transfers of value rather than profits through production.

For some time, scholarship on the historical geography of capitalism has emphasized that the processes Marx described as "primitive accumulation" do not represent a moment of capital's past so much as a continuous and necessary feature of its self-expansion. As this body of theory has argued, the profitable production of commodities for sale on global markets has relied on a shifting mix of sources lying outside the "abode" of production itself.[2] These insights have often pointed toward the constitutive dependencies between extraction in the colonies and accumulation proper in the metropole. Less visible in such accounts, however, is the interplay between these paired processes within those spaces that occupy a subordinate status in the global order.

From this perspective, the history of capitalism in Egypt has exhibited several recognizable patterns across the past two centuries. Foremost among them is the state's involvement, not merely as the guarantor of arrangements that comprise "the market" but directly within the process of production itself. State violence, under many guises, has been crucial to suppressing the costs of production for capitalist enterprise. Second, as a claimant upon the profits of production—whether directly through public ownership or indirectly through taxation—the state has frequently sought to supplement the capital requirements of production with rents extracted from Egypt's position in global trade and geopolitics. Third, even as these rent-seeking strategies have functioned as a kind of primitive accumulation in reverse, they have rarely satisfied the country's needs for capital. Shortfalls were repeatedly met with foreign borrowing. As a kind of prosthetic to capital, debt can postpone current costs in favor of future profits. That possibility has frequently allowed accumulation crises abroad to reappear as potential solutions to fiscal woes within Egypt.

All these means of acquiring and employing capital have bound spaces of power and accumulation inside Egypt to the world around them in complex ways that have often defied the confines of present-day national borders.

COLONIAL CAPITALISM IN EGYPT REVISITED

Egypt's journey through the nineteenth century is sometimes told as the story of an autonomous region drawn into the capitalist world economy. It is better understood as a transition from one set of imperial arrangements to another. Within the Ottoman Empire's "command economy," Egypt was a crucial supplier of grain for both the Sultan's military and the holy cities of the Hijaz.[3] Alongside the cultivation of these strategic commodities, networks of internal commerce had woven a rich tapestry of localized specializations in fine handicrafts and particular foodstuffs.[4] Nevertheless, Egyptian grain remained the chief attraction for rival powers in the Mediterranean. In the decade prior to the Napoleonic invasion of 1798, Ottoman efforts to prevent the movement of Egyptian wheat and rice to Europe had become a source of growing tensions with France.[5] Grandiose imperial pretensions notwithstanding, it was in part to acquire Egyptian grain that Napoleon's army invaded in 1798.[6]

Following the Anglo-Ottoman campaign, Egypt was left in the hands of the deputy commander of the Ottoman forces that were sent to expel the French in 1801. As the new Ottoman *wali* (governor), Mehmed Ali Pasha sought to secure an autonomous dynasty for his family by establishing a disciplined conscript army. He waged a series of campaigns, first on behalf of the sultan in the Arabian Peninsula and Greece, and then against Istanbul's armies in his conquest of Greater Syria.[7] To fund his military ventures and state-building projects, the pasha made two fateful decisions.

First, together with an English entrepreneur named Thomas Waghorn, Mehmed Ali developed an overland route between Europe and British India. By channeling the traffic and commerce through Egyptian ports and transportation networks, Waghorn's company and the Egyptian government agreed to share in the rents generated from the country's unique location.[8] Second, in 1821 the pasha began to compel peasants in the Nile Delta to grow long-staple cotton for sale to the textile mills of northern England.[9] While Egypt had for centuries produced agricultural goods for export, the forced conversion of farmland to cotton was no simple matter of substituting one crop for another. It entailed a fundamental shift in the objectives of the work Egyptian farmers performed. Istanbul's main interest in Egyptian grain lay in its utility as food. By contrast, cotton would be sold for money that could then buy other things. The new military-fiscal state accordingly seized as much of that monetary value as possible.[10]

Turning cotton into money required that Egypt enter a world market dominated by cheap, slave-grown fiber from the United States. To compete with the horrific productivity of the American South, Mehmed Ali's government attempted to segment the market by promoting long-staple strains that fetched higher prices than the "upland" variety comprising the bulk of US exports. Until the late 1830s, the pasha also enforced a monopoly over the crop. Control over the annual harvest allowed the government to improve its margins by dictating lower farmgate prices and negotiating higher export prices with foreign merchants.[11] And while Egypt's new regime could not replicate the American "cotton kingdom," it found other ways to boost profits through outright coercion.[12] The corvée, an annual tax in labor time, had existed for centuries. Mehmed Ali radically expanded its use.[13] Although the corvée was nominally labor contributed for public works, in subsequent decades Egypt's ruling classes frequently diverted conscripts onto their own private estates.[14]

In consolidating his rule, Mehmed Ali had murdered the old Mamluk elite and abolished the existing system of tax farming (*iltizam*). His early efforts to establish a new revenue regime encountered numerous challenges. Peasants were often reluctant to grow cotton; rather than meet the government's demands, many abandoned their land. Foreign merchants, meanwhile, were eager to see the monopoly system abolished. Following the worldwide economic crisis of 1836–37, during which cotton prices tumbled, Mehmed Ali relinquished state control of the crop in favor of direct land taxes.[15] By foregoing a share of its potential profits, the government was able to shield itself from some of the hazards of global price volatility.

Implementing this revenue system, however, required two key groups of intermediaries. First, to extend cash-crop cultivation and enforce its tax demands upon the peasantry, the new regime granted tax-exempt or lightly taxed lands to rural notables and members of the pasha's family. Over time, they became the nucleus of a large landholding class that controlled vast swaths of the countryside and dominated Egyptian politics for the better part of the next century.[16] Second, to manage the seasonal transactions of the cotton crop, the government permitted foreign merchants and bankers to operate in inland villages. This growing cohort of Greek, Levantine, and Jewish immigrants formed a merchant class whose firms enjoyed a lasting influence over Egyptian commerce.

Throughout his long reign, Mehmed Ali funded his various projects without taking on debt.[17] Those arrangements shifted under his successors. The pasha's death in 1848 coincided with a major economic crisis in Western Europe; capital and labor were idled with few opportunities for profitable employment. The resolution to this impasse entailed a new marriage between high finance and the built environment. With novel financial instruments that deferred current profits by securing claims upon future wealth, capital was pooled and channeled into feats of construction and engineering on a colossal scale.[18] Most famously, this "spatial fix" gave rise to Baron Haussmann's authoritarian reconstruction of modern Paris.[19] The midcentury crisis also spurred a reconception of European colonies as potential sites for investment at higher rates of profit than metropolitan markets could offer.[20] One result was a spectacular proliferation of large-scale infrastructures across the globe.[21]

In this context, Mehmed Ali's successors welcomed the overtures of foreign financiers. Hoping to secure Egypt's role as a global thoroughfare, Sa'id Pasha in 1854 granted Ferdinand de Lesseps the concession to excavate a maritime canal through the Isthmus of Suez. A new joint-stock corporation, La Compagnie Universelle du Canal de Suez, announced a public offering of shares across Europe. When skittish investors left roughly 40 percent of the shares unsubscribed, Sa'id was forced to purchase them.[22] In these same years, the Egyptian government took on additional loans to fund the reengineering of rural landscapes in service of cotton. It constructed dams and canals to extend perennial irrigation for the summer cotton crop and built a network of railways to move the harvest to Alexandria for export.[23] These loans were premised on an optimistic wager. So long as revenues grew faster than the interest on the debt, that wager would pay off. If not, the debtor would owe all the same.

In the 1860s, world events induced a disastrous miscalculation. During the American Civil War, the Union blockade of Confederate ports created a global cotton shortage.[24] Under Isma'il Pasha, who came to power in 1863, the Egyptian government banked on inflated cotton prices to contract more loans. When the war ended and cotton prices fell, Egypt faced a serious revenue shortfall. Over the next decade, the government scrambled to meet its obligations. Isma'il intensified his reliance on both corvée and slave labor as he established sugar plantations and processing factories in Upper Egypt.[25] Many poorer farmers fled the tax collectors, so the government transferred their plots to wealthier proprietors who could pay.[26] Others borrowed heavily from local moneylenders to cover tax rates that now exceeded what their farms could sustain. In 1871, sacrificing long-term revenue for short-term gains, the government enacted the Muqabala Law, which offered to confer full property rights and a permanent future discount to farmers who paid five years' worth of land tax in advance. Still, Egypt took on new loans from Europe to make current payments.[27] And in 1875, Isma'il sold the government's remaining Suez Canal shares to the British government.

By 1876, the country was effectively bankrupt. Representatives of the primary bondholders seized control of the state's finances. Empowered to make debt repayment its foremost priority, the new Caisse de la Dette Publique imposed devastating budget cuts.[28] These austerity measures provoked widespread popular outrage and gave rise to a movement for fiscal sovereignty and constitutional rule led by the Egyptian military officer Ahmad 'Urabi Pasha.[29] Fearing that if the revolt succeeded, Egypt would choose to default, the British government found a pretext in 1882 to invade.[30] Although it nominally remained an Ottoman province, Egypt became a "veiled protectorate" governed by a staff of foreign "advisers" from the British consulate in Cairo. The British occupation thus ensured that meeting foreign debt obligations would remain an overriding imperative of the Egyptian state. Roughly half of the state's annual revenue would thereafter flow directly to the bondholders.[31]

The British explained Egypt's bankruptcy as a symptom of "Oriental despotism." Their histories of Egypt's recent past conveniently avoided mention of the foreign banks that had profited from the country's misfortunes. They thus attributed to failures of Egyptian statecraft and moral judgment a range of structural problems that resulted from the government's crippling foreign debt. Self-serving as it was, this diagnosis also formed the basis of the agrarian policies that appeared, for a time, to inaugurate a reversal in Egypt's economic condition. Central to the occupation's vision of a profitable symbiosis between the peasantry and the foreign bondholders was an explicit class critique of the khedivial regime. By monopolizing public resources for private gain, they argued, the Mehmed Ali dynasty and its retainers had undermined the very conditions for agricultural production.[32]

Over the next two decades, British administrators saw the small family farm, with its abundant supply of uncompensated child labor, as an ideal site for the cultivation of cheap raw cotton.[33] The British made no attempt to alter the unequal distribution of agricultural land. Rather, by standardizing ownership rights, reassessing tax rates, extending rural transport, and, most of all, improving supplies of irrigation water, they hoped to unleash the untapped productivity of smallholders whose efforts had once been thwarted by the predations of so-called khedivial despotism.[34]

As in the past, this program of "economic development" would require considerable capital outlays to construct new infrastructures, reclaim land, and purchase livestock and machinery. But the bankruptcy arrangements imposed after 1876 restricted the Egyptian state's ability to contract new loans. The British, therefore, attempted to make the occupation a colonial laboratory for foreign investment through private enterprise.[35] Most significantly, British consul-general Lord Cromer worked to promote the employment of European capital in mortgage loans to Egyptian farmers.[36]

These efforts to forge novel attachments between farmers in the colonies and metropolitan financiers again refigured a shortage of capital in Egypt as the solution to economic problems elsewhere. By the late nineteenth century, decades of competitive investment in industrialization, especially in Europe and the United States, had led to the protracted global slump of overproduction and falling commodity prices known as the Great (or Long) Depression of 1873 to 1896.[37] As idle funds accumulated in London, Paris, and Brussels, proponents of agricultural banking argued that Egypt's farms represented an attractive frontier for investment. By the late 1890s, the occupation's utopian vision of agrarian finance appeared to be succeeding. Egypt briefly enjoyed worldwide renown as a model for colonial development.[38] Initially, Egypt's new banks focused their business mainly on loans against landed property or commercial goods. But as foreign investment flooded the country, many of these institutions started to dabble in more lucrative, but risky, financial instruments. By the height of the boom in 1905 and 1906, several leading banks were borrowing money on renewable short-term credit from Europe to make loans on the stock certificates of Egyptian companies, many of which were themselves involved in financial transactions of other sorts.[39] The abundance of cheap credit gave rise to a massive financial bubble and a steady inflation of both land values and share prices.

In the autumn of 1906, the Bank of England decided to raise its benchmark interest rate. Once the flow of easy money from Europe dried up, the vast edifice of leveraged debts came crashing down.[40] British officials insisted that this was merely a short-lived corrective to an excess of stock speculation. But by the summer of 1907, the Arabic press was reporting a near-total interruption of rural credit. The result was a massive wave of defaults by the very class of smallholders the British had long claimed to champion.[41]

Outraged by the occupation's refusal to acknowledge or address the real extent of the crisis, a new generation of Egyptian writers and activists in this moment began to articulate a vision of independence that would inform their program of economic nationalism for the next several decades. The defining "malady" of Egypt's colonial condition, they argued, was neither poverty nor underdevelopment.[42] Rather, the country's reliance on foreign capital had rendered the lives of ordinary Egyptians both less stable and less free. Embracing Egypt's designation as an "agricultural country" and a producer of raw cotton, they called for establishing a national bank and a network of cooperative associations that might together expand the supply of national capital.[43]

World War I in fact created the conditions for such a territorialization of capital. But thanks to a little-known act of monetary subterfuge, this economic nationalist vision was realized in travestied form. The declaration of a protectorate in the summer of 1914 gave Britain unprecedented powers to regulate agricultural production and to control the country's financial institutions.

Soaring global demand for cotton combined with wartime import restrictions to deliver the growing money supply that economic nationalists advocated. The rising value of Egyptian pounds in circulation, however, redounded to the British war effort rather than to the benefit of Egyptians. In April 1916, in consultation with the Bank of England, the protectorate's British advisers determined that paper banknotes in Egypt would be backed not by deposits of gold, but by British treasury bonds; each pound printed thereby became an immediate loan from Egypt to the British government.[44] Because British debt was denominated in pounds sterling, this effectively took Egypt off the international gold standard and placed it on a sterling exchange standard. The ensuing devaluation of Egyptian currency inflicted vicious inflation on ordinary consumers. It also helped to bind Egypt more tightly within the economic geography of the British Empire after the war. Egypt's debts to British banks had been the main impetus behind decades of "veiled" colonial rule. Now, Britain's inability or unwillingness to pay its debts to Egypt became another reason that their colonial relationship could not be severed.[45]

NATIONAL DEVELOPMENT IN EGYPT REVISITED

Despite British efforts to rejuvenate its financial and political power in Egypt, the end of World War I inaugurated a gradual decline of European imperialism, and with it the demise of a world economy managed through imperial institutions. While the four decades before the war were a golden age for imperial globalization—characterized by a dramatic growth of world trade, the expansion of international finance, heightened migration, and massive overseas investments—these foundations of an imperial world economy now began to encounter serious opposition.[46] Like Ireland and India, Egypt became a major site of anticolonial resistance to the British Empire. In 1919, a nationalist uprising swept the country. Three years later Britain granted Egypt a limited form of independence.

Subsequently, nationalists tried to create or to control institutions that might advance the project of Egyptian sovereignty. They believed that a meaningful independence required a reconfiguration of the political-economic arrangements that enabled capital accumulation on an imperial scale. They soon began to challenge the privileges that foreign capital enjoyed by creating institutions whose activities were organized on a national scale.

While ideas about development had been a discursive component of Egyptian nationalism since the early twentieth century, during World War I they started to become institutional fixtures of the nationalist project. The Commission on Commerce and Industry, convened in 1916 by Egyptian minister of finance Isma'il Sidqi, was an early attempt to promote such a program.[47] The resumption of foreign imports after the war blunted, for a time, the urgency of the commission's proposals. But its central ideas—economic diversification, agricultural improvement, and state support for limited industrialization—proved remarkably durable.[48]

In these years, economic life in Egypt was dominated by three forces: landed oligarchs, foreign capital, and an emerging bourgeoisie that included foreign residents, their descendants, and a smaller group that began to champion an Egyptian national identity. In 1920, Tal'at Harb established a holding company that became the most important industrial initiative of this period: Bank Misr. Harb and his circle stood to benefit from the gathering pace of nationalist sentiment and anti-British boycotts in the interwar period.[49] Still, they continued to pursue a variety of joint ventures with foreign capitalists. Businessmen like Harb did not form an aspiring bourgeoisie that failed to create national industries that could wrest control of capitalist enterprise from foreign hands. Rather, they represented an assortment of oligarchs who prioritized the accumulation of monopoly rents and profits.[50]

However, this did not mean there were no links between nationalist politics and efforts at capitalist restructuring. National elites did advance a vision of economic sovereignty and worked to reconfigure Egypt's material relations with the wider imperial world, even if their efforts did not always entail an unambiguous project of import-substitution industrialization. Rather than any devotion to re-creating Egypt in the image of industrial England, many proponents of economic nationalism had a different aim: to reduce Egypt's dependence on uneven movements of finance, trade, and prices during an age of global economic turmoil. They perceived the obstacle to genuine independence as the contradiction between the production of what they considered "national" wealth and its circulation beyond Egypt's borders.[51] Their solution was to develop mechanisms to territorialize the circulation of profits from agriculture, commerce, and industry within the boundaries of their emerging independent nation-state.

This orientation toward nationally scaled accumulation took on several forms. First, landowners and their allies tried to limit the power of foreign merchants in the cotton trade. In 1924, Ibrahim Rashad, the founder of Egypt's first department for agricultural cooperatives, observed, "If the wealth of the country increases and then seeps into the hands of foreigners . . . it remains lost wealth of which our only share is the toil it took to produce it."[52] Informed by such arguments, policy makers linked to the large landholding class devised methods to displace foreign export houses and put growers in direct contact with spinners in Europe.[53]

Second, economic nationalists sought to eliminate the privileges that foreigners had long enjoyed. In February 1930, when Egypt's capitulation agreement with Italy expired, Prime Minister Isma'il Sidqi's government introduced a three-tiered tariff system, resulting in higher duties on imported cotton textiles and a considerable decline in textile imports over the next decade.[54] As tariffs were the government's chief revenue source, the reforms were primarily intended to generate state income and only secondarily to promote domestic industries.[55] Nevertheless, they helped to foster an environment in which projects like Tal'at Harb's Misr Spinning and Weaving Company would begin to grow.[56]

Third, nationalists advocated the moral and material reform of the peasantry. The Great Depression of the 1930s precipitated a collapse of cotton prices and incomes from its cultivation, which highlighted the extent of rural immiseration. To regenerate the production of surplus value in the countryside, state reformers began to intensify a project of rural governmentality seeking to transform Egyptian cultivators into healthy, rational, growth-oriented subjects. To achieve these goals, they devised institutions including cooperatives, agricultural banks, clinics, schools, model villages, and rural social centers.[57] These reforms aimed to furnish both the resources and the technical knowledge required to produce a new Egyptian peasant. Yet none of them presented a serious challenge to the large landholders who remained the dominant fraction of the country's ruling class. If anything, they ascribed rural poverty to factors like peasant backwardness and land scarcity, thereby avoiding any discussion of social inequality.[58] That tide would soon begin to turn.

Between 1929 and 1937, real income per capita dropped by roughly 9 percent, the largest such decline in half a century.[59] The agricultural recession had two major effects. First, entrepreneurs emboldened by the achievement of tariff autonomy began to invest more heavily in manufacturing.[60] The gradual divergence between the interests of large landowners and industrialists meant that the interwar program of balanced development began to unravel. It was at this point that growing numbers of Egyptian intellectuals and policy makers began to see industrialization as the telos of a development project that would subordinate the countryside to the needs of urban centers.[61]

Second, landowners began to lease their properties on a much greater scale. Whereas in 1939 less than 11 percent of all owned land was leased, by 1952 that proportion increased to 75 percent. According to the Ministry of Agriculture, the revenue that landowners earned from cultivation was one-third less than income they earned from renting their properties.[62] In this moment, reformers and activists began debating the question of land redistribution more openly.[63] By 1944, an agrarian reform plan was presented to the Egyptian Senate. The following year, the liberal Mirrit Ghali's *al-Islah al-zira'i* (Agrarian reform) and Marxist Ahmad Sadiq Sa'd's *Mushkilat al-fallah* (The peasant problem) were published.[64] These early proposals represented contending ideological poles in a budding debate about land reform. In the coming decade, the redistribution of land would become an important source of political legitimacy.

By the late 1940s, two lessons had become evident to Egyptian reformers, intellectuals, and political activists. First, the exploitation of rural laboring populations had generated deep-seated grievances that needed to be addressed. For more than four decades, critics of the existing agrarian order had protested that producing classes were the principal generators of wealth but did not retain an equitable share of its value. In the aftermath of World War II, most major opposition groups developed positions on agrarian reform, although the government and large landholders opposed them. Second, after decades of experimentation in creating national banks and industries had achieved only moderate success, it became clear that any project of national capital formation was inseparable from asserting national sovereignty. Political and economic independence needed to go hand in hand.

In this context, a politicized faction of the Egyptian army—the Free Officers—seized control of the state in 1952 and ultimately brought Gamal Abdel Nasser to power. What became known as Nasserism proposed that the twin problems of national independence and capital formation, on the one hand,

and the creation of a mass consumer society of workers and peasants, on the other, could be addressed together. Like their contemporaries elsewhere, the Free Officers believed they could harness the powers of the state to promote industrialization and growth while socializing many of the costs of reproducing Egyptian labor.[65] To achieve this objective, the Nasserist regime drew on ideas from the previous decade to fashion three redistributive mechanisms: public services (education, health, family planning); price controls (subsidies, rent ceilings); and wealth redistribution (land reform, asset seizures, and public employment). These policies shifted onto the Egyptian state a larger share of the costs of delivering improvements in the livelihoods of those groups that formed Nasser's political base. While politicians and businessmen had begun to promote such policies during the interwar period, any nationally scaled fix to Egypt's crisis would require substantial funds that earlier governments lacked but that the Free Officers aggressively pursued.

The Nasserist state drew from a mixture of sources to fund its social welfare programs. The first was centrally planned pricing. Through a countrywide network of agricultural cooperatives, state officials supplied credit and farm inputs and compelled farmers to deliver key export crops, like cotton and rice. The government purchased those crops at fixed farmgate prices and resold them for more on international markets. As in Mehmed Ali's monopoly system, the net result was a transfer of value from farmers to the state. This expropriation of agrarian wealth provided an important source of foreign exchange that the state used to subsidize its industrialization program.[66]

The second source of funding was foreign aid and debt. At the height of the Cold War, Nasser and his cohort successfully manipulated superpower rivalries to secure fiscal assistance. Egypt became a major beneficiary of Soviet foreign aid, including discounts on arms and semimanufactured goods, support for iron and steel manufacturing, and the construction of the Aswan High Dam.[67] Low-interest loans were repaid by primary goods such as cotton, rice, and fruits for which the state monopolized trade.[68] By 1970, Egypt sent 61 percent of its exports to Soviet Bloc countries and received 34 percent of its imports from them.[69] While aid and favorable trade with the USSR drew Egypt into the Soviet orbit, Nasser also received support from its superpower rival. The US Office of Food for Peace created by Public Law 480 of 1954 allowed Egypt to buy wheat and other grains with Egyptian pounds. Between 1956 and 1967,

Egypt became one of the largest recipients of the program, which accounted for nearly 70 percent of total US assistance to Egypt.[70]

The third source of funding involved natural and strategic rents. After the 1956 Suez Crisis—when Israel, France, and Britain invaded Egypt in response to Nasser's decision to nationalize the Suez Canal—Egypt gained access to considerable revenues from the tolls on this important global transit route. By 1967 they totaled more than 3,000 percent of the 1955 level, when the Egyptian government received a merely symbolic royalty.[71] At the same time, Egypt's petroleum industry began to grow. With the creation of a national oil company in 1956, the country's subsoil resources too became a vital source of rents for the state.

The fourth, and most important, source of funding was the expropriation of assets through land reform and nationalization of private businesses. After 1956, the regime began to nationalize a wide range of enterprises—commercial banks, insurance companies, and textile factories, in addition to the Suez Canal Company itself.[72] Some estimates valued shares and physical assets transferred to public ownership between 1952 and 1966 at close to E£700 million.[73]

Awash with new revenues, the state proceeded with its program of industrial development and social welfare. Between 1952 and 1969, the Free Officers implemented land reform, eventually setting a 50 *feddan* ceiling on ownership. In targeting large landowners, these policies ultimately gave rise to a class of rich peasants—those owning 5 to 50 *feddans* of land—who emerged as a newly dominant force in the countryside.[74] While the reforms redistributed less than 13 percent of the country's cultivated area to a fraction of the rural population, they also established rent controls on agricultural land that benefited many poorer tenants.[75] The poorest peasants who constituted a majority of Egypt's rural working population—landless migrant workers (*'ummal al-tarahil*)—saw fewer opportunities for social mobility in the countryside. Many began to find seasonal jobs in the construction and maintenance of public works. They remained crucial to the viability of export-oriented agriculture, yet their seasonal movements now created labor shortages that contributed to economic crises in 1961 and again in 1964–65.[76]

In the cities, many elements of the commercial and industrial bourgeoisie that had started to emerge before 1952 were expropriated or absorbed into a new state-produced class that disproportionately captured the benefits of capital accumulation. The economic backbone of the regime became what critics called the state bourgeoisie—a class of officials across various ministries, public-sector companies, and general organizations and authorities.[77] The expansion of free education aimed to produce a national public that could fulfill various laboring roles in an industrial society—from household care work, to government jobs, to industrial and service employment.[78] Successive employment drives in the 1960s brought close to one million Egyptians into the public sector, where they received corporatist representation in state-run trade unions.

The balance sheet of Nasserism was decidedly mixed. For many, the regime's policies offered healthcare and education, security of land tenure, guaranteed jobs, and unprecedented social mobility. But maintaining these benefits came at a price. Politically, the program reinforced the state's authoritarian tendencies by requiring the population to sacrifice political freedoms for material gains. Dissent by communists, Islamists, and others was brutally repressed. Moreover, as an ambitious experiment in using the levers of the state to manage the costs of reproducing Egyptian labor, the project soon began to reveal its heavy costs. Continuing to extract a surplus from its population while delivering immediate consumption gains and financing a military intervention in North Yemen after 1962 simply proved too expensive, even as the state offset some of its costs through new rents. By 1964–65, Egypt was facing deficits in its budget and balance of payments, which its existing fiscal structure could not resolve. Like his ambitious forebears a century beforehand, Nasser turned to foreign lenders for help. However, negotiations with the International Monetary Fund (IMF) over a stabilization plan in 1966 soon stalled. That same year, in response to mounting tensions over Egypt's involvement in the conflict in North Yemen, the Lyndon Johnson administration halted Public Law 480 food aid to Nasser's government.[79] Moreover, Egypt was on the brink of a major conflict—the 1967 Arab-Israeli War—that fatally damaged the Nasserist project.

Egypt's loss in the 1967 war was both a political and an economic catastrophe. Conventional histories of the period have argued ad nauseam that the crushing defeat of Egyptian forces sowed new doubts about the promise of

Arab Nationalism.[80] But the war's outcome was no less devastating for the economic system that had allowed Nasser's "Arab Socialism" to deliver material improvements to broad sectors of Egyptian society.

Nasser had ordered the closure of the Suez Canal on June 5, 1967, and it remained shut for the next eight years, halting the flow of tolls that the government had obtained since nationalization. Israel's occupation of the Sinai deprived Egypt of its primary sites of petroleum production. Revenues from tourism, which had grown steadily through the 1960s, likewise plummeted after the war.[81] The dramatic constriction of rents overburdened the state as it faced the staggering cost of repairing and replacing all that had been destroyed. Most significant was the tremendous outlay on new equipment for the army and air force. Military expenditures over the next six years rose by more than 600 percent.[82] Meanwhile, as the interruption of US food aid continued, the government was forced to pay the full cost of the grain imports that were crucial to its subsidy regime.[83]

NEOLIBERALISM IN EGYPT REVISITED

Anwar al-Sadat confronted this precarious situation upon Nasser's death in 1970. Within four years, he launched an *infitah* or "open door" program to restructure his country's economy in an international environment less supportive of developmentalism and import-substitution industrialization. In the early 1970s, a sequence of shocks began to reconfigure existing arrangements for managing global flows of finance, capital, and goods that had existed under the Bretton Woods system. Chief among them was the delinking of the US dollar from the gold standard in 1971, which encouraged currency speculation and an offshore dollar-denominated financial sector. This effective devaluation of the US dollar was also linked to another shock, the 1973 oil price hike. Oil-rich Arab states reaped tremendous windfalls from both the price increases and the subsequent partial or full nationalization of their petroleum industries.[84] Awash with oil profits, Gulf states began to recycle their earnings into European dollar-denominated accounts, which contributed to a significant growth of a private banking sector on a global scale.[85] By the end of the 1970s, loans from private banks accounted for 60 percent of the global South's debt.[86] International financial institutions such as the IMF began to fashion a new regime of debt management. These shocks helped to reshape the transnational networks of finance in which the Egyptian state soon became enmeshed.

In Egypt, Sadat's ability to avert an economic crisis has sometimes been credited to his liberalization program after the 1973 Arab-Israeli War. Far more consequential were the implications of the war itself for restoring and improving Egypt's access to rents, loans, and foreign aid. Thanks to its emerging alliance with the United States, Egypt was able to reap substantial rewards from the oil boom that the war itself had helped to generate.[87] Two years of negotiations, mediated by Washington, resulted by October 1975 in the reopening of the Suez Canal and the return of the Sudr oil fields in the Sinai Peninsula to Egyptian control.[88] Annual petroleum exports quadrupled over the next five years; by the end of the decade they accounted for roughly 22 percent of Egypt's GDP.[89] Linked to the oil boom, canal revenues rose from E£86.2 million in 1965 to E£400 million by 1980. The diplomatic rapprochement with Western governments and the easing of restrictions on foreign investment contributed to a surge in tourism, which by 1980 brought in another E£500 million.[90] While these enhanced rents provided much-needed foreign exchange, they were dwarfed by the surge in cash remittances from Egyptian workers who migrated to the Gulf after 1973. By 1980, the annual value of those remittances stood close to E£1.9 billion.[91]

As was the case for the US Civil War–era cotton boom a century prior, the windfall that ensued from the 1973 war created additional complications. First, the resulting economic dislocation accelerated the decline of cotton cultivation. The waning importance of cotton was part of a general eclipse of agriculture by other sources of export revenue and a steady out-migration of rural workers. It was also emblematic of the uneven nature of economic liberalization. Throughout the 1970s, the government's monopoly over the purchase of cotton remained in place. Even as inflation and higher oil prices raised the costs of labor and agricultural inputs, the prices farmers received for the crop remained well below the export price.[92] As farmers watched their profit margins dwindle, many stopped growing cotton. Between 1970 and 1976, production fell by close to 30 percent, while exports fell by more than half.[93]

Second, while the surge in state revenues did forestall an economic crisis, it did not reduce deficit spending. Throughout the 1970s, government expenditures continued to outstrip revenues.[94] In December 1976, Egypt negotiated a deal with the IMF, which required cuts to food subsidies. Key support groups of the Nasserist state, like students and public employees, rebelled against this proposal. The implementation of this plan in January 1977 prompted two days of massive protests, which pushed the government first to impose a curfew and then to reverse its agreement with the IMF.[95] Sadat's government abandoned its plan to slash subsidies. Indeed, it increased them as it realized that public provisioning might be linked to its own survival.[96] Paradoxically, during the *infitah*, Egypt's subsidy program grew immensely and began to outstrip spending on other services, like health and education. Thanks to rising revenues from oil, the Suez Canal, and US aid, public spending grew from 48 percent of GDP in 1974 to 61 percent in 1981.[97] The failure to secure an IMF loan did not immediately precipitate a more serious fiscal crisis. But the government was only deferring an inevitable set of problems.

As Egypt continued to borrow over the course of the 1980s, it staggered toward an external debt crisis. The regime was again able to offset some of the mounting fiscal pressures by leveraging Egypt's role in international affairs. Through the signing of the Egyptian-Israeli Peace Treaty in March 1979, Egypt secured access to substantial new streams of military financing and foreign aid from the United States.[98] A decade later, after the government received considerable debt relief in exchange for supporting American forces during the First Gulf War, it was able to accommodate the dictates of global debt managers. In 1991, President Hosni Mubarak, Sadat's successor, oversaw the negotiation of a structural adjustment agreement with the IMF. For the next two decades, the Mubarak regime pushed a program of privatization, deregulation, free trade, and financial expansion. Policy makers and international financial institutions celebrated Egypt for its successful economic liberalization. In reality, Egypt's neoliberal reforms were less about adhering to free-market principles than redistributing resources and concentrating them in the hands of a new class of business cronies.

Official statistics representing economic growth, budget deficits, and inflation portrayed an image of a thriving Egyptian economy in the 1990s. Behind the fog of macroeconomic data, however, was a story about the state subsidizing financiers and urban developers operating in the country's major growth sectors. The state rescued commercial banks, sold public land cheaply, and built infrastructure to support private-sector development benefitting an emerging group of capitalists with close ties to Mubarak's National Democratic Party. Rather than generating an economic revival through fiscal prudence and privatization, Egypt's version of neoliberalism entailed a "multi-layered political readjustment of rents, subsidies, and the control of resources."[99] In the 1990s and 2000s, politically connected tycoons continued to benefit enormously from those networks of support, while the meager job opportunities they provided were insufficient to make up for the decline in public employment.

While Egypt's neoliberal transformation in some ways resembled late-nineteenth-century patterns of financial dependence, what has distinguished the last thirty years is the changing geographic configuration within which these transformations have occurred. Those spaces of accumulation to which Egypt now belongs are increasingly orientated toward centers of power in Arab Gulf states. As Adam Hanieh's chapter in this book indicates, Gulf capital has extended into key sectors across the region, including agribusiness, banking, real estate, and urban development.[100] Since the coup d'état of 2013 that brought Field Marshall 'Abd al-Fattah al-Sisi to power, Gulf capital and military enterprises have increasingly collaborated on major development projects in Egypt. Gulf states have also aggressively intervened in Yemen, Syria, Libya, and beyond. These military ventures have inflicted a massive destruction of life and property that will likely create future investment opportunities.

We began this chapter by considering how, over the course of the long nineteenth century, Egypt shifted from one set of imperial arrangements to another. We conclude by once again reflecting on those political-economic spaces that have formed the shifting contours of the history of capitalism in Egypt. In the nineteenth century, Egypt was transformed from a vital node in an Ottoman system of resource management to a commodity frontier and an attractive destination for metropolitan finance in a British-centered imperial world economy.[101] In the twentieth century, amid a global consolidation of the nation-state form, Egypt's postindependence rulers mobilized new political constituencies and exploited Cold War rivalries. They built a developmentalist state geared toward the nationally scaled pursuit of growth. By the end of the century, Egypt joined many states in its embrace of free-market policies that went hand-in-hand with a tendency toward the regionalization of hegemonic power centered on the Arab Gulf states. Over the course of more than two centuries, these changing configurations of political-economic power have been shaped by dynamics situated at once within and beyond the country's borders.

The narrative that we have sketched here suggests that a historical investigation of these shifting spatial configurations to which different regions in Egypt have belonged might offer one way out of a seeming impasse in approaches to the study of capitalism. For decades, this field of scholarship has been shaped by a generative tension between an emphasis on the large-scale, patterned regularities of capital accumulation and an attention to the nuances of local, concrete experience. We see this tension not so much as a problem to be solved but as a reason to reconsider how we frame the stories we tell. At no point in history were the lives of producers, traders, and politicians across the uneven spaces of accumulation within Egypt merely reflections of "global" processes originating elsewhere. Nor were they so uniquely different from those of people in other parts of the world as to render those experiences incommensurable. The story we have presented examines how those lives were embedded in shifting configurations of power, violence, accumulation, and dependence that have existed on multiple scales and that have repeatedly transformed the realities of social and economic life in modern Egypt. This does not mean that undertaking a history of Egypt or any part of the Middle East must simultaneously be a history of the whole world. Nor does it mean that capitalism in Egypt can or should be understood either as a distinct national or regional "type" or as an alternative lifeworld defined by differences that elude meaningful comparison. Rather, it means paying attention to how those lives were stitched into wider geographies of power and accumulation and how those geographies have been produced, over and again, throughout history. For that reason, the history of capitalism in Egypt and the history of global capitalism might be better understood as vantages onto a single, interconnected story.

Chapter 7

STATE, OIL, AND WAR IN THE FORMATION OF IRAQ

Nida Alahmad

THE STUDY OF IRAQI POLITICS AND POLITICAL ECONOMY, AT least within the English-speaking world, has long been defined by Hanna Batatu's *The Old Social Classes and the Revolutionary Movements of Iraq* as one characterized by class-based political movements and struggles.[1] Since its publication, the majority of academic works on Iraq have been diplomatic and political histories, while political economy studies of Iraq since the early 1980s have been dominated by rentier state theory.[2] The fall of the Ba'thist regime in 2003 brought questions regarding Iraq's national identity, sectarianism, and whether Iraq is a colonial invention and thus an artificial state, to the forefront of scholarship.[3] Scholars have also reexamined the Ba'thist era in terms of governance, the party's involvement in the daily lives of Iraqis, and the legacies of the Iran-Iraq War.[4] But the political economy of social classes that Batatu introduced forty years ago has not been revisited.

Building sociologically detailed accounts of Iraq's political economy has become increasingly more difficult since Batatu's work. Consequently, a metanarrative on state politics and the role of the state has predominated in forming the nature of inquiry of Iraq and its political economy. This is not due to its role as "the center of gravity"[5] in Iraqi politics; it is an effect of the state's restrictions on academic research of and in Iraq.

Three themes—the state, oil, and war—have shaped both Iraqi politics and Iraqi studies over the past decades. These themes emerge from Iraq's modern history and its representation in academia. The shifts in the study of Iraq can be traced to two interrelated factors: access to primary source material, and the political context of the time. Limited access to primary sources and restrictions on academic freedom inside Iraq especially during the Ba'thist period (1963–2003) resulted in the production of political and diplomatic histories that do not, because they could not, draw heavily on empirical or archival sociological investigations.[6] Despite these difficulties, a small number of Iraqi economists, notably Isam Al-Khafaji and Abbas Al-nasrawi, addressed questions of political economy particularly in relation to state policies and class formation during this period.[7] But questions of political economy were generally dominated by the emergence of rentier state theory (RST) as a framework to understand the political economy of oil-dependent states in the Middle East during the 1970s and 1980s. This was also manifested in studies on Iraq, particularly during the 1980s. In their joint and separate reviews of Iraq's historiography, Marion-Farouk Sluglett and Peter Sluglett also point out the emergence of academic work with political agendas supportive of the Iraqi Ba'thist regime. The Slugletts were among many scholars whose work was critical of the regime. But perhaps the most famous anti-Ba'thist was Kanan Makiyya, who mirrored the pro-Ba'thist writings in his absolutist portrayal of the regime.[8] Because of this political polarization, "scholars and policy makers alike have tended to simplify the complexities and ambiguities of this 35-year [Ba'thist] period, arguing that the former regime erased both society and politics, leaving post-invasion Iraq a blank slate."[9]

Studies of Iraq underwent a major shift following the 2003 US invasion. While many archival materials were destroyed or lost during the 2003 war, some of the Ba'th party archives are now available for scholarly investigation.[10] Official restrictions on academic freedom no longer exist. However, over the past decade Iraq has been suffering from violent conditions that pose new challenges. Opportunities and restrictions on access to primary sources and fieldwork are shaped by the same political circumstances that have informed recent scholarship on Iraq. These include the collapse of state institutions and immediate disorder following the 2003 invasion; the de-Ba'thification of Iraqi society; sectarian violence that culminated in civil war in 2006; the threats of the Islamic State (IS) to erase Iraq's borders that were established, according to its rhetoric, by colonial powers; the new political system of federalism and consociationalism; and the constant negotiations on the Kurdish region's position in Iraq's political and economic life.

I argue that state, oil, and war are interrelated themes rather than bounded categories that determine certain political economy effects. They are markers in historical processes that, since the late nineteenth century, involved the formation of social relations organized by conceptual categories such as class, sect, nation, and gender. These social relations have informed and constituted one another within particular material and historical contexts. In what follows I elaborate on the links between the state and oil, trace the impact of wars and armed conflicts, and discuss the transformation of social relations, particularly class.

STATE

The high political stakes that emerged as a result of the 2003 war prompted debates on whether the Iraqi state is an artificial entity. The standard artificiality argument is that the Iraqi state was the result of French and British colonial imposition of borders based on the 1916 Sykes-Picot Agreement, which led to Britain establishing Iraq under a League of Nations mandate in 1920. Academics and political commentators from a wide spectrum of political orientations, 2003 war proponents and apologists, Arab nationalists, and IS have all made this argument.[11] In fact, the current Iraqi borders were produced, like borders anywhere else, over time, rather than in one event. Their construction did not start with the colonial maps, nor did it end with them. It involved "a lot of work and a lot of violence"[12] by colonizing armies and officers, colonized peoples and leaders, nationalists, national governments, and neighbors who were constructing and (re)drawing their own boundaries too.[13] Processes of modern state building, consolidation, and expansion were already underway during the nineteenth century under the Ottoman Empire. Iraq's political economy has since been entangled with efforts to consolidate state power through various methods of expanding the state's reach through infrastructure, development projects, land and population control.

Infrastructure Networks

In Iraq, infrastructure has been instrumental in extending the state's reach and control, facilitating movements of people, ideas, and goods over space and time in ways that caused many fundamental changes in the power dynamics among people and localities. Due to this role, the state as a site of political contestation and the facilitator of economic activities has been very prominent in modern Iraqi history.

The opening of the Suez Canal in 1869 and the introduction of steam navigation on the Tigris and Euphrates rivers in 1858 enabled Iraq to become a cash crop exporter.[14] These events marked the initiation of Iraq's integration into the world economy. Yusuf Ghanima, a prominent Iraqi financial and political figure during the Monarchical period (1921–1958), suggested that the Suez Canal "brought life to our trade and connected it to Europe and the whole civilized world. In other words, and I borrow Bismarck's words when he described the Suez Canal as the spine of the British Kingdom, I can say here that it is the spine of Iraq's trade as well."[15] The opening of the canal encouraged and made possible the transformation of Iraq's agricultural practices, especially in the middle Euphrates and the southern regions, from ones focused on subsistence to ones focused on profit making. Iraq's exports, mainly to India and Europe, included grains, dates, wool, leather, and opium, among other primary products. Most of its imports consisted of consumer goods. Also imported were industrial products not available in Iraq. Among the most significant was the steam water pump used for agriculture; by the end of the nineteenth century, there were twelve such pumps in all of Iraq.[16]

One indirect consequence of the multifaceted transformation of trade and agricultural practices was the introduction of industrial machinery and factories. The first machine-operated workshop in Iraq was in Baghdad and dedicated to repairing imported ships and industrial equipment. A more direct consequence was the transformation of the nature of wealth. For example, the Baghdadi Jewish Sassoon family became financially prominent due to international trade opportunities in silk, cotton, and opium.[17] The newly introduced naval lines also encouraged the stations along the Tigris river. These stations serviced ships and passengers, and grew into cities with time.[18]

In contrast to the flourishing service industry along the path of the naval lines, the service industry that catered to Shi'i pilgrims traveling from Iran and India to visit the shrine cities of Najaf and Karbala suffered after the launch of the Iraqi Railways. Between 1919 and 1924, British and Iraqi governments introduced regulations to manage the entry and length of stay of pilgrims. This was one component of enforcing the state's territorial control and demarcating its borders. These developments, and the introduction of railway and taxi services, encouraged pilgrims to buy cheap train tickets. They no longer had to stop at different localities along the way, spending money on services and accommodation.[19]

Significant infrastructure expansion also took place in the 1950s[20] and later in the 1970s, due to increased oil revenues and the emergence of the developmentalist welfare state. The accomplishments of the 1950s, 1970s, and early 1980s suffered tremendously in the following decades. The Iran-Iraq War (1980–1988) as well as the 1991 Gulf War and the era of international economic sanctions (1991–2003) decimated the economy and infrastructure. Weak state control of the borders helped turn interstate roads, some built in the 1980s in war-related efforts, into smuggling routes that contributed to a "war economy."[21]

The example of electricity in post-2003 war Iraq best illustrates how infrastructure is a node of economic and political power. Rehabilitation of the national grid after the Iran-Iraq War was postponed and the damages suffered during this period were compounded by the effects of over a decade of comprehensive international economic sanctions. Within days of the occupation of Baghdad in April 2003, American engineers arrived as part of a team in charge of restoring, in this order, electricity, water, and sewage systems. The team's task was complicated by the fact that the oil industry's production capacity was radically diminished due to the extreme reduction in electricity supply after the occupation. The particularity of the electricity-oil interdependence was also shaped by the ramifications of the 1990s sanctions. Sanctions and wars limited oil refinery capacity, resulting in the production of an excess residue known as "heavy fuel oil," which was used to run thermal power plants and produce 54 percent of Iraq's electricity.[22]

The electricity-oil interdependence created opportunities for criminal and political sabotage. The immediate and radical reduction in post-2003 electrical supply was due to criminal activities: fifty electrical transmission towers were damaged due to the preinvasion bombing, and by mid-June 2003 looters who sold precious metals to Iran and Kuwait had destroyed seven hundred such towers.[23] Criminal activities were soon combined with insurgency-inflected sabotage. The electricity and oil infrastructures were heavily reliant on each other and physically met in many spots where they fed energy into each other. These spots became attractive targets for an insurgency that was trying to undermine the new state-building project. Between 2003 and 2006, oil and electricity infrastructure was subjected to over three hundred attacks and multiple criminal assaults. Electricity generation and supply did not improve until 2008, after the end of the 2006 civil war. It is still a major problem in Iraq until this day.[24] Thus, infrastructure was not only interdependent on networks that facilitate "everyday life," including economic activities; they were themselves "a *political terrain* for the negotiation of moral-political questions."[25]

Developmental Projects

The history of development has recently been revisited by many scholars who aim at constructing a narrative that is *wider* in covering the scope of practices involved and actors affected; *deeper* in understanding the nuance, contradictions, and interplay of ideas and on-the-ground policies; and *longer* in its historical roots.[26] This new historical contextualization decenters the dominance of the term *development* in its normative and paradigmatic meaning, which is discussed and critiqued in the introduction of this volume. A distinction that might help in forming an historically nuanced understanding of developmental practices is between "'development' as an immanent process (in which 'crisis' must be seen as something intrinsic to the process itself) and 'development' as an intentional, usually state-directed, practice."[27] Seen this way and looking back to the early industrialization and colonial histories, states have often introduced development in response to crises brought about by capitalist transformations.[28] Taking this wider definition of development, it is possible to trace developmental efforts in Iraq from the late Ottoman period to the present, demonstrating that the state has always responded to material and social crises through, among other things, developmental projects.

Midhat Pasha, the governor (*wali*) of Baghdad (1869–72), was the first Ottoman governor to introduce grand developmental projects: modern public schools, a tram line, the first hospital in Iraq, Iraq's first newspaper, modern urban planning, and land reforms.[29] While his projects were grand in their ambition, they were part of multiple Ottoman attempts that started before his term in office and continued after he left Iraq to centralize governance and establish deeper and wider control of the state.

Midhat Pasha commissioned a Belgian engineer to build the city of al-Nasiriyya, in southern Iraq, the first Iraqi city to follow a modern grid plan. Currently Iraq's fourth largest city, it was named after Nasir al-Sa'dun, one of the first tribal leaders to become an Ottoman government official. Al-Sa'dun was the *mutasarrif* (district governor) of the newly established administrative unit of Liwa' al-Muntafiq (Muntafiq District) with its administrative capital at al-Nasiriyya.[30] The city was built with Ottoman orders, European expertise, and Iraqi labor to house the newly appointed governor, who was instrumental in the creation of large-scale private land ownership in southern Iraq.

Modern education was another way that the state has sought to expand its control over the country. It introduced discipline, ideas, and skills that would contribute to the creation of a modern state order. The first modern schools in Iraq were sponsored by the Dominican priests in Mosul, followed by the first Ottoman public school (also in Mosul) in 1861, and, in 1865, the Jewish community's school in Baghdad.[31] With the expansion of the administrative state structure in the 1920s, and the increasing ties to the global economy, the advantages of modern education as a tool for upward social mobility became clear to the population. For example, members of the urban Jewish community had a Western style education (a curriculum based on the French model, though the principal language of instruction in communal schools was Arabic) and were often multilingual. Their skills and education allowed them to occupy many professional positions that became available in the 1920s in education, law, and medicine as well as in the state bureaucracy and private-sector companies. A British account noted: "After the British occupied Iraq and the new administration was formed, the number of government officials required was large. The only educated and capable elements in the country being the Jews, a great number of the officials were drawn from their ranks."[32]

Modern education affected the landscape of political movements in Iraq and the composition of its political elite; it contributed to class transformation in the country in different time periods. When first introduced, it helped create a new educated (often urban) middle class: the *effendiyya*. Members of this class participated in national and ideological movements in Iraq that crossed communal and sectarian boundaries.[33] Another social and class transformation was the rise of lower-middle-class Sunni officers into the ranks of government and the military with the establishment of the

Iraqi state. Ottoman schools, which started to open during the second half of the nineteenth century, were both military and civilian. Military schools were numerous in Baghdad and often attractive for Sunni families of humble backgrounds. The government paid all student expenses at these boarding schools, which offered a path to the military college in Istanbul as well as future military and state careers. Between 1923 and 1941, most of Iraq's prime ministers were graduates of military colleges.[34]

Increased oil rent in the monarchical 1950s led to surges in developmental projects, of which education had been the most significant.[35] The state's interest in education continued through the Republican era (1958–1962) when, for example, primary education became compulsory. The most significant expansion of the educational system took place after the Ba'thist takeover, during the 1970s and early 1980s. The Iraqi developmental state manifested most prominently after the oil industry's nationalization in 1972. The educational system during the early Ba'thist period focused on eradicating illiteracy and, as a 1974 Ba'th Party document states, on "science and technology in education . . . to provide [the] personnel required in the various fields of development."[36] Free public education was established, and universities were founded in major cities in Iraq's north, center, and south. Illiteracy was reduced from 55 percent to 11 percent between 1980 and 1988.[37]

As before, public education helped transform social and economic relations in the 1980s. The military draft for the Iraq-Iran war reduced the number of men in the civilian labor force. Women, now literate, with many holding professional qualifications, filled a significant gap in the labor force. As one labor official noted: "Arabs are a problem; foreigners are a [political] problem—we have to use Iraqi women."[38] The war also meant that foreign, especially Egyptian, labor was imported. These laborers tended to be unskilled and uneducated; they also suffered unemployment when they remained stuck in Iraq during the sanctions era.[39]

Even though the Iran-Iraq War resulted in a significant increase of women in the labor force, it also diminished the developmental capacity that allowed women to become professionals to begin with. The war, and later sanctions, led to the deterioration of previously sponsored state projects, including the educational system. Until recently, the state was not able to recover the 1970s educational success record. Illiteracy in Iraq was at 74 percent in 2000 and 43 percent in 2013.[40]

The implementation and later deterioration of state-sponsored developmental projects set new socioeconomic and political trends in motion, including further class transformations and class-based politics. An example that illustrates the persistence of such trends are the dynamics of the 2006 civil war. A major player in the civil war was the Mahdi Army, the military wing of the Sadrist movement. The membership in this movement and its militia drew heavily on residents of Sadr City, a neighborhood on the outskirts of Baghdad. Sadr City was first founded as Thawra [Revolution] City during the early Republican era. It was an urban development project that sought to organize the shantytown (*sarifa*, pl. *sarayif*) established by rural migrants from southern Iraq during the monarchical period after the implementation of the 1933 Law Governing the Rights and Duties of Cultivators (see below). Thawra City, later renamed Saddam City and now Sadr City, is an example of the co-constitution of economic transformations, state-led developmental projects, and political power and contestation. The state's development of the *sarayif* reflected "efforts at social control rather than urban integration," thus doing little to transform the socioeconomic positions of their residents. The *sarayif* were always home for both secular and Islamist proletarian movements, most famously the Communist Party of Iraq (CPI), as well as for those breaking the law.[41]

Urban developments during the early Ba'thist period included land distribution schemes in Baghdad to civil servants. This led to the emergence of new middle-class neighborhoods that were mixed in their sectarian composition. Those neighborhoods, unlike the cohesive and historic center of civil disobedience, Sadr City, became prone to the devastating effects of the civil war and attacks from all sides. The sanctions and civil war drove many of the inhabitants of middle-class civil servants' neighborhoods, "the technically skilled population that was both the product and the basis of a modern state," into exile.[42] The same circumstances coupled with the lack of social and financial capital left the youth of Sadr City little hope for social mobility through now deteriorated education or the impoverished army. Instead of migrating, during the 1990s they were left with menial jobs and criminal activities as the only viable economic choices. The Sadrist movement was, as a result, partly defined by its working-class and urban poor composition, in sharp contrast to other Shi'i political parties who were in exile during the Ba'thist period and closer to the religious establishment and the Shi'i merchant and landed class.[43]

Land and Population Control

Land, both as a territory and as a taxable commodity, was significant to the Ottoman state's efforts in expanding its territorial control and rationalizing its bureaucracy to increase its tax revenues. Tribal confederations posed a major challenge standing between the state and access to land. Only 9 percent of the population during the late nineteenth and early twentieth centuries lived in urban centers; the majority were spread across nomadic, semisettled, and sedentary tribes.[44] Tribes in central and southern Iraq formed confederations that controlled territories and imposed tariffs, for example, on ships passing through what they considered to be their territories. Intertribal raids and revolts against forms of state control were common, especially in the southern and mid-Euphrates regions. Ottoman governors used different tactics, including the cooptation of tribes against one another and cutting water sources to the Marshes where insurgent tribes would hide, with various degrees of success.[45]

The Ottoman Land Code of 1858 was introduced to Iraq during the governorship of Midhat Pasha in 1871. Within the Ottoman legal framework, discussed in detail by Kristen Alff in this volume, land that was not *mulk* (privately owned) or *waqf* (Islamic endowment) belonged to the state and was referred to as *miri*. The Land Code of 1858 introduced a new kind of land holding: *tapu*. *Tapu* gave legal and heritable rights of usufruct to individuals, while the ultimate ownership of the land remained in the hands of the state.[46] While it is generally accepted that the main purpose of introducing this Land Code was to generate tax revenue, al-Wardi suggests another related reason—population control. In his memoirs, Midhat Pasha considered different reasons why southern Iraq was beset with tribal unrest: that they were Shi'i while the Ottoman rulers were Sunni, and the desire to evade taxes. The pasha thought that these were not convincing reasons: "'It is not possible that these large numbers of people revolt and spill their own blood just to obey the orders of their tribal shaykhs [leaders]. If one were to look at the state of affairs, it will appear to him that the source of conflict is land.'"[47] His solution was to transfer the holdings of public lands to the tribes within the new *tapu* system. He set up a bureau for land registration, hoping that this would transform the tribes into productive citizens and put an end to the chronic conflicts among them.[48]

The introduction of the *tapu* system as part of a plan to extend state control over tribal lands can be best illustrated in the example of Midhat Pasha and Nasir al-Sa'dun that was mentioned briefly above. Midhat Pasha convinced Nasir al-Sa'dun, the leader of the Sa'dun tribe, to become the governor of the new district of al-Muntafiq and built a new city named after Nasir al-Sa'dun, al-Nasiriyya, as its administrative center. At the same time, the Land Code of 1858 was introduced to the land of al-Muntafiq, but many tribes were reluctant to register in the land bureau. Al-Muntafiq was, up until that point, effectively tribal land. The actual (rather than legal) control over a tribal land did not rely on legal demarcations and enforcement but on the ability of the tribe to defend its territory against other tribes and the government. The Sa'duns were not reluctant to register in the *tapu* system, and most of the Muntafiq was eventually registered as property of the Sa'duns. A tribe that historically produced the leaders of the Muntafiq confederation now turned into land owners.

With the implementation of the Land Code of 1858, the Sa'duns accumulated considerable wealth, until the turn of the century when their tribesmen (now tenants) refused to pay rents. In consequence the Sa'duns leased the land to small sectional tribal shaykhs, causing further splits and tensions within the Muntafiq. The tensions (sometimes armed) continued through to World War I when land tenants completely refused to pay their dues to their new landlords.[49] These events marked the weakening of one of the biggest and strongest tribal confederations in southern Iraq and the middle Euphrates.[50]

While the introduction of the Land Code in Iraq succeeded in the weakening of tribal power, this did not automatically translate into an expansion of the state's administrative control over land and/ or tribes. The continuous intertribal disputes, brought about by the Land Code policies, proved the inability of the central government to bring these territories or the tribes generally under its administrative control and led to the suspension of issuing further land deeds (*tapu*) in 1881.[51]

The Mandate and monarchical governments were more successful in enforcing changes to land ownership, land use, and the management of the tribal people through advanced technologies of violence and heightened administrative capacities. The Mandate (1920–1932) and independent monarchy (1932–1958) granted tribal leaders land ownership in exchange for political support or neutrality. Urban political elites acquired property in a similar manner. These processes resulted in the concentration of large landownership among a few families.[52]

Laws in 1926 and 1932 that encouraged the use of irrigation pumps and continuous cultivation of land created economic and legal incentives to cultivate cash crops rather than the traditional subsistence crops. Landowners had insufficient knowledge of cultivation for commercial agriculture and sought to make profit without intensifying their capital investments. Consequently, these laws encouraged year-round overcultivation, which created environmental problems with land salination.[53] New laws facilitating the private acquisitions of public (*miri*) land by those who cultivated a plot of land for fifteen continuous years encouraged the installment of water pumps and cultivation of *miri* land by wealthy individuals and large private acquisitions by a handful of families.[54]

These new incentives and ownership structures transformed the relationship between land, labor, and tribes. However, the introduction and implementation of the 1933 Law Governing the Rights and Duties of Cultivators would be one of the most influential. It led to one of the most significant population movements that was not generated by war or political violence in Iraqi history. The law placed extreme financial burdens on farmers, including a prohibition on leaving the land if a farmer was in debt to the owner or the government. Implementation of this law initiated the mass exodus from the south to the outskirts of Baghdad and Basra, where the working class of these cities and their principal abodes, the *sarayif*, began to take shape.[55]

The Republican era, initiated by the 1958 Free Officers' coup and overthrow of the monarchy, came on the heels of countrywide protests, led mainly by the CPI, against social and economic inequalities. Policies in this period redistributed ownership of agricultural land and ended tribal authority over land and people in southern Iraq that took root since the 1871 introduction of the Land Code and subsequent reinforcement of these policies during the Mandate and independent monarchy eras.

Tribal authority over land and people reemerged in a new form in the late 1980s and early 1990s. As war, debt, and sanctions weakened the state's capacity to establish order, tribes began to function as state auxiliaries. An early indicator of these changes was when Saddam Hussein met with tribal leaders in the early 1990s and apologized for the land reforms of the Republican and Ba'thist eras. New policies and legal arrangements allowed tribes to resolve disputes and maintain order locally. Tribal paramilitary units were introduced and linked to the Presidential Palace and the Ministry of Interior.[56] This new formulation meant that the authority of tribal shaykhs was neither protective, as in the early Ottoman period, nor predatory, as under the Mandate and monarchy. In the new configurations, tribal shaykhs acted as auxiliaries of the state in return for benefits, including employment and tolerance of smuggling activities, that consolidated the new power of those shaykhs.[57]

Another effect of the sanctions was the introduction of the food rationing system as a new method of welfare distribution and population control. Within three weeks of the sanctions' imposition, the government improvised a system of food distribution and rationing that it eventually improved. The Ministry of Trade ran the system, which sought to ensure effective distribution and provision of sufficient caloric intake for the population. It succeeded in preventing mass hunger by providing at least one thousand calories per day to every Iraqi.[58]

One reason for this success was the "localization of governance" in the program's implementation. Localization also enabled new forms of control and resistance. Distributors were local shopkeepers and grocery store owners. Local Ba'th Party committee members enforced regulations and monitored retailers and distributors. Distributors and party agents were held responsible to their communities officially, in addition to the informal accountability measures that came with being neighbors and members of the same small communities. By 1995 local popular committee members were elected by people in their districts. Three years later, in response to complaints of distributors' fraud, the Ministry of Trade introduced a system of local referendum. Families registered would cast votes of confidence on the performance of the agents they were registered with. If the agent received less than half the votes, they would lose their position.

Local ties and formalized votes of confidence hampered the government's attempts to use food rationing system as a form of punishment. The government faced resistance from local agents and sometimes party committee members. The government use the withdrawal of rations as a form of collective punishment against deserters, opposition group members, and absentee public sector employees. If a person was found guilty of one of these three crimes, his or her family would be deprived of their rations until the person surrendered to the authorities, was arrested, or died. Punishments were sometimes evaded, reduced, or waved by family members who petitioned the government and forged alliances with sympathetic agents and party committee members.[59]

OIL

Since the 1980s rentier state theory (RST) has dominated scholarly writing on the significance of oil in Iraq's politics and political economy. This literature emerged in the 1970s and coincided with the commencement of Ba'thist rule. The variations and origins of this literature, as well as its limitations, are explicated by Adam Hanieh and Timothy Mitchell in this volume. In the Iraqi case, the framework's dominance resulted in its basic theses penetrating into understandings of state power[60] and Iraqi political histories. One main premise of RST is the conviction that the Iraqi state, particularly during the Ba'thist period, was able to enhance its power and separate itself from social relations and pressures. The state, in this view, acted *upon* society in an authoritarian, if not totalitarian, manner and become the center of power thanks to the abundant oil rents that it came to control.

The increased national income as a result of the nationalization of Iraq's oil industry in 1972 and the fact that most of it was now derived from oil rent allowed Iraq to fit into the paradigmatic definition of a rentier state. As the RST paradigm increasingly and causally linked state-controlled oil rent to authoritarian political systems, it became ubiquitous in the literature on Ba'thist Iraq.[61] The difficulties of doing field research during this period and the limitations on academic freedom in Iraq, coupled with RST's explanatory framework, flattened studies of Iraq into a simplistic and exclusive focus on the regime's political system.

The dominance of RST is problematic at multiple levels. It depicts a misplaced causality between oil and democracy[62] and between state formation and the oil industry.[63] As discussed in Adam Hanieh's chapter in this book, it creates a false binary between state and society, obscuring complicated social and political relationships that produce and reproduce categories such as state and class. Moreover, as Hanieh and Mitchell argue in their chapters, the paradigm's methodological approach focuses on the "national" as an enclosed and autonomous sphere of social relations that reproduce themselves independently from global connections.

Iraq offers many examples that exemplify the arguments of these critiques. While the developmental state of the 1970s was possible due to the nationalization of the oil industry, the surge in development and infrastructure projects in the 1950s was facilitated by oil rent granted to the state by oil companies hoping to avoid nationalization. In 1951 Iran passed legislation to nationalize its oil industry. At that time, the Iraq Petroleum Company (IPC) was owned by a consortium of American, British, Dutch, and French companies. Acting in part to help improve the position of the Iraqi monarchy and avoid a repeat of the Iranian nationalization, the IPC increased the Iraqi government's share in oil revenues.

Oil played a critical role in subsequent wars that Iraq became involved in. Arguably, while the U.S. "tilted" toward Iraq during the Iran-Iraq War, it in fact pursued, along with its regional allies, a dual containment approach. An example where oil was directly used as weapon in the war by regional powers was the Saudi glut policy, which was to flood the international oil market with oil, driving the oil prices down during the 1980s, causing serious financial burdens on both waring countries. Iraq's oil minister at the time commented: "Were it not for the oil glut, which may have been inspired and planned to prolong the Gulf war and wear down Iraq, the Gulf war would now be over."[64] After the end of Iran-Iraq War, oil continued to play a role in conflicts that Iraq was involved in. Complex oil-smuggling networks during the sanctions period included foreign companies, facilitation by foreign states, rebel groups, and the Iraqi government. These networks highlight the global dynamics essential for oil to circulate and acquire value and meaning.[65]

Certainly oil played a major role in Iraq's political economy, albeit not in the manner portrayed by RST. The expansion of the modern Iraqi state's capacities, through infrastructural expansions and developmental projects and public health advances, was the result of increased state revenues due to oil rent. At the same time, oil had a destructive effect in its a role in providing the incentive for a dual-containment approach during the Iran-Iraq War. Oil rents also financed the war for both Iraq and Iran, as well as the Gulf countries. Oil rents led to the emergence of a new class of construction contractors from Sunni provincial backgrounds who were engaged in building various state projects, in contrast to the urban contractor class that existed during the monarchical period.[66]

Oil workers from various ethnic and sectarian backgrounds were among the critical actors in Iraq's trade unions and social movements that animated the protests led by the CPI in the late 1940s and 1950s.[67] The legacy of these unions and their activism was later considered by the state as a threat to its war-weakened control during the mid-1980s, leading to abolition of these unions. If oil rents financed policing mechanisms, as the standard RST story goes, it also financed the wars that led to the destruction of these mechanisms, thus making possible the subsequent inventions of new forms of social control such as the rationing system and the tribal policies of the 1990s.

Despite its limitations, RST remains a powerful paradigm that has adopted many forms since it was first articulated by Mahdavi in 1970. It entered the mainstream of political science in the late 1990s and early 2000s. Using statistical regressions, leading US political science journals published articles testing the relationship between oil and democracy as postulated by RST. This interest in translating knowledge about the Middle East into a set of variables that would allow for an easy comparison with a larger number of countries developed around the same time that democracy promotion in the Middle East became a central element in President George W. Bush's policy of a "forward strategy of freedom."[68] The power of this approach, in other words, is not in its explanatory function, but in its ability to persist as a simple abstraction of complicated realities that makes an intervention at a large scale possible. For example, a question that circulated in policy discussions over the US-led state-building project in post-2003 Iraq was how to manage oil rent differently in order to enhance the chances of democracy.

CONCLUSION

State, oil, and war are three interrelated thematic markers that help us understand Iraq's political economy. They encapsulate historical processes that entailed, since the nineteenth century, the co-constitution and reconstitution of social relations such as class, sect, nation, and gender within particular material and historical contexts. These themes are *not*, as many have argued, definitive causes of certain political and political economy effects.

Only a brief historical overview confirms the prominence of war and armed violence. During the Ottoman period armed tribal revolts and armed government responses to these revolts were common. The British Mandate of 1920 came on the heels of Britain's victory and Ottoman defeat in World War I. Multiple insurgencies and successful and unsuccessful coups d'état have taken place from the establishment of the Iraqi state to the present. During the past four decades Iraq went through three devastating interstate wars (1980–88; 1991; 2003), and one civil war (2006). Each has radically altered the country's social, economic, and political fabric.

The Iran-Iraq War's impact on the political economy cannot be overstated. It altered the composition of the labor force, diverted investments away from civilian infrastructures and developmental projects into military expenditures, and created huge amounts of debt. The effect of poor wartime investment in repairing, updating, and extending Iraq's civilian infrastructure and developmental projects was compounded by the 1991 war and a decade of comprehensive international sanctions. Wars and sanctions led to shrinking state control over territories outside the center. This led to new forms of social control that influenced political economic interactions: the localization of state functions such as food distribution is one example. Another was the delegation of maintaining order to tribal groups and allowing them, in return, to run smuggling activities along the borders.

War reconstruction was only possible after 2003 when the sanctions were lifted. But in its initial stages, reconstruction funds were drained by mismanagement, corruption, and security needs to combat an insurgency that targeted reconstruction sites, prominently the electrical grid.[69] Iraq's political economy continues to be negotiated through popular protests against corruption and inefficiencies,[70] as well as negotiations over political arrangements and their impact on oil wealth distribution.[71] The infrastructural destruction caused by years of conflict is yet to be repaired.

Putting political economy in a longer historical perspective avoids the trap of falling prey to the analytical tyranny of oil. While oil rent played a major role in enhancing the consolidation of state power from the 1950s to the 1970s through endeavors such as expanding the state bureaucracy and developmental and infrastructural projects, these efforts have their roots in the late nineteenth century. We can no longer depict oil rent as the singular factor in the state's capacity to coopt and oppress political life by virtue of its financial independence from society. Simple portrayals of states that operate in isolation from global contexts and are the center of political power ruling over a helpless people obscure much more complicated and intricate historical phenomena.

Taking these phenomena seriously is crucial to understanding mechanisms of power and control. For example, a focus on oil or regime type will not reveal why certain neighborhoods were more immune than others to destruction in the 2006 civil war. Nor would such a focus help us understand what enabled paths of state-sanctioned smuggling operated by tribes, political groups, and criminal networks along the borders during the sanctions era. RST's methodological nationalism understands Iraq through its regime types, contained within the state's official boundaries. Such a conception cannot account for the regional and international links forged in the late Ottoman period that would transform Iraq's infrastructure, agricultural practices, and forms of wealth. Methodological nationalism cannot account for the depth of an international political economy of oil that played a significant role during the Iran-Iraq War.

A critical understanding of Iraq's political economy must consider a longer historical view that stretches deeper than the nationalization of oil and the British colonial intervention. Processes of state building, infrastructure construction, developmental projects, and population and territorial control were set in motion during the Ottoman period. Integration into the world market began in the second half of the nineteenth century alongside the processes of building modern state structures that support and manage new global realities as they manifested in Iraq. A long historical view decenters the colonial experience as the setting for a state that appears at once artificial and at the center of gravity of all politics. This perspective makes clear that the Iraqi state is not something to be "fixed" because it is an artificial or an ill-conceived colonial invention. Rather, it is rather a dynamic sociological phenomenon with meaningful historical roots.

Chapter 8

COLONIAL CAPITALISM AND IMPERIAL MYTH IN FRENCH NORTH AFRICA

Muriam Haleh Davis

DID FRANCE OBTAIN ECONOMIC BENEFITS FROM HER NORTH African colonies? Did capitalist interests play a decisive role in decolonization? These have been major questions in the historiography of the Maghreb over the last two decades, in part inspired by "business history" based on company archives and in part following Jacques Marseille's postulation of a "divorce" between empire and metropolitan capital after 1930.[1] A detailed, empirically rich concern for the actions of large-scale employers (*le patronat*, see below), sits uneasily with a second major theme in recent scholarship: a tendency to explain economic policies by "colonial myths," "colonial ideas," or other discursive formations that appeal to the mythology of the French civilizing mission.[2] In both cases, scholars largely agree that there was no singular logic of capital that preordained France's pattern of domination in the region. Economic historians have thus turned their attention to specific industries and interests that won handsome gains from empire while also popularizing the imperial venture in metropolitan France. This highlights both the "relative autonomy" of the French state and its responsibility for managing the contradiction between accumulation and legitimization, even as the historical tensions between nationalism and empire played themselves out in the political economy of the French colonial empire.[3] Recent scholarship on the "history of economic life" in the French colonial empire offers a partial reprieve from this dichotomy, although its call for a "more expansive approach" does not fundamentally question the nature of colonial capitalism, but instead seeks to focus on human actors and draws attention to the social embeddedness of economic activity.[4]

I argue that a narrow focus on empirically based economic history, on the one hand, or on lofty notions of imperial grandeur, on the other, make the same fundamental mistake: they fail to account for the colonial political economy as a key site, not only for redistributing material goods and organizing access to the means of production, but also for shaping the moral orders and political subjectivities that buttressed imperial rule. As scholars of the French Revolution have pointed out, the link between economic structures and prevailing notions of virtue and patriotism is hardly unique to French North Africa.[5] Indeed, regimes of capital and regimes of meaning overlap considerably, although their relationship has certain particularities in colonial contexts, especially in cases of intensive settler colonialism like Algeria.

France's early attempts to gain a foothold in the Maghreb began in the Ottoman period. As North Africa was gradually and unevenly incorporated into Europe's economic orbit, the concessions granted to European subjects dovetailed with predominant notions of Oriental despotism and the allegedly degenerate economic forms embodied in piracy, environmental degradation, and "white slavery." Diplomatic and economic penetration were inseparable during the nineteenth century. Over the course of the twentieth century, France wavered between protectionist and more liberal economic policies, a debate that was often entangled with the question of empire. If the British Empire is best known for adopting a liberal policy based on the "imperialism of free trade," French policy imagined links between economic expansion and possibilities of cultural exchange in non-European territories.[6] This was especially the case under the Second Napoleonic Empire (1852–70), when Saint-Simonian policy advocated more "liberal" methods of colonization.

Under the Third Republic (1870–1940), France resumed its protectionist tendencies and introduced the developmentalist vision that came to be associated with "modern" imperialism.[7] Paul Leroy-Beaulieu's *De la colonisation chez les peuples modernes* exemplifies this transition from a liberal form of empire to a focus on territorial expansion. First written in the final year of the Second Empire, it was subsequently published in 1874 and a second edition appeared in 1882. Leroy-Beaulieu advocated that private capitalists invest in infrastructure, which would allow them to amass considerable fortunes in North Africa thanks to contracts granted by the French state.[8]

As a settler colony and a legal extension of France, Algeria differed fundamentally from the protectorates established in Tunisia and Morocco. The experiences of establishing a settler colony in Algeria between 1870 and 1914 served as both a blueprint and a warning for other policies in North Africa. The figures of the employer (*patron*), the settler (*colon*), and the peasant (*fellah*) came to dominate the imaginaries of colonial planners. This had important ramifications for the political economy of empire in the interwar period, when a rural proletariat emerged alongside an intransigent settler population who systematically refused any economic or political reform of the colonial system.

During the interwar period, the world economic crisis changed France's economic policies drastically, introducing the high point of agrarian capitalism. Increased production of North African wine stood in flagrant contradiction with metropolitan economic interests. Yet the symbolic importance of wine, which represented "proof" of the French identity of the Algerian soil, ensured the state's continued support. At the same, time, the need for irrigation introduced a system of "hydrocapitalism" that anchored North African dependence on France.[9] The end of World War I provided the historical context for a dialogue between communism and anticolonial nationalism. During this period the gap between the logics of capitalism and empire was most evident, but the trope of investment as a sacrifice for *La Plus Grande France* was as much a discursive as an economic argument for modernization.

While the Fifth Republic inaugurated by De Gaulle in 1958 was eager to distance itself from Vichy's economic tradition of planning for obvious moral reasons, recent scholars have pointed to certain economic continuities, and not only in the colonies.[10] The "second colonial occupation" of the Maghreb faced accusations that the empire cost far too much, even with the discovery of oil in Algeria and the continued exploitation of phosphates in Tunisia and Morocco. This reoriented France's policy away from North Africa and toward Europe, while patterns of dependence indelibly influenced the forms of postcolonial rule that emerged. Although the transition between the colonial and postcolonial periods is often understood as a rupture, late colonial development projects had strange afterlives after independence. The approach to the political economy of the French colonial empire elaborated here allows us to see the continuities of certain cultural values and economic policies into the postcolonial era.

THE EARLY CONQUEST OF THE MAGHREB, 1830–1860

For French imperial historiography, 1830 has been the watershed for the history of North Africa, which continues to be problematically defined through the chronology of French conquest. As Isabelle Grangaud and M'hamed Oualdi argue, colonial historiography has been largely unable to attend to the ways that the precolonial legacy is "incrusted, constantly maneuvered, reinterpreted and molded" within the modern period.[11] Focusing on North-South relations has often obscured the ways that economic transactions, from the smuggling of goods and people, cross the borders of French North Africa, Egypt, and sub-Saharan Africa. Highlighting precolonial Mediterranean networks of trade, Joshua Schreier demonstrates that the central commercial role of Jews offers a window into these activities.[12] We should be attentive to how French imperialism transformed rather than erased precolonial structures of land tenure, tribal organization, or trading networks.

Historians have typically considered the conquest of Algeria in 1830 the beginning of France's so-called second colonial empire, successor to its colonial empire in the Atlantic world and the continental empire of Napoleon Bonaparte. Algeria was thus a crucial link between the so-called old colonies and the "new imperialism" that took shape in the late nineteenth century. As Jennifer Sessions has pointed out, the conquest of Algiers had a certain economic logic in addition to the (failed) attempt to bolster Charles X's prestige at home: metropolitan officials hoped that by conquering this Ottoman Mediterranean littoral, they would gain an entry point to the trans-Saharan trade routes into the African continent.[13] The desire to control trade in the Mediterranean also derived from historical preoccupations that married economic and civilizational concerns. France's civilizational ideology had long focused on the backwardness of the Ottoman Empire, whose moral degeneracy was expressed by a particular economic practice: piracy.[14] Lastly, the French saw their invasion of Algeria as a noble attempt to protect North Africa from so-called white slavery while also hoping to restore the "Granary of Rome" and save ancient Latin North Africa from environmental ruin.[15]

The colonization of Algeria unfolded in the context of increased anxieties about the cultural impact of industrialization in Europe. French politicians thus hoped that "agriculture and civic virtue would flourish in place of the corruptions of urban, industrial life" on the southern shore of the Mediterranean.[16] The French relationship to the soil thus surpassed the narrowly economic possibilities for agrarian capitalism. From the Saint-Simonian dream of marrying European rationality with Arab labor to attempts at delimiting tribal lands in the 1850s (*cantonment*), developing a relationship to the soil though agriculture and private property was fundamental for the civilizing mission. This policy had devastating effects for Algerian pastoralists and agro-pastoralists whose grazing lands were dramatically reduced.

The colonial conquest of Algeria had profound implications for Tunisia and Morocco. While the expanding European economic interests in Morocco and Tunisia did not involve colonial settlement to the same degree, like Algerians, Moroccans and Tunisians first experienced conquest through their country's integration into European circuits of commerce and capital investment. Having infiltrated the North African coastline, the French were able to pressure Hussein Bey of Tunisia into ending government monopolies on agricultural products. A wily mix of diplomacy and force opened Tunisian markets. The effects of economic integration were ruinous for local artisans as cheaply manufactured goods started arriving from Europe. In Morocco, the advance of informal empire after the 1844 Battle of Isly provoked a defensive reaction, especially from religious circles, as commercial penetration by European powers increased.[17] After the Tétouan War of 1860, "Morocco was transformed into another subaltern state feeding European expansion by offering raw materials, cheap labor, and unprotected markets."[18]

While Tunisia and Morocco both became French protectorates, they had profoundly different social and economic formations. Morocco had been historically closed to the West, while Tunisia had long been a site of trans-Mediterranean immigration and commerce. Yet in both countries, European economic power expanded through a regime of capitulations that granted foreigners immunity from North African legal codes as well as payment of certain taxes. Urban lower classes were impoverished by the new sources of competition, while a rising local commercial bourgeoisie made considerable profit as commercial intermediaries.[19]

In 1863 the Husaynid Bey of Tunis, Muhammad III al-Sadiq, took out a loan from the Paris-based Emile Elanger & Co. at an exorbitant interest rate. Six years later in 1869, this unrepayable debt led to the formation of an International Finance Commission, composed of French, Italian, and British nationals to supervise Tunisia's economy. In 1881, Tunisia's inability to repay the debt led to the establishment of a French protectorate, consecrated by the Treaty of Bardo. This echoed developments in Morocco, where after the Tétouan War, the Moroccan state was made to pay an indemnity of 100 million pesetas, payable only in specie, thus undermining the government's economic stability.[20]

In both Morocco and Tunisia, European ambitions dovetailed with indigenous hopes and projects for modernization. Politicians like the governor of the Moroccan city of Tétouan, Muhammad al-Saffar, and Tunisia's prime minister Khayr al-Din admired the West and adopted economic, military, and political reform policies based on the European model.[21] Economic policies in the nineteenth century are hard to explain by any singular account of colonial capitalism. The capitulations system and its economic protections for European subjects, competition among European states, the expansion of markets, and commercial penetration and related attempts to abolish local monopolies all contributed to eroding local economic and social structures. This set the stage for formal colonization. Thus, military confrontations worsened an already untenable imbalance of economic power in the region, leading to an erosion or elimination of native sovereignty.

ESTABLISHING A SETTLER COLONY IN ALGERIA

The official pretext for the French invasion at Sidi-Ferruch on July 5, 1830, was the infamous "fly-whisk incident" of 1827, when Ottoman governor of Algiers Husayn Dey allegedly struck French consul Pierre Duval in a verbal altercation over unpaid French debts to the Regency. Of course, France's decision to invade had little to do with this insolent gesture. The initial conquest did not translate into any certainty as to what economic or political vision should be implemented in Algeria. Many officials supported a limited colonization (*occupation restreinte*) that would restrict French presence to the coastal areas. The colonial doctrines of assimilation and association also presented differing economic blueprints for the role of French capital. The Saint-Simonians, who had initially attempted to bring their vision to Egypt, viewed the Algerian

Arabs as a foil for the French proletariat, proposing that Europeans assume tasks such as industry while the Arabs were to engage in agriculture.[22] They also advocated industrialization, encouraging massive capital investment in the domains of infrastructure and communication.[23]

France's loss of Alsace-Lorraine in the Franco-Prussian War of 1871 prompted the arrival of a new wave of settlers and accelerated the need to construct centers of colonization inhabitable for Europeans. The French state offered lucrative construction contracts, leading to significant clientelism and corruption.[24] Native agriculturalists, progressively expelled from the most fertile land, lost their livelihoods to European settlers, many of rural origin who had been displaced from Alsace-Lorraine. The expropriation of tribal lands began in earnest with the 1865 *sénatus-consulte*. The alleged lack of private property among Muslims justified both legislations. By the first decade of the twentieth century, the measures reduced Muslim-owned land from 2.5 million to 1,967,955 million hectares.[25] The French parliamentarian Auguste Warnier invoked civilizational notions of backwardness to justify this dispossession, arguing that "land fallen into a state of Arab communism prepares the observer for the desolate spectacle of the interior of Africa."[26] Native millenarian revolts and colonial designs on the most fertile lands were part of a singular logic.

Fearing even more severe repression due to the fall of Napoleon III after the Franco-Prussian War, the 1871–72 Muqrani revolt channeled fragmented opposition to colonial rule through the structures of the Rahmaniyya Sufi brotherhood. When this uprising was severely defeated, Kabyle society was further devastated by the 1873 Warnier Law, which replaced the *sénatus-consulte*. These land seizures—as well as the colonial myth that Berbers were more "civilized" than their Arab counterparts—largely explain the predominance of Berber immigration to France in the early twentieth century.[27]

These measures built on royal orders of 1844 and 1846, which had bypassed Islamic laws and allowed perpetual leases, a common arrangement governing European land use, to constitute a transfer of ownership.[28] Introduction of private property and speculation made land into a form of capital by regularizing land tenure arrangements that were, in fact, marked by an uncertainty that did not correspond to a clear distinction between private and public ownership.[29] Monetarization of the Algerian economy led to the political disenfranchisement of traditional political elites as *hubus* (pious endowment) properties were effectively turned over the colonial state, diminishing the standing of traditional sources of authority such as mosques or *zawiyas* (Sufi lodges). More significantly, those traditional elites who maintained their prestige and wealth in colonial society generally did so by inserting themselves into the colonial state, for example by ensuring their children spoke French or working for the French administration.[30] As rural Algerians lost their land, many were transformed into rural proletarians or sharecroppers (*khammès*, or someone who retained a fifth of the crop). This population grew considerably after World War I and began migrating to France in large numbers, first as military conscripts and then as workers to replace young Frenchmen slaughtered in the war.

The introduction of dry farming and the mechanization of agriculture intensified these dramatic changes. Algerian farmers had traditionally consumed the majority of the foodstuffs that they produced and stored excess grain as insurance against bad harvests. Their entrance into a market economy ended this practice, so when drought or other factors impaired the harvest, they were forced to purchase grain at high prices.[31] At the same time, the expansion of credit and the low cost of native labor made Algeria a fertile ground for European capitalist agriculture, which benefitted from French markets for Algerian goods. Despite the historical importance of Saharan trade networks that connected the Sahelian space to the Algerian Tell, as well as local markets, the region's incorporation into the world economy changed the contours of these relations.[32] Algeria increasingly exported crops to Europe and imported virtually everything consumed in the colony. Small and medium landholders sought to specialize in crops with a high exchange value on the French market. Credit structures facilitated access to loans for European settlers but not for Algerian farmers, who therefore found it impossible to transition to mechanized agriculture.[33]

In many ways, the political economy of Algeria was fashioned through two figures that came to represent the patriotism of economic activity rather than its propensity for generating profits. These figures decisively influenced the trajectory of decolonization. The *patronat*, difficult to translate into English, denotes the heads of large business interests, either public or private. It thus only partially overlaps with the bourgeoisie as a class category. In France, the *patronat* is often portrayed as a politico-economic actor, a key interlocutor of the government, and an active supporter of imperial expansion. Yet by the late nineteenth century, investing in North Africa was also a matter of national pride. As the president of the Bône-Guelma Railway Company claimed while addressing the National Assembly in 1878, the construction of the railroad granted a "patriotic satisfaction" since, in addition to its benefits for the company, it would contribute "above all" to France.[34] The state secured these contracts in an attempt to encourage investments up until decolonization. René Damien expressed doubts regarding the economic viability of building a large metal plant in Bône in 1961, but stated, "If the government tells us that political reasons that are more imperative than economic reasons dictate the installation of this factory, it will find steelmakers ready, as always, to fulfill their obligation."[35] According to this patriotic discourse, steelmakers were ready to accept risky financial conditions to help protect the existence of French Algeria.[36]

The other hero of French Algeria, who has received considerably more scholarly attention, was the *petit colon* or settler who lived a more modest existence than the *gros colon* or wealthy landowner. Unlike in Tunisia or Morocco, the Algerian settlement model was a family farm that would encourage an abiding attachment to the soil. By the sweat of his brow, the European farmer would make Algeria French. While already represented in the myth of the "Granary of Rome," the symbolism of the *colon* intensified when wine became the economic mainstay of the colony following the 1863 Phylloxera plague in France. Replanting vines outside the Hexagon by grafting European vines onto the roots of Phylloxera-resistant wine species and Louis Pasteur's discoveries regarding the role of yeasts in alcoholic fermentation permitted widespread wine cultivation and production in warm climates like Algeria. As agrarian capitalism became dominant after 1910, vineyards supplanted Algeria's historical vocation of growing soft wheat (*blé tendre*), and its economy was restructured to serve the needs of the French market. As historian of Algerian wine Hilbert Isnard argues, "wine growing put in place the structures that conditioned the existence of modern Algeria."[37] It influenced patterns of Algerian migration, created an agricultural subproletariat, organized regional spaces, and introduced an elaborate system of credit. Consequently, wine was the motor of the colonial economy before the discovery of oil, equaling 66 percent of the value of Algerian exports in 1933.[38]

After World War II Algerian wine threatened to undermine France's wine markets. Facing pervasive overproduction, wine growers from the Midi region objected to state support for Algerian "medicinal" wine.[39] Yet this did not hamper the French state's decision to offer subventions for Algerian wine, largely due to the settler lobby and the ideological importance of the product. France continued to be the largest market for Algerian wines until 1967 due to Algeria's limited but politically significant position in the European Economic Community. Only in 1968, six years after Algerian independence, did pressure from metropolitan wine interests finally prevail.

The conventional economic history of wine in Algeria posits contrasting French and Algerian identities due to metropolitan hostility to Algerian wine production. Most scholars agree that political interests trumped market logic.[40] Settlers understood their identity as literally rooted in the Algerian soil, and were largely sympathetic to versions of right-wing Poujadism, a political ideology that rejected urban (and economic) modernity in favor of the imagined traditional values of the French countryside.[41] French economic protection enabled this ideology, which formed the crux of the far-right opposition to De Gaulle. Pierre Lagaillarde, a founder of the right-wing Secret Armed Organization (OAS), exemplifies this "settler environmentalism."[42] He believed that French Algeria was rooted in the Algerian soil and called on De Gaulle "to undertake decisions and acts with the humanist spirit that inspired the speech of Constantine so that France can show its fraternity to the farmers (*fellahs*) of Algeria that I have learned to love because their land resembles my land, and because their suffering was that of my father."[43]

The devastation of the rural world coincided with major insurrections against the colonial regime (Emir Abdelkader in 1832, Bu Ziyan in 1849, al-Muqrani in 1871). While relying on Sufi networks or couched in millenarian terms, market dependency, partial self-sufficiency, and revolt were correlated.[44] Julia Clancy-Smith has argued that Bu Ziyan's revolt demonstrated how millenarian revolts became a preferred mode of action as a foil to the colonial state's "profane" mode of power, a form of resistance that was not limited to Algeria but instead had a pan-Islamic coloring.[45] This of course foreshadowed decolonization; the colonial world that Frantz Fanon famously described as a Manichean place that represented a zero-sum game between colonized and colonizer was reflected in both economic and legal terms, resulting in a severe social fragmentation that, according to some observers, makes it difficult to speak of a shared subaltern position among Algerian intellectuals.[46]

ALGERIA AS MODEL OR COUNTERMODEL?

In the late nineteenth century, opinion regarding the financial value of the colonies definitively shifted, largely thanks to the publication of Paul Leroy-Beaulieu's *De la colonisation chez les peuples modernes*. Leroy-Beaulieu had considerable investments in Tunisia, so his argument that France had too long ignored the needs of her colonies may have also likely signaled some degree of self-interest. He claimed that colonial development could be mutually beneficial rather than merely exploitative, echoing some of the older arguments of the Saint-Simonians. Moreover, while he was a proponent of laissez-faire in metropolitan France, he advocated a form of economic interventionism in the colonies.[47] Under the Third Republic, while political leaders such as Jules Ferry defended colonization using economic arguments, most liberal economists opposed colonization.[48] A shift away from assimilation and toward association would be fundamental for the policies of Hubert Lyautey in Morocco, as well as the economic doctrine of *mise en valeur* (development or, more literally, value creation) as espoused by Alfred Sarrault. In both of these visions of colonial development, administrators discarded the hope of making Algerians into Frenchmen and postulated a vision in which natives would evolve within their specific cultural frameworks.[49]

Colonial officials and native populations in Morocco and Tunisia closely watched France's experience in Algeria, often referred to as a *regime du sabre*, or "government by the sword." France legally incorporated Algeria as three departments in 1848. In 1870, the French state transferred their governance from the Ministry of War to the Ministry of the Interior. The incorporation and shift in governance were mirrored by economic arrangements: in 1884, Algeria and France formed a free trade zone. This was not immediately possible in Morocco and Tunisia due to the interests of other European powers. In Tunisia, France had to settle for most favored nation treatment until 1890. This status evolved as France achieved tax exemptions for most products by 1928 (except wine, tobacco, and salt).[50] In contrast, the 1906 Act of Algeciras opened Morocco to multiple European interests, although France was the primary beneficiary. Regardless of the plural economic ties that bound Tunisia and

Morocco to other European countries, they were most dependent on France. At the end of the colonial period, four-fifths of Algeria's foreign trade was with France, while the numbers were just over 50 percent for Morocco and Tunisia. Exchanges among the three Maghreb countries represented a mere 2 percent of their total foreign trade.[51] In 1913, France consecrated 10 percent of its outflow of capital to empire, of which 61.5 percent went to the Maghreb and two-thirds of that to Algeria.[52]

The French were anxious not to repeat their Algerian mistakes in Tunisia and Morocco. Several financial measures were specific to the Algerian territory. First, a 1900 law granted Algeria financial autonomy, although the financial delegates who voted on expenditures were overwhelmingly European. Second, special taxes known as the *impôts arabes* aided the French state's appropriation of Algerian wealth, as local farmers steadily lost ownership and use of their land over the course of the nineteenth century. Moreover, other parts of French North Africa resolutely rejected the Algerian model of offering land to Frenchmen as a safety valve to ease class tensions in the metropole. In Tunisia, so-called official colonization did not begin until the late 1890s, and many land owners preferred to hire Italian, rather than Tunisian (Muslim), labor. Hubert Lyautey, the first resident general of Morocco, was horrified by the riffraff who had been attracted to settle in Algeria and preferred to encourage a "gentleman farmer" class of inhabitants.[53] Yet certain patterns could not be avoided; the influx of settlers and the spread of capitalist modes of production drastically transformed the landscape in Morocco, as cities such as Tangiers and Casablanca became new hubs for foreign trade. The creation of shantytowns—or *bidonvilles*—around major urban centers in the 1920s would become an important factor in recruitment for the nationalist cause in Algeria and Morocco. As Jim House writes, "Uneven economic development existed as much within each colonial territory as between colony and metropolis."[54]

Under the facade of local rule provided by the protectorates, Tunisia and Morocco generally avoided the large-scale violence that had defined the occupation of Algeria in the mid- to late nineteenth century. They also had larger mineral resources to exploit: Tunisia's Gafsa Phosphate Company was formed in 1897; the Moroccan Sharifian Office of Phosphates was established in 1920. In both countries, the phosphate mines and related railway lines became at once the mainstay of the colonial economy as well as the centers of interwar trade union organizing.[55] Unlike Algeria and Tunisia, which had relied on some degree of official state-led colonization targeted to attract individual settlers, Morocco's protectorate remained beholden to large capitalist interests, a result of loans issued by European banks in the early twentieth century. Consequently, large-scale capital continued to flow into Morocco right until decolonization, while capital investment in Algeria and Tunisia tapered off in 1910 and 1930, respectively.[56]

The facade of native sovereignty in Tunisia and Morocco did not stop the French state from unleashing forms of economic violence in these protectorates. An 1885 law based on the Australian Torrens Act aided the confiscation of native lands in Tunisia. As official colonization accelerated in the twelve years prior to the Great War, more than 250,000 hectares of land were transferred from Tunisian to French control.[57] Tunisians who were able to retain their land formed an elite who turned toward liberal professions and invested in education. From the ashes of the Mamluk-era mercantile classes, then, came another privileged class who appropriated the values of modernity and democracy, even as they resented their exclusion from the upper echelons of the state administration.[58] Such frustrations fueled the formation of the Young Tunisians, the country's first nationalist party. However, the Young Tunisians looked down on the rowdier political style of labor unions. Indigenous trade unions first formed in the 1920s and culminated in establishing a national federation, the General Union of Tunisian Workers (UGTT), in 1946.

Similarly, in Morocco, the introduction of land registration and European purchase of *melk* (privately owned) lands went hand in hand with official colonization. Sale of indigenous-owned land was accelerated in 1919, when a decree made collective lands the property of those occupying them. The state seized the land of local tribes, compensating them at low prices and often resettling them on their remaining territory. Such French attempts to sedentarize tribes by stripping them of their domains bolstered the ability of powerful chiefs (protected by the French state) to exploit members of their own tribe, leaving individuals with no option but exodus or poverty.[59] In 1913, Europeans occupied 73,000 hectares, skyrocketing to one million hectares by 1953.

THE "BLOOD TAX" AND THE CHANGING ECONOMICS OF COLONIAL RULE (1914–1945)

The Great War demanded new economic, political, and human sacrifices from France's North African territories. After French West Africa, the most substantial aid for the war effort came from Algeria. Due to France's de facto monopoly on Algerian foodstuffs, the metropole saved 770 million francs when compared to purchasing grain, wine, tobacco, and sheep at market prices from 1915 to 1919.[60] Moroccan agricultural trade boomed during the war. Yet along with such economic opportunities, Maghreb countries were expected to pay a so-called blood tax and sacrifice their lives for the *patrie* by sending Muslim troops to war. As Minister of War Adolphe Messimy wrote in 1909, "Africa has cost us heaps of gold, thousands of soldiers, and streams of blood. We do not dream of demanding the gold from her. But the men and the blood, she must repay them with interest."[61] One hundred and forty thousand Algerians and 24,300 Moroccans were recruited during World War I to fight on the western front; an additional 144,000 worked in the coal mines, fields, and factories of France.[62] The racial logic of colonial conscription and the military division of labor dovetailed with colonial stereotypes. Moreover, colonial policies were implanted in the metropole during World War I and undermined labor movements. Hostility toward colonial workers in French factories led European workers to see themselves as a "white" working class.[63] Colonial expertise and structures continued to shape the organization of North African labor in France well after World War II.[64]

North Africans were thus unaffected by the general spirit of 1917 and learned their own lessons from the Russian Revolution. Messali Hadj first organized Algerian factory workers in France and in 1929 formed the left-nationalist North African Star (Étoile Nord-Africaine, ENA).[65] Despite Hadj's own uneasy relationship with the French Communist Party, the focus of the ENA's program on land redistribution and class struggle drew heavily on communist doctrine, blending elements of Islam and Marxism. The internal contradictions of the colonial system, the narrow economic possibilities it offered to North Africans, the Great Depression of the 1930s, and the Popular Front government's failures disappointed the hopes of radical labor activists and nationalists for reform. Hence, the ENA was often at odds with reformist advocates of assimilation.

A pervasive shift in official thinking about the political economy of empire occurred with the 1923 publication of Albert Sarraut's *La mise en valeur des colonies*, which advocated state investment in infrastructure to secure moral, economic, and political profits.[66] Large-scale expansion of ports, roads, railways, electrification, and hospitals was impossible for private capitalists or colonial governments to undertake. So, the French state would need to finance them. In lobbying for metropolitan funds, Sarraut rejected the long-standing view that the colonies should be financially autonomous. While he failed to procure funding for his ambitious program, Sarrault popularized the notion of *mise en valeur.* Although by the early 1930s his ambitious program seemed less feasible due to the Depression, his conviction that it was necessary to inject large amounts of capital into the colonies became the new orthodoxy in the postwar period.

Despite Sarrault's vision, the economic historian Jacques Marseille has argued that there was, in fact, a major shift in the relationship between metropolitan imperial policy and capital in the 1930s. Until then, the French state had ensured a favorable climate for private industries, often by protecting markets, which helped noncompetitive companies make a profit. Certain industries, he admits, benefitted enormously from the colonies, but he argues that this was not true across the board. Industrial capital, he argues, became "divorced" from empire after the 1930s. Paradoxically, "at the moment that empire finally seemed like a privileged domain for French capitalism, it at the same time and contradictorily became a troublesome reminder of its past."[67] During the interwar period, "if empire was in fact a millstone around the neck of French capitalism and economic development, many were not only unaware of this fact, but believed the opposite."[68]

The political economy of the French Maghreb was thus dramatically reconfigured in the 1930s. Notions of economic competition and free trade began undermining traditional colonial protectionism. As France faced the nascent globalization of its markets, planners both in the metropole and Algeria looked to California as a model of colonial agriculture for Morocco and Algeria. They reoriented agricultural production toward high-value products, such as oranges.[69] Between 1930 and 1933, prices for soft wheat, a Maghreb staple, fell by 55 percent.[70] Increased production of wine and citrus required extensive irrigation, which deepened the dual economic structures that gave colonizer and colonized unequal access to the means of production.[71] Moreover, because wine and citrus relied on seasonal Muslim wage labor, the number of rural proletarians, who traveled to the cities to find work in the off-season, exploded in the interwar period and accelerated throughout the Maghreb after World War II.[72] This population became a pillar of support for Algerian independence.

TOWARD THE "SECOND COLONIAL OCCUPATION": VICHY AND THE POSTWAR PERIOD

In October 1958, during the Algerian war of independence, France's president Charles De Gaulle announced a plan for the social and economic development of Constantine. He promised 15 billion francs in public works and urban development, construction of housing for 1 million individuals, creation of 400,000 new jobs, education of two-thirds of Algerian children, redistribution of 250,000 hectares of land to Muslim farmers, and recruitment of one-tenth of metropolitan cadres (civil servants) from Muslim Algerians. Industrialization and completing the modernization of North Africa's economy and population were the major themes of the postwar period. The transformation of the French civilizing mission into a "modernizing mission" was the discursive frame for the post–World War II "second colonial occupation" of Africa, accompanied by massive capital investments in industrialization, social engineering, education, and agriculture, concurrent with Europe's postwar reconstruction. Not everyone agreed with the economic logic of these investments. On the pages of *Paris Match*, Raymond Cartier argued that the skyrocketing cost of developing the colonies was a burden on the metropole, the beginning of an argument that would take his name (Cartierism).

After World War II, European integration posed an additional threat to colonial capitalism. With the Treaty of Rome in 1957, the falling trade barriers across Europe were a bad omen for colonial economies uncompetitive with their European metropoles. The discovery of oil in Algeria 1956 was a bright spot, but the cost of building pipelines to export it to Europe meant that the financial boon would not be palpable for a few years. De Gaulle sought to present himself as the first economic modernizer. But, in fact, economic modernization plans for North Africa began in 1946 with the Balensi Plan's agricultural modernization scheme. While colonial developmental visions were interrupted by World War II, the Vichy era foreshadowed postwar efforts at large-scale industrialization and development.[73]

Samir Saul has recently asked the question, Did the changing economics of empire after World War II determine the trajectory of decolonization? Based on data from individual branches of industry, he criticizes Marxist approaches, which, he argues, share with defenders of colonialism the "conviction that the functioning of metropolitan economies and their aptitude to overcome crisis depended on [France's] overseas possessions."[74] According to Saul, French economic interests (public or private) were not the main drivers of decolonization. Jacques Marseille also maintains that political rather than economic calculations explain the French colonial commitment to French Algeria in the postwar period. Indeed, the post–World War II economic policies undeniably had political effects; the Algerian National Liberation Front (FLN), for example, viewed French development projects as the infrastructure for a "pilot state" in the Third World.[75]

The continuities between colonial and nationalist visions of development are striking. In Morocco the Secteurs de Modernization du Paysannat played a key role in the postcolonial agricultural modernization, as did the Algerian Sociétés Agricoles de Prévoyance. The need to create a new, industrial civilization after colonialism, or plans for mass housing such as the million villages program introduced by Algeria's president Houari Boumediene, also have certain parallels with colonial projects. When independence actually came, the flight of the European settlers meant the exodus of needed capital and expertise. North Africa was now left with economic needs that were primarily filled through the policy of cooperation with France.

Mineral extraction in Tunisia and Morocco, and hydrocarbons in Algeria, allowed these countries to survive economically. Algeria's socialist experiment attempted to diversify its trading partners with revolutionary bravado. Tunisia, although fundamentally committed to a liberal economic program, briefly experimented with Destourian socialism, which it abandoned in 1969 due to opposition from large Muslim olive growers and the World Bank. In fact, Tunisia took many of the same steps as Algeria to decolonize its economy. But it did so much more slowly due to Habib Bourguiba's pro-Western orientation. Morocco, in contrast, couched its economic program in terms of *promotion nationale* rather than socialism, borrowing heavily from the United States and tying its economic interests to the West.

The possibility of massive profits in mineral extraction, agrarian capitalism, and certain industrial sectors in the postwar period should not lead us to conclude that the construction or protection of markets was an activity separate from cultivating the French moral vision of the "imperial spirit." Asking if myths of grandeur or profits drove the French colonial empire in North Africa is the wrong question. French planners in France and Algeria consistently envisioned economic reforms as the way to cultivate certain subject positions, calm the passions of nationalism, or even as a form of propaganda. French colonial historians have been tempted to frame colonial investment as an irrational commitment, in part because they have been insufficiently critical of the fundamental tenant of the civilizing mission: that France was exceptional in its commitment to grandeur and enlightenment. Emphasizing France's economic "sacrifices" in establishing these values comes with certain political dangers. It can serve as ammunition, for example, in recent arguments that France should resist calls for colonial "repentance."[76] The notion of French exceptionalism also obfuscates the ways colonial capitalism was always imbricated in certain assumptions about civilization.

Chapter 9

LEBANON BEYOND EXCEPTIONALISM

Ziad M. Abu-Rish

FOR THE MOST PART, LEBANON HAS BEEN CONSPICUOUSLY ABSENT from the literature on the comparative political economy of the Middle East and North Africa, particularly in scholarship on state building, economic development, and social mobilization. Lebanon's exclusion or exceptionalization stems from two historical features of its political economy. First, the postcolonial development trajectory of Lebanon coalesced around a laissez-faire and service-based model. This contrasts with the majority of postcolonial states whose political economies pursued state-led development and organized closed economies based on either primary goods or manufacturing. Second, violent militia mobilizations coupled with repeated foreign military interventions throughout its prolonged civil war were particularly intense in Lebanon. Scholars typically lump the Lebanese Civil War into a broader history of alleged sectarian violence dating back to the nineteenth century.[1] The ubiquity of civil war and sectarianism as a marker, research topic, and analytical framework in the study of Iraq, Libya, Syria, or Yemen (along with more comparative studies of the region) since 2011 should not obscure the fact that historically scholars considered Lebanon to be uniquely sectarian and exceptionally violent.[2] They argued that sectarianism either prevented the establishment of effective state institutions or strained and led to the collapse of government authority.[3]

A subset of scholars compounded this problem with uncritical narratives about the political economy of Lebanon. One current argues that the Lebanese state is the product of a power-sharing compromise between notables of different sects, and its institutions were therefore never meant to stand above society let alone intervene in the economy.[4] A second group takes more seriously the role of Lebanese state institutions in providing the administrative and legal framework for the liberalized movement of goods and capital but claims such arrangements were the inevitable product of decision making by a network of political and economic elites.[5]

An important group of historians, anthropologists, sociologists, and political scientists have applied critical political economy to study Lebanon—notwithstanding the lack of consensus on the definition of political economy, which theoretical approach is most effective, or the conclusions to be drawn from this orientation. Some have taken political economy itself as the subject of inquiry. Others have turned to political economy to explain historical change or sociopolitical praxis. Collectively, they have challenged traditional research, rejected exceptionalist framings, and provided the building blocks to reconceptualize the histories of the territories that constitute present-day Lebanon and its relationship to regional and global history.

I draw on this literature to present an alternative reading of modern state, market, and class formation in Lebanon anchored in three premises. First, as the introduction to this volume argues, state, market, and class formation are co-constitutive. Class struggle and state power in Lebanon were intrinsic to the making of its economy, not separate or irrelevant to it. Second, historical periodization must consider the operation of different scales of time and the simultaneity of change and continuity across them. Historical legacies matter, but so too do structural transformations and political contingencies. Finally, state, market, and class formation in Lebanon were not separate from regional and global dynamics, but central to them. The question is not the effects of preformed global and regional dynamics on state, market, and class formation in Lebanon, but how dynamics in Lebanon contributed to regional and global dynamics and vice-versa. This chapter historicizes the trajectory of Lebanon's postcolonial political economy by eschewing culturalist and deterministic analysis. It highlights how political economy sheds light on key junctures in historical and contemporary Lebanon and demonstrates how the case of Lebanon advances our understanding of the region's political economy.

THE PRE–WORLD WAR I OTTOMAN SETTING (1831–1914)

The current territory of the Lebanese Republic is an amalgamation of the Ottoman *mutasarrifiyya* (a subprovince directly responsible to Istanbul) of Mount Lebanon and parts of the *vilayet* (province) of Beirut and the *sanjaks* (ordinary subprovinces) of Hama, Damascus, and Hawran. The modern forms of political economy and their attendant dynamics initially emerged in these territories during the last century of the Ottoman Empire. Because Lebanon's territory featured late nineteenth- and early twentieth-century dynamics common across the Middle East and North Africa, engaging its pre–World War I political economy challenges exceptionalist narratives that have contributed to Lebanon's exclusion from comparative political economy studies.

During the nineteenth century, two overarching processes undergirded the integration of the territories and people that would constitute Lebanon into the modern world system. The first was the introduction of techniques of governance that permitted the state to intervene into subjects' daily lives.[6] The second was the shift from subsistence to market production.[7] Both processes were uneven in time and space, resulting in heterogeneous patterns of cultural identification, political affiliation, land ownership, capital accumulation, and labor relations.[8] A key effect of the transformation of Ottoman rule and the shift to market production was the redefinition of social categories: slavery and tax farming were abolished; new urban business, rural landholding, and rural and urban wage-earning classes began to form; and the relationship of Ottoman subjects to one another and to the sultan increasingly came to be defined through a negotiated—however unequally—set of rights and responsibilities.

Peasants—the overwhelming majority of the local population—along with rural and urban landed elites increasingly turned to production for the world capitalist market. The rise and fall of the silk economy is the most studied aspect of this transformation.[9] Silk production entailed two primary activities: sericulture—planting mulberry trees to host silkworms—and silk reeling—establishing workshops and other infrastructure to process silk. French and local investors spurred a dramatic expansion in sericulture between the 1840s and 1880s. Previously, silk production had not been a significant part of the region's economy. However, the entry of Chinese and Japanese silk into the world market coupled with the Long Depression of 1873–96 caused the local silk economy to decline precipitously. Consequently, large numbers of landowners and peasants turned to new crops, tobacco in particular.

A second key element of the pre–World War I period is the influx of European investment capital in the form of loans, concessions, and monopolies.[10] The development of the railway, tramway, road, port, telegraph, and urban amenities like water, lighting, and electricity systems was tied to the emerging global commodity markets. Yet they were also profit-generating enterprises in their own right.[11] Such infrastructure further linked the history of these territories to a broader pattern of European investment and political interference in the region.

In response to the decline of the silk economy and the global depression, large numbers of residents of Mount Lebanon and nearby areas emigrated to the Americas, a third key element in the pre–World War I transformations.[12] This process began in the 1880s and accelerated between 1890 and 1915. A significant number of these émigrés returned.[13] New transportation and communication infrastructure greatly facilitated migration, return, and flows of information and capital between local communities and the diaspora. Return migration transformed home villages and towns, as returnees brought back capital, purchased land, built houses, educated their children, and embodied new gender norms and relations.[14] Consequently, the emergence of a middle class in the territories that would become Lebanon followed a slightly different trajectory than other parts of the Middle East.[15]

A final key element in the pre–World War I transformations was the rise of Beirut as a major port city and, in 1888, a provincial capital, a development linking modern statecraft, commodity markets, and infrastructural investments.[16] Only in the 1830s and 1840s did the central government and local inhabitants begin to transform Beirut into a major port.[17] This was not due to the much-mythologized inherent Lebanese entrepreneurial spirit, but to the same processes that spurred the creation of other new ports and provincial capitals throughout the Middle East.[18]

WORLD WAR I AND THE POSTWAR SETTLEMENT (1914–1920)

World War I brought famine, disease, and conscription to Lebanon, producing demographic, socioeconomic, and political crises. The Entente powers imposed a crippling blockade on the eastern Mediterranean, resulting in food shortages, price hikes, and hoarding, culminating in famine.[19] Ottoman fiscal policies and grain requisition aggravated the crisis. Ottoman wartime conscription exacerbated the loss of life. In addition, some local urban, rural, and foreign elites compounded the blockade through hoarding and speculation in wheat and other basic foodstuffs, thereby accumulating vast wealth. Estimates vary, but most historians agree that Mount Lebanon was hit hardest with a death toll of approximately 50 percent of its residents. Surrounding areas, including Beirut, fared only slightly better.[20] Wartime also hastened the decline of the silk economy, especially as the Ottoman military requisitioned mulberry and other trees for timber. In contrast, the wartime blockade created a boom in demand for tobacco, which intensified its cultivation.[21]

At the end of World War I, the British and French occupied the former majority Arab provinces of the now collapsed Ottoman Empire. Meanwhile, pursuing the "Open Door Policy" articulated at the turn of the century, the US government sought to end the prewar system of imperial trading preferences and secure access for US businesses. While the Entente powers made multiple promises of self-determination or statehood, none were honored. The quasi-colonial mandate system, legitimated by the League of Nations, emerged from these ashes and maneuvers. The April 1920 San Remo Conference sanctioned British occupation of what would become Iraq, Jordan, and Palestine, and French occupation of territories that today constitute Lebanon and Syria. The French declared the State of Greater Lebanon on September 1, 1920, incorporating predominantly Sunni and Shi'i areas adjacent to Mount Lebanon.[22] A 1926 constitutional proclamation consecrated Lebanon as distinct from Syria and changed its name to the Lebanese Republic.

THE COLONIAL PERIOD (1920–1943)

Attention to political economy reveals otherwise obscure continuities and ruptures across the precolonial and colonial periods. The integration of Lebanon and the surrounding region into the modern world system intensified, marked by the territorial encaging of specific spaces, people, and resources. Several other elements of change and continuity are worth considering.

In addition to the French Army and the mandatory bureaucracy, local urban and rural elites, comprising notables, businessmen, landlords, tribal shaykhs, village heads, and religious leaders, served as a third pillar of French colonial rule.[23] The colonial state consolidated these alliances through the distribution of resources, such as subsidizing religious schools and charities, granting former Ottoman imperial lands, providing credit and access to equipment, and buttressing elite violence that sought to contain "unruly" opposition.

Thus, French policies contributed to the formation of the political and economic elite that became the future ruling class of Lebanon, reorganizing and nourishing its familial, regional, and sectarian composition.[24] Some families in the new state maintained their late Ottoman political and economic status. Others experienced a precipitous decline. At the same time, war and colonialism created opportunities for middle or middle-lower classes to consolidate new financial and political resources.

The Lebanese Republic reconfigured relationships between the individual and the collective, the local and the foreign, the public and the private, and the people and the state. Beyond the production and instantiation of the new category of "Lebanese citizen," it also reconfigured categories of citizenship along sectarian, gender, and class lines. The French privileged Maronite politicians and communities, created a confessional system of representation, and shaped the emergence of two dominant, yet competing, parliamentary coalitions of the National Bloc and the Constitutional Bloc—in large part through an alliance with leaders of the former. Members of the French High Commission and local elites expanded electoral participation, which remained nevertheless exclusive to male citizens. The constitution and other institutional arrangements guaranteed the autonomy of religious officials in adjudicating matters of marriage, divorce, and inheritance.[25] Thus, the personal status system became another layer of gender differentiation—both between women and men within a given sect, as well as between women across sects. This gendering of citizenship facilitated the formation of diverse and internally contentious women's movements.[26]

The French alliance with local urban and rural elites, the new land tenure regime based on a cadastral survey, a land registry, and a land code all enshrined class differences in the new politico-legal system. Certain corporate interests were legally recognized while others were denied. For example, the French High Commission maintained Ottoman laws or passed new laws recognizing foreign and local business interests individually and collectively, among them laws governing chambers of commerce (1910), patents (1924), foreign corporations (1926), contracts (1932), and commercial transactions (1942). However, the lack of a labor code meant that labor interests were subject to the Ottoman Law of Associations (1909)—legislation too broad to regulate labor relations. A 1934 law built on Ottoman precedents requiring workplace associations to group workers, employees, managers, and owners into a single organization. As a result, labor was a legally invisible collective interest, even as the ranks of wage earners in general and urban workers in particular increased significantly.[27] The simultaneous invisibility and growing ranks of laborers mobilized a labor movement that coalesced around the issue of securing a comprehensive labor code.[28] As was the case with the women's movements, cleavages in the labor movement resulted in compromises, negotiations, and alliances with the state bureaucracy, politicians, and other movements.

Two principles undergirded French economic policy in Lebanon (and Syria) during the colonial period: economic stabilization and self-sufficiency.[29] The French Mandate sought to soften the blow of colonialism while responding to the fiscal, monetary, and economic instability of the immediate postwar period, but locally generated revenue was to cover state expenditures. Except for continuing military subsidies, the Mandate paid for itself, even during the Depression of the 1930s and World War II.

These policy principles resulted in specific institutional arrangements. First, the monetary and customs systems of Syria and Lebanon were unified.[30] Second, monopolies and concessions established centralized control over key aspects of the economy.[31] Third, the budgetary structure was reorganized to prioritize self-sufficiency and cooptation.[32] The Mandate was funded by three basic budgets, which reflected the tripartite (French, Mandate, and Lebanese) bureaucratic organization of colonial Lebanon.

The colonial period also featured a shifting and dynamic landscape of power relations. In the 1920s, military repression and state patronage were the pillars of colonial rule. However, in the 1930s, movements demanding political and social rights started to challenge these pillars. Key Depression-era developments transformed relations among the French High Commission, local elites, and popular groups and produced a colonial welfare state.[33] At the same time, the size and scope of the French colonial and local state bureaucracies significantly expanded.

The colonial political regime generated both the reproduction and shifts in local hierarchies of power. Elite and popular groups simultaneously challenged and integrated into the system, while the political regime channeled struggles away from revolt and insurgency and into the new bureaucracy. These developments instantiated Lebanon as a nation-state in people's everyday practices. By the eve of World War II there was a near-complete integration of the population into the Lebanese nation-state as both a bureaucracy and identity, notwithstanding their uneven sets of rights and privileges across regions, classes, genders, and sects. As opposition to French rule and calls for independence escalated, demands for restructuring political representation and economic privilege increased. People increasingly understood the stakes as control over Lebanon rather than questioning Lebanon as a nation-state.

The Allied invasion of Lebanon and Syria in 1941 overthrew the Vichy colonial government and facilitated the emergence of new alliances and institutional arrangements that reconstituted the local, regional, and global balance of power. The British garrisons in Lebanon and Syria incorporated them into the Anglo-American dominated war effort, while the pro-Vichy sympathies of many French colonial officials undermined French power in both countries. The movement of goods, capital, and people became subject to the Anglo-American Middle East Supply Centre (MESC).[34] MESC's economic management influenced state institutional arrangements and capacities differentially across the Middle East.[35] In Lebanon, MESC promoted the port of Beirut as a hub of regional trade.

In this context, the Constitutional Bloc increasingly took up an anti-French posture and built up an alliance with relatively excluded Sunni, Shiʿi, and Druze politicians as well as popular sectors of society. The British and US governments invested in Lebanese local affairs, each with their own preferences and stakes in relationships among politicians and businessmen. Eventually, local mobilizations, elite jockeying, and wartime exigencies of maintaining a stable Lebanon and Syria combined to produce the Constitutional Bloc's electoral defeat of the National Bloc in 1943, British and US backing of formal political independence for Lebanon, and the evacuation of all foreign troops in 1946. Thus, World War II facilitated the transition from colonial rule to independence and formed a key conjuncture in state, market, and class formation.[36]

THE POSTINDEPENDENCE PERIOD (1943–1975)

How should the postcolonial history of Lebanon be periodized? Some consider the period from 1943 to 1975 a single unit; this approach sees little fundamental change across this period,[37] or collapses it into a teleology: a series of external shocks, beginning with the 1948 influx of Palestinian refugees and culminating in the post-1973 oil boom, leading directly to the civil war.[38] Others identify the three-month rebellion or civil war of 1958, its terminology depending on analytic preference and political worldview, as a pivot dividing the period of independence from the civil war.[39] This rebellion undermined the incumbent elements of the late-Mandate-era political elite, leading to the election of President Fu'ad Shihab and the crystallization of a new political formation around him. Scholars have conventionally identified the presidencies of Shihab (1958–64) and his successor Charles Helou (1964–70), as the period when Lebanon temporarily and ineffectively followed regional trends in state-led economic development.

A political economy perspective offers alternative periodizations. Some emphasize the 1950 dissolution of the customs union with Syria as a key moment.[40] Others highlight shifts in financial regulation, such as the 1948 French-Lebanese monetary accord and establishment of a central bank in 1964.[41] I argue that the prevailing features associated with the Lebanese postcolonial political economy were institutionalized by 1955: an open, laissez-faire, service-based economy along with renewed labor and women's mobilizations, resulting in the Labor Code (1946) and women's suffrage (1953).[42]

Regardless of periodization, post-1958 policies featured important continuities with the preceding period. Banking reform, nationalization of public utilities, state-led rejuvenation of the agricultural sector, and the social security system have their origins in debates and struggles that preceded 1958. Some emerged in the 1943–55 period, while others, such as calls for nationalizing electricity (1931) and water (1936) date back to the Mandate era. Thus, many policies associated with the Shihabist period cannot be reduced to the ideological preferences of a particular presidential regime or an emulation of regional trends. They were part of a longer history of local debates and mobilizations over the trajectory of state and market formation.

Four other elements of continuity and rupture in the Lebanese postindependence period are noteworthy. Foremost is the transformation of state institutional arrangements.[43] These include the dramatic expansion of the scope and efficacy of the state as well as the nature of its intervention into people's everyday lives. From 1943 to 1975, the number of ministries nearly tripled compared to the late colonial period.[44] Between 1946 and 1970, ordinary budget expenditures increased from 52 million liras to approximately 628 million liras.[45]

The transformation of state institutions was not only administrative and budgetary; it also represented a qualitative shift in the scope, reach, capacity, and efficiency of the state bureaucracy. Lebanese bureaucrats established direct links with significantly larger segments of the population, further extending the reach of state institutions across the geography of Lebanon and deeper into the lives of its citizens.[46] This involved stricter curricular supervision over private education alongside the introduction and expansion of secondary and university public education, the reclamation of a majority of the country's infrastructure from primarily foreign concessions, the development of a state-managed labor arbitration system, the inauguration of a social security project, and much more. These transformations emphasize how central state institutional expansion was during the 1943–75 period, including in economic sectors often assumed to be devoid of state intervention, like trade and banking.[47] These institutional developments challenge the standard narrative that there was never a unified state, and that Lebanon was constituted of disparate sects, classes, and foreign agents.

A second element of postindependence Lebanon is its changing relationship to the regional and world economies. This period featured capital flight from several neighboring states. Syria is the most discussed example, initially in response to political instability and later to the rise of an authoritarian populist regime.[48] Equally important is Palestinian capital flight in the wake of Zionist depopulation and dispossession in 1948.[49] Some Syrians and Palestinians invested capital in Lebanon before the Nakba. Yet the subsequent influx of capital was of a fundamentally different order of magnitude. New waves of urban and rural labor migration into Lebanon, primarily Palestinian and Syrian, also accompanied this capital influx.[50] Two additional factors were equally significant. First, recipients of petroleum royalties and oil-related wealth from the Arabian Peninsula deposited funds in Lebanese banks or invested in Lebanon. Second, new patterns of Lebanese labor migration to the Arabian Peninsula as well as East African countries created new sources of remittance flows.[51] These latter two developments began in earnest during the 1950s and surged in the first half of the 1970s.

The changing sectoral composition of Lebanon's postindependence economy is a third element. Lebanon departed from its previous history as well as contemporary regional trends.[52] One calculation of Lebanon's net national product between 1950 and 1965 shows that agriculture declined from 19.7 to 11.6 percent, manufacturing remained relatively stable moving slightly from 13.5 to 13.1 percent, and trade increased from 28.8 to 30.6 percent.[53] Statistics for the 1970s are more difficult to compare to the earlier years, primarily due to the substitution of gross domestic product (GDP) for net national product. Nevertheless, overall trends indicate that the sectoral share of agriculture and trade exhibited a continuous pattern of decline and growth respectively, while the share of manufacturing grew significantly, even if it was subordinate to trade. Equally important are changes in the share of specific commodities in export, import, and entrepôt trade, and the share of specific trading partners in both the type of trade and the commodities traded. For example, manufacturing goods as a share of exported goods increased from 46.24 percent in 1951 to 74.27 percent in 1973.[54] At the same time, the respective shares of exports to oil-producing Arab countries as opposed to other Arab countries was 7.43 and 41.28 percent in 1951 but 50.33 and 6.40 percent in 1973.[55] The share of goods exported from Lebanon to the United States during that same time period declined from 25.44 to 5.39 percent.[56] That manufacturing maintained its relative position at least until 1965 or that oil-producing Arab countries overtook their Arab counterparts only beginning in the late 1960s challenges linear and simplistic claims about developmental exceptionalism in Lebanon. Considering these factors would contribute to a more nuanced and complicated understanding of the dynamics that led to Lebanon's postindependence developmental trajectory.

Shifting class composition is the final element of change in the postindependence economy. Lebanon experienced a similar pattern of accelerating rural-urban migration as other countries in the region. The timing and context for this acceleration matters. The primary push factor appears to be the collapse of the rural economy in the mid-1950s. A supplementary factor was the series of repeated Israeli military strikes and raids on Lebanese border areas, particularly after 1967. The resulting patterns of rural emigration are one of the most understudied elements of this period. However, several scholars have addressed the consequences of this migration for urban development, labor activism, and urban politics.[57]

The 1960s and 1970s featured some of the most sustained and militant urban labor mobilizations, while the Communist Party of Lebanon established a broad base in rural areas, especially the south.[58] Most research on these mobilizations has sought to account for their role in the eruption of the civil war. Equally important—yet understudied—is how their patterns, institutional bases, and discursive framings compare to labor mobilizations throughout the colonial and early postindependence periods. Conventional wisdom holds that these later mobilizations were an inevitable result of the stifling of industry and agriculture in favor of trade. But these mobilizations also intersected with the collapse of the agricultural sector and the expansion of manufacturing.

THE CIVIL WAR, 1975–1990

The Lebanese Civil War casts the longest shadow on scholarship on Lebanon. There is a tendency to view the civil war as the culmination of Lebanese history, with the preceding period(s) posited as explanatory. Some highlight the protracted fifteen-year civil war as exemplifying Lebanon's weak national identity, state institutions, and economic development compared to other regional countries. The predominant characterizations of the civil war are first, as a violent manifestation of irreconcilable sectarian and ideological differences coupled with multiple forms and sources of foreign intervention, and second, as the complete breakdown of national authority and with it the network of state institutions. Scholars with a political economy orientation privileged class over sect or ideology to explain the eruption and prolonged character of militia violence. While they exposed the social inequalities that fueled civil strife, they tended toward class determinism.

The outbreak and prolonged nature of the civil war were not inevitable. They were products of structural and contingent factors, as well as the strategies and decisions of historical actors. What we call the Lebanese Civil War was a series of wars that overlapped and intersected in important ways, yet nevertheless represented different sets of geographies, actors, grievances, resources, and calculations. Different material conditions, balances of power, and strategic logics obtained across Lebanon throughout the period. These wars did share a broader set of patterns and had a cumulative effect.

Perhaps the most significant economic development of this period is the emergence of a militia economy. Large institutionalized militias monopolized resources and violence in their spheres of operation.[59] This unfolded unevenly over time and space and manifested in two broad phases.[60] From 1976 to 1983, local armed militias and national state institutions coexisted in the aftermath of a two-year war (1975–76). A key transformation was the increasing dominance of militias and the shift from banditry to more routinized forms of resource extraction. In the second phase, from 1983 to 1990, national institutions totally broke down. The armed forces splintered, and the Lebanese lira collapsed. This phase featured a more direct relationship between militias and the people living in their territories; militias paid fighters' salaries, provisioned basic goods and services, and charged residents for protection.

Including the militia economy in the analysis shifts the narrative from a focus on multiple battles and patterns of alliances as merely a function of chaos to how, when, and why militias sought to maximize and monopolize resources. It also partly explains the intensity of violence that accompanied struggles over ports and other infrastructure. The material structures that the war gave birth to and fed off of shed light on relationships between militias and their territories. Selective trade and other forms of cooperation between competing militias were vital to securing food supplies, creating a division of labor in the production and export of drugs, and maintaining a modicum of banking networks.[61] It is also crucial to account for differences among militias: geographic, organizational, and strategic differences, as well as variations in institutional capacities, resource bases, and foreign patrons. Each of these factors produced divergences in militia relationships to people as well as the remnants of state institutions.

The legacies of the war have left important marks on the present. A critical mass of leading politicians and businessmen in postwar Lebanon successfully managed, navigated, and benefited from the war's militia economy.[62] The civil war reflected the fault lines of the past. It also generated the scaffolding of Lebanon's postwar business and political classes as well as their relationship to Syria, Saudi Arabia, Iran, and the United States.

CONCLUSION: TOWARD A POLITICAL ECONOMY OF POSTWAR LEBANON

In this conclusion I briefly note some key features of the postwar era.[63] First, militia leaders translated their civil war power into strategic positions in the postwar order.[64] They oversaw the transition from the militia economy to one in which state institutions played a central role. The control and exchange of resources took place under the purview of the legal frameworks of a postwar settlement that incorporated representatives of almost all remaining militias. Certainly, corruption was widespread and nonstate collectives continued to selectively deploy violence. However, the postwar era featured an end to the militia economy, even as the militias transferred their relative political and economic strength into the postwar order.

Second, leading politicians and businessmen—many of them former militia leaders—shaped reconstruction and stabilization programs to maintain and in some cases bolster their positions.[65] Rafiq al-Hariri's restructuring of the Lebanese political economy is the most prominent example.[66] During his premiership (1992–98 and 2000–2004), he anchored postwar reconstruction and development in a liberal monetary policy, low levels of taxes and tariffs (including the introduction of the VAT), and the privatization of state enterprises. This period witnessed the selling, leasing, and contracting out state functions to the private sector, including telephone and postal service, electricity generation, waste management, road construction and maintenance, and gas and oil distribution. Key cabinet members and parliamentarians profited from the reconstruction and privatization programs, enriching themselves and their allies by manipulating the bidding process and contract terms. The quintessential example is Hariri's awarding a private real estate corporation, Solidere, the exclusive right to rebuild and develop the Central Beirut District. This included the transfer of all property to the company, issuing shares—by judicial valuation—to the original owners of those assets, and company ownership of new surface area created by landfills. As the dominant politician overseeing the postwar reconstruction and development programs, Hariri and his network were responsible for the lion's share of such corruption until his assassination. Other politicians and businessmen profited also from the postwar order—the majority of them militia leaders who successfully transitioned into the new landscape and bolstered their power and wealth through directing state-financed contracts to themselves and their allies.

Third is the reorientation of capital accumulation practices. As Adam Hanieh's chapter in this volume demonstrates, loans, grants, and investments originating from the ruling families of Saudi Arabia, Kuwait, the United Arab Emirates, and Qatar were the primary sources of foreign aid and direct investment. International financial institutions such as the World Bank and external powers such the Islamic Republic of Iran served as important junior poles in this reorientation.

Other developments crucial to Lebanon's postwar economy include the end of the Israeli occupation of the south in 2000, the Syrian withdrawal in 2005, the Israeli war of 2006, and the post-2011 influx of Syrians fleeing repression and destruction. The Israeli and Syrian withdrawals made new sources and greater amounts of foreign patronage from the Gulf available. The post-2006 period featured an unprecedented entry of Qatari capital in the form of postwar reconstruction aid. We cannot yet fully understand the long-term impact of the war in Syria on the Lebanese economy. While government officials, politicians, and businessmen continue to scapegoat Syrian refugees for infrastructural breakdown, rising unemployment, and financial instability, no one has adequately analyzed the capital and aid flows accompanying Syrian displacement into Lebanon, let alone the economics of the military operations of Hizballah and the Lebanese Army—whether in border regions or inside Syria.

Lebanon's postwar economy featured many of the same patterns that characterized other regional states in the 1990s and 2000s, particularly the combination of policies that liberalized trade regulation; privatized state properties, enterprises, and services; and cut various social provisions. The resulting increase in unemployment and poverty rates and decrease in purchasing power have been devastating for everyday people. The role of foreign direct investment from the Gulf is crucial. Just as the comparative analysis of Egypt, Syria, and Tunisia by Max Ajl, Bassam Haddad, and Zeinab Abul-Magd in this book reveals important differences in neoliberal restructuring, the specificities of the unfolding of these processes in Lebanon are significant. Three analytic keys can help us understand these specificities.

First is the post–World War II divergence of Lebanon's developmental trajectory from that of other MENA states, coupled with the neoliberal context of post–civil war reconstruction. Post-1990 local practices of capital accumulation qualitatively distinguish the contemporary organization of capitalist relations from the early postindependence period of open, laissez-faire, and service-based development. Lebanon's avoidance of the regional and global trend of state-led economic development makes it a productive site for exploring the historical variations of economies in which the private sector plays the primary role of wealth generation.

Second, neoliberalism in Lebanon is different than in Egypt, Morocco, Tunisia, and Turkey—the major regional sites of imposed neoliberal restructuring. Its distinctive features are a relatively small manufacturing sector at the time of the launch of the neoliberal project, the historical entrepôt role of Beirut (however diminished by the civil war), and migration and remittance flows that long pre-date and far exceed those of the post–World War II Arab labor migration patterns.

The nature of public debt in Lebanon is also significant. Loan conditionalities and deepening debt burdens are a hallmark of neoliberal restructuring. Lebanon's public debt is one of the largest in the region (and world) relative to GDP.[67] However, this debt was initially exclusively reliant on a (narrow) domestic base.[68] The local baking sector holds more than 50 percent of gross public debt, with the main politically connected banks holding more public debt than the overall banking sector average.[69]

A negligible fraction of foreign public debt is in the form of bilateral or multilateral loans.[70] In fact, the overwhelming majority of Lebanon's gross public debt is in the form of publicly traded debt instruments: treasury bills and Eurobonds. Significantly high interest rates on government debt made it possible for local banks to offer relatively high interest rates on time-deposit accounts while still profiting from government debt.[71] Combined with the banking secrecy law, these interest rates attracted significant sums of capital from both the local population and the Lebanese diaspora. These differences make Lebanon a productive site for exploring the variations of neoliberalism. Do these differences have analytical significance and amount to a qualitatively different forms of neoliberalism?

Lebanon's significant infrastructural breakdown since 2015 is the third analytic key.[72] The waste management and electricity sectors have collapsed, and other sectors—most notably water—have also been in crisis. These infrastructure failures and the political crises that accompany them point to possible transformations in Lebanon's postwar political economy. Some have overemphasized corruption as the cause of infrastructural breakdown. But corruption alone is not an effective explanation, as it has long been integral to the postwar order and does not necessarily lead to infrastructural breakdown in and of itself.[73] What about Lebanon has changed such that existing networks of political and economic elites are willing to precipitate a breakdown in infrastructure unprecedented since the end of the civil war? Some have pointed to political polarization around geostrategic rivalries between the United States and Saudi Arabia on the one hand and Russia and Iran on the other. A critical political economy approach would demand a deeper inquiry, including assessing the erosion of external sources of revenue and the resulting intensification of conflict over domestic sources, as well as investigating how the Lebanese economy is linked to other national and regional economies.

Lebanon's economic specificities in the modern period have a regional function. The Beirut port, the banking sector, and the real estate sector are clear examples. We can make little sense of the most recent debates, struggles, and patterns in the political economy of Lebanon—including both the most recent economic crisis and the 2019–20 popular uprising—absent understanding the changing nature of its linkages with other economies. Lebanon's exclusion from comparative and regional analyses has reinforced reductive understandings of state, market, and class formation. Considering how local particularities are articulated with regional and global political economy is more fruitful than continuing to insist on Lebanon's exclusion or exceptionalization.

Chapter 10

THE US-ISRAELI ALLIANCE

Joel Beinin

THE DOMINANT CURRENTS IN THE ZIONIST MOVEMENT HAVE BEEN closely attuned to the culture, electoral politics, and political economy of the United States since before the establishment of the state of Israel. Israel's mode of capital accumulation has shifted from social democratic state-led development with a strong collective component to individualistic neoliberal capitalism. But the symbiotic relationship with the United States has remained constant, despite significant periodic tensions.

The US-Zionist/Israeli relationship has been shaped by Protestant theological support for Jewish restoration in the Holy Land, feelings of obligation to the survivors of the Holocaust, the political power of Jewish voters and donors to the Democratic Party, and a strategic alliance whose origins are in the Cold War but continues well beyond it. After the June 1967 War, the relationship deepened into a many-faceted alliance first proclaimed publicly by President Ronald Reagan. Beginning in the 1980s, the personnel, technology, finance, and production of the two countries' hi-tech and military/security industrial sectors became more closely intertwined. President George W. Bush's Global War on Terror enhanced intelligence, military, and domestic policing collaboration, which continued into the Obama era and beyond. Through these manifold relations, the political discourses of the two countries on Middle East issues have come to resemble each other on many issues. Nonetheless, Israel has never been simply a subservient client state, as differences over matters such as Israel's perceived security needs, Iran, and the Occupied Palestinian Territories highlight.

Protestant notions of Jewish Restoration to Zion have been "endemic to American culture," since the early colonial period.[1] In 1891, six years before the founding of the World Zionist Organization, Rev. William Blackstone submitted a petition to President Benjamin Harrison urging him to help persecuted Russian Jews by supporting their settlement in Palestine. Blackstone believed that restoration of Jewish rule in Palestine was a precondition for the second coming of Jesus. While most Protestants do not embrace this premillennial dispensationalist eschatology, Blackstone's proposal was not eccentric. Over four hundred prominent industrialists, big-city mayors, congressional leaders, editors and publishers of major periodicals, prominent Christian clergymen, and the chief justice of the Supreme Court endorsed the "Blackstone Memorial," as it became known. Christians United for Israel exemplifies this political theology today.

American Jews have become a wealthy and politically effective community, prominently represented among professionals, Wall Street, the media, Hollywood, and the intelligentsia. There have always been prominent Jewish non-Zionists and critics of Israel. But Israel boosters are better organized, better funded, and more influential in public culture and the political arena. Largely due to pressure from Zionist lobbyists and concern to secure Jewish funding for the Democratic Party and the Jewish vote in New York and other key states, President Truman recognized the State of Israel on May 14, 1948.[2]

Cultural affinities and the electoral and financial clout of the Israel lobby are substantial elements in the US-Israel relationship. But, overemphasizing these factors alone obscures the material and strategic components in the alliance and its function as a pillar of the US empire in the Middle East.

BEGINNINGS OF THE STRATEGIC RELATIONSHIP

The early steps in institutionalizing the US-Israel strategic relationship were managed by the head of CIA Counterintelligence, James Jesus Angleton. From 1951 he assumed responsibility for relations with Israel's secret services, headed the CIA's Israel Desk, and supervised its Israel station. Angleton overcame his initial suspicions about the pro-Soviet sentiments of some socialist Zionists when Israeli intelligence operatives delivered to him the complete text of Nikita Khrushchev's secret speech to the 20th Congress of the Communist Party of the Soviet Union denouncing Stalin's crimes, the first to reach the West. Subsequently Angleton zealously pursued intelligence cooperation with Israel, becoming, as Mossad chief Meir Amit put it, "the biggest Zionist of the lot."[3]

Consequently, Angleton did not vigorously investigate the likelihood that from 1957 to 1978 Israel diverted (i.e., stole) over 330 kilograms of highly enriched uranium from a Pennsylvania firm established and managed by a group of devoted Zionists—the Nuclear Materials and Equipment Corporation (NUMEC).[4] He apparently believed that continued intelligence cooperation with Israel was more important than upholding official US policy opposing nuclear proliferation. The NUMEC affair highlights the persistent tensions in the US- Israel relationship while it continued and deepened nonetheless.

When its leaders deem it necessary and possible, Israel acts without Washington's approval and even in opposition to US interests. The most notorious instance is the attack on the USS *Liberty* during the June 1967 War, in which Israeli air and naval forces killed 34 crewmen and wounded 171. Until the administration of President Donald Trump, Washington officials publicly criticized Israel's settlement project in the West Bank and East Jerusalem and its moves to annex those territories as well as the Syrian Golan Heights. Former secretary of defense James Mattis and former CIA director David Petraeus declared that Israel's failure to accommodate Palestinian rights was a liability in their area of responsibility when they served as commanders of the US Central Command.[5]

As is the case with the other major US regional ally, Saudi Arabia, the alliance with Israel has costs. It persists and has intensified because, on balance, Israel is a strategic asset. On March 2, 2011, Chairman of the Joint Chiefs of Staff Adm. Mike Mullen testified before Congress that the alliance with Israel "is of extraordinary value" and "absolutely critical" to US national security.[6] Secretary of Defense Robert Gates concurred.

MILITARY AID IS NOT A GIFT TO ISRAEL; IT IS A BONANZA FOR US ARMS MANUFACTURERS

From its earliest days, Israel sought a publicly acknowledged security relationship with the United States.[7] That began to emerge in 1962 when, despite its concerns about Israel's nuclear program, the Kennedy administration announced it would supply Israel with defensive Hawk ground-to-air missiles. In 1966 President Johnson approved the sale of 200 Patton tanks and 48 Skyhawk jet bombers, a significant enhancement to Israel's offensive capacity. However, they arrived only after Israel's overwhelming victory in the June 1967 War.

Israel is the largest recipient of US aid since World War II—a total of $228.7 billion through 2020 (in constant 2017 dollars).[8] The 2016 Memorandum of Understanding (MOU) secured $38 billion in US military aid to Israel from FY 2019 to 2028. Until then, uniquely among aid recipients, Israel could spend 26.3 percent of its military aid domestically and $400 million annually on jet fuel. Over the course of the MOU, Israeli domestic expenditures will be phased out. In FY 2019 fuel expenditures were discontinued. This amounts to a potential $10.2 billion enhancement to the sales of US arms producers.[9]

When the US government supplies military equipment to a foreign country, it buys the materiel from American producers and then delivers it as aid or through the Foreign Military Sales program. An important collateral advantage of all foreign military sales and aid is providing American arms manufacturers with sufficient orders to keep open production lines that could not be profitably sustained if they supplied only US forces. Thus, military aid is also a jobs and profits program. In addition, Israel's regular deployment of US military equipment tests its effectiveness under battle conditions and promotes future sales to other countries.

Although the United States maintains Israel's "Qualitative Military Edge" over all its Arab neighbors, they nonetheless seek to maintain credible militaries. From 2006 to 2015 the United States *gave* Israel $3.33 billion in military aid (in trend-indicator value expressed in US dollars at constant 1990 prices, the measure used by the authoritative Stockholm International Peace Research Institute). In the same period, it *sold* weapons valued at over $16.3 billion to the United Arab Emirates, Saudi Arabia, Kuwait, Qatar, and Oman. It also provided over $6 billion in military aid to Egypt and Iraq.[10] Only about $25 billion of the $110 billion in arms sales President Trump announced during his May 2017 visit to Saudi Arabia represented new contracts in process; many of the agreements were reached in the Obama era.[11] Nonetheless, even this reduced figure is substantial. Military sales to oil-rich Arab countries recycle petrodollars into the US economy, reduce the balance of payments deficit, and provide employment for thousands of trainers, technicians, and maintenance workers.

ISRAEL AS A COLD WAR STRATEGIC ASSET

The first qualitative breakthrough in US-Israeli military relations occurred after Israel demonstrated its military prowess in the 1967 War. The 1969 Nixon Doctrine conceded that the antiwar movement had made it politically impossible to repeat Vietnam-style foreign military interventions (at least until the administration of President George W. Bush reached different conclusions). Consequently, President Nixon and Secretary of State Kissinger sought to arm and train "regional influentials" to maintain a pro-American status quo. In the Gulf, the Two Pillars Policy (Saudi Arabia and Iran) expressed this new strategy.

During the September 1970 Palestinian-Jordanian civil war, Israel's regional role was on display: it warned Syria not to intervene. Subsequently, the Nixon administration came to see Israel as "the key to combating Soviet influence in the Arab world."[12] US military aid to Israel skyrocketed, from $360 *million* in 1968–70 to $1.5 *billion* in 1971–73. Following its victory over Egypt and Syria in the October 1973 War, Israel received an additional $2.6 billion in military aid.[13]

During the 1980 presidential campaign, Ronald Reagan proclaimed Israel to be "the only remaining strategic asset in the region on which we can rely" (having "lost" Iran after its 1979 revolution).[14] On November 30, 1981, the Reagan administration approved an MOU for security collaboration with Israel, only to suspend it on December 18 to chastise Israel for annexing the Syrian Golan Heights. However, the bombings of the US Embassy and Marine Corps barracks in Beirut in April and October 1983 and the subsequent withdrawal of US forces from Lebanon rendered Israel indispensable. In November 1983 the MOU provisions were mostly implemented.[15]

By annexing the Golan Heights, Israel overreached and was rebuked (until the Trump administration recognized the annexation). However, its strategic value overcame the Reagan administration's pique, and military cooperation deepened qualitatively. In 1984, the United States began constructing installations to preposition military equipment that Israel could "lease." Its value has increased from an initial $100 million to $1.8 billion by 2014.[16] Haifa became the principal eastern Mediterranean port of call for the Sixth Fleet. In 1987 the Reagan administration designated Israel a major ally, giving it privileged access to US weaponry; this was upgraded to "major non-NATO ally" in 1989, the year that designation was enacted into law. Joint US-Israeli military exercises began in 1984. They were regularized in 2001 as the biennial Juniper Cobra war games. The March 2018 edition of Juniper Cobra focused on responding to a potential Iranian missile attack.[17]

During the Cold War, US officials routinely examined Soviet military equipment captured by Israel, most notably an Iraqi MIG-21 and a Syrian MIG-23 flown to Israel by their defecting pilots in 1966 and 1989 respectively.[18] The 1983 bombing of the US Embassy in Beirut decimated the CIA's Lebanon station, resulting in increased reliance on Israeli intelligence, as revealed in the 1985–87 Iran-Contra Affair.

STATE, CAPITAL, AND POLITICS

In the 1970s and 1980s Israel became a major arms producer and exporter, enabling, although not without some conflict, the strategic collaboration established during the Reagan era to extend beyond the Middle East. The largest firms of Israel's military-industrial sector are the state-owned Israel Aerospace Industries (IAI) and Rafael Advanced Defense Systems, and IMI Systems (formerly Israel Weapons Industries), which was originally publicly owned but privatized in 2005. In 2011 the privately owned Elbit bought out IAI's 30 percent share of the Elisra Group, which specializes in electronic warfare, and in 2018 it acquired IMI Systems, making it Israel's largest producer of land-based military systems.[19] Altogether, Israel boasts 700 military-industrial firms. About 80 percent of their production is exported.[20]

In the mid-1980s, Israel's military-industrial sector employed 65,000 people. That number declined to about 50,000 by 2002 due to budget cuts. But this was more than offset by the growth of the hi-tech sector. In 2019, over 307,000 people were employed in hi-tech, 8.7 percent of the workforce.[21] A very substantial proportion of Israeli hi-tech is linked to the Israeli and US military and homeland security/surveillance sectors. The tendency toward privatization and monopolization of Israel's military-industrial sector and its close relationship with the privately owned hi-tech and homeland security/surveillance sectors exemplify Israel's full participation in the global neoliberal political economy, aggressively promoted by the governments led by Prime Minister Benjamin Netanyahu since 2009.

Naftali Bennett, a former officer in Israel's elite General Staff Reconnaissance Unit (Sayeret Matkal), software entrepreneur, and Netanyahu chief-of-staff, is the poster boy for the fusion of militarism, hi-tech, and rightwing politics. In 2012 Bennett left the Likud to lead a succession of right-wing parties and hold several ministries in Netanyahu-led coalition governments.

ISRAEL AS GLOBAL ARMS MERCHANT

During the 1960s Israel sought to overcome its diplomatic isolation by training domestic security and military forces and purveying arms throughout Africa.[22] Its relationship with the Democratic Republic of the Congo (DRC, then Zaire) began in 1963–64. Military dictator Mobutu Sese Seko (1965–97) earned his parachute wings in Israel. After a hiatus in their relations, Israel became a major arms supplier to the DRC in 1983.

Israel supported Portugal in its African colonial wars. In the mid-1970s and 1980s, in collaboration with the CIA and South Africa, it trained and armed the FNLA and UNITA in the postindependence Angolan civil war. Israel and South Africa collaborated on developing both conventional and nuclear weapons. Substantial evidence supports suspicions that they jointly detonated a nuclear device in the South Atlantic on September 22, 1979.[23]

Several African countries broke relations with Israel after the 1973 Arab-Israeli War. Consequently, Latin America became the principal market for its military exports. Shortly after the fraudulent 1972 presidential election that triggered a civil war, Israel provided extensive "anti-guerilla security assistance" to El Salvador, including the first jet fighters in Central America.[24] Israel supplied and trained the forces of Argentina during the generals' dirty war (1974–83) and Chile under the CIA installed junta (1973–90).

Israel began supplying arms to Nicaraguan dictator Anastasio Somoza in 1974. Military support escalated as Somoza was making his last stand against the Sandinista guerilla movement in 1978–79. Following the victory of the Sandinistas, a deputy director of the Mossad ensconced himself in Tegucigalpa, Honduras, to manage the Mossad's arming and training of the Contras who sought to overthrow the revolutionary government.[25] The Boland Amendment prohibited the United States from aiding the Contras. Nonetheless, the Reagan administration facilitated Israel's arms supply to the Contras, the full dimensions of which were only partially exposed in the Iran-Contra Affair.[26]

After the Cold War, Israel continued to arm states engaged in ugly conflicts: Azerbaijan, South Sudan, Rwanda as it committed a genocide of Tutsis in 1994, and most recently Myanmar, as it ethnically cleansed its Rohingya Muslims.[27] By 2012–18 Israel was the world's tenth largest arms exporter with annual sales averaging nearly $7 billion.[28] In this period, Asia became Israel's foremost market, led by India, Azerbaijan, and Vietnam.[29]

There have been periodic frictions over Israeli military exports. President Carter believed that Israel likely did conduct a nuclear test with South Africa in 1979 and almost certainly wished that it not develop nuclear weapons.[30] But Israel–South Africa military cooperation buttressed the Reagan administration's policy of "constructive engagement" in opposition to the boycott, divestment, and sanctions (BDS) demanded by the international antiapartheid movement.

Israel has been selling arms to China since 1981 and is its second largest supplier after Russia. The United States objects to Israel supplying China with American-manufactured arms components and blocked the sale of a Phalcon radar aircraft in 1995. In 2005 a crisis erupted over a drone sale.[31] These frictions have had no long-term consequences on US-Israel relations or on Israel's flourishing military and commercial relations with China.

JOINT DEVELOPMENT OF WEAPONS

Israel and the United States have jointly developed weapons systems since the secret 1986 agreement on Israeli participation in research for President Reagan's Strategic Defense Initiative (Star Wars). From 1988 to 2002 Israel received about $1 billion in research and development (R&D) grants for the Arrow antimissile missile produced by Boeing and IAI.[32] In 1996, Israel began coproduction of the Nautilus tactical high-energy laser with Northrop Grumman as lead contractor. But in 2005, after $300 million had been spent, the Nautilus was discontinued due to its high cost and mediocre performance.[33]

Lockheed Martin (LMT) is the world's largest arms manufacturer by sales volume. Lockheed Martin Israel was established in 2014.[34] It operates offices in Tel Aviv and Beersheba, where the Israeli government is promoting military-oriented hi-tech development.

LMT has been arming Israel since 1971. Its F-16 fighter jets have been the mainstay of its Air Force since 1980. Israel purchased an updated and customized version, the Sufa, in 2004. That year LMT completed an industrial collaboration valued at $1.45 billion with some forty Israeli firms in the military, hi-tech, venture capital, and R&D sectors.

LMT is the lead contractor, with Northrup Grumman and British BAE as secondary partners, for the notoriously overbudget and underperforming F-35 stealth fighter jets. Israel has contributed prominently to the project and will acquire at least 50 F-35I Adirs, with Israeli-customized avionics. LMT's coproduction agreements with Israeli enterprises for F-35 components have an anticipated value of over $4 billion. In 2014 IAI opened a new production line to manufacture over 800 pairs of F-35 wing skins valued at $2.5 billion. Cyclone, an Elbit subsidiary, produces F-35 aerostructures. Elisra provides its electronic warfare suite. Rafael manufactures the F-35's advanced weapons and sensors. The F-35 and many other US military aircraft use the Joint Helmet Mounted Cueing System, a digital eye piece developed by Elbit and Rockwell-Collins.[35] LMT vice-president for customer requirements, retired US Air Force Gen. Gary North, proclaimed, "There's a part of Israel in every F-35 that's ever been built."[36] In December 2017 Israel became the first country outside the United States to deploy operational F-35s, a good news advertisement for the much-maligned aircraft.

LMT is expanding its R&D collaborations with Israeli institutions. Its joint venture with Bynet Data Communications Ltd. will construct the Israel Defense Forces (IDF) Intelligence Corp's Negev technology campus, known as the 5/9 project.[37] In 2014 LMT and Yissum Research Development, a subsidiary of the Hebrew University in Jerusalem, agreed to cosponsor joint research in quantum information and material sciences. LMT has the option to purchase exclusive licenses to products resulting from the partnership.[38] LMT is partnering with Dell EMC and Ben-Gurion University on cybersecurity research.

Israel has similarly extensive relationships with Boeing, the second-largest global arms manufacturer based on 2015 revenue. Boeing has maintained an office in Tel Aviv since 1969. Israel's national carrier, El Al, has operated an all-Boeing fleet since the 1960s, and the Israeli Air Force has used aircraft and helicopters manufactured by Boeing and its predecessor firms since the 1970s. In 2003 former IAF commander and former ambassador to the United States David Ivry became president of Boeing Israel.[39]

Boeing's F-15I, a dual-seat ground attack aircraft initially acquired by Israel in 1998, was the first US military jet coproduced with Israeli firms: Elisra (electronic warfare suite), Elta (secure radios), IAI (structural subassemblies), and Cyclone (external fuel tanks). Israeli firms supply parts for many other Boeing commercial and military products, including the Apache Longbow helicopter, and the 737, 777, and 787 airliners. In 2002 Boeing designated Elta, which manufactures the electronics support system for Boeing's Nimrod maritime surveillance aircraft, its Supplier of the Year.

In addition to joint development and coproduction, the US military and many domestic security agencies and local police forces employ Israeli-designed and manufactured equipment. From the 1960s to the 1990s, IMI's Uzi submachine gun was the standard weapon of the US Secret Service. Israel has advanced far beyond producing such basic firearms and now specializes in hi-tech weapons, avionics, lasers, military software, population control systems, and drones.

In 1994 Rafael began working with General Dynamics, the manufacturer of the Bradley Fighting Vehicle, to develop its Reactive Applique Armor Tiles for use on General Dynamics products. In 2005 General Dynamics received a $37.8 million contract modification to fit Rafael's add-on armor to Bradley Fighting Vehicles and armored personnel carriers deployed in Iraq.[40]

In 2011 US forces in Afghanistan began using the Israeli-manufactured Skystar-180, an aerostat reconnaissance system that demonstrated its value during Israel's 2014 assault on Gaza. The US Army approved the Skystar-180 for purchase the next year. Since 2010, five NATO countries have deployed Israeli-manufactured drones in anti-Taliban operations in Afghanistan.[41]

In March 2015 the US Marine Corps awarded Elbit a $73.4 million contract for new laser systems.[42] The US Army uses the Iron Fist Light Configuration active protection system for light and medium armored vehicles designed and manufactured by IMI Systems.[43] The Jewish Virtual Library, an Israel lobby-aligned website that may exaggerate such matters, lists over a dozen other Israeli manufactured weapons systems employed by US military and domestic security forces.[44]

ANTITERRORISM AND HOMELAND SECURITY IN THE POST-9/11 ERA

The conjuncture of the second Intifada, which erupted in the fall of 2000; al-Qa'ida's September 11, 2001, terrorist attacks in New York and Washington, DC; and the 2003 US invasion of Iraq elevated US-Israeli military and security collaboration to a new level with a focus on radical Muslim groups and Iran. In 2008 the CIA and Mossad collaborated in assassinating 'Imad Mughniyya, who was allegedly responsible for the 1983 Beirut embassy bombing and many other attacks on military and civilian targets.[45] In 2010 the United States established "unusually tight collaboration" with Israel in "Operation Olympic Games," which launched the Stuxnet computer worm that disabled some one thousand Iranian nuclear centrifuges at Natanz.[46] In 2017 Israeli cyber operators penetrated a cell of ISIS bomb makers in Syria and learned they could make explosives resembling laptop computer batteries that would evade detection by airport screening devices. Israel shared the information with the United States, which then banned laptops in carry-on luggage on flights from eight Muslim-majority countries.[47]

Israel is a world leader in the "new military urbanism"—crowd control, border surveillance, and counterterrorism—that burgeoned after 9/11.[48] It advertises its extensive experience in the post-1967 Occupied Palestinian Territories to promote its techniques and equipment to increasingly militarized police forces and the thriving homeland security market. Israel's homeland security sector comprises 600 firms, of which 300 export training services and goods, mainly surveillance technologies, with an annual value of $3 billion.[49]

Israel is a leading global supplier of drones to armed forces, police, and security agencies. A promotional video by the American subsidiary of Elbit, the principal supplier of tactical drones to the Israeli military, advertises its "Proven Technology, Proven Security" and "10+ years securing the world's most challenging borders."[50] As a subcontractor for Boeing, Elbit provided camera and radar systems for the George W. Bush administration's Strategic Border Initiative. In 2004 Elbit's Fort Worth, Texas, subsidiary, EFW Inc., leased two Hermes 450 drones, along with ground control stations, operational crews, and support personnel, to US Customs and Border Protection for its Arizona Border Control Initiative.[51] In 2014 Elbit won a $145 million contract from the US Department of Homeland Security to supply electronic sensing technology for the (pre-Trump) barrier along the US-Mexico border.[52]

IWI US offers courses in firearms use, Krav Maga (hand-to-hand combat), and weapons repair at campuses in Texas and Pennsylvania.[53] IWI has collaborated with the Metropolitan College of New York's MPA in Emergency and Disaster Management. In the mid-2000s the curriculum included a ten-day trip to Israel.[54] In 1999 IMI Systems established an Academy for Advanced Security and Anti-Terror Training, offering services to "military, law enforcement, government agencies and commercial clients worldwide."[55]

Presaging post-9/11 policing collaborations, in 1992 Georgia State University and state law enforcement agencies established the Georgia International Law Enforcement Exchange (GILEE) to support Atlanta's bid for the 1996 Olympic Games.[56] Its mission statement's first priority is "to enhance inter-agency cooperation between State of Georgia law enforcement agencies and the police force of the State of Israel." GILEE has sponsored 330 programs and 180 delegations to Israel involving 24,000 participants. GILEE's director, Robert Friedmann, holds an endowed chair at Georgia State and is close to right-wing Zionists.

Since 9/11 thousands of US police officers, sheriffs, and agents from the Border Patrol, Immigration and Customs Enforcement, Transportation Security Administration, and Federal Bureau of Investigation have trained with the Israeli military and police forces. Israel has particularly close ties with the Los Angeles and New York police departments.[57] In 2012 the New York Police Department opened an office at the Sharon District headquarters of the Israeli police in Kfar Saba.[58] In addition to promoting Israeli techniques of militarized policing, underwritten trips to Israel create a strategic social base of support for Israel well beyond the "usual suspects" of the Israel lobby.

Over 200 senior American law enforcement professionals have participated in the Anti-Defamation League (ADL)–sponsored weeklong National Counter-Terrorism Seminar in Israel since it began in 2004.[59] ADL's Advanced Training School in Extremist and Terrorist Threats in Washington, DC, has graduated over 1,100 law enforcement executives and commanders from 250 agencies since it was established in 2003. Over 130,000 law enforcement professionals have attended ADL Law Enforcement and Society training programs in several major American cities since 1999.

The Jewish Institute for National Security Affairs (JINSA), whose board of advisors includes over fifty mainly non-Jewish retired generals, admirals, and police chiefs, also sponsors trips and trainings promoting military and counterterrorism collaboration, including an annual trip of retired generals and admirals.[60] In 2009 it sent members of the National Bomb Squad Commanders Advisory Board to Israel. Its Law Enforcement Exchange Program brings Israeli counterterrorism and intelligence experts to the United States to train law enforcement officers. JINSA also operates an IDF Leadership Education Program to educate Israeli military officers about American culture and the foreign policy-making process so they become more effective lobbyists for Israel's interests.

US military officers closely observed the tactics of Israeli forces as they reconquered the West Bank in 2002 in the course of suppressing the second Intifada. Eyal Weizman reported that "an Israeli paratrooper who participated in the battle of Jenin told me that there were US officers (dressed in IDF uniform) present as spectators within the rubble of the refugee camp" during the last stages of the battle.[61] A Joint Chiefs delegation visited Israel in May 2002 to "make changes to the (Marine) Corps' urban war-fighting doctrine to reflect what worked for the Israelis."[62]

In 2003 Israeli commandos and intelligence forces trained US special forces at Fort Bragg, North Carolina, to use aggressive counterinsurgency tactics in Iraq "that echo(ed) Israeli operations in the occupied territories," including "assassination squads against guerrilla leaders" and "sealing off centers of resistance with razor wire and razing buildings from where attacks [were] launched against US troops."[63] Israeli military consultants also visited Iraq. US Army units reportedly underwent training at the IDF's antiterror school and subsequently returned to Iraq.[64] That visit was not explicitly confirmed. But Deputy Chief of Staff for Doctrine, Concepts, and Strategy for the US Army Training and Doctrine Command Lt. Gen. Michael Vane acknowledged, "We recently travelled to Israel to glean lessons learned from their counterterrorist operations in urban areas." Vane considered Israel's "experience . . . pivotal as U.S. forces tried to confront the proliferating urban insurgencies on the streets of Iraq's cities."[65]

In 2005 the IDF began building Baladia at its Tze'elim base east of the Gaza Strip—an Arab-style city with modules that can be reconfigured for specific missions of house-to-house combat. During a December 2006 visit, Lt. Gen. H. Steven Blum, chief of the National Guard Bureau, praised Baladia as "a world-class site." US Marines, UN security forces, and other foreign militaries have used the facility.[66]

In the most recent US military adventure in the Middle East, Israel provided satellite imagery and other intelligence to support the 2014 aerial campaign against the Islamic State in Iraq.[67]

SILICON VALLEY AND BEYOND

Israeli and US commercial corporations, technology, and personnel are closely interconnected. Since 2000, Israel has been the largest US trading partner in the Middle East.[68] Between 50,000 and 200,000 Israelis and over 100 Israeli firms make their home in Silicon Valley.[69] Nearly 100 Israeli firms are listed on the NASDAQ; only China has more.[70] Dozens of US hi-tech enterprises maintain R&D facilities in Israel. Leading firms invest substantially in Israel and regularly acquire local startups.

Intel has invested $17 billion in Israel since 1974, more than any other American firm. It employs over 10,000 people, 60 percent of them in R&D. Intel is planning an additional $5 billion investment in its Kiryat Gat manufacturing facility. In 2017 Intel bought Mobileye, which makes sensors and cameras for driverless vehicles, for $15.3 billion, perhaps the largest single foreign acquisition in Israeli history.[71]

Hewlett-Packard Israel was established in 1998 as a subsidiary of the American firm, which split into H-P Enterprise and H-P Inc. in 2015. An Israeli subsidiary, EDS, supplies the Ministry of Defense and police with biometric cards used at checkpoints throughout the West Bank to verify the identities of Palestinians (the Basel System). H-P Inc. is the exclusive provider of PCs and peripherals to the IDF. H-P Enterprise was the sole provider of servers to the IDF until 2017, when Cisco won the contract.[72]

In 1964 Motorola established an R&D center in Israel, its first outside the United States. Motorola Solutions Israel has contracts worth $193 million to supply a Wide Area Surveillance System and encrypted smartphones to the Ministry of Defense.[73] Microsoft established an Israeli R&D center in 1991 and expanded it substantially in 2006. Between 2014 and 2017 Microsoft acquired five Israeli startups for at least $550 million.[74]

PayPal acquired Fraud Sciences for $169 million in 2008 and built a fraud and risk detection center around it in Tel Aviv. In 2015 PayPal bought Cy-Active for $60 million. It became the base for its cybersecurity center near Beersheba.[75]

Corporate links are extensive even in traditional industries. Israeli apparel manufacturer Delta Galil is a major supplier of Victoria's Secret, Calvin Klein, Tommy Hilfiger, Nike, and Hugo Boss brands, and retailers like Walmart, Target, and others.[76]

ISRAEL IN US POLITICS

In 2016 J. J. Goldberg, editor-at-large and former editor-in-chief of the *Forward*, related that a report of the Center for Responsive Politics listing the top donors to 527s (independent campaign entities) and super-PACs "knocked my socks off."[77] "Eight of the 36 Republican bigs were Jewish, and of the 14 Democrats, only one was *not* Jewish."[78] At the same event, Stephanie Schriock, president of Emily's List, which funds pro-choice Democratic women running for elected office, explained how money and pro-Israelism became linked in the Democratic Party:

> I started as a finance director. . . . And I would come on a congressional race, I am a 20-something kid who also knows nothing beyond the state borders, let alone overseas, and you thought about where you are going to go to raise the money that you needed to raise to win a race. And you went to labor, you went to the choice community, and you went to the Jewish community. But before you went to the Jewish community, you had a conversation with the lead AIPAC [American Israel Public Affairs Committee] person in your state and they made it clear that you needed a paper on Israel. And so you called all of your friends who already had a paper on Israel—that was designed by AIPAC—and we made that your paper. . . .
>
> The poor campaign manager would come in, or the policy director, and I'd [say], "Here is your paper on Israel. This is our policy." We've sent it all over the country because this is how we raise money. . . . These candidates who were farmers, schoolteachers, or businesswomen ended up having an Israel position without having any significant conversations with anybody.[79]

Do these and similar stories mean that everything in the previous pages was superfluous, that the US-Israel relationship is shaped by Jewish Zionist political donors? Not exactly.

Jews are highly disproportionately represented among political activists and donors. One study estimated that in the 2016 election cycle Jews donated about 50 percent of all money raised by the Democratic Party and 25 percent of that raised by the Republican Party.[80] The precise amounts are unverifiable but substantial. Many, though not all, major Jewish donors exercise their considerable influence to keep politicians in line on Israel.

Sheldon Adelson was the single largest funder of the Republican Party in the 2012 and 2016 elections. His $82.5 million made him the second largest donor to either party in the 2016 election cycle.[81] The party's second largest Jewish donor, Paul Singer, gave $26 million. Adelson and Singer are pro-Israel superhawks. Republican candidates groveled for their contributions. But this does not fully explain the party's Israel policy.

Evangelical Protestants and the Tea Party are unwaveringly pro-Israel on their own (often antisemitic) terms. Christians United for Israel is by far the largest American pro-Israel organization, claiming a membership of 8 million in 2020.[82] Many are Republican activists. The Republican Party's social base and its neoconservative ideologues have transformed the coolness of the Eisenhower-era party into a passionate embrace of Israel, especially the right-wing elements that have dominated politics for most of the time since Benjamin Netanyahu first became prime minister in 1996. The bond is based on a toxic cocktail of premillennial dispensationalism, support for an aggressive global US military posture, belligerent antiterrorism, and Islamophobia, especially antipathy to Iran.

AIPAC is the largest component of the Israel lobby based in the Jewish community. Although AIPAC was historically bipartisan, its strenuous efforts to defeat the 2015 Iran nuclear deal and support for President Trump's abrogation of the agreement in 2018 aligned it more closely with the Republican Party. Nonetheless Democratic Israel hardliners like Senator Chuck Schumer remain AIPAC enthusiasts. AIPAC claims a membership of over 100,000 and has an annual budget of some $70 million, of which about $3.5 million is spent on lobbying. Its political clout comes from directing allied political action committees and bundlers to funnel donations to approved candidates.

Neoconservative intellectuals, prominent among them Jews who served in the George W. Bush and/or Ronald Reagan administrations, wielded great influence in reorienting the Republican Party towards Israel. The most prominent are William Kristol, Douglas Feith, Elliott Abrams, and Paul Wolfowitz, the "brains" behind the 2003 invasion of Iraq. However, it is not necessary to be Jewish to be a pro-Israel militarist. John Bolton, Patrick Gaffney, Gary Bauer, and Michael Flynn largely share the views of their Jewish colleagues.

Neoconservative political ideas and operatives circulate between Israel and the United States (equally the case for Democrats and liberal Zionists). Richard Perle served in the Reagan administration and chaired the Defense Policy Board Advisory Committee until he resigned over a financial scandal in 2003. He led a study group, commissioned by an Israeli think tank, the Institute for Advanced Strategic and Political Studies, that submitted the infamous "A Clean Break: A New Strategy for Securing the Realm" report to Benjamin Netanyahu's 1996 election campaign. Perle's report advocated abandoning the Palestinian-Israeli "peace process" and other aggressive policies, including removing Saddam Hussein from power. Sheldon Adelson is the largest investor (reportedly $50 million) in Israel's largest circulation daily, *Yisrael Hayom* (Israel Today), and his spouse, Miriam Adelson, is its publisher. Its editorial policy prioritizes praising Netanyahu, and it endorsed Trump for president. Republican political consultant Frank Luntz's report, "The Israel Project's 2009 Global Language Dictionary," has been used by both the Israeli government and its American supporters. Luntz also met with the Republican Governors Association to advise them on how to counter the Occupy Wall Street movement.[83] The late Arthur Finkelstein consulted for Benjamin Netanyahu, Ariel Sharon, Avigdor Lieberman, and Jerusalem mayor Nir Barkat as well as a host of Republicans.

The Republican Party's embrace of Israel is largely due to a shared global right-wing agenda. But the Democratic Party's relationship with Israel is more complex. Jews have been part of its social base since the New Deal. Barack Obama received 78 percent of the Jewish vote in 2008 and 69 percent in 2012. Since the 1960s, only African Americans have comprised a more consistently Democratic demographic.

American public culture mainly comprehends the State of Israel as a response to the Holocaust and the moral legatee of the Jewish victims of Nazi mass murder. After World War II, establishing a haven for Jewish survivors was an antifascist and humanitarian cause concentrated on the left of the political spectrum. President Truman's support for Israel in 1948 was largely instrumental. But it was a sincere conviction for icons of the left-liberal camp of his era: Eleanor Roosevelt, Bayard Rustin, Reinhold Niebuhr, Walter Reuther, Hubert Humphrey, Henry Wallace, and the Progressive Party. For older Democrats, Jews and non-Jews alike—Joe Biden, Chuck Schumer, Diane Feinstein, Ben Cardin, Bob Menendez, Ron Wyden, Nancy Pelosi, and Steny Hoyer—viewing Israel as a refuge for persecuted Jews is consistent with avidly pursuing AIPAC-directed campaign contributions. Younger Democrats with higher aspirations like senators Cory Booker, Kamala Harris, and Jeff Merkley and the mayors of New York and Los Angeles, Bill De Blasio and Eric Garcetti, may be more instrumentally "pro-Israel." Neither group acknowledges the Palestinian Nakba.

Hillary Clinton's unwavering pro-Israelism dates from her 2000 Senate campaign in New York. Pro-Israel Jews donated massively to her 2008 and 2016 presidential campaigns. Haim and Cheryl Saban are long-time friends of the Clintons. They were the ninth largest contributors to the Democratic Party's 2016 campaign, with $16.3 million.[84] Haim Saban unabashedly acknowledges, "I'm a one-issue guy and my issue is Israel."[85] Saban and like-minded donors were concerned about the growing influence of the campaign for BDS against Israel. Clinton sought to assuage them by writing a letter to Saban promising to "make countering BDS a priority" during the 2016 campaign.[86]

CONCLUSION: IT'S THE EMPIRE, STUPID

From the 1940s to the present, conventional wisdom in Washington has held that control of the Middle East and its hydrocarbon resources is vital for sustaining the informal global American empire. No other country in the region can support that objective with the combination of technical, intelligence, and military capacities; a network of personal, business, and institutional relationships; and unwavering enthusiasm for American hegemony in the Middle East that Israel offers; Saudi Arabia is a distant second. Moreover, influential sectors of domestic public opinion actively promote the US-Israeli alliance.

Every president from Nixon to Obama regarded Israel's occupation of the West Bank and the Gaza Strip and violations of Palestinian rights as destabilizing. Hence, they advocated a settlement freeze and Israeli withdrawal from the Occupied Palestinian Territories. Presidents likely would have pushed Israel harder to compromise with the Palestinians absent the political clout of the lobby. But Israel's strategic value during the Cold War and the Global War on Terror and its Obama-era extension secured it significant immunity from pressure to accept any peace agreement its leadership considered ill advised.

President Obama was fully committed to what William Appleman Williams called "Empire as a Way of Life" with the US-Israeli alliance in a prominent role.[87] However, Obama sought to avoid an armed confrontation with Iran by concluding the 2015 nuclear agreement despite the vociferous objections of Benjamin Netanyahu and his American supporters. In contrast, President Trump's withdrawal from that agreement and his inauguration of a US Embassy in Jerusalem asserted the strategic commitment of his administration and its funder-in-chief, Sheldon Adelson, to realigning the Middle East around a belligerent anti-Iranian front in concert with its domestic base of hardline militarists, white nationalists, Jewish and evangelical Protestant Likudniks, and regional allies Israel, Saudi Arabia, the United Arab Emirates, and Egypt. The United States stands with Israel against Palestinian rights and maintains warm relations with Arab autocratic regimes (and pre-1979 Iran), because, despite their sometimes significant costs, these relationships have been essential to sustaining a pro-American order in the Middle East.

Chapter 11

REPERCUSSIONS OF COLONIALISM IN THE OCCUPIED PALESTINIAN TERRITORIES

Samia Al-Botmeh

AT THE HEART OF THE FACTORS THAT HAVE SHAPED THE DEVELOPMENT of the Palestinian political economy over the past fifty years is Israeli colonialism. In both the period from 1967 to 1993, when the West Bank and Gaza Strip were under direct Israeli control, and the post-Oslo Accords period, from 1994 to 2017, colonial policies and structural changes led to the underdevelopment of the Palestinian economy. This colonial context has been described as a process of Palestinian de-development, underdevelopment, dispossession, and skewed or pauperized development. Whatever term we choose, Palestinian political economy has been trapped in dependency on external sources for growth and its productive capacity has been severely eroded. This has affected all aspects of economic life, particularly the capacity of the economy to generate employment. However, the process of underdevelopment commenced well before 1967, and even before the Nakba of 1948.

Britain gradually established its colonial rule over Palestine from its military conquest in 1917 to the establishment of the League of Nations Mandate in 1920. In the Mandate era, the political economies of the indigenous Palestinians and Zionist settlers were never entirely separate, despite labor Zionist efforts to accomplish this objective.[1] But the combination of the British policy of limited investment, labor Zionist exclusivism, and relatively high Zionist capital imports led to the subordination of the Arab sector despite efforts of some Palestinian "men of capital" to build a national economy.[2] The Nakba prompted considerable capital flight from Palestine to Lebanon and elsewhere. Therefore there was barely any local capital to invest in the West Bank and the Gaza Strip after the Arab-Israeli War of 1948.

Under the Jordanian occupation of the West Bank, (1949–67), the government invested relatively little in its economy, except for the tourist sector in Jerusalem and Bethlehem. The West Bank represented about half of Jordan's population, 40 percent of its gross domestic product (GDP), and 34–40 percent of its agricultural production. But only one-third of all Jordanian investment was directed to the West Bank. There was little industrial growth. In 1961 agriculture remained the primary productive sector, employing nearly 65,000 workers or 37.6 percent of the labor force, while mining, quarrying, and manufacturing (primarily small-scale industry and handicrafts) employed under 20,000 workers or 11.5 percent of the labor force. Services, of which tourism comprised a large share, employed 40 percent of the labor force and amounted to 56 percent of the West Bank's GDP.[3]

The Gaza Strip was overburdened by the sudden influx of over 200,000 refugees after the Nakba, three times more than its local population. The refugees had no productive resources, and most of them could not be absorbed into Gaza's limited agricultural sector. UNRWA, not the Egyptian administration, became the principal provider of services, employment, and transfer payments. Egypt undertook a more active economic development role after the 1956 Arab-Israeli war. Gaza's economy grew modestly, but it remained weak, primarily agricultural, and dependent on external income sources.[4]

Thus from early in the twentieth century to 1967, the political economy of Arab Palestine was shaped by colonial subordination that set it on a trajectory of structural dependency. This continues to characterize economic relations between Israelis and Palestinians to this day.

THE POLITICAL ECONOMY OF THE OCCUPIED PALESTINIAN TERRITORIES: 1967–1993

Following its occupation of the West Bank, including East Jerusalem, and the Gaza Strip in June 1967, Israel sealed its control over the entire territory of British Mandate Palestine. Shortly after the war, the Israeli government adopted decisions with long-term repercussions for economic development: the annexation of East Jerusalem and an open borders policy between Israel and the

West Bank and Gaza Strip, while the Israeli military maintained control over external borders and the resource base of the occupied Palestinian territories (OPT). In addition, this new phase of colonization led to the displacement of a further 200,000 Palestinians from the West Bank into Jordan. Consequently, the sectoral composition, productive base, employment and wage levels, trade links, capacity to conduct financial intermediation, and infrastructural base of the economy of OPT underwent major structural changes for the worse.[5] These colonial measures further entrenched the dependency of the Palestinian economy on external sources of growth and eroded its productive capacity, with detrimental repercussions for all aspects of economic life.

Legal Structures and Control over Resources

In 1981, in an effort to circumvent the growing popularity of the Palestine Liberation Organization (PLO), the Israeli government set up the Civil Administration to manage social and economic affairs. The Civil Administration's power formally derived from and was subordinate to the military area commander. Israeli military orders controlled every aspect of the social, economic, and political life of the Palestinians in the OPT. Natural resources, including water, land, and energy, were placed under Israeli control. Israel confiscated vast areas of land and established "security zones" that cut Palestinians off from use of large swaths of land. By 1995, Israel had confiscated or controlled 73 percent of the land of the West Bank and Gaza Strip.[6] Israel also froze the volume of water that could be drawn from wells at their 1967 levels until 1994, causing severe constraints on agriculture.[7]

All Palestinian economic activities required permits from the Israeli military governor. Everything from starting a new venture or expanding an old one, the construction of any building, the transportation of goods, or any export and import activities required a permit. This system damaged all economic sectors, particularly manufacturing, which remained confined to Israel's declining industries and found limited scope for expansion in employment as a result of Israeli-imposed limitations.[8] Israel's administrative, legal, and resource restrictions were complemented by measures that deprived Palestinians of economic policy tools including control over trade, monetary, and fiscal affairs. These constraints combined with political measures to destroy the productive base of the Palestinian economy and prevent its organic growth.

The annexation of East Jerusalem initiated the attempt to separate the Gaza Strip and the West Bank from its capital city. The city's Palestinians were still able to conduct business with the rest of the OPT residents, despite their altered legal and fiscal status. Only a handful of Palestinian Jerusalemites accepted Israeli citizenship. Hence, the vast majority were legally defined merely as residents of the city of Jerusalem, but subject to Israeli taxes and economic administration.[9]

Trade, Monetary, and Fiscal Economic Tools

While the Israeli authorities kept bridges and border crossings with Jordan open, they imposed an "involuntary one-sided partial customs union" arrangement on the West Bank and Gaza Strip.[10] According to this arrangement, exchanges between Israeli and Palestinian traders were not subject to any internal trade barriers. Nevertheless, goods did not move freely. Trade between the OPT and the rest of the world was subject to the Israeli trade regime. Thus, Israeli customs and other trade barriers operated along the external borders of the combined "customs union" area.[11]

As a result of this imposed customs union, tariffs with the rest of the world increased approximately fourfold.[12] This, along with the other nontariff barriers that Israel applied, led to a rise in the cost of capital and intermediary goods for Palestinian producers, wiping out any competitive edge they might have had due to cheaper labor costs. As a result, a large number of enterprises closed and there were major losses in employment. Palestinian trade was confined to the Israeli market and isolated from global trade. As trade between Israel and the West Bank and Gaza Strip soared, Israeli imports flooded West Bank and Gaza Strip markets.[13]

The occupation dismantled the financial system in the OPT; Palestinian, Arab, and British banks were all closed shortly after the 1967 war.[14] This further reduced employment and brought the finance sector to a screeching halt. Only after the Palestinian Authority's (PA) assumption of powers in 1994 did the financial sector resume limited and conditional operation.[15] The OPT's fiscal affairs were similarly brought under Israel's control. Through a series of military orders, Israel revamped the tax system and introduced new procedures of tax assessment and collection. These measures sought to increase the revenue accruing to the Israeli treasury and to align the territories' tax system with

Israel's.[16] The private sector in the West Bank and Gaza Strip was stunted and its capacity to grow and generate jobs paralyzed.

Labor Market Convergence

The most dramatic change in the wake of the Israeli occupation was the opening of the Israeli market to Palestinian workers. Labor relations with Israel played, and still play, an important role in the economic development of the OPT. Following the opening of the borders between Israel and the OPT, Palestinian workers poured into the Israeli market, attracted by higher wages and escaping severe unemployment. Israel's construction and agriculture sectors attracted unskilled male workers. The number of Palestinian workers in Israel rose from zero in 1967 to 66,000 in 1975; to 109,000 in 1987; and to 116,000 in 1992.[17]

Palestinian unskilled labor migration to Israel was coupled with skilled labor migration to the oil-rich Arab states and the United States. Income from the earnings of workers in Israel, as well as remittances from Palestinians working abroad, contributed to raising standards of living in the OPT. These remittances enabled Palestinians to maintain high consumption levels, despite the erosion of their productive sectors.

Aggregate and Sectoral Economic Performance

GDP is a problematic measure of economic performance because it is an aggregate statistic that reveals little about the structure of an economy or its class dynamics. Nonetheless, it is widely used by economists as an indicator of broad trends. In the Oslo era the UN Development Programme began to include Palestine in its annual *Human Development Report*, a better gauge of social welfare.[18] According to the report, Palestinian human development indicators have just barely advanced from 2010 to 2019.[19]

Israeli subjugation of the Palestinian economy has shaped the composition and pattern of four phases of GDP growth between 1967 and 1993. From the start of the occupation in 1967 until 1975, growth rates increased rapidly, driven mainly by two major new sources: the opening of the Israeli market for Palestinian workers, and the 1970s oil boom in the petroleum-rich Arab states. As a result, GDP (in constant 1986 new Israeli shekels), nearly doubled from NIS 689.3 million in 1968 to NIS 1,355.1 million in 1975.[20] Because GDP growth rate exceeded population growth, real per capita GDP rose by nearly two-thirds from US$573.5 in 1968 to US$962 in 1975. During the second phase, from 1975 until the early 1980s, growth rates slowed due to the contraction in demand for labor in Israel following the 1979 oil shock. Nonetheless, because remittances from Palestinians working in the petroleum-rich Arab states continued at a high level until crude oil prices collapsed in 1985–86, by 1980, real per capita GDP rose nearly one-third to US$1,303.[21]

During the third phase, from the early 1980s until 1987 when the first intifada began, real growth stagnated. Not only did remittances from the Arab petroleum-rich states decline, but the Israeli economy was mired in stagnation and hyperinflation in the mid-1980s. From 1980 to 1987, GDP grew by about 3.6 percent per annum in the West Bank and 1.6 percent per annum in the Gaza Strip. However, GDP growth rates were similar to population growth rates. So real GDP per capita was virtually stagnant during this period.[22]

The fourth and final phase was marked by the outbreak of the first intifada in 1987 through the US-led war on Iraq, or Gulf War I, in 1991, and concluded with the 1993 Oslo Accords. In this period, except for construction, labor demand in Israel decreased exponentially. The intifada contributed to reduced labor supply and lower rates of economic growth as a result of strikes, periodic border closures, higher costs of movement, and the increased enforcement of taxes on firms. The short-run impact of the Gulf War was drastic due to the closure of the border for forty days in early 1991, followed by permanent losses due to the expulsion of Palestinians from several Gulf states, particularly Kuwait. The PLO's support of Saddam Hussein's linkage of Iraqi withdrawal from Kuwait to Israeli withdrawal from the OPT appeared to endorse Iraq's invasion of Kuwait, in opposition to the stance of the vast majority of Palestinians in Kuwait who opposed it. Income levels began to deteriorate for the first time since 1967. In 1991, the estimated real GDP per capita (US$1,259) was slightly less than GDP per capita in 1987 (US$1,274). This decline resulted in higher unemployment rates.[23]

Economic growth in the OPT has a tendency toward increasing consumption and declining investment. Income gains from labor in Israel and remittances from abroad increased total and per capita consumption in the West Bank and Gaza Strip. Real per capita consumption rose by 130 percent between 1968 and 1989.[24] While Palestinians maintained high levels of consumption, which improved standards of living, due to Israel's draconian measures financial resources were not channeled into productive economic investment. Accumulation patterns restricted growth to only a few sectors and limited the economy's capacity to absorb a growing labor force.[25]

Agriculture, the predominant productive sector before 1967, increased its productivity and output from 1969 to 1986. Nevertheless, the sector experienced major adverse transformations. Its share in GDP declined from an annual average of 36 percent in the West Bank and 29 percent in the Gaza Strip in 1970–76 to an annual average of 26 percent and 19 percent, respectively, in 1985–87. Another setback was the constriction of land under cultivation. By 1989, the cultivated area in the West Bank dropped by 14 percent below its pre-1967 level, and employment in this sector suffered.[26]

From 1967 to 1993, manufacturing was the weakest sector with a GDP share as low as 5–6 percent. The number of industrial establishments in the West Bank decreased from 2,927 in 1965 to 2,462 in 1987, and employment consequently decreased. In the Gaza Strip, however, the number of industrial establishments increased from 768 in 1960 to 793 in 1987. Overall, the number of industrial establishments in the OPT declined by 440.

Israeli measures, including restrictions on imports of machinery and other inputs or production, limited industrial production capacity in the West Bank and Gaza Strip. Therefore, a high proportion of manufacturing in the OPT was necessarily linked to the Israeli economy through subcontracting arrangements with Israeli firms, particularly in the textile and ready-to-wear clothing industry. Israeli firms subcontracted the collation of clothing segments to Palestinian enterprises, while Israeli companies were in charge of the design and sale processes. Palestinians worked for wages lower than their Israeli counterparts, incentivizing Israeli firms to subcontract to Palestinian businesses. Israeli firms reaped higher profits than Palestinian entrepreneurs because of the higher value added in the design and production of segments than in the assembly phase and the markup in the marketing. These subcontracting arrangements limited the decline in the number of industrial establishments in the West Bank. But because wages were lower in the Gaza Strip than the West Bank, Israeli companies targeted the Gaza Strip to exploit cheaper Palestinian labor, which increased the number of manufacturing establishments there.[27]

The size of industrial establishments, measured in terms of workers employed, remained small over this period. Average employment per establishment in the West Bank was 7.7 persons in 1987; only about 7 percent of the total industrial firms employed more than 10 persons. This pattern reflected the small family-based workshop and labor-intensive nature of Palestinian industrial establishments. In the Gaza Strip, the average number of employees per establishment stood at approximately 2; only 6 percent of industrial establishments employed more than 10 persons. The principal products were food processing, textiles and clothing, leather products, wood products, plastics, chemicals, and olive oil soap. Many, if not most, medium- and larger-scale manufacturing firms operated well below full capacity, which limited new job creation.[28]

Expansion in the service sector partly compensated for this contraction in the agricultural and manufacturing sectors in overall GDP. The skewed nature of the economy in favor of consumption constrained the development of producer services while promoting wholesale and retail trade services. Thus growth and contribution to GDP as well as employment were concentrated in distributive rather than productive services. Branches of other services, such as storage, telecommunication, and transport, experienced either marginal or no growth, with meager contributions to GDP and employment.

The economic patterns in the OPT from 1967 to 1993 were paradoxical. Productive sectors, usually the drivers for sustainable growth, eroded. At the same time, GDP growth levels were high, financed through remittances from the Israeli labor market or Arab Gulf states. Thus, Palestinians maintained reasonable standards of living, but only by relying on external sources. This rendered the economy deeply vulnerable and precarious. The entrenchment of dependency on external sources combined with the erosion of productive capacity undermined the Palestinian economy's organic ability to generate employment.

THE OPT IN THE POST–OSLO PEACE ACCORDS PERIOD, 1994–2017

The broad features of the political economy of the West Bank and Gaza Strip in the post–Oslo Accords period were largely defined by five factors. First were the Oslo Peace Accords and the political status of the OPT. The series of agreements between Israel and the PLO was initiated with the signing of the

Oslo Declaration of Principles in September 1993.[29] These agreements were intended to govern a five-year transition. Moreover, the Declaration of Principles stipulated that issues of sovereignty over land and natural resources, the disposition of settlements and settlers, the status of Jerusalem, and the nature of the Palestinian entity to be established were to be addressed only in the final status negotiations. The Oslo agreement gave the PA, established as a result of the agreements, functional jurisdiction over the high-density Palestinian population centers but limited the scope of Palestinian control over the economy as well as Palestinian access to national resources, such as water and land. Israel retained legal authority over zoning, building, and land registration.

These agreements permitted Israel to remain in control of the borders of the West Bank and Gaza Strip with the rest of the world, as well as of major sections of the OPT. The West Bank was divided into three areas, A, B, and C, with varying degrees of control by Israel and the PA. Area C came under the full control of Israel; Area B was under PA civil control and joint Israeli-PA security control; in Area A the PA exercised full civil and internal security control. However, even in Area A, Israel retained full control of the Population Register. Israel refused to permit issuing Palestinian currency, postage stamps, and passports, underlining its ultimate control over all the areas of the OPT. Areas A and B consist of some 227 separate geographical areas. Travel between the West Bank and Gaza Strip became increasingly difficult after 1991 and is now nearly impossible. Thus, Oslo transformed the West Bank into noncontiguous isolated enclaves separated by areas under complete Israeli jurisdiction.[30]

Israel's control of land in the West Bank and Gaza Strip facilitated its confiscation of resources and its building of new settlements, encroaching further on the possibility of an integrated national economy. By 1984, Israeli confiscated or controlled an estimated 41 percent of West Bank land. This figure rose to 60 percent in 1991 and 73 percent in 1998. Much of this consists of agricultural lands that Israel has degraded by building bypass roads and settlements.[31]

A second factor that influenced political and economic life in this period were closures and restrictions on movement. *Closure* refers to the overall restrictions placed on the movement of labor, goods, and factors of production between the West Bank and Gaza Strip and Israel as well as between Palestinian localities within the West Bank and Gaza Strip.[32] Closures were first introduced during the 1991 Gulf War; the Oslo Accords legalized and institutionalized closure as a policy measure. An elaborate system of movement restrictions, checkpoints, roadblocks, and trenches enables these closures. Israel deploys its closure policy to randomly restrict, if not altogether halt, the movement of Palestinian labor and goods inside and outside the OPT.

This land fragmentation process has divided the West Bank into three main areas (north, central, and south). Hundreds of roadblocks and checkpoints have further fragmented West Bank space into ten smaller segments or enclaves; Israeli authorities channeled Palestinians through manned checkpoints in order for them to move between the trisections and in and out of the enclaves. This system of control and separation immobilized economic growth and employment generation.

A third factor shaping Palestinian economy in the post-Oslo period is the Apartheid Wall (hereafter, the Wall), which mostly consists of a sixty-meter-wide electronic fence with paved paths, barbed-wire fences, and ditches flanking it on either side, and in urban areas is an actual eight- to nine-meter-high concrete wall. Israel's 2002 decision to build the Wall between the West Bank and Israel on a route that departs from the 1967 Armistice Line (known as the Green Line) has further damaged the Palestinian economy in violation of international law.[33] About 85 percent of the Wall runs inside the West Bank, effectively annexing 9.5 percent of the territory and isolating 150 Palestinian West Bank communities from their agricultural lands located in closed military zones between the Wall and the Green Line.[34] Although there is no physical barrier in the Jordan Valley, since 2006 Israel has barred Palestinians from entering or using at least 85 percent of the area, which comprises about 30 percent of the West Bank.[35]

In the Gaza Strip, despite Israel's withdrawal of its settlements and military bases in 2005, the conditions of colonial control and subjugation continue. There has been a barrier around the Gaza Strip since 1994. In addition, Israel has imposed a security belt 300 meters wide around the border, effectively confiscating about 15.8 percent of the Gaza Strip's total area. Those who approach the barrier risk being shot, which renders about 25 percent of its agricultural land unusable.[36] The Israeli government has applied a tight siege policy on the Gaza Strip, which has had devastating effects on all aspects of life, social, political, and certainly economic.

A fourth factor in shaping the post-Oslo economy has been the political split between Fatah and Hamas as well as the Israeli wars on Gaza. Fatah, historically led by Yasser Arafat, was formed in 1959 and is the largest party within the PLO. Hamas is an Islamist political party formed by the Gaza branch of the Muslim Brotherhood in 1988.

Hamas's victory in the 2006 parliamentary elections left the West Bank under Fatah control and the Gaza Strip under Hamas control. Despite Hamas's electoral victory, the international community, at the insistence of the United States and Israel, supported the "secular" West Bank government (Fatah) and halted aid to the Gaza Hamas "Islamist" government. International aid to the Gaza Strip was channeled through international and civil society organizations. In June 2007, the Israeli government imposed a total siege on the Gaza Strip, isolating it from the rest of the world. By 2009, Israel's siege had left the Gaza economy crippled, with 80 percent of its inhabitants dependent on assistance.[37]

Between 2008 and 2014, Israel launched three wars on the Gaza Strip. During the first, which lasted for 23 days in 2008–09, Israeli forces killed 1,440 Palestinians. During the second eight-day invasion in November 2012, Israeli forces killed 167 Palestinians. Numerous houses and public buildings, including schools, health centers, and mosques, were damaged or destroyed. In July 2014, Israel launched another assault on the Gaza Strip during which its forces skilled more than 2,100 people, destroyed 20,000 homes, and displaced half a million people.[38] The Palestinian Central Bureau for Statistics estimated that Israel's 2008–9 assault on the Gaza Strip destroyed at least US$1.4 billion worth of buildings, roads, pipes, power lines, and other infrastructure.[39] According to the IMF, as a result of the 2014 assault on the Gaza Strip, local GDP declined by 32 percent for the third quarter of the year and 15 percent for the entire year, an estimated loss of US$200 million.[40]

A fifth factor in the post-Oslo period was the PA's neoliberal policies and Salam Fayyad's so-called statehood plan. On its establishment in 1994, the PA adopted an economic program inspired by the globally ascendant model of neoliberal governance promoted by the World Bank and International Monetary Fund. The pillars of this program include free trade, cuts in government spending, removing restrictions on foreign investments, and promoting the private sector (see the Introduction to this book). Although the PA adopted these policies with the 1994 Protocol on Economic Relations (Paris Agreement), the premiership of Salam Fayyad, who formed a caretaker government in 2007, accelerated and broadened the scope of their implementation.

Fayyad aimed to forge "sound" and "viable" PA institutions that would realize a Palestinian state by 2011. The plan focused on public order and the rule of law and sought to guarantee the security of Israel. It envisioned providing effective service delivery as the means of gaining legitimacy among citizens and investors. Finally, the plan emphasized the promotion and growth of the private sector as a driver for economic prosperity.[41]

Fayyad's reform scheme improved financial management and supported a new Palestinian security force (trained by US Army General Keith Dayton). Yet economic prosperity, and more importantly, a Palestinian state, remained elusive. Strengthening the rule of law entailed the containment of Palestinian popular resistance and facilitating Israel's colonial interests and control. The attempt to realize a Palestinian state by placing neoliberal "good governance" on par with "political sovereignty" failed miserably.

In reaction to these failed policies, as well as the failure of the Oslo Peace Accords to deliver peace or liberation, Palestinians opted for strengthening their resistance strategies. These included marches against land confiscation in villages adjacent to the Apartheid Wall and the formation of the boycott, divestment, and sanctions (BDS) movement in 2005.[42]

In addition to its political role as a resistance strategy, the BDS movement could play an important economic role in the OPT. The movement's call to boycott Israeli products may provide an avenue for encouraging Palestinian production. A September 2011 UNCTAD report calculated the benefits to the Palestinian economy from switching from Israeli imports to local production. It estimated the loss to the Palestinian economy due to importing from Israel to be US$500 million annually. If these revenues were invested in the Palestinian economy, real GDP could increase by US$630 million. This growth in the production base could create 45,000 new jobs.[43] Based on these estimates, a boycott of US$1 billion could create nearly 90,000 jobs and reduce dependence on Israel, thus impairing Israel's ability to squeeze out more political concessions from the Palestinians.[44]

Economic Policies: Trade, Fiscal, and Monetary Affairs

The Oslo Peace Accords gave Israel sole control over the borders of the West Bank and Gaza Strip, as well as the collection of import taxes and the value added tax (VAT). The Protocol on Economic Relations formalized the de facto customs union that had existed since 1967 between the OPT and Israel. The new arrangements added some elements of a free trade area and allowed the PA to trade with a number of Arab and Muslim majority countries via Jordan and Egypt. However, trade was restricted to certain basic goods and commodities such as foodstuffs. Trade with Arab countries remained minimal: Arab countries in 1996 accounted for 5 percent of Palestinian exports and grew to only 6 percent in 2007. Similarly, imports from Arab countries were 0.3 percent of the total in 1996 and rose to only 1 percent in 2007. As a result, in 2008, Israel remained the main trading partner for the West Bank and Gaza Strip, receiving 89 percent of its exports, while 74 percent of imports originated in Israel.[45] While the direction of trade for the OPT has not changed much since 1993, the magnitude of the trade fluctuated, mainly as a result of movement restrictions and other political factors. Until 1998, as the incidence of closures increased in a given month, total trade (exports plus imports) declined.[46]

Israeli subcontracting investment in Palestinian industries, such as garment assembly, are limited in scope and technological content. The main Palestinian trading partner with Israel is the PA, since nearly 40 percent of imports from Israel are utilities, including electricity, fuel, and water.[47] Israeli-Palestinian "joint ventures" since the 1990s have entailed collaboration between suppliers of certain key commodities, such as gasoline and cement.[48] The PA has designated one Palestinian company or public sector institution to purchase these commodities from Israel, thereby establishing monopolies.

Oslo allowed the financial sector to reemerge after more than two decades. By the end of 2007, twenty-two banks with 162 branches were licensed for operation in the OPT.[49] A Palestine Monetary Authority was established to supervise the activities of these banks. It has some functions of a central bank, but not the right to issue a national currency. Accordingly, the new Israeli shekel and Jordanian dinar remain in use as legal tenders in the West Bank and Gaza Strip, with losses to the Palestinian economy. Palestinian seigniorage, the revenue a government makes from issuing currency, is retained by the Bank of Israel and the Central Bank of Jordan. From 1970 to 1987, the value of Palestinian seigniorage revenues retained by the Bank of Israel in constant 1987 US dollars rose from $0.7 billion to $1.8 billion.[50] In 2012, Palestinian seigniorage retained by the issuers of the three circulating currencies (new

Israeli shekels, Jordanian dinars, and US dollars) ranged from US$364 million to US$384 million, or 3.2 to 3.4 percent of Palestinian GDP that year.[51]

Israel's movement restrictions and the siege on the Gaza Strip have also jeopardized the financial sector. Forced to shut their doors during closures, and fearing defaults due to uncertain and precarious conditions, banks became extra cautious in extending credit to borrowers. Until 2000, approximately 60 percent of bank credit represented short-term overdrafts.[52] Limited access to credit constrained investments in the private sector and its capacity to generate employment.

Fiscal affairs in the post–Oslo Accords era redefined Palestinian economic dependence on Israel. The Paris Protocol required Israel to transfer income tax from Palestinians working in Israel, VAT on goods purchased in Israel by Palestinian firms, and custom duties on Palestinian imports to the PA. These transfers account for a majority of the PA's budget: in 1999, they equaled 60 percent of the PA's tax revenues.[53] However, the system of revenue transfer gives Israel control over significant parts of Palestinian public revenues. The Israeli government has weaponized these revenues to force PA compliance with its political and security concerns.[54]

Overall Economic Performance in the Post–Oslo Peace Accords Period

The political economy of the post-Oslo period is characterized by four distinct phases: growth in 1994–1999, destruction in 2000–2002, relative recovery in 2003–2007, and fluctuation in 2008–2017. The average real annual rates of growth of GDP for the four phases are: 8.5 percent, -10 percent, 11.7 percent, and 5.8 percent.[55] The growth phase was a period of political and economic optimism, during which Israeli restrictive measures were minimal. The destruction period is associated with heavy-handed Israeli military raids into the cities and villages of the West Bank and Gaza Strip following the start of the second intifada in 2000. These raids damaged infrastructure, business establishments, and private homes. Closures and other movement restrictions were heavily applied. The third stage marks the recovery from this destruction and is associated with a high level of foreign assistance. The fourth phase is associated with the three Israeli wars on Gaza and recovery from these wars through an influx of large sums of financial aid.

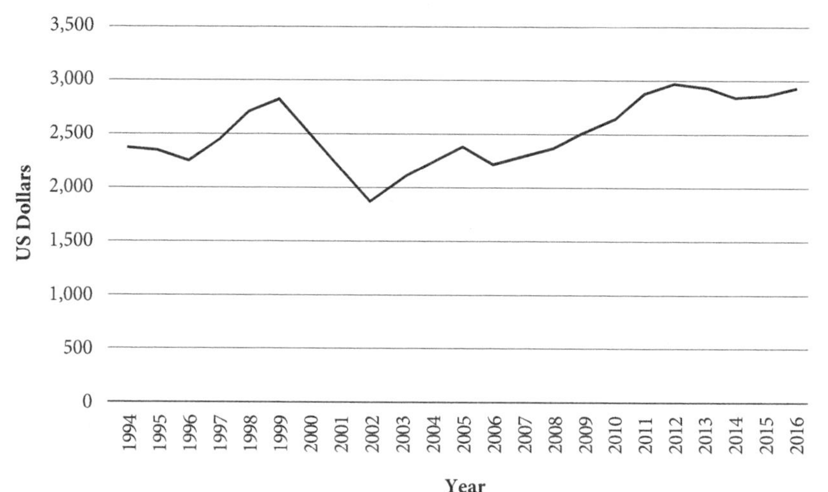

FIGURE 1. Real GDP per capita (2010 constant prices). Source: Palestinian Central Bureau of Statistics, National Accounts, 2018.

Population growth has outstripped whatever real GDP growth was achieved throughout this period. As a result, real GDP per capita in 2016 (US$2,923) was only 23 percent higher than in 1994 (US$2,361) (see Figure 1).

The growth of the Palestinian economy has been driven by three major components: trade in goods and services, the export of Palestinian laborers to Israel, and aid. Growth in trade has been inward oriented: GDP growth has consistently exceeded growth in exports. In 1994, trade accounted for 86 percent of Palestinian GDP; imports of goods and services represented about 72 percent, and exports of goods and services represented some 14 percent of GDP. This share has altered minimally over the years, so that by 2016 trade accounted for 75 percent of GDP with imports accounting for 60 percent and exports 20 percent.[56]

At the same time, Palestinian employment in Israel declined. The share of those employed in Israel as a proportion of total employment fell from an average of 18.4 percent in 1994–1999 to 9.5 percent in the period 2003–2007 to 11 percent in 2008–2017. In addition, unemployment rates were on the rise, particularly among women, who experience one of the highest unemployment rates in the world, particularly in the Gaza Strip (see Figure 2).

FIGURE 2. Unemployment rates in the OPT (%). Source: Palestinian Central Bureau of Statistics, Labor Force Surveys (various years).

During the post-Oslo period the Palestinian economy's productive base further eroded. The shares of agriculture, construction, and manufacturing in the GDP have all declined. In 1994, agriculture accounted for 13.2 percent of GDP; by 2017, its share was only 3.4 percent, while manufacturing declined from 25 to 20 percent. The construction sector has also been shrinking. In 1994, this sector accounted for 14 percent of GDP, declining to 8 percent in 2017. On the other hand, the contribution of the services sector as well as public administration and defense rose from 68 percent in 1994, to 75 percent in 2017.[57] This decline in the productive capacity of the Palestinian economy meant that employment in these sectors also declined, as Figure 3 illustrates, particularly in the agricultural sector.

Following its establishment in 1994, the PA extended permits and licenses to Palestinian firms that the Israeli Civil Administration had previously denied. Consequently, the number of firms registered from 1994 to mid-1995 (3,028 in the Gaza Strip and 5,442 in the West Bank) was much larger than the total for the entire decade of the 1980s (1,745 in the Gaza Strip and 4,846 in the West Bank), indicating the potential interest in private sector development.[58] Establishment of new firms has become easier. However, investing under a regime of closures, restrictions on trade, an economic siege on Gaza, interruptions to the production process, and disruptions in the supply of inputs means higher transaction costs, higher production costs, and lower sales and profits. These factors have further undermined the capacity of the economy to generate long-term, stable forms of employment. Real wages in the OPT have declined since 2000 (see Figure 4), undermining standards of living and families' capacities to meet basic needs.

In light of this adverse climate, the Palestinian manufacturing sector has concentrated on producing low-value, labor-intensive goods for Palestinian and Israeli markets. Until the second intifada, small Palestinian enterprises served as subcontractors for larger Israeli firms that designed and marketed goods. Given the costs and risks of dealing with Palestinian firms under closure, Israeli importers and businesses turned to more stable markets elsewhere, even if at a higher cost. The impact on employment has been devastating.

The situation in the Gaza Strip has been far worse, particularly after the siege on the Strip in 2007. The Palestine Trade Center, established in 1998 as a nonprofit organization with a mandate to promote exports, and the Palestinian Federation of Industries estimate that 98 percent of Gaza's industrial operations have become inactive as a result of the siege.[59] In addition, the halt in exports and the prohibition on importing inputs of production for

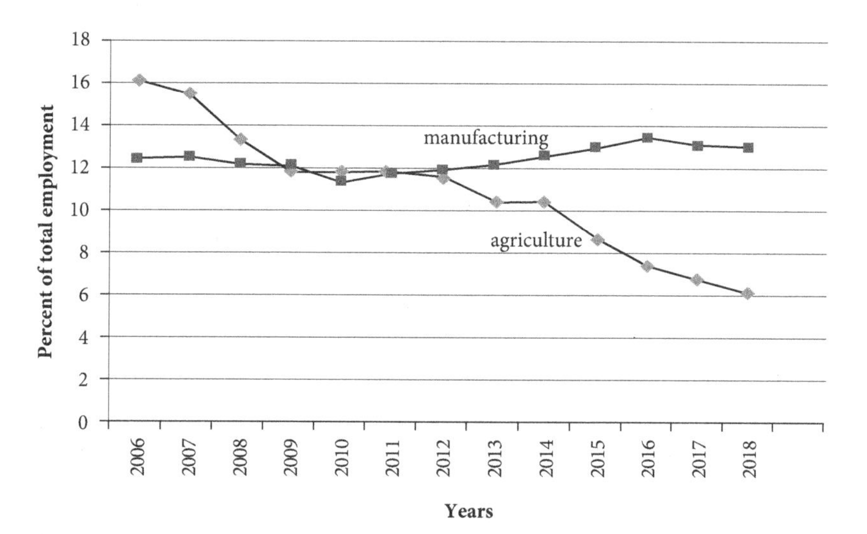

FIGURE 3. Employment in the productive sectors (%). Source: Palestinian Central Bureau of Statistics, Labor Force Surveys (various years).

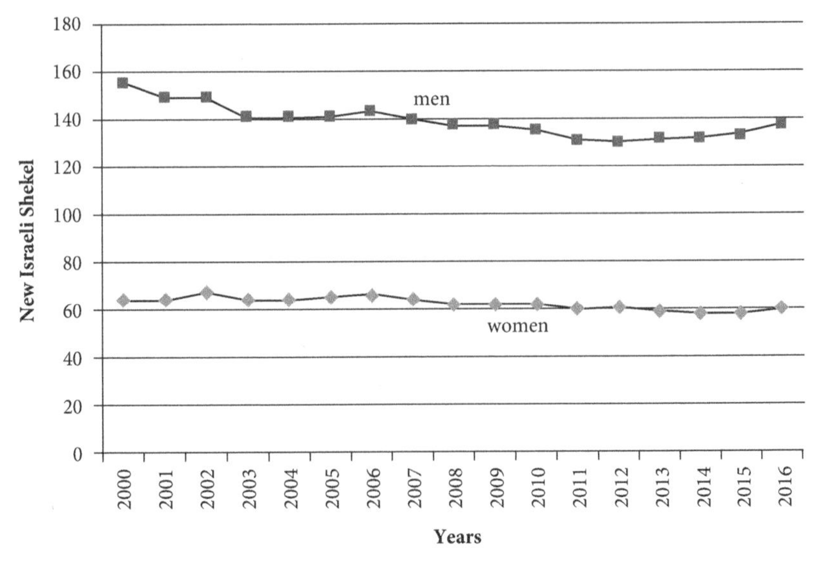

FIGURE 4. Real daily wages in the OPT. Source: Palestinian Central Bureau of Statistics, Labor Force Survey (various years).

agriculture led to the loss of more than 40,000 jobs in the agricultural sector. Because of Israel's restrictions, fishermen have been restricted to 3–6 nautical miles off the coast, causing overfishing and loss in productivity.[60]

The Applied Research Institute–Jerusalem estimated the costs of Israel's occupation to the Palestinian economy at US$6.897 billion in 2010 and US$9.458 billion during 2014.[61] More comprehensive figures covering the entire period since 1993 are not available but can be roughly extrapolated from these two years. These bleak economic conditions led to declining standards of living in the OPT.

Despite expectations of economic prosperity and donor support following the signing of the Oslo Accords, consumption-based poverty rates in the occupied Palestinian territory rose from 14 percent in 1995 to 24 percent in 1996. This was due to the sluggish economic recovery, the increase in the number of closures in the OPT, and the slow disbursement of donor funds. Furthermore, fluctuating Israeli demand for Palestinian labor affected the earnings and livelihoods of a large number of Palestinian households.[62] Following the outbreak of the second Intifada and the sudden decline in economic activity, poverty rates jumped to 51 percent in 2002.[63]

Even with the relative calm that prevailed after 2003, rates of poverty remained high, mainly due to the effect of the expanding Wall as well as continued restrictions on economic activity and labor mobility. As a result of the international boycott of the PA following the 2006 parliamentary elections and the subsequent suspension of aid to the OPT, the number of people living in deep poverty, calculated as less than US$0.50 a day, doubled from 500,000 to over 1 million.[64] According to the Palestinian Central Bureau of Statistics, by 2008 over half of all Palestinians were living in poverty, 46 percent in the West Bank and 79 percent in the Gaza Strip.[65]

Inequality in the West Bank and Gaza Strip has increased since the 1990s.[66] The Lorenz curve, a measure of inequality showing the proportion of income earned by any given percentage of the population, was worse in the Gaza Strip compared to the West Bank in the 1990s. However, by 2017, inequality deepened in both areas. The more equitable distribution of resources in the Gaza Strip reflects the high poverty among the population.[67]

Enormous infusions of foreign aid, particularly since the second intifada, have sustained the Palestinian economy. Before 1994, aid was mostly limited to UN agencies, especially UNRWA, which has provided assistance to Palestinian refugees since 1949. Between 1994 and 1999, international donors disbursed approximately US$6 billion to the OPT, or about US$420 million per annum (equivalent to about US$200 per capita per year).[68] This aid aimed to assist the peace process and "postconflict" reconstruction, starting with infrastructural projects during the 1990s.

Following the second intifada, in an attempt to mitigate the impact of Israel's violent response, aid rose sharply to US$1 billion per annum or US$320 per capita in 2002. The World Bank has argued that this is the highest sustained rate of per capita disbursement to any aid recipient since World War II.[69] However, in the post–second Intifada period, development projects shifted to institution building in the 1990s and governance reforms after 2004. Both priorities were in line with Washington Consensus directives, rather than with needs of the Palestinian economy. Following the second intifada, donors pressured the PA to undergo wide-ranging reforms of the very institutions that these same donors had themselves designed a few years earlier.[70]

Donor assistance was hence directed away from "development" aid toward government budget support and institutional reform, which increased from 2.6

percent of total assistance before the second intifada to more than 40 percent in the post-intifada period. The main sources of the boost in budget support are the European Union, the World Bank, and Arab donors.[71] This increased budget support came with greater donor influence on internal Palestinian budgetary decision making and a wide range of economic and political conditions. The latter were justified on the basis of fighting corruption despite the fact that in August 2004, the European Anti-Fraud Office announced that there had been "no evidence that the EU non-targeted budget assistance was used to finance illegal activities, including the financing of terrorism," a conclusion reaffirmed in their 2005 assessment.[72]

Aid continued to rise slowly, and by August 2008 the PA had received US$1.2 billion in foreign aid, amounting to 28 percent of GDP. However, since 2009, aid has steadily declined to below US$600 million during 2016.[73] Over the past twenty-five years, while aid may have addressed certain humanitarian and developmental concerns and helped sustain Palestinians' survival of colonialism, it has never challenged it. As Sahar Taghdisi-Rad notes,

> by "working around" the conflict, the actual donor behaviour on the ground does not take into account the forces of conflict *even after* the outbreak of the Intifada and intensification of the conflict elements. By failing to incorporate such significant considerations in donor programmes and projects, these programmes and projects fail to address the needs and weaknesses of the Palestinian economy and their origins, while creating a state of aid dependency and making the Israeli occupation less costly [for Israel] and more sustainable.[74]

CONCLUSION

The Palestinian economy's development trajectory is typical of a colonized economy: it has been held hostage to the requirements and interests of the colonial power. The tremendous costs of Israel's colonization to the Palestinian economy have meant a persistent underdevelopment process comparable to other colonial contexts, like British India or French Algeria. In the Palestinian case, this process eroded productive capacity, at times masked by rises in GDP growth rates and per capita income levels. The destruction of the productive capacity of the Palestinian economy has had enormous negative repercussions for sectoral distribution, labor market structures, standards of living, and stability of growth rates.

The Oslo political framework devastated the Palestinian economy. Standards of living came to reflect the lack of productive capacity previously masked by high growth rates driven by labor exports. The Oslo Accords did not place the Palestinians in control of their natural resources, borders, and land zoning or allow free mobility of labor and goods. They rendered most of the PA's newly acquired powers, such as setting tax rates, establishing banks, and controlling waste collection, insignificant. The fundamentals governing the operation of the Palestinian economy remained unchanged. Rather than altering the structure of the relationship between the Palestinians as a colonized people and the Israelis as the colonizers, the Oslo Accords intensified this relationship, resulting in further dependence on the Israeli economy and international aid, as well as major structural distortions to the Palestinian economy.

Notes

INTRODUCTION

1. Louis Althusser brought this term into the Marxian tradition in his essay "Contradiction and Overdetermination" in *For Marx* (New York: Pantheon Books, 1969).

2. Timothy Mitchell, *Rule of Experts: Egypt, Techno-Politics, Modernity* (Berkeley: University of California Press, 2002), 19–53; Jennifer Derr, *The Lived Nile: Environment, Disease, and Material Colonial Economy in Egypt* (Stanford, CA: Stanford University Press, 2019).

3. Hanan Hammad, *Industrial Sexuality: Gender, Urbanization, and Social Transformation in Egypt* (Austin: University of Texas Press, 2016).

4. Brian Merchant, *The One Device: The Secret History of the iPhone* (New York: Little, Brown and Company, 2017).

5. Hanna Batatu, *The Old Social Classes and the Revolutionary Movements of Iraq: A Study of Iraq's Old Landed and Commercial Classes and of Its Communists, Ba'thists, and Free Officers* (Princeton, NJ: Princeton University Press, 1978).

6. Fareed M. A. Hassan, *Tunisia: Understanding Successful Socioeconomic Development* (Washington, DC: World Bank, 2005), ix–x.

7. The 2010 Country Brief has been removed from the World Bank's website but is quoted in Alex Callinicos, "The Return of the Arab Revolution," *International Socialism*, April 1, 2011 http://isj.org.uk/the-return-of-the-arab-revolution/#130analysis18; World Bank, World Development Indicators, 2015.

8. UNDP, *Human Development Index*, http://hdr.undp.org/en/content/human-development-index-hdi.

9. United Nations Development Programme and Arab Fund for Economic and Social Development, *Arab Human Development Report 2003* (New York: UN Publications, 2003), 139.

10. Nazih Ayubi, *Over-Stating the Arab State: Politics and Society in the Middle East* (London: I. B. Tauris, 1995).

11. The term was coined by Hossein Mahdavy, in "The Pattern and Problems of Economic Development in Rentier States: The Case of Iran," in *Studies in the Economic History of the Middle East*, ed. M. A. Cook (Oxford: Oxford University Press, 1970). Another well-known exposition of the theory is Hazem Beblawi and Giacomo Luciani, eds., *The Rentier State: Nation, State and the Integration of the Arab World* (London: Croom Helm, 1987).

12. Bertell Ollman, *Dance of the Dialectic: Steps in Marx's Method* (Urbana: University of Illinois Press, 2003), 202.

13. Harry S. Truman, Inaugural Address, January 20, 1949.

14. Daniel Lerner, *The Passing of Traditional Society: Modernizing the Middle East* (Glencoe, IL: Free Press, 1958), 79.

15. Begum Adalet, *Hotels and Highways: The Construction of Modernization Theory in Cold War Turkey* (Stanford, CA: Stanford University Press, 2018).

16. Joe Stork, *Middle East Oil and the Energy Crisis* (New York: Monthly Review Press, 1975); Abbas Alnasrawi, *Arab Nationalism, Oil, and the Political Economy of Dependency* (New York: Greenwood, 1991), 89–108; Timothy Mitchell, *Carbon Democracy: Political Power in the Age of Oil* (London: Verso, 2011), 173–99.

17. Fred Halliday, *Arabia Without Sultans* (London: al-Saqi, 2001); Robert Vitalis, *America's Kingdom: Mythmaking on the Saudi Oil Frontier* (Stanford, CA: Stanford University Press, 2007); Toby Craig Jones, *Desert Kingdom: How Oil and Water Forged Modern Saudi Arabia* (Cambridge, MA: Harvard University Press, 2010); Adam Hanieh, *Capitalism and Class in the Gulf Arab States* (New York: Palgrave Macmillan, 2011) and *Money Markets, and Monarchies: The Gulf Cooperation Council and the Political Economy of the Contemporary Middle East* (Cambridge: Cambridge University Press, 2018). *PEME*'s bibliography lists Stork's works but does not discuss them.

18. Janet Abu-Lughod, *Before European Hegemony: The World System A.D. 1250–1350* (Oxford: Oxford University Press, 1989).

19. Kenneth Pomeranz, *The Great Divergence: China, Europe, and the Making of the Modern World Economy* (Princeton, NJ: Princeton University Press, 2000).

20. Beshara Doumani, *Rediscovering Palestine: Merchants and Peasants in Jabal Nablus, 1700–1900* (Berkeley: University of California Press, 1995); Sarah Shields, *Mosul Before Iraq: Like Bees Making Five-Sided Cells* (Albany: State University of New York Press, 2000).

21. Hala Fattah, *The Politics of Regional Trade in Iraq, Arabia and the Gulf, 1745–1900* (Albany: State University of New York Press, 1997), 7.

22. Lord Cromer, *Modern Egypt* (New York: Macmillan, 1908), vol. 2, 180.

23. Weekly radio address as reported in the *Washington Post*, November 17, 2001.

24. Gérard Davet and Fabrice Lhomme, *Un président ne devrait pas dire ça . . .* (Paris: Stock, 2016), 595.

25. Gayatri Chakravorty Spivak, "Can the Subaltern Speak?" in *Marxism and the Interpretation of Culture*, ed. Cary Nelson and Lawrence Grossberg (Urbana: University of Illinois Press, 1988), 296.

26. "An American Proposal," quoted in Leo Panitch and Sam Gindin, *The Making of Global Capitalism: The Political Economy of American Empire* (London: Verso Books, 2012), 67.

27. Michel Aglietta, *A Theory of Capitalist Regulation: The US Experience* (London: Verso, 1976); Robert Boyer, *The Regulation School: A Critical Introduction* (New York: Columbia University Press, 1990); Stephen Marglin and Juliet Schor, eds., *The Golden Age of Capitalism* (Oxford: Clarendon Press, 1990).

28. David S. Painter, "The Marshall Plan and Oil," *Cold War History* 9, no. 2 (2009): 160, 163, 164, 167.

29. Andrew Glyn, Alan Hughes, Alain Lipietz, and Ajit Singh, "The Rise and Fall of the Golden Age," in Marglin and Schor (eds.), *The Golden Age of Capitalism*, 39–125.

30. Bent Hansen, *Egypt and Turkey: Political Economy of Poverty, Equity, and Growth* (Oxford: Oxford University Press for the World Bank, 1991), 6–9. According to Ali Kadri, *The Unmaking of Arab Socialism* (London: Anthem, 2016), 74, in Egypt, Syria, and Iraq, key economic indicators of growth were about as good or better for the 1960–80 period than for 1980–2011, when Washington Consensus policies prevailed. But the 1980–88 Iran-Iraq War and the 2003 US invasion of Iraq make comparison difficult.

31. John Williamson, "In Search of a Manual for Technopols," in *The Political Economy of Policy Reform*, ed. John Williamson (Washington, DC: Institute for International Economics, 1994), 26–28.

32. John Williamson, "Democracy and the Washington Consensus," *World Development* 21, no. 8 (1993): 1329.

33. John Walton and David Seddon, *Free Markets and Food Riots: The Politics of Global Adjustment* (Oxford: Blackwell, 1994), 39–40. Slightly different figures on page 172.

34. Talal Asad and Roger Owen, *Review of Middle East Studies* 1 (1975): 1. Owen's influential essay in the inaugural issue, "The Middle East in the Eighteenth Century: An Islamic Society in Decline: A Critique of Gibb and Bowen's *Islamic Society and the West*," 101–12, exemplified this project.

35. André Gunder Frank, *Capitalism and Underdevelopment in Latin America: Historical Studies of Chile and Brazil* (New York: Monthly Review, 1969); Immanuel Wallerstein, *Capitalist Agriculture and the Origins of the European World-Economy in the Sixteenth Century* (Berkeley: University of California Press, 2011).

36. Samir Amin, *Accumulation on a World Scale: A Critique of the Theory of Underdevelopment* (New York: Monthly Review, 1974), and *The Arab Nation: Nationalism and Class Conflict* (London: Zed, 1978).

37. Huri İslamoğlu-İnan and Çağlar Keyder, "Agenda for Ottoman History," *Review* 1, no. 1 (1977): 31–56. The edited version was reprinted in Huri İslamoğlu-İnan, ed., *The Ottoman Empire and the World-Economy* (Cambridge: Cambridge University Press, 1987), 42–62, along with Huri İslamoğlu-İnan's critique in her Introduction to the book, 1–24.

38. Shuhdi 'Atiyya al-Shafi'i, *Tatawwur al-haraka al-wataniyya al-misriyya, 1882–1956* (Cairo: al-Dar al-Misriyya, 1957) and Ra'uf 'Abbas, *al-Haraka al-'ummaliyya fi misr, 1899–1952* (Cairo: Dar al-Katib al-'Arabi, 1967) are Marxist and Nasserist examples respectively.

39. Vladimir Borisovich Lutsky, *Modern History of the Arab Countries* (Moscow: Progress, 1969).

40. Batatu, *The Old Social Classes*; Eric Davis, *Challenging Colonialism: Bank Misr and Egyptian Industrialization, 1920–1941* (Princeton, NJ: Princeton University Press, 1983); Ervand Abrahamian, *Iran Between Two Revolutions* (Princeton, NJ: Princeton University Press, 1982); Joel Beinin and Zachary Lockman, *Workers on the Nile: Nationalism, Communism, Islam, and the Egyptian Working Class, 1882–1954* (Princeton, NJ: Princeton University Press, 1987).

41. Robert Vitalis, *When Capitalists Collide: Business Conflict and the End of Empire in Egypt* (Berkeley: University of California Press, 1995).

42. Sherene Seikaly, *Men of Capital: Scarcity and Economy in Mandate Palestine* (Stanford, CA: Stanford University Press, 2016).

43. Ted Swedenburg, *Memories of Revolt: The 1936–1939 Rebellion and the Palestinian National Past* (Fayetteville: University of Arkansas Press, 2003).

44. James Toth, *Rural Labor Movements in Egypt and Their Impact on the State, 1961–1992* (Gainesville: University Press of Florida, 1999); Reem Saad, "State, Landlord, Parliament and Peasant: The Story of the 1992 Tenancy Law in Egypt," in *Agriculture in Egypt: from Pharaonic to Modern Times*, ed. Alan K. Bowman and Eugene Rogan (Oxford: Oxford University Press for the British Academy, 1999); Stephanie Cronin, *Tribal Politics in Iran: Rural Conflict and the New State, 1921–1941* (London: Routledge, 2006); Charles W. Anderson, "State Formation from Below and the Great Revolt in Palestine," *Journal of Palestine Studies* 47, no. 1 (Autumn 2017): 39–55 and "From Petition to Confrontation: The Palestinian National Movement and the Rise of Mass Politics, 1929–1939," (PhD diss., New York University, 2013).

45. Kenneth Cuno, *The Pasha's Peasants: Land, Society and Economy in Lower Egypt, 1740–1858* (Cambridge: Cambridge University Press, 1992); Doumani, *Rediscovering Palestine*; Kristen Alff, "The Business of Property: Levantine Joint-Stock Companies, Land, Law, and Capitalism Around the Mediterranean, 1850–1925," (PhD diss., Stanford University, 2019).

46. Judith E. Tucker, *Women in Nineteenth-Century Egypt* (Cambridge: Cambridge University Press, 1985).

47. In Joan Wallach Scott, *Gender and the Politics of History* (New York: Columbia University Press, 1988), 28–50.

48. Deniz Kandiyoti, "Bargaining with Patriarchy," *Gender and Society* 2, no. 3 (1988): 274–90; Mervat F. Hatem, "Economic and Political Liberation in Egypt and the Demise of State Feminism," *International Journal of Middle East Studies* 24, no. 2 (1992): 231–51; Elizabeth Thompson, *Colonial Citizens: Republican Rights, Paternal Privilege, and Gender in French Syria and Lebanon* (New York: Columbia University Press, 2000); and Akram Khater, *Inventing Home: Emigration, Gender, and the Middle Class in Lebanon, 1870–1920* (Berkeley: University of California Press, 2001).

49. This trend was heralded by a special section of *International Labor and Working-Class History* 60 (October 2001) on "Labor History in the Ottoman Middle East, 1700–1922" curated by the late Donald Quataert. Quataert's *Miners and the State in the Ottoman Empire: The Zonguldak Coalfield, 1822–1920* (New York: Berghahn, 2006) is also notable. Joel Beinin, *Workers and Peasants in the Modern Middle East* (Cambridge: Cambridge University Press, 2001), sought to summarize the literature to that point.

50. Karen Pfeifer, "How Tunisia, Morocco, Jordan and Even Egypt Became IMF 'Success Stories' in the 1990s," *Middle East Report* 210 (Spring 1999): 23–27, offered an early critique of the Washington Consensus. See also Ray Bush, ed., *Counter-Revolution in Egypt's Countryside: Land and Farmers in the Era of Economic Reform* (London: Zed, 2002); and Julia Elyachar, *Markets of Dispossession: NGOs, Economic Development, and the State in Cairo* (Durham, NC: Duke University Press, 2005).

51. See also Bassam Haddad, *Business Networks in Syria: The Political Economy of Authoritarian Resilience* (Stanford, CA: Stanford University Press, 2011), 32.

52. Firat Bozçalı, "The Illegal Oil Trade Along Turkey's Borders," *Middle East Report* 261 (Winter 2011): 24–29, and "Borderwork: Smuggling, Techno-legal Politics and the Making of National Borders in the Kurdish Borderlands of Turkey," (PhD diss., University of Michigan, 2017).

53. On the earlier period see Hammad, *Industrial Sexuality,* discussed above. On the later period see M. Laetitia Cairoli, *Girls of the Factory: A Year with the Garment Workers of Morocco* (Gainesville: University Press of Florida, 2011); Leila Zaki Chakravarti, *Made in Egypt: Gendered Identity and Aspiration on the Globalised Shop Floor* (New York: Berghahn, 2016).

54. Mehran Kamrava and Zahra Babar, eds., *Migrant Labor in the Persian Gulf* (New York: Columbia University Press, 2012); Abdulhadi Khalaf, Omar AlShehabi, and Adam Hanieh, eds., *Transit States: Labour, Migration and Citizenship in the Gulf* (London: Pluto, 2014); Andrea Grace Wright, "Migratory Pipelines: Labor and Oil in the Arabian Sea," (PhD diss., University of Michigan, 2015).

55. See also Zeinab Abul-Magd, *Militarizing the Nation: The Army, Business, and Revolution in Egypt* (New York: Columbia University Press, 2017); and on ports and shipping, Laleh Khalili, *Sinews of War and Trade: Shipping and Capitalism in the Arabian Peninsula* (London: Verso, 2020).

56. Laleh Khalili, *Time in the Shadows: Confinement in Counterinsurgencies* (Stanford, CA: Stanford University Press, 2012); Ilana Feldman, *Police Encounters: Security and Surveillance in Gaza under Egyptian Rule* (Stanford, CA: Stanford University Press, 2015).

57. Eric Gobe, "The Gafsa Mining Basin between Riots and a Social Movement: Meaning and Significance of a Protest Movement in Ben Ali's Tunisia," (Paris: HAL Working Paper, 2010); Hafidh Tabbabi, *Intifadat al-hawd al-manjami bi-qafsa, 2008* (Tunis: al-Dar al-Tunisiyya li'l-Kitab, 2012); Anne Alexander and Mostafa Bassiouny, *Bread, Freedom, Social Justice: Workers and the Egyptian Revolution* (London: Zed,

2014); Habib Ayeb and Ray Bush, "Small Farmer Uprisings and Rural Neglect in Egypt and Tunisia," *Middle East Report* 272 (Fall 2014): 2–10; Hèla Yousfi, *L'UGTT, une passion tunisienne: Enquête sur les syndicalistes en révolution 2011–2014* (Tunis: Editions Mohamed Ali/IRMC, 2015); Joel Beinin, *Workers and Thieves: Labor Movements and Popular Uprisings in Tunisia and* Egypt (Stanford, CA: Stanford University Press, 2016).

58. See also Aaron Jakes, *Egypt's Occupation: Colonial Economism and the Crises of Capitalism* (Stanford, CA: Stanford University Press, 2020); and Kristen Alff, "Levantine Joint-Stock Companies, Trans-Mediterranean Partnerships, and Nineteenth-Century Capitalist Development," *Comparative Studies in Society and History* 60, no. 1 (January 2018): 150–77.

CHAPTER 1

1. Maxime Rodinson, *Islam and Capitalism*, trans. Brian Pearce (New York: Pantheon, 1973), xii–xviii, 67–68.

2. Kenneth Cuno, *The Pasha's Peasants: Land, Society and Economy in Lower Egypt, 1740–1858* (Cambridge: Cambridge University Press, 1992); Beshara Doumani, *Rediscovering Palestine: Merchants and Peasants in Jabal Nablus, 1700–1900* (Berkeley: University of California Press, 1995).

3. Rodinson, *Islam and Capitalism*, xvii.

4. Peter Gran, *The Rise of the Rich: A New View of Modern World History* (Syracuse, NY: Syracuse University Press, 2009), 49–54.

5. Peter Gran, *Islamic Roots of Capitalism in Egypt, 1760–1840* (Syracuse, NY: Syracuse University Press, 1998).

6. S. D. Gottein, *A Mediterranean Society: The Jewish Communities of the Arab World as Portrayed in the Documents of the Cairo Geniza*, Gustave E. Von Grunebaum Center of Near Eastern Studies (Berkeley: University of California Press, 1978).

7. Jessica Goldberg, *Trade and Institutions in the Medieval Mediterranean* (Cambridge: Cambridge University Press, 2012); Gottein, *A Mediterranean Society.*

8. Sebouh David Aslanian, *From the Indian Ocean to the Mediterranean: The Global Trade Networks of Armenian Merchants from New Julfa* (Berkeley: University of California Press, 2010).

9. Gran, *Islamic Roots of Capitalism in Egypt*, 18.

10. Rodinson, *Islam and Capitalism*, 28–58.

11. Gran, *Islamic Roots of Capitalism in Egypt*, 12–13.

12. Gershon Shafir, *Land, Labor and the Origins of the Israeli-Palestinian Conflict, 1882–1914* (Berkeley: University of California Press, 1996); Roger Owen, *The Middle East in the World Economy, 1800–1914* (London: I. B. Tauris, 2002).

13. Walter Johnson, *River of Dark Dreams: Slavery and Empire in the Cotton Kingdom* (Cambridge, MA: Belknap Press of Harvard University Press, 2013).

14. Isabelle Guérin, "The Political Economy of Debt Bondage in Contemporary South India " in *Bonded Labour and Debt in the Indian Ocean World*, ed. Gwyn Campbell and Alessandro Stanziani (New York: Routledge, 2013).

15. Henry Bernstein, "'The Peasantry' in Global Capitalism: Whom Where and Why?," *Socialist Register* (2001).

16. Michael Löwy, "Marx and Weber: Critics of Capitalism," *New Politics* 11, no. 2 (42, Winter 2007) https://newpol.org/issue_post/marx-and-weber-critics-capitalism/.

17. Löwy, "Marx and Weber: Critics of Capitalism."

18. Halil İnalcik and Donald Quataert, eds. *An Economic History of the Ottoman Empire, Volume Two: 1600–1914* (Cambridge: Cambridge University Press, 1997), 103–42.

19. Engin Deniz Akarlı, "Gedik: A Bundle of Rights and Obligations for Istanbul Artisans and Traders, 1750–1840," in *Law, Anthropology, and the Construction of the Social: Making Persons and Things*, ed. Alain Pottage and Martha Mundy (Cambridge: Cambridge University Press, 2004), 168.

20. Akarlı, "Gedik," 169.

21. Richard van Leeuwen, *Notables and Clergy in Mount Lebanon: The Khazin Sheikhs and the Maronite Church (1736–1840)* (Leiden: E. J. Brill, 1994), 67.

22. Kenneth Cuno, "Origins of Private Ownership of Land in Egypt," *International Journal of Middle East Studies* 12 (1980): 251.

23. Jane Hathaway, *The Politics of Households in Ottoman Egypt: The Rise of the Qadağlıs*, Cambridge Studies in Islamic Civilization (Cambridge: Cambridge University Press), 13–14.

24. Cuno, *The Pasha's Peasants*, 26.

25. Jane Hathaway and Karl Barbir, *The Arab Lands under Ottoman Rule: 1516–1800*, 2nd ed. (London: Routledge, 2013), 50, 229.

26. Murat Çizakça, "Evolution of Domestic Borrowing in the Ottoman Empire," in *East Meets West—Banking, Commerce and Investment in the Ottoman Empire*, ed. Ian L. Fraser, Phillip L. Cottrell, and Monika Pohle Fraser (New York: Routledge, 2016); Ali Yaycioglu, *Partners of the Empire: The Crisis of the Ottoman Order in the Age of Revolutions* (Stanford, CA: Stanford University Press, 2016), 29–30.

27. Ariel Salzmann, "An Ancien Régime Revisited: 'Privatization' and Political Economy," *Politics & Society* 21, no. 4 (December 1993): 205.

28. Fawwaz Traboulsi, *A History of Modern Lebanon* (London: Pluto, 2007), 16–18, 34.

29. André Raymond, "The Economic Crisis of Egypt in the Eighteenth Century" in *The Islamic Middle East, 700–1900*, ed. Abraham L. Udovitch (Princeton, NJ: Darwin, 1981).

30. Cuno, *The Pasha's Peasants*, 60–63.

31. Alan Mikhail, *Nature and Empire in Ottoman Egypt: An Environmental History* (Cambridge: Cambridge University Press, 2011), 3–4.

32. Kenneth Cuno, "Egypt's Wealthy Peasantry, 1740–1820: A Study of the Region of Al-Mansura," in *Land Tenure and Social Transformation in the near East*, ed. Tarif Khalidi (Beirut: American University of Beirut Press, 1984), 314–15.

33. Amy Singer, *Palestinian Peasants and Ottoman Officials: Rural Administration around Sixteenth-Century Jerusalem* (Cambridge: Cambridge University Press, 1994), 91–94.

34. Joel Beinin, *Workers and Peasants in the Modern Middle East* (Cambridge: Cambridge University Press, 2001), 28–29.

35. Alan Richards, *Egypt's Agricultural Development, 1800–1980: Technical and Social Change* (Boulder, CO: Westview, 1982), 12.

36. Doumani, *Rediscovering Palestine*, 131–35.

37. Doumani, *Rediscovering Palestine*, 135–40; Kenneth M. Cuno, "Salam Contract and the Transformation of the Agricultural Sector in Ottoman Egypt," *Annales* 4 (2006): 4.

38. Ömer Lüfti Barkan, *Süleymaniye Cami Ve İmaret İnşaat (1550–1557)*, 2 vols. (Ankara: Türk Tarih Kurumu Basımevi, 1972–1979).

39. Doumani, *Rediscovering Palestine*, 134–35.

40. Quoted in Traboulsi, *A History of Modern Lebanon*, 55.

41. Lorenzo Trombetta, "The Private Archive of the Sursuqs, a Beirut Family of Christian Notables: An Early Investigation," *Rivista Degli Studi Oriental* 82, no. 1–4 (2009).

42. Traboulsi, *A History of Modern Lebanon*, 59.

43. Mikhail, *Nature and Empire in Ottoman Egypt*, 3–4.

44. Akram F. Khater, *Inventing Home: Emigration, Gender, and the Middle Class in Lebanon* (Berkeley: University of California Press, 2001), 28–31.

45. Khater, *Inventing Home*, 29.

46. Leeuwen, *Notables and Clergy in Mount Lebanon*, 67.

47. Thomas Philipp, *The Syrians in Egypt, 1725–1975*, Berliner Islamstudien, Number 3 (Stuttgart: Franz Steiner, 1985), 2, 9, 22, 25.

48. Trombetta, "Private Archive of the Sursuqs," 202.

49. Kristen Alff, "Levantine Joint-Stock Companies, Trans-Mediterranean Partnerships, and Nineteenth-Century Capitalist Development," *Comparative Studies in Society and History* 60, no. 1 (2018): 155.

50. Jacob N. Landau, *Jews in Nineteenth-Century Egypt*, Routledge Library Editions: Society of the Middle East (London: Routledge, 2016), 10.

51. Kristen Alff, "The Business of Property: Levantine Joint-Stock Companies, Land, Law, and Capitalist Development around the Mediterranean, 1850–1925" (PhD diss., Stanford University 2019), 50.

52. Richards, *Egypt's Agricultural Development*, 19–21.

53. David Harvey, "The 'New' Imperialism: Accumulation by Dispossession," *Socialist Register* 40 (2004): 76.

54. Alff, "Business of Property," 156.

55. Akram F. Khater, "'House' to 'Goddess of the House': Gender, Class, and Silk in 19th-Century Mount Lebanon," *International Journal of Middle East Studies* 28, no. 3 (1996): 326.

56. Khater, "'House' to 'Goddess of the House,'" 327.

57. Khater, "'House' to 'Goddess of the House,'" 329–34.

58. Samir Kassir, *Beirut*, trans. M. B. Debvoise (Berkeley: University of California Press, 2010), 127.

59. Alff, "Business of Property," 59.

60. Rosa Luxemburg, *The Accumulation of Capital*, trans. Agnes Schwarzschild (London: Routledge, 2003); Aaron Jakes, "Boom, Bugs, Bust: Egypt's Ecology of Interest, 1882–1914," *Antipode* (2016): 1–25.

61. Owen, *Middle East in the World Economy*, 248.

62. Alff, "Business of Property," 101.

63. Alff, "Business of Property," 101.

64. Alff, "Business of Property," 225.

65. Robert L. Tignor, *State, Private Enterprise and Economic Change in Egypt, 1918–1952* (Princeton, NJ: Princeton University Press, 1984), 7.

66. Robert Vitalis, *When Capitalists Collide: Business Conflict and the End of Empire in Egypt* (Berkeley: University of California Press, 1995), xviii.

67. Beinin, *Workers and Peasants in the Modern Middle East*, 26.

68. Philipp, *Syrians in Egypt*, 93; Gabriel Baer, *A History of Landownership in Modern Egypt 1800–1950* (Oxford: Oxford University Press, 1962), 62.

69. Alff, "Business of Property," 98.

70. Alff, "Business of Property," 96–102.

71. Beinin, *Workers and Peasants in the Modern Middle East*, 55.

72. Phillip S. Khoury, *Urban Notables and Arab Nationalism: The Politics of Damascus 1860–1920* (Cambridge: Cambridge University Press, 1983), 41–42.

73. Kenneth Cuno, "Was the Land of Ottoman Syria Miri or Milk? An Examination of Juridical Differences within the Hanafi School," *Studia Islamica* 81 (June 1995): 148–50.

74. Michael Gilsenan, *Lords of the Lebanese Marches: Violence and Narrative in an Arab Society* (Berkeley: University of California Press, 1996), 69–78; Haim Gerber, *The Social Origins of the Modern Middle East* (Boulder, CO: Lynne Rienner, 1987), 84.

75. Linda Schatkowski Schilcher, "The Hauran Conflicts of the 1860s: A Chapter in the Rural History of Modern Syria," *International Journal of Middle East Studies* 13, no. 2 (1981).

76. Richards, *Egypt's Agricultural Development*, 233.

77. Richards, *Egypt's Agricultural Development*, 35; Beinin, *Workers and Peasants in the Modern Middle East*, 55–56.

78. Richards, *Egypt's Agricultural Development*, 69.

79. Eric Davis, *Challenging Colonialism: Bank Misr and Egyptian Industrialization, 1920–1941* (Princeton, NJ: Princeton University Press, 1983), 26–27.

80. Khater, "'House' to 'Goddess of the House,'" 328–29.

81. Martha Mundy and Richard S. Smith, *Governing Property, Making the Modern State: Law Administration and Production in Ottoman Syria* (London: I. B. Tauris, 2007), 235.

82. Alff, "Business of Property," 114–15.

83. Mundy and Smith, *Governing Property, Making the Modern State*, 57–99.

84. Mundy and Smith, *Governing Property, Making the Modern State*, 57–99; "United Egyptian Lands, Ltd" and "Sidi Salem Estates of Egypt, Ltd.," *The Statist*, 58 (December 8, 1906), 1071.

85. Samir Saul, *La France et L'Égypte de 1882 à 1914, Intérêts économiques et implications politiques* (Paris: Institut de la gestion publique et du développement économique, Comité pour l'histoire économique et financière de la France, 1997), 5–8.

86. "The United Egyptian Lands, Ltd.," *Times of London*, December 10, 1906.

87. Alff, "Business of Property," 136–42.

88. Mikhail, *Nature and Empire in Ottoman Egypt*, 199.

89. Alff, "Business of Property," 176–77.

90. "Diary of Archibald Crawfold," in Nicholas Z. Ajay, *Mount Lebanon and the Wilayah of Beirut, 1914–1918: The War Years* (Washington, DC: Georgetown University Press, 1972), 147.

91. Alff, "Business of Property," 248.

CHAPTER 2

1. John Gallagher and Ronald Robinson, "The Imperialism of Free Trade," *Economic History Review* New Series 6, No. 1 (1953): 1–15.

2. Roger Owen, *The Middle East and the World Economy, 1800–1914* (London: I. B. Taurus, 1993); Zeinab Abul-Magd, *Imagined Empires: A History of Revolt in Egypt* (Berkeley: University of California Press, 2013); Alan Richards, *Egypt's Agricultural Development, 1800–1980: Technical and Social Change* (Boulder, CO: Westview, 1982); Alexander Schölch, *Egypt for the Egyptians! The Socio-Political Crisis in Egypt, 1878–82* (London: Ithaca, 1981).

3. E. R. J. Owen, *Cotton and the Egyptian Economy: 1820–1914* (Oxford: Clarendon, 1969).

4. Abul-Magd, *Imagined Empires*, 122–46; Jennifer L. Derr, *The Lived Nile: Environment, Disease, and Material Colonial Economy in Egypt* (Stanford, CA: Stanford University Press, 2019), 75–98.

5. Joel Beinin, *Workers and Peasants in the Modern Middle East* (Cambridge: Cambridge University Press, 2001), 84.

6. Joel Beinin and Zachary Lockman, *Workers on the Nile: Nationalism, Communism, Islam, and the Egyptian Working Class, 1882–1954* (Princeton, NJ: Princeton University Press, 1987), 291–92.

7. Beinin and Lockman, *Workers on the Nile*, 285–362.

8. Hanan Hammad, *Industrial Sexuality Gender, Urbanization, and Social Transformation in Egypt* (Austin: University of Texas Press, 2016); Nancy Reynolds, *A City Consumed: Urban Commerce, the Cairo Fire, and the Politics of Decolonization in Egypt*

(Stanford, CA: Stanford University Press, 2012); Mona Russell, "Marketing the Modern Egyptian Girl: Whitewashing Soap and Clothes from the Late Nineteenth Century to 1936," *Journal of Middle East Women's Studies* 6, no. 3 (2010): 19–57; Karin van Nieuwkerk, *"A Trade Like Any Other": Female Singers and Dancers in Egypt* (Austin: University of Texas Press, 1995).

9. According to Philip Khoury, "Local industry in Syria centered on cement, food-processing, cigarettes, cotton-spinning and textiles, which were labor-intensive and could, up to a point, face foreign competition." "The Syrian Independence Movement and the Growth of Economic Nationalism in Damascus," *Journal of the British Society for Middle Eastern Studies* 14, no. 1 (1988): 27.

10. Philip Khoury, *Syria and the French Mandate: The Politics of Arab Nationalism 1920–45* (Princeton, NJ: Princeton University Press, 1987), 624–26.

11. Philip Khoury, "Continuity and Change in Syrian Political Life: The Nineteenth and Twentieth Centuries." *American Historical Review* 96, no. 5 (December 1991): 1374–95.

12. Khoury, *Syria and the French Mandate*, 619–30.

13. Raymond Hinnebusch, *Authoritarian Power and State Formation in Ba'thist Syria* (Boulder, CO: Westview, 1990), 1–7; Steven Heydemann, *Authoritarianism in Syria: Institutions and Social Conflict 1946–1970* Ithaca, NY: Cornell University Press, 1999), 12–16; Patrick Seale, *The Struggle for Syria: A Study in Post-War Arab Politics, 1945–1958* (London: I. B. Tauris, 1988).

14. Malcolm H. Kerr, *The Arab Cold War: Gamal 'Abd al-Nasir and His Rivals, 1958–1970*, 3rd ed. (London: Oxford University Press, 1971).

15. Hanna Batatu, *Syria's Peasantry, the Descendants of Its Lesser Rural Notables, and Their Politics* (Princeton, NJ: Princeton University Press, 1999), 144–154.

16. Abdel-Jawed Zouari, "European Capitalist Penetration of Tunisia, 1860–1881: A Case Study of the Regency's Debt Crisis and the Establishment of the International Financial Commission" (PhD diss., University of Washington, 1998), 10–11.

17. Zouari, "European Capitalist Penetration of Tunisia," 259–71.

18. Noureddine Dougui, *Histoire d'une grande entreprise coloniale: La Compagnie des Phosphates et du chemin de fer de Gafsa, 1897–1930* (Tunis: Faculté des lettres de la Manouba, 1995); Abdesslem Ben Hamida, *Le syndicalisme tunisien de la Deuxième Guerre mondiale à l'autonomie interne* (Tunis: Université de Tunis, 1989), 118.

19. Jean Poncet, *La colonisation et l'agriculture européennes en Tunisie depuis 1881* (Paris: Impr. Nationale, 1962); Habib Attia, "Les hautes steppes tunisiennes de

la société pastorale à la société paysanne" (PhD diss., Université Paris Diderot–Paris 7, 1977).

20. Mohamed Moncef M'Halla, "Le developpement du capitalisme dans la Tunisie coloniale (1881–1936)" (PhD diss., Université Paris Diderot–Paris 7, 1979); Hassen El-Annabi, "La Crise de 1929 et ses conséquences en Tunisie" (PhD diss., University of Tunis, 1975).

21. Hassine Raouf Hamza, "Eléments pour une réflexion sur l'histoire du Mouvement National pendant l'entre-deux-guerres: la scission du Destour de mars 1934," *Les Mouvements Politiques et Sociales Dans La Tunisie Des Années Trente* (Tunis: CNUDST, 1987), 51–78.

22. 'Arousiyya Triki, *al-Haraka al-yusifiyya fi tunis, 1955–1956* (Sfax, Tunisia: Maktabat 'Ala al-Din, 2011).

23. Max Ajl, "Farmers, Fellaga, and Frenchmen" (PhD diss., Cornell University, 2019), 56–210.

24. Mahmoud Abdel-Fadil, *Development, Income Distribution and Social Change in Rural Egypt (1952–1970)* (Cambridge: Cambridge University Press, 1976); Ellen Kay Trimberger, *Revolution from Above: Military Bureaucrats and Development in Japan, Turkey, Egypt, and Peru* (New Brunswick, NJ: Transaction, 1978), 41–43.

25. Anouar Abdel-Malek, *Egypt: Military Society; the Army Regime, the Left, and Social Change under Nasser* (New York: Random House, 1986); Robert Tignor, *Capitalism and Nationalism at the End of Empire: State and Business in Decolonizing Egypt, Nigeria, and Kenya, 1945–1963* (Princeton, NJ: Princeton University Press, 1998).

26. Mervat Hatem, "Economic and Political Liberation in Egypt and the Demise of State Feminism," *International Journal of Middle East Studies* 24, no. 2 (May 1992): 231–51.

27. Laura Bier, "The Family Is a Factory: Gender, Citizenship, and the Regulation of Reproduction in Post-War Egypt," *Feminist Studies* 36, no. 2 (2010): 404–32.

28. Joel Beinin, "The Communist Movement and Nationalist Political Discourse in Nasirist Egypt," *Middle East Journal* 41, no. 4 (1987): 568–84.

29. Timothy Mitchell, *Rule of Experts: Egypt, Techno-Politics, Modernity* (Berkeley: University of California Press, 2002), 153–78.

30. Max Ajl, "The Political Economy of Thermidor in Syria: National and International Dimensions," in *Syria: From National Independence to Proxy War*, ed. Linda Matar and Ali Kadri (Cham, Switzerland: Springer, 2019), 209–45.

31. Bassam Haddad, *Business Networks: The Political Economy of Authoritarian Resilience* (Stanford CA: Stanford University Press, 2012), 36–60.

32. Habib Belaid, "La crise de l'autonomie syndicale au Maghreb, 1956–1965: de l'alliance avec les partis nationaux au contrôle par les Etats indépendants" (PhD diss., Université de Paris 1, 1982), 222–28, on mines, 137, 258–365, 413–14.

33. Max Ajl, "Farmers, Fellaga, and Frenchmen" (PhD diss., Cornell University, 2019), 246–85.

34. Lars Rudebeck, "Developmental Pressure and Political Limits: A Tunisian Example," *Journal of Modern African Studies* 8, no. 2 (1970): 173–98; Fadhila Amrani, "La réforme agraire" (PhD diss., FDSE, 1979).

35. Amrani, "La réforme agraire;" Khalil Zamiti, "Culture, idéologie de la modernité et obstacles au développement en Tunisie" (PhD diss., Paris V, 1973).

36. Eva Rana Bellin, *Stalled Democracy: Capital, Labor, and the Paradox of State-Sponsored Development* (Ithaca, NY: Cornell University Press, 2002).

37. Rida al-Zuwari, *al-Sira' al-tabaqi fi tunis, 1956–1980* (Sfax, Tunisia: Dār Ṣāmid lil-Nashir, 2009).

38. Jeremy Sharp, "Egypt: Background and U.S. Relations," (Washington, DC: Congressional Research Service, March 2019), 26–27, https://fas.org/sgp/crs/mideast/RL33003.pdf.

39. Raymond Hinnebusch, *Egyptian Politics under Sadat: The Post-Populist Development of an Authoritarian-Modernizing State* (Cambridge: Cambridge University Press, 1985); Samia Sa'id Imam, *Man yamluk misr? dirasa tahliliyya lil-usual al-ijtima'iyya li-nukhbat al-infitah al-iqtisadi fi al-mujtama' al-misri, 1974–1980* (Cairo: Dar al-Mustaqbal al-'Arabi, 1986).

40. Ibrahim al-'Isawi, *Fi islah ma afsadahu al-infitah* (Cairo: Kitab al-Ahali, 1984).

41. Haddad, *Business Networks*, 32 and 175, and "The Political Economy of Development," 131–35 in Hinnebusch, *Syria: Revolution from Above*.

42. Haddad, *Business Networks*, 32 and 175, and "The Political Economy of Development," 131–35 in Hinnebusch, *Syria: Revolution from Above*.

43. Volker Perthes, *The Political Economy of Syria Under Asad* (London: I. B. Tauris, 1995).

44. Burleigh Hendrickson, "Imperial Fragments and Transnational Activism: 1968 (s) in Tunisia, France, and Senegal" (PhD diss., Northeastern University, 2013); Ajl, "Farmers, Fellaga, and Frenchmen," 408–24.

45. Ridha Gouia, "Régime d'accumulation et modes de dépendance: le cas de la Tunisie" (PhD diss., University of Tunis, El Manar, 1988).

46. Mahmoud Ben Romdhane, "L'Accumulation du capital et les classes sociales en Tunisie depuis l'indépendance" (PhD diss., University of Tunis, Tunis, 1981).

47. Ray Bush, ed., *Counter Revolution in Egypt's Countryside* (London: Zed, 2002); Reem Saad, "State, Landlord, Parliament and Peasant: The Story of the 1992 Tenancy Law in Egypt," in *Agriculture in Egypt: From Pharaonic to Modern Times*, ed. Alan K. Bowman and Eugene Rogan (Oxford: Oxford University Press, 1999); reports of the Land Center of Human Rights, 2000–2008, Cairo, www.lchr-eg.org/.

48. Samer Soliman, *The Autumn of Dictatorship Fiscal Crisis and Political Change in Egypt under Mubarak* (Stanford, CA: Stanford University Press, 2011).

49. Zeinab Abul-Magd, "The Brotherhood's Businessmen," *Egypt Independent*, February 13, 2012; Avi Asher-Schapiro, "The GOP Brotherhood of Egypt," *Salon*, January 25, 2012.

50. Zeinab Abul-Magd, *Militarizing the Nation: Army Business and Revolution in Egypt* (New York: Columbia University Press, 2017).

51. Joel Beinin, *Workers and Thieves: Labor Movements and Popular Uprisings in Tunisia and Egypt* (Stanford, CA: Stanford University Press, 2016).

52. Eberhard Kienle, ed., *Contemporary Syria: Liberalization between Cold War and Cold Peace* (London: British Academic, 1994).

53. Hinnebusch, *Authoritarian Power and State Formation in Ba'thist Syria.*

54. Despite the legal form of "private" ownership, often these social carriers of private property are beholden to the regime. But even loyal private business partners of state officials can brandish their economic power while declaring allegiance. See Haddad, *Business Networks*, 63–67.

55. For an elaborate treatment, see John Waterbury, "Twilight of the State Bourgeoisie," *International Journal of Middle East Studies* 23, no. 1 (1991): 1–17; Bassam Haddad, "Syria's State Bourgeoisie: An Organic Backbone for the Regime," *Middle East Critique* 21, no. 3 (2012): 231–57.

56. Bassam Haddad, "The Political Economy of Syria: Realities and Challenges," *Middle East Policy* 18, no. 2 (2011): 46–61.

57. Sami Zemni, "The Tunisian Revolution: Neoliberalism, Urban Contentious Politics and the Right to the City," *International Journal of Urban and Regional Research* 41, no. 1 (January 2017): 70–83.

58. Karen Pfeifer, "Neoliberal Transformation and the Uprisings in Tunisia and Egypt," in *Political and Socio-Economic Change in the Middle East and North Africa*, ed. Roksana Bahramitash and Hadi Salehi Esfahani (New York: Palgrave Macmillan, 2016), 21–73.

59. Leila Baghdadi, Sonia Ben Kheder, and Hassen Arouri, "In Search of A New Development Model for Tunisia: Assessing the Performance of the Offshore Regime,"

Working Papers 1118, Economic Research Forum, 2017, https://ideas.repec.org/p/erg/wpaper/1118.html; Loes Debuysere, "Between Feminism and Unionism: The Struggle for Socio-Economic Dignity of Working-Class Women in Pre-and Post-Uprising Tunisia," *Review of African Political Economy* (2018): 1–19.

60. Benzina Naceur, "Changement technologique et développement agricole" (These de 3ème Cycle, Aix-Marseille II, 1985); Jean Jacques Perennes, *L'eau et les hommes au Maghreb: Contribution a une politique de l'eau en Mediterranee* (Paris: Karthala, 1993).

61. Habib Ayeb, "Social and Political Geography of the Tunisian Revolution: The Alfa Grass Revolution," *Review of African Political Economy* 38, no. 129 (2011): 467–79.

62. Mathilde Fautras, "Injustices foncières, contestations et mobilisations collectives dans les espaces ruraux de Sidi Bouzid (Tunisie) : aux racines de la 'révolution,'" *Justice Spatiale*, no. 7 (January 2015), http://www.jssj.org/article/injustices-foncieres-contestations-et-mobilisations-collectives-dans-les-espaces-ruraux-de-sidi-bouzid-tunisie-aux-racines-de-la-revolution/.

63. Beinin, *Workers and Thieves*, 85–92.

64. Habib Ayeb, "Food Issues and Revolution: The Process of Dispossession, Class Solidarity, and Popular Uprising: The Case of Sidi Bouzid in Tunisia," in "The Food Question in the Middle East," ed. Malak Rouchdy and Iman Hamdy, special issue, *Cairo Papers in Social Sciences* 34, no. 4 (2017): 86–110; Linda Matar, *The Political Economy of Investment in Syria* (London: Palgrave Macmillan UK, 2016); Beinin, *Workers and Thieves*, 97–134.

65. Abul-Magd, *Militarizing the Nation*, 228–41.

66. Dietrich Rueschemeyer, Evelyn Huber Stephens, and John D. Stephens, *Capitalist Development and Democracy* (Chicago: University of Chicago Press, 1992).

67. Corinna Mullin and Brahim Rouabah, "Decolonizing Tunisia's Border Violence: Moving Beyond Imperial Structures and Imaginaries," *Viewpoint Magazine*, February 1, 2018, https://www.viewpointmag.com/2018/02/01/decolonizing-tunisias-border-violence-moving-beyond-imperial-structures-imaginaries/.

68. Jihen Chandoul, "The IMF Has Choked Tunisia. No Wonder the People Are Protesting," *The Guardian*, January 17, 2018, http://www.theguardian.com/commentisfree/2018/jan/17/imf-tunisia-people-rioting-2011-economic-reforms; Jihen Chandoul, "La propriété des terres dans le nouveau code d'investissement: vers une recolonisation agricole?" *Observatoire Tunisien de l'Economie*, May 9, 2014, http://economie-tunisie.org/fr/observatoire/analysiseconomics/recolonisation-agricole-code-d%E2%80%99investissement.

69. Max Ajl, "Development by Popular Protection and Tunisia: The Case of Tataouine," *Globalizations* 16, no. 7 (2019): 1215–31.

CHAPTER 3

1. Pedro van Meurs, "Iraq 5th Bid Round: Summary and Preview," June 1, 2018, https://vanmeursenergy.com/documents/Iraq-Fifth-Bid-Round-Summary.pdf. Average production costs across all fields in the three largest MENA producers—Iran, Iraq, and Saudi Arabia—are estimated at around US$10 per barrel. See http://graphics.wsj.com/oil-barrel-breakdown/.

2. Gregory Nowell, *Mercantile States and the World Oil Cartel, 1900–1939* (Ithaca, NY: Cornell University Press, 1994); Stephen Longrigg, *Oil in the Middle East: Its Discovery and Development*, 3rd ed. (London: Oxford University Press, 1968); Daniel Yergin, *The Prize: The Epic Quest for Oil, Money, and Power* (New York: Simon & Schuster, 1991).

3. John Blair, *The Control of Oil* (New York: Pantheon, 1976), 81–85; Nowell, *Mercantile States*, 270–75.

4. Robert Vitalis, *America's Kingdom: Mythmaking on the Saudi Oil Frontier*, 2nd ed. (London: Verso, 2009).

5. Christopher F. Jones, *Routes of Power: Energy and Modern America* (Cambridge, MA: Harvard University Press, 2014); Matthew Huber, *Lifeblood: Oil, Freedom, and the Forces of Capital* (Minneapolis: University of Minnesota Press, 2013).

6. Calculated from BP Statistical Review of World Energy, 1st ed., 1951, and 67th ed., 2018, https://www.bp.com/en/global/corporate/energy-economics/statistical-review-of-world-energy.html.

7. Huber, *Lifeblood*.

8. Geoffrey Supran and Naomi Oreskes, "Assessing ExxonMobil's Climate Change Communications (1977–2014)," *Environmental Research Letters* 12, no. 8 (2017).

9. Three other firms are sometimes counted as "supermajors" alongside the big four—Total, Conoco-Philips, and Eni. Today the large state-owned firms—those of Saudi Arabia, Kuwait, and Iran, alongside two Chinese firms—and the privatized Russian producer Lukoil rival or exceed the size of the US and European multinationals.

10. Timothy Mitchell, *Carbon Democracy: Political Power in the Age of Oil* (London: Verso, 2012).

11. For a detailed studies of the Iranian oil struggle, which shaped the oil politics of the rest of the region, see Katayoun Shafiee, *Machineries of Oil: An Infrastruc-*

tural History of BP in Iran (Cambridge, MA: MIT Press, 2018); Mark Gasiorowksi, ed., *Mohammad Mosaddeq and the 1953 Coup in Iran* (Syracuse, NY: Syracuse University Press, 2004); and Ervand Abrahamian, *The Coup: 1953, the CIA, and the Roots of Modern U.S.-Iranian Relations* (New York: New Press, 2013).

12. Brandon Wolfe-Hunnicutt, "Embracing Regime Change in Iraq: American Foreign Policy and the 1963 Coup d'état in Baghdad," *Diplomatic History*,39, no 1 (2015): 98–125.

13. Samir Saul, "Masterly Inactivity as Brinksmanship: The Iraq Petroleum Company's Road to Nationalization," *International History Review* 29 (2007): 746–92; Christopher Dietrich, "'Arab Oil Belongs to the Arabs': Raw Material Sovereignty, Cold War Boundaries, and the Nationalisation of the Iraq Petroleum Company, 1967–1973," *Diplomacy and Statecraft* 22, no 3 (2011): 450–79.

14. Hossein Mahdavy, "The Pattern and Problems of Economic Development in Rentier States: The Case of Iran," in *Studies in the Economic History of the Middle East*, ed. M. A. Cook (Oxford: Oxford University Press, 1970).

15. Adam Hanieh, *Capitalism and Class in the Gulf Arab States* (New York: Palgrave Macmillan, 2011).

16. Hazem Beblawi and Giacomo Luciani, eds., *The Rentier State* (New York: Croom Helm, 1987); Kiren Aziz Chaudhry, *The Price of Wealth: Economies and Institutions in the Middle East* (Ithaca, NY: Cornell University Press, 1997); Jill Crystal, *Oil and Politics in the Gulf: Rulers and Merchants in Kuwait and Qatar*, 2nd ed. (Cambridge: Cambridge University Press, 1995); Lisa Anderson, "The State in the Middle East and North Africa," *Comparative Politics* 20, no. 1 (October 1987): 9, which suggests that the concept of the rentier state was one of the major concepts that scholars of the Middle East had contributed to the discipline of political science.

17. Mitchell, *Carbon Democracy*.

18. Mitchell, *Carbon Democracy*, 173–99.

19. Huber, *Lifeblood*, 97–127; Abbas Alnasrawi, *Arab Nationalism, Oil, and the Political Economy of Dependency* (Westport, CT: Greenwood, 1991).

20. Peter Gowan, *The Global Gamble: Washington's Faustian Bid for World Dominance* (London: Verso, 1999); Robert Meister, "Liquidity," in Benjamin Lee and Randy Martin, eds., *Derivatives and the Wealth of Societies* (Chicago: University of Chicago Press, 2016), 143–73; Dick Bryan and Michael Rafferty, *Capitalism with Derivatives: A Political Economy of Financial Derivatives, Capital and Class* (New York: Palgrave Macmillan, 2006).

21. Andrew J. Bacevich, *America's War for the Greater Middle East: A Military History* (New York: Random House, 2016).

22. On the need for new ways to represent and imagine the place of the human in this pellicular "critical zone" see Alexandra Arènes, Bruno Latour, and Jérôme Gaillardet, "Giving Depth to the Surface: An Exercise in the Gaia-graphy of Critical Zones," *Anthropocene Review* 5, no. 2 (2018): 120–35.

23. Intergovernmental Panel on Climate Change, "Global Warming of 1.5°C: An IPCC Special Report," http://www.ipcc.ch/report/sr15/. To reach "net zero" by 2050, any remaining human-caused emissions of carbon dioxide would need to be balanced by removing CO_2 from the air, using techniques that have yet to be proven at large scale.

24. Ellen Gray, "NASA Finds Drought in Eastern Mediterranean Worst of Past 900 Years," March 1, 2016, https://www.nasa.gov/feature/goddard/2016/nasa-finds-drought-in-eastern-mediterranean-worst-of-past-900-years.

25. Save the Tigris, "Iraq Without Rivers: Disaster Becomes a Reality," March 18, 2018, http://www.savethetigris.org/iraq-without-rivers-disaster-becomes-a-reality/.

26. Jean-Daniel Stanley and Pablo L. Clemente, "Increased Land Subsidence and Sea-Level Rise are Submerging Egypt's Nile Delta Coastal Margin," *GSA Today* 27, no. 5 (May 2017): 4–11, http://www.geosociety.org/gsatoday/archive/27/5/article/GSATG312A.1.htm.

CHAPTER 4

1. James T. Quinlivan, "Coup-Proofing: Its Practice and Consequences in the Middle East," *International Security* 24, no. 2 (1999): 131–65.

2. Mehran Kamrava, "Military Professionalization and Civil-Military Relations in the Middle East," *Political Science Quarterly* 115, no. 1 (2000): 68.

3. Hisham Sharabi, "Parliamentary Government and Military Autocracy in the Middle East, *Orbis*, no. 4 (1960): 338–55.

4. P. J. Vatikiotis, *The Egyptian Army in Politics* (Bloomington: Indiana University Press, 1961), 240.

5. Joseph La Palombara, *Bureaucracy and Political Development* (Princeton, NJ: Princeton University Press, 1963), 31.

6. Lucien Pye, *Armies in the Process of Political Modernization* (Cambridge, MA: Center for International Studies, Massachusetts Institute of Technology, 1959), 16.

7. This is not unique to the global South. The US Army Corps of Engineers has built many large infrastructure projects, including the Panama Canal, commercial harbor facilities, and hydroelectric plants.

8. Elizabeth Picard, "Arab Military in Politics: From Revolutionary Plot to Authoritarian Regime," In *The Arab State,* ed. Giacomo Luciani (Berkeley: University of California Press, 1990), 181–219.

9. Lahcen Achy, "The Breakdown of the Arab Authoritarian Bargain," Carnegie Middle East Center, January 9, 2012, http://carnegie-mec.org/2012/01/09/breakdown-of-arab-authoritarian-bargain-pub-46414.

10. Having signed a peace treaty with Israel in 1979, Sadat needed to redirect the energies of an army that spent the three previous decades nominally mobilized for war. With NASPO it expanded into agriculture, food processing, electronics, facility maintenance, and mining. Transparency International, *The Officers Republic: The Egyptian Military and Abuse of Power,* 2018, https://ti-defence.org/publications/the-officers-republic/, 9.

11. Abu Ghazala formed these networks during his time as defense attaché in the US embassy. Robert Springborg, "The President and the Field Marshal: Civil-Military Relations in Egypt Today," *Middle East Report,* no. 147 (Summer 1987): 4–16.

12. Philippe Droz-Vincent, "From Political to Economic Actors: The Changing Role of Middle Eastern Armies," in *Debating Arab Authoritarianism: Dynamics and Durability in Nondemocratic Regimes,* ed. Oliver Schlumberger (Stanford, CA: Stanford University Press, 2007), 195–211.

13. Fred Lawson, "Neglected Aspects of the Security Dilemma," in *The Many Faces of National Security in the Arab World,* ed. Rex Brynen, Bahgat Korany, and Paul Noble (London: Palgrave Macmillan, 1993), 109; Timothy Hoyt, *Military Industry and Regional Defense Policy: India, Iraq, and Israel* (New York: Routledge, 2006), 124.

14. Bassam Haddad, *Business Networks in Syria: The Political Economy of Authoritarian Resilience* (Stanford, CA: Stanford University Press, 2011); Shana Marshall and Joshua Stacher, "Egypt's Generals and Transnational Capital," *Middle East Report,* no. 262 (Spring 2012): 12–18.

15. Sevket Pamuk, "Estimating Economic Growth in the Middle East Since 1820," *Journal of Economic History* 66, no. 3 (2006): 809–27.

16. Gu Guan-Fu, "Soviet Aid to the Third World: An Analysis of Its Strategy," *Soviet Studies* 35, no. 1 (1983): 71–89.

17. East Asian governments protected firms from competitive imports through trade restrictions and subsidized firms' loss-making prices so they could gain market share overseas. Dani Rodrik, "Getting Globalization Right: The East Asian Tigers," *OECD Insights,* May 3, 2012, http://oecdinsights.org/2012/05/03/getting-globalization-right-the-east-asian-tigers/.

18. "US Embassy Cables: Egyptian Military's Influence in Decline, US Told," *The Guardian*, February 3, 2011, https://www.theguardian.com/world/us-embassy-cables-documents/171176.

19. Hicham Bou Nassif, "Wedded to Mubarak: The Second Careers and Financial Rewards of Egypt's Military Elite, 1981–2011," *Middle East Journal* 67, no. 4 (Autumn 2013): 509–30.

20. Yezid Sayigh, "Above the State: The Officers' Republic in Egypt," Carnegie Endowment for International Peace, 2012, https://carnegie-mec.org/2012/08/01/above-state-officers-republic-in-egypt-pub-48972.

21. Jesse Dillon Savage and Jonathan Caverley, "When Human Capital Threatens the Capitol: Foreign Aid in the Form of Military Training and Coups," *Journal of Peace Research* 54, no. 4 (2017): 542–57.

22. Heightened internal violence in Algeria spilling over from Libya and Mali sometimes means conscripts are used as security guards for military and state-owned enterprises, such as gas installations, as opposed to regular factory or service jobs. This was also the case in the mid-1990s, when fighting between the military and the FIS was at its height.

23. Anne Marie Baylouny, *Privatizing Welfare in the Middle East: Kin Mutual Aid Associations in Jordan and Lebanon* (Bloomington: Indiana University Press, 2010), 57–58.

24. Gordon Adams, *The Politics of Defense Contracting: The Iron Triangle* (New Brunswick, NJ: Transaction, 1982), 24.

25. Marshall and Stacher, "Egypt's Generals."

26. The Egyptian military manufactures air conditioners under license from the Chinese multinational firm Hisense, and owns a 10 percent share in the Gulf-based Kharafi Group subsidiary, the Arab Company for Computer Manufacturing. Marshall and Stacher, "Egypt's Generals."

27. A 1994 US government report cites the "brokers" and "independent contractors" employed by US defense firms to fulfill secondary contract obligations in Egypt, language that sounds suspiciously like the "fixers," "agents" and "intermediaries" that have historically permeated the region's arms trade. Whereas official government channels once handled these obligations, the relationships are now between individual officers, their agents, and American defense firm executives. GAO Report, "Military Exports: Concerns over Offsets Generated with US Foreign Military Financing Program Funds," GAO/NSIAD-94-127, June 22, 1994, 19.

28. Zeinab Abul-Magd and Elke Grawert, eds., *Businessmen in Arms: How the Military and Other Armed Groups Profit in the MENA Region* (Lanham, MD: Rowman & Littlefield, 2016).

29. Aron Lund, "The Factory: A Glimpse into Syria's War Economy," Century Foundation, February 2018, https://tcf.org/content/report/factory-glimpse-syrias-war-economy/?agreed=1#easy-footnote-bottom-22.

30. According to the company, MEDSA was formed in response to increasing demand from private banks for armed security. But in fact, the Jordanian police pressured the banks to install complicated security systems and frameworks that would require armed personnel (thus creating "demand" for the creation of MEDSA). See Virginie Collombier, "Private Security . . . Not a Business Like Any Other," *Arab Reform Initiative* (September 2011), https://www.arab-reform.net/en/node/573.

31. Shana Marshall, "Jordan's Military-Industrial Complex and the Middle East's New Model Army," *Middle East Report*, no. 267 (Summer 2013): 42–45.

32. When Iraq invaded in 1991, the majority of Kuwaiti soldiers were foreigners, including many Palestinians and Jordanians, whose governments sided with Iraq. Their questionable loyalty resulted in a massive postwar purge of nearly all non-Kuwaiti Arabs, with long-lasting negative impacts on their economies.

33. Nicholas Watt, "'Sandhurst Sheikhs': Calls to Stop Training Cadets from Gulf States with Bad Rights Records," *The Guardian*, January 22, 2016, https://www.theguardian.com/uk-news/2016/jan/22/sandhurst-sheikhs-calls-to-stop-training-cadets-from-gulf-states-with-bad-rights-records.

34. Jonathan Nitzan and Shimshon Bichler, "Bringing Capital Accumulation Back In: The Weapondollar-Petrodollar Coalition—Military Contractors, Oil Companies and Middle East 'Energy Conflicts,'" *Review of International Political Economy* 2, no. 3 (Summer 1995): 446–515.

35. Ed Crooks, "Five Charts That Explain Saudi Arabia's Importance to the Global Arms Trade," *Financial Times*, October 22, 2018, https://www.ft.com/content/dd836c34-d60b-11e8-a854-33d6f82e62f8.

36. Lockheed Martin, 2018 Annual Report on US Securities and Exchange Commission Form 10-K, https://investors.lockheedmartin.com/static-files/141388f7-0aec-492e-8fb1-9884c4d91ee2, 83.

37. Keith Webster, "It's Time to Update US Defense Export Policies," *Defense News*, August 13, 2018, https://www.defensenews.com/top-100/2018/08/09/its-time-to-update-us-defense-export-policies/.

38. US International Trade Commission, "Assessment of the Effects of Barter and Countertrade Transactions on U.S. Industries: Report on Investigation No. 332-185 Under Section 332 of the Tariff Act of 1930." USITC Publication 1766 (October 1985), https://www.usitc.gov/publications/332/pub1766.pdf, 45.

39. Chris Hedges, "Serbs Said to Ship Arms to Libya in Effort to Evade U.N. Sanctions," *New York Times*, November 7, 1996, https://www.nytimes.com/1996/11/07/world/serbs-said-to-ship-arms-to-libya-in-effort-to-evade-un-sanctions.html.

40. Oleg Shchedrov, "Russia Writes Off Libya's Cold War Debt in Exchange for Contracts," *New York Times*, April 17, 2008, https://www.nytimes.com/2008/04/17/business/worldbusiness/17iht-rusbiz.4.12106999.html.

41. Spencer Ackerman, "Libyan Rebels Want to Trade Oil for Guns," *Wired*, April 1, 2011, https://www.wired.com/2011/04/libyan-rebels-want-to-trade-oil-for-guns/.

42. Frederic S. Pearson, "The Priorities of Arms Importing States Reviewed," *Arms Control* 9, no. 2 (1988): 179.

43. Chris Thompson, "Planned International Technology Transfer: The 'Economic Offset' Example in Saudi Arabia," *Digest of Middle East Studies* 3, no. 1 (1994): 8.

44. M. A. Ramady, *The Saudi Arabian Economy: Policies, Achievements, and Challenges* (New York: Springer, 2005), 284–86.

45. Ahmed Al Omran and Peggy Hollinger, "Saudi Arabia Beefs Up Plans for Domestic Defence Industry," *Financial Times*, March 15, 2018, https://www.ft.com/content/88427260-2765-11e8-b27e-cc62a39d57a0.

46. Khaled Fahmy, *All the Pasha's Men* (Cairo: American University in Cairo Press, 2002).

47. John P. Dunn, *Khedive Ismail's Army* (New York: Routledge, 2005), 68–70.

48. Mark Kagan, "Iraq's Case: The International Missile Trade and Proliferation," in *The International Missile Bazaar: The New Suppliers' Network*, ed. William C. Potter and Harlan W. Jencks (Boulder, CO: Westview, 1994), 181.

49. R. Jeffrey Smith, "Dozens of U.S. Items Used in Iraq Arms," *Washington Post*, July 22, 1992.

50. Mark Kagan, "Iraq's Case," 192.

51. Vision 2030, https://vision2030.gov.sa/en/node/226. See also Souhail Karam, "Saudi Arabia Opens Military Supply to Local Firms," *Reuters News Agency*, February 7, 2010, https://www.reuters.com/article/idUSLDE616043.

52. Florence Gaub and Zoe Stanley-Lockman, "Defense Industries in Arab States: Players and Strategies," *European Union Institute for Security Studies* (March

22, 2017), Chaillot Paper no. 141, https://www.iss.europa.eu/content/defence-industries-arab-states-players-and-strategies.

53. Tom Kington, "Algeria to Beef Up Defense with Leonardo Helicopter Deal," *DefenseNews*, August 19, 2016, https://www.defensenews.com/air/2016/08/19/algeria-to-beef-up-defense-with-leonardo-helicopter-deal/; Dalia Ghanem Yazbeck, "The Algerian Army: Cooperation, Not Intervention," *l'Istituto per gli Studi di Politica Internazionale,* December 7, 2017, https://www.ispionline.it/it/pubblicazione/algerian-army-cooperation-not-intervention-19132.

54. Plans for new Saudi defense production are to be partially financed by revenue from the IPO of Saudi Aramco. Shana Marshall, "The New Politics of Patronage: The Arms Trade and Clientelism in the Arab World," (PhD diss., University of Maryland, 2012), http://hdl.handle.net/1903/12970.

55. David Harvey explains the dynamics of the growth imperative, barriers to accumulation, and how they are overcome in "The Geography of Capitalist Accumulation: A Reconstruction of the Marxian Theory," *Antipode* 7, no. 2 (1975): 9–10.

56. John Dowdy and Elizabeth Oakes, "Defense Outlook 2017: A Global Survey of Defense-Industry Executives," McKinsey and Company, April 2015, https://www.mckinsey.com/industries/aerospace-and-defense/our-insights/defense-outlook-2017-a-global-survey-of-defense-industry-executives.

57. Kagan, "Iraq's Case," 187.

58. Kagan, "Iraq's Case," 185.

59. GAO, "Military Exports: Concerns over Offsets Generated with U.S. Foreign Military Financing Program Funds," GAO/NSIAD-94-127, June 22, 1994.

60. Metin Gurcan, "Turkish Defense Industry at Critical Juncture," *Al-Monitor,* May 25. 2018, https://www.al-monitor.com/pulse/originals/2018/05/turkey-defense-industry-at-critical-juncture.html.

61. İsmet Akça, *Military-Economic Structure in Turkey: Present Situation, Problems and Solutions* (Istanbul: TESEV, 2010).

62. "Military Exports: Concerns Over Offsets Generated with U.S. Foreign Military Financing Program Funds." *US General Accounting Office,* June 1994.

63. Jonathan Nitzan and Shimshon Bichler, *The Global Political Economy of Israel* (London: Pluto, 2002), 280.

64. For examples, see Nitzan and Bichler, *The Global Political Economy of Israel,* 281–83.

65. Michael Knights, "Future Development of GCC Air Forces; Part 2," Air Combat Information Group (ACIG), December 18, 2003.

66. Ivan Gale, "UAE Wants Its Fighters Its Own Way." *The National* (UAE), September 29, 2009; David Fulghum and John Morrocco, "UAE's F-16s Will Be Envy of USAF Pilots," *Aviation Week & Space Technology*, March 13, 2000, 24–25.

67. Gillian Rich, "Defense Stocks Rally as U.S. Exit from Iran Deal Adds to Mideast Tension," *Investor's Business Daily*, May 9, 2018, https://www.investors.com/news/defense-stocks-rally-iran-nuclear-deal-middle-east-conflict.

68. General Electric supports eleven, Boeing and Lockheed Martin each support six, Northrop Grumman four, and Raytheon three. They are often among the top-tier contributors. See Rick Carp, "Who Pays for Think Tanks?" *FAIR*, July 2013, https://fair.org/extra/who-pays-for-think-tanks.

69. Bahrain Watch, "Your Western Think Tank Funding Cheatsheet for the Qatar-GCC Conflict," June 12, 2017, https://bahrainwatch.org/blog/2017/06/12/qatar-gcc-think-tank-cheatsheet.

70. Jeremy Herb, "Lawmakers Press Trump to Approve Drone Sales to Jordan, UAE," *CNN*, April 17, 2017, https://www.cnn.com/2017/04/17/politics/congress-sales-drones-jordan-uae-trump/index.html.

71. The Gulf states have gone one step further. Since 2015, the UAE, Saudi Arabia, and Qatar have all founded their own well-funded and fully staffed think tanks in downtown DC. These are, respectively, the Arab Gulf States Institute in Washington/AGSIW, the Arabia Foundation, and the Gulf International Forum.

72. Anthony H. Cordesman and Abdullah Toukan, "National Security Economics of the Middle East: Comparative Spending, Burden Sharing, and Modernization," Center for Strategic and International Studies, March 23, 2017), https://www.csis.org/analysis/national-security-economics-middle-east-comparative-spending-burden-sharing, 15.

73. World Bank, World Development Indicators, https://data.worldbank.org/indicator/?tab=all.

74. The six largest investors are the United Kingdom, United States, Belgium, France, the UAE, and Saudi Arabia.

75. Shana Marshall, "The Egyptian Armed Forces and the Re-Making of an Economic Empire," (Washington DC: Carnegie Endowment for International Peace, 2015), https://carnegieendowment.org/files/egyptian_armed_forces.pdf.

76. Clarion Events, "EDEX 2018: Egypt Locally Produced 1,200 M1A1 Abrams Main Battle Tanks," December 5, 2018, https://www.egyptdefenceexpo.com/news/edex-2018-egypt-locally-produced-1200-m1a1-abrams-main-battle-tanks.

CHAPTER 5

1. Nelida Fuccaro, "Rethinking the History of Port Cities in the Gulf," in *The Persian Gulf in Modern Times: People, Ports, and History*, ed. L. Porter (New York: Palgrave-Macmillan, 2014).

2. Ahmad Kanna, *Dubai: The City as Corporation* (Minneapolis: University of Minnesota Press, 2011); Pascal Menoret, *Joyriding in Riyadh: Oil, Urbanism, and Road Revolt in Saudi Arabia* (Cambridge: Cambridge University Press, 2014); Farah Al-Nakib, *Kuwait Transformed: A History of Oil and Urban Life* (Stanford, CA: Stanford University Press, 2016); Johan Mathew, *Margins of the Market Trafficking and Capitalism across the Arabian Sea* (Berkeley: University of California Press, 2016).

3. Rosie Bsheer "W(h)ither Arabian Peninsula Studies?" in *Handbook of Contemporary Middle East and North African History*, ed. Jens Hansen and Amal Ghazal (Oxford: Oxford University Press, 2017).

4. Hossein Mahdavy, "The Patterns and Problems of Economic Development in Rentier States: The Case of Iran," in *Studies in the Economic History of the Middle East*, ed. M. Cook. (London: Oxford University Press, 1970), 429.

5. Lisa Anderson, "The State in the Middle East and North Africa," *Comparative Politics* 20, no. 1 (October 1987): 9.

6. Joel Migdal, *Strong Societies and Weak States: State-Society Relations and State Capabilities in the Third World* (Princeton, NJ: Princeton University Press, 1988), 4.

7. Mahdavy, "Patterns and Problems," 428.

8. Mahdavy, "Patterns and Problems," 436.

9. Hazem Beblawi and Giacomo Luciani, eds., *The Rentier State: Nation, State and the Integration of the Arab World* (London: Croom Helm, 1987); Theda Skocpol, "Rentier State and Shi'a Islam in the Iranian Revolution," *Theory and Society* 11, no. 3 (1982): 46–82; M. Ross, "Does Oil Hinder Democracy?" *World Politics* 53, no. 3 (April 2001): 325–61.

10. M. Goswami, "Rethinking the Modular Nation Form: Toward a Sociohistorical Conception of Nationalism," *Comparative Studies in Society and History* 44, no. 4 (2002):794.

11. See Robert Vitalis, *America's Kingdom: Mythmaking on the Saudi Oil Frontier* (Stanford, CA: Stanford University Press, 2007); Timothy Mitchell, *Carbon Democracy: Political Power in the Age of Oil* (London: Verso, 2011); Adam Hanieh, *Money, Markets, and Monarchies: The Gulf Cooperation Council and the Political Economy of the Contemporary Middle East* (Cambridge: Cambridge University Press, 2018); David Spiro, *The*

Hidden Hand of American Hegemony: Petrodollar Recycling and International Markets (Ithaca, NY: Cornell University Press, 1999).

12. Karl Marx, *Capital* (London: Penguin, 1990), vol. 1, chapter 1, section 4, "The Fetishism of Commodities and its Secret,"163–77.

13. I borrow this insight from David McNally, "Staples Theory as Commodity Fetishism: Marx, Innis and Canadian Political Economy," *Studies in Political Economy* 6 (Autumn 1981): 35–64.

14. Mitchell, *Carbon Democracy*; Hanieh, *Money, Markets, and Monarchies.*

15. Max Weber, *Economy and Society: An Outline of Interpretive Sociology* (Berkeley: University of California Press, 1978), 54–55.

16. Richard Norton, *Civil Society in the Middle East*, vol. 2 (Brill: Leiden, 2001), x.

17. Hugo Radice, "The Developmental State under Global Neoliberalism," *Third World Quarterly* 29, no. 6 (2008): 1157.

18. Derek Sayer, *The Violence of Abstraction: The Analytic Foundations of Historical Materialism* (Oxford: Basil Blackwell, 1987), 96–111.

19. Neil Davidson, "The Necessity of Multiple Nation-States for Capital," *Rethinking Marxism: A Journal of Economics, Culture & Society* 24, no. 1 (2012): 26–46.

20. Bertell Ollman, *Dance of the Dialectic: Steps in Marx's Method* (Urbana, IL: University of Illinois Press, 2003), 202.

21. Toby Jones, *Desert Kingdom: How Oil and Water Forged Modern Saudi Arabia* (Cambridge, MA: Harvard University Press, 2010).

22. Laleh Khalili, *Sinews of War and Trade: Shipping and Capitalism in the Arabian Peninsula* (London: Verso, 2020).

23. Yasser Elsheshtawy, *The Evolving Arab City: Tradition, Modernity and Urban Development* (Routledge: New York, 2008); Kanna, *Dubai.*

24. Omar Shehabi and S. Suroor, "Unpacking 'Accumulation by Dispossession,' 'Fictitious Commodification,' and 'Fictitious Capital Formation': Tracing the Dynamics of Bahrain's Land Reclamation," *Antipode* 4, no. 1 (2015): 835–56.

25. Calculated by author from an analysis of Qatar Stock Exchange data.

26. Jill Crystal, *Oil and Politics in the Gulf: Rulers and Merchants in Kuwait and Qatar* (Glasgow: Cambridge University Press, 1995).

27. Hanieh, *Money, Markets, and Monarchies.*

28. Hanieh, *Money, Markets, and Monarchies*, 157.

29. Hanieh, *Money, Markets, and Monarchies*, 187.

30. Hanieh, *Money, Markets, and Monarchies*, 136–38.

31. Migdal, *Strong Societies and Weak States*, 5.

32. Gulf Labour Markets and Migration, "Percentage of Nationals and Non-nationals in Employed Population in GCC Countries," http://gulfmigration.eu/percentage-of-nationals-and-non-nationals-in-employed-population-in-gcc-countries-national-statistics-latest-year-or-period-available/.

33. World Bank Group, "Migration and Remittances: Recent Developments and Outlook," Migration and Development Brief, no. 31, April (Washington DC: World Bank, 2017), 4.

34. Mohammed Dito, "Kafala: Foundations of Migrant Exclusion in GCC Labour Markets," in *Transit States: Labour, Migration and Citizenship in the Gulf*, ed. Abdulhadi Khalaf, Omar AlShehabi, and Adam Hanieh (London: Pluto, 2014).

35. A. N. Longva, *Walls Built on Sand: Migration, Exclusion and Society in Kuwait* (Boulder, CO: Westview, 1997), 100.

36. Dito, "Kafala."

37. Abdulhadi Khalaf, "The Politics of Migration," in *Transit States: Labour, Migration and Citizenship in the Gulf*, ed. Abdulhadi Khalaf, Omar AlShehabi, and Adam Hanieh (London: Pluto, 2014).

38. In Bahrain and Kuwait, migrant workers are permitted to join established unions (but not to form their own). In practice, however, there is a great deal of reluctance from these unions to recruit or ally with migrant workers.

39. Michelle Buckley, "Construction Work, 'Bachelor' Builders and the Intersectional Politics of Urbanisation in Dubai," in *Transit States: Labour, Migration and Citizenship in the Gulf*, ed. Abdulhadi Khalaf, Omar AlShehabi, and Adam Hanieh (London: Pluto, 2014).

40. Akhbar24, "al-dakhli: tarhil 1.2 milyun makhalif wa-mukhalafa" [Interior Ministry: Deportation of 1.2 Million Violators], Akhbar24, July 30, 2015, https://akhbaar24.argaam.com/article/detail/227266/.

41. R. Anderson, "Illegal Workers in Saudi Face Prison, SAR50,000 Fine as Crackdown Begins," *GulfNews*, July 30, 2017, http://gulfbusiness.com/illegal-workers-saudi-face-prison-sar50000-fine-crackdown-begins/.

42. Vitalis, *America's Kingdom*.

43. Abdulhadi Khalaf, "Labor Movements in Bahrain," *MERIP Reports* 132 (1985): 24–29.

44. These figures record the percentage of the labor force aged 15–24 out of work but actively seeking a job. World Development Indicators Database, databank .worldbank.org.

45. See Hanieh, *Money, Markets, and Monarchies*, ch. 7.

CHAPTER 6

1. In questioning the analytical utility of a category like "Egyptian capitalism," we suggest that the same doubts might easily extend to other national typologies. By contrast, see Sven Beckert and Christine Desan, *American Capitalism: New Histories* (New York: Columbia University Press, 2018).

2. Nancy Fraser argues that the exploitation of wage labor in the "hidden abode" of commodity production depends fundamentally on diverse forms of appropriation that lie in "realms that are more hidden still." See Nancy Fraser, "Behind Marx's Hidden Abode: For an Expanded Conception of Capitalism," *New Left Review*, no. 86 (2014): 57. See also Nancy Fraser and Rahel Jaeggi, *Capitalism: A Conversation in Critical Theory* (Cambridge: Polity, 2018); David Harvey, *The New Imperialism* (Oxford: Oxford University Press, 2003); Rosa Luxemburg, *The Accumulation of Capital*, trans. Agnes Schwarzschild (New York: Routledge, 2003); Jason Moore, *Capitalism in the Web of Life: Ecology and the Accumulation of Capital* (New York: Verso, 2015).

3. Alan Mikhail, *Nature and Empire in Ottoman Egypt: An Environmental History* (Cambridge: Cambridge University Press, 2011); Zoe Griffith, "Egyptian Ports in the Ottoman Mediterranean, 1760–1820" (PhD diss., Brown University, 2017).

4. For a rich tableau of this diversity of domestic production, drawn from a creative reading of 'Ali Pasha Mubarak's encyclopedic *al-Khitat al-tawfiqiyya*, see Jacques Berque, *Egypt: Imperialism and Revolution*, trans. Jean Stewart (New York: Praeger, 1972), chapter 1.

5. Griffith, "Egyptian Ports," 54, 191–210.

6. Peter Gran, *Islamic Roots of Capitalism: Egypt, 1760–1840* (Austin: University of Texas Press, 1978), 8–11.

7. Khaled Fahmy, *All the Pasha's Men: Mehmed Ali, His Army, and the Making of Modern Egypt* (Cairo: American University Press, 2002), 246.

8. On Barak, *On Time: Technology and Temporality in Modern Egypt* (Berkeley: University of California Press, 2013), chapter 1.

9. Edward Roger John Owen, *Cotton and the Egyptian Economy, 1820–1914: A Study in Trade and Development* (Oxford: Clarendon, 1969), 28–30.

10. Helen Rivlin, *The Agricultural Policy of Muhammad 'Ali in Egypt* (Cambridge, MA: Harvard University Press, 1961).

11. Sven Beckert, *Empire of Cotton: A Global History* (New York: Alfred A. Knopf, 2014), 132; Owen, *Cotton and the Egyptian Economy*, 28–44.

12. On the "cotton frontier" in the American South, see Walter Johnson, *River of Dark Dreams: Slavery and Empire in the Cotton Kingdom* (Cambridge, MA: Belknap, 2013); Philip McMichael, "Slavery in Capitalism: The Rise and Demise of the U.S. Ante-Bellum Cotton Culture," *Theory and Society* 20, no. 3 (1991).

13. Mikhail, *Nature and Empire*, 242–90.

14. Nathan Brown, "Who Abolished Corvée Labour in Egypt and Why?," *Past and Present*, no. 144 (1994).

15. Owen, *Cotton and the Egyptian Economy*, 58; Alan Richards, *Egypt's Agricultural Development, 1800–1980* (Boulder, CO: Westview, 1982), 24–25.

16. Ra'uf 'Abbas, *al-Nizam al-ijtima'i fi misr fi zill al-milkiyya al-zira'iyya al-kabira, 1837–1914* (Cairo: Dar al-Fikr al-Hadith 1973); Raouf Abbas and Assem El-Dessouky, *The Large Landowning Class and the Peasantry in Egypt, 1837–1952*, trans. Amer Mohsen and Mona Zikri (Syracuse, NY: Syracuse University Press, 2012); 'Ali Barakat, *Tatawwur al-milkiyah al-zira'iyah fi misr wa-atharuhu 'ala al-haraka al-siyasiyya, 1813–1914* (Cairo: Dār al-Thaqafah al-Jadidah, 1977); 'Asim Dasuqi, *Kibar mullak al-aradi al-zira'iyya wa-dawruhum fi al-mujtama' al-misri, 1914–1952* (Cairo: Dar al-Shuruq, 2007).

17. Arthur Edwin Crouchley, *Investment of Foreign Capital in Egyptian Companies and Public Debt* (New York: Arno, 1977), 12; R. Hanbury Brown, *History of the Barrage at the Head of the Delta of Egypt* (Cairo: F. Diemer, 1896); Mikhail, *Nature and Empire*, chapter 6.

18. David Harvey, *Marx, Capital, and the Madness of Economic Reason* (London: Profile, 2017), chapter 4; Darcy Grimaldo Grigsby, *Colossal: Engineering Modernity—Suez Canal, Statue of Liberty, Eiffel Tower, and Panama Canal* (Pittsburgh, PA: Periscope, 2012).

19. David Harvey, *Paris, Capital of Modernity* (London: Routledge, 2003); David Harvey, *The Limits to Capital* (New York: Verso, 2006); David Harvey, *Rebel Cities: From the Right to the City to the Urban Revolution* (London: Verso, 2012).

20. Duncan Bell, *Reordering the World: Essays on Liberalism and Empire* (Princeton, NJ: Princeton University Press, 2016), 211–36; John Stuart Mill, *Principles of Political Economy with Some of Their Applications to Social Philosophy*, repr., 5th ed., vol. II (New York: D. Appleton and Company, 1882); Bernard Semmel, *The Rise of Free Trade*

Imperialism: Classical Political Economy, the Empire of Free Trade, and Imperialism (Cambridge: Cambridge University Press, 1970).

21. Ravi Ahuja, *Pathways of Empire: Circulation, "Public Works" and Social Space in Colonial Orissa (c. 1780–1914)* (Hyderabad: Orient BlackSwan, 2009); Manu Goswami, *Producing India: From Colonial Economy to National Space* (Chicago: University of Chicago Press, 2004).

22. Crouchley, *Investment of Foreign Capital*, 14–15; Zachary Karabell, *Parting the Desert: The Creation of the Suez Canal* (New York: Vintage, 2003), chapter 11; Luxemburg, *Accumulation of Capital*.

23. Jennifer Derr, *The Lived Nile: Environment, Disease, and Material Colonial Economy in Egypt* (Stanford, CA: Stanford University Press, 2019); Owen, *Cotton and the Egyptian Economy*; Ahmad Shokr, "Beyond the Fields: Cotton and the End of Empire in Egypt, 1919–1956" (PhD diss., New York University, 2016); Ehud Toledano, "Social and Economic Change in the 'Long Nineteenth Century,'" in *The Cambridge History of Egypt*, ed. M. W. Daly (Cambridge: Cambridge University Press, 1998), 261.

24. Sven Beckert, "Emancipation and Empire: Reconstructing the Worldwide Web of Cotton Production in the Age of the American Civil War," *American Historical Review* 109, no. 5 (2004).

25. Zeinab Abul-Magd, *Imagined Empires: A History of Revolt in Egypt* (Berkeley: University of California Press, 2013); Derr, *Lived Nile*; Timothy Mitchell, *Rule of Experts: Egypt, Techno-Politics, Modernity* (Berkeley: University of California Press, 2002); Martina E. Rieker, "The Sa'id and the City: Subaltern Spaces in the Making of Modern Egyptian History" (PhD diss., Temple University, 1997). As Rosa Luxemburg observed roughly a century ago, "The forced labour of the fellaheen was to compete with the Southern States of the Union where slavery had been abolished." Luxemburg, *Accumulation of Capital*, 412.

26. Mitchell, *Rule of Experts*, 62–66. For a history of the laws that sanctioned the appropriation of abandoned land from 1847 onwards, see Kenneth M. Cuno, *The Pasha's Peasants: Land, Society, and Economy in Lower Egypt, 1740–1858* (New York: Cambridge University Press, 1992), 189–97.

27. David S. Landes, *Bankers and Pashas: International Finance and Economic Imperialism in Egypt* (Cambridge, MA: Harvard University Press, 1958).

28. Edwin W. Kemmerer, "The Fiscal System of Egypt," *Publications of the American Economic Association* 1, no. 3 (1900).

29. Juan Cole, *Colonialism and Revolution in the Middle East: Social and Cultural Origins of Egypt's 'Urabi Movement* (Princeton, NJ: Princeton University Press, 1993); Alexander Schölch, *Egypt for the Egyptians! The Socio-political Crisis in Egypt, 1878–1882* (London: Ithaca, 1981).

30. A. G. Hopkins, "The Victorians and Africa: A Reconsideration of the Occupation of Egypt, 1882," *Journal of African History* 27, no. 2 (1986); Alexander Schölch, "The 'Men on the Spot' and the English Occupation of Egypt in 1882," *Historical Journal* 19, no. 3 (1976).

31. Kemmerer, "Fiscal System of Egypt"; Edward Roger John Owen, *The Middle East in the World Economy, 1800–1914* (London: I. B. Tauris, 2002), 128–35.

32. The National Archives (UK), FO 78/3565: Earl of Dufferin to Earl of Granville, "General Report by the Earl of Dufferin Respecting Reorganization in Egypt," (February 6, 1883); Aaron Jakes, "The Scales of Public Utility: Agricultural Roads and State Space in the Era of the British Occupation," in *The Long 1890s in Egypt: Colonial Quiescence, Subterranean Resistance*, ed. Marilyn Booth and Anthony Gorman (Edinburgh: Edinburgh University Press, 2014).

33. This association between cotton and peasant smallholding was common across much of the "empire of cotton" in the late nineteenth century. See also Andrew Zimmerman, *Alabama in Africa: Booker T. Washington, the German Empire, and the Globalization of the New South* (Princeton, NJ: Princeton University Press, 2010).

34. Aaron Jakes, *Egypt's Occupation: Colonial Economism and the Crises of Capitalism* (Stanford, CA: Stanford University Press, 2020), chapter 1.

35. Robert L. Tignor, *Modernization and British Colonial Rule in Egypt, 1882–1914* (Princeton, NJ: Princeton University Press, 1966), 367.

36. Aaron Jakes, "Boom, Bugs, Bust: Egypt's Ecology of Interest, 1882–1914," *Antipode* 49, no. 4 (2017); Jakes, *Egypt's Occupation*, chapter 3.

37. Giovanni Arrighi, *The Long Twentieth Century: Money, Power, and the Origins of Our Times* (New York: Verso, 1994), 171–72; P. J. Cain and A. G. Hopkins, *British Imperialism, 1688–2000*, 2nd ed. (New York: Longman, 2002), 309; Eric Hobsbawm, *The Age of Empire, 1875–1914* (New York: Vintage, 1989), 52.

38. Edwin W. Kemmerer, *Report on the Agricultural Bank of Egypt to the Secretary of War and to the Philippine Commission* (Washington, DC: Government Printing Office, 1906); Emily Rosenberg, *Financial Missionaries to the Word: The Politics and Culture of Dollar Diplomacy, 1900–1930* (Durham, NC: Duke University Press, 2003).

39. Jakes, "Boom, Bugs, Bust," 1051–52.

40. Jakes, *Egypt's Occupation*, chapter 5.

41. Jakes, *Egypt's Occupation*, chapter 7.

42. Muhammad Tal'at Harb, *'Ilaj misr al-iqtisadi wa-mashru' bank al-misriyin aw bank al-umma* [1912] (Cairo: Matba'at Dar al-Kutub, 2002).

43. Jakes, *Egypt's Occupation*, chapter 8.

44. L. G. Roussin, "The Present Monetary Regime in Egypt," *L'Égypte Contemporaine* (February 1924): 1; Ministère des Finances, *Recueil des documents relatifs à la guerre publiés au "Journal Officiel" du 1er Août 1916 au 31 Juillet 1917* (Cairo: Imprimerie Nationale, 1920), 878.

45. Jakes, *Egypt's Occupation*, Conclusion; Mohammed Ali Rifaat, *The Monetary System of Egypt: An Inquiry into Its History and Present Working* (London: George Allen & Unwin, 1935).

46. V. I. Lenin, *Imperialism: The Highest Stage of Capitalism* (New York: Pathfinder, 2002); Erez Manela, *The Wilsonian Moment: Self-Determination and the International Origins of Anticolonial Nationalism* (Oxford: Oxford University Press, 2007); Pankaj Mishra, *From the Ruins of Empire: The Intellectuals Who Remade Asia* (New York: Farrar, Straus and Giroux, 2012); Joseph Schumpeter, *Imperialism and Social Classes: Two Essays by Joseph Schumpeter*, trans. Heinz Norden (New York: Meridian, 1955).

47. Commission de la Commerce et de l'Industrie, *Rapport de la Commission du Commerce et de l'Industrie* (Cairo: Imprimerie Nationale, 1918).

48. Robert L. Tignor, *State, Private Enterprise, and Economic Change in Egypt, 1918–1952* (Princeton, NJ: Princeton University Press, 1984), 55–58.

49. Nancy Reynolds, *A City Consumed: Urban Commerce, the Cairo Fire, and the Politics of Decolonization in Egypt* (Stanford, CA: Stanford University Press, 2012), chapter 3.

50. Robert Vitalis challenges Eric Davis's view that interwar business coalitions were motivated by a commitment to incubating Egyptian-owned industries. While we find Vitalis's political-economic analysis compelling, our research suggests a less cynical relationship between nationalist discourse and interwar accumulation strategies. See Eric Davis, *Challenging Colonialism: Bank Misr and Egyptian Industrialization, 1920–1941* (Princeton, NJ: Princeton University Press, 1983); Robert Vitalis, *When Capitalists Collide: Business Conflict and the End of Empire in Egypt* (Berkeley: University of California Press, 1995).

51. Jakes, *Egypt's Occupation*; Shokr, "Beyond the Fields."

52. Ibrahim Rashad, "Al-Ta'awun al-zira'i wa-atharuhu fi istiqlalina al-iqtisadi wa-ruqiyina al-ijtima'i," *al-Majalla al-zira'iyya al-misriyya* (1924): 24; Shokr, "Beyond the Fields," chapter 1.

53. Yusuf Nahhas, *al-Qutn fi khamsin 'amm* (Cairo: Dar al-Nil, 1954); Ellis Goldberg, *Trade, Reputation, and Child Labor in Twentieth-Century Egypt* (New York: Palgrave Macmillan, 2004), 77–83.

54. A greater degree of fiscal autonomy was secured after the 1937 Montreux Convention.

55. Shokr, "Beyond the Fields," 187.

56. John Waterbury, *The Egypt of Nasser and Sadat: The Political Economy of Two Regimes* (Princeton, NJ: Princeton University Press, 1983), 59–60; Hanan Hammad, *Industrial Sexuality: Gender, Urbanization, and Social Transformation in Egypt* (Austin: University of Texas Press, 2016), 6.

57. Shokr, "Beyond the Fields," chapter 1; Omnia S. El Shakry, *The Great Social Laboratory: Subjects of Knowledge in Colonial and Postcolonial Egypt* (Stanford, CA: Stanford University Press, 2007); Amy J. Johnson, *Reconstructing Rural Egypt: Ahmed Hussein and the History of Egyptian Development* (Cairo: American University in Cairo Press, 2004), chapter 3.

58. El Shakry, *Great Social Laboratory*, 115–19.

59. Bent Hansen, "Income and Consumption in Egypt, 1886/1887 to 1937," *International Journal of Middle East Studies* 10, no. 1 (1979): 29.

60. Edward Roger John Owen, "Egypt in the World Depression: Agricultural Recession and Industrial Expansion," in *The Economies of Africa and Asia in the Inter-war Depression*, ed. Ian Brown (London: Routledge, 1989), 137–51.

61. Ali al-Gritly, "The Structure of Modern Industry in Egypt," *L'Égypte Contemporaine* 38 (1947).

62. Abbas and El-Dessouky, *Large Landowning Class*, 125.

63. Edward Roger John Owen, "The Ideology of Economic Nationalism in Its Egyptian Context: 1919–1939," in *Intellectual Life in the Arab East, 1890–1939*, ed. Marwan R. Buheiry (Beirut: American University in Beirut Press, 1981), 8–9.

64. Mirrit Ghali, *al-Islah al-zira'i: al-milkiyya, al-ijar, al-'amal* (Cairo, 1945); Ahmad Sadiq Sa'ad, *Mushkilat al-fallah* (Cairo: Dar al-Qarn al-'Ishrin li'l-Nashr, 1945).

65. John Waterbury, "The 'Soft State' and the Open Door: Egypt's Experience with Economic Liberalization," *Comparative Politics* 18, no. 1 (1985).

66. Mahmoud Abdel-Fadil, *Development, Income Distribution and Social Change in Rural Egypt, 1952–1970: A Study in the Political Economy of Agrarian Transition* (Cambridge: Cambridge University Press, 1975), 82–108.

67. Samer Soliman, *The Autumn of Dictatorship: Fiscal Crisis and Political Change in Egypt under Mubarak* (Stanford, CA: Stanford University Press, 2011), 27, 48.

68. Waterbury, *Egypt of Nasser and Sadat*, 395–99.

69. Bent Hansen and Karim Nashashibi, *Foreign Trade Regimes and Economic Development: Egypt*, vol. 4, Special Conference Series on Foreign Trade Regimes and Economic Development, National Bureau of Economic Research (New York: Columbia University Press, 1975), 22, cited in Waterbury, *Egypt of Nasser and Sadat*, 395.

70. Jean-Jacques Dethier and Kathy Funk, "The Language of Food: PL 480," *Middle East Report*, no. 145 (1987); Samantha Gayathri Iyer, "The Paradox of Poverty and Plenty: Egypt, India, and the Rise of U.S. Food Aid, 1870s to 1950s" (PhD diss., University of California, Berkeley, 2014).

71. Waterbury, *Egypt of Nasser and Sadat*, 68.

72. Anwar Abdel-Malek, "The Crisis in Nasser's Egypt," *New Left Review*, no. 45 (1967): 71.

73. *Egypt, Military Society: The Army Regime, the Left and Social Change Under Nasser* (New York: Random House, 1968), 151–55; Charles Issawi, *Egypt in Revolution: An Economic Analysis* (London: Oxford University Press, 1963), 60–61.

74. Alan Richards, "Egypt's Agriculture in Trouble," *Middle East Report*, no. 84 (1980); Richards, *Egypt's Agricultural Development*, 179.

75. Abdel-Fadil, *Development, Income Distribution and Social Change*, 9–10.

76. James Toth, *Rural Labor Movements in Egypt and Their Impact on the State, 1961–1992* (Cairo: American University in Cairo Press, 1999).

77. Mahmoud Hussein, *Class Conflict in Egypt, 1945–1970* (New York: Monthly Review, 1973); John Waterbury, "Twilight of the State Bourgeoisie?," *International Journal of Middle East Studies* 23, no. 1 (1991); Ahmad Shokr, "Reflections on Two Revolutions," *Middle East Report*, no. 265 (2012).

78. Laura Bier, *Revolutionary Womanhood: Feminisms, Modernity, and the State in Nasser's Egypt* (Stanford, CA: Stanford University Press, 2011), chapter 2; Waterbury, *Egypt of Nasser and Sadat*, 234–46.

79. Dethier and Funk, "Language of Food," 24.

80. For example, Fouad Ajami, *The Arab Predicament: Arab Political Thought and Practice since 1967* (Cambridge: Cambridge University Press, 1992).

81. Eliyahu Kanovsky, "The Economic Aftermath of the Six Day War," *Middle East Journal* 22, no. 2 (1968).

82. Ray Bush, *Economic Crisis and the Politics of Reform in Egypt* (Boulder, CO: Westview, 1999), 15.

83. Bush, *Economic Crisis*, 21.

84. Iraq nationalized its petroleum industry in 1972 but was marginal to Western circuits of capital.

85. Peter Gowan, *The Global Gamble. Washington's Faustian Bid for World Dominance* (London: Verso, 1999), 19–25; Adam Hanieh, *Capitalism and Class in the Gulf Arab States* (New York: Palgrave Macmillan, 2011), 39–48; Vanessa Ogle, "Archipelago Capitalism: Tax Havens, Offshore Money, and the State, 1950s-1970s," *American Historical Review* 122, no. 5 (2017).

86. Philip McMichael, *Development and Social Change: A Global Perspective* (Thousand Oaks, CA: Pine Forge, 1996), 118.

87. Timothy Mitchell, *Carbon Democracy: Political Power in the Age of Oil* (London: Verso, 2011), 181–86.

88. "Israel Signs Protocol of New Pact on Sinai," *New York Times* (October 11, 1975).

89. Waterbury, *Egypt of Nasser and Sadat*, 197–98; Edward Roger John Owen, "Sadat's Legacy, Mubarak's Dilemma," *MERIP Reports* 117 (1983).

90. Waterbury, *Egypt of Nasser and Sadat*, 198.

91. Waterbury, *Egypt of Nasser and Sadat*, 198.

92. Jean-Jacques Dethier, "Trade, Exchange Rate, and Agricultural Pricing Policies in Egypt," in *World Bank Comparative Studies* (Washington, DC: World Bank, 1989), 191–97.

93. Marie-Christine Aulas, "Sadat's Egypt: A Balance Sheet," *MERIP Reports* 107 (1982): 10; Dethier, "Trade, Exchange Rate, and Agricultural Pricing," 196.

94. Soliman, *Autumn of Dictatorship*, 39.

95. Husayn 'Abd al-Raziq, *Misr fi 18 wa 19 yanayir* (Cairo: Dar Shuhdi, 1985), 229–31; Waterbury, *Egypt of Nasser and Sadat*.

96. Waterbury, *Egypt of Nasser and Sadat*, 213.

97. Soliman, *Autumn of Dictatorship*, 39–40.

98. Jason Brownlee, *Democracy Prevention: The Politics of the U.S.-Egyptian Alliance* (New York: Cambridge University Press, 2012), 36.

99. Mitchell, *Rule of Experts*, 272–304; Tamer El Gindi, "The Inequality Puzzle in Egypt: What Do We Really Know?," *Arab Studies Journal* 25, no. 2 (2017).

100. Hanieh, *Capitalism and Class*, chapter 6; Adam Hanieh, *Money, Markets, and Monarchies: The Gulf Cooperation Council and the Political Economy of the Contemporary Middle East* (Cambridge: Cambridge University Press, 2018), chapters 4–6.

101. We borrow the term "commodity frontier" from the work of Jason W. Moore. He develops this concept at length in Moore, *Capitalism in the Web of Life*. See, also, Jakes, "Boom, Bugs, Bust."

CHAPTER 7

I would like to thank Joel Beinin and Sherene Seikaly for their insightful comments and feedback during the writing and editing process. I also want to thank Arang Keshavarzian for his suggestions that improved this piece. My colleagues Jamie Allinson, Iain Hardie, and Marc Geddes read earlier drafts and provided helpful comments. Part of the research for this chapter was done with support of the Marie Sklodowska-Curie grant no.658988 PS-Iraq.

1. Hanna Batatu, *The Old Social Classes and the Revolutionary Movements of Iraq: A Study of Iraq's Old Landed and Commercial Classes and of Its Communists, Ba'thists and Free Officers* (London: Saqi, 2004 [1978]).

2. For political histories, see Marion Farouk-Sluglett and Peter Sluglett, *Iraq Since 1958* (London: I. B. Tauris, 2003 [1987]); Charles Tripp, *A History of Iraq* (Cambridge: Cambridge University Press, 2002 [2000]); Phebe Marr, *The Modern History of Iraq* (Boulder, CO: Westview, 2004 [2003]). Most political histories embrace the rentier state theory. For a political economy study see Isam al-Khafaji, "State Incubation of Iraqi Capitalism," *Middle East Report* 16 (1986).

3. On sectarianism, see Fanar Haddad, *Sectarianism in Iraq: Antagonistic Visions of Unity* (London: Hurst & Company, 2011). For studies of nationalism and refutation of the artificial state thesis see Reider Visser, "Proto-Political Conceptions of Iraq in Late Ottoman Times," *International Journal of Contemporary Iraqi Studies* 3, no. 2 (2009): 143–54; Abbas Kadhim, *Reclaiming Iraq: The 1920 Revolution and the Founding of the Modern State* (Austin: University of Texas Press, 2012); Sara Pursley, "'Lines Drawn on an Empty Map': Iraq's Borders and the Legend of the Artificial State (Part 1)," *Jadaliyya*, June 2, 2015a, http://www.jadaliyya.com/Details/32140/%60Lines-Drawn-on-an-Empty-Map%60-Iraq's-Borders-and-the-Legend-of-the-Artificial-State-Part-1; Sara Pursley, "'Lines Drawn on an Empty Map': Iraq's Borders and the Legend of the Artificial State (Part 2)," *Jadaliyya*, June 3, 2015b, http://www.jadaliyya.com/Details/32153.

4. For example, Dina Rizk Khoury, *Iraq in Wartime: Martyrdom, and Remembrance* (Cambridge: Cambridge University Press, 2013); Joseph Sassoon, *Saddam Hussein's Ba'th Party: Inside an Authoritarian Regime* (New York: Cambridge University Press, 2012).

5. Tripp, *History of Iraq.*

6. Marion Farouk-Sluglett and Peter Sluglett, "The Historiography of Modern Iraq," *American Historical Review* 29 (1991): 1408–21.

7. Al-Khafaji published a number of influential pieces in the 1980s, including a piece in 1986 that was commented on in the same issue by Hanna Batatu. Isam al-Khafaji, "State Incubation of Iraqi Capitalism," *Middle East Report* 142 (1986): 4–9, 12; Hanna Batatu, "State and Capitalism in Iraq: A Comment," *Middle East Report* 142 (1986): 10–12. For an example of Alnasrawi's work on Iraq during this period, see Abbas Alnasrawi, *The Economy of Iraq: Oil, Wars, Destruction of Development and Prospects, 1950–2010* (Westport, CT: Greenwood, 1994).

8. Kanan Makiya, *Republic of Fear: The Politics of Modern Iraq* (Berkeley: University of California Press, 1998 [1989]).

9. Peter Harling, "Beyond Political Ruptures: Towards a Historiography of Social Continuity in Iraq," in *Writing the Modern History of Iraq: Historiographical and Political Challenges*, ed. Jordi Tejel, Peter Sluglett, Riccardo Bocco, and Hamit Bozarslan (Hackensack, NJ: World Scientific, 2015 [2012]), 61.

10. See, for example, the Iraq archival collections at the Hoover Institution, particularly the Ba'th Arab Socialist Party of Iraq's collection, https://www.hoover.org/library-archives/collections/iraq. More recently the *New York Times* removed 15,000 documents of Islamic State's archives from Iraq. It published some of them and plans to make them available for research. The Middle East Studies Association's Committee on Academic Freedom objected to the removal of the documents from Iraq in a letter of September 25, 2018, to the *New York Times* and George Washington University: https://mesana.org/advocacy/committee-on-academic-freedom/2018/09/25/research-partnership-between-the-new-york-times-and-george-washington-university.

11. A radical and clear example comes from policy advisor Peter Galbraith and his call to divide Iraq, e.g., Peter W. Galbriath, *The End of Iraq: How American Incompetence Created a War Without End* (New York: Simon and Schuster, 2006), an argument that rests on the claim that Iraq is artificially composed of three separate groups (Kurds, Sh'ia, and Sunni). More subtle examples in academic work that suggest that Iraq's

present has been strongly conditioned by its failed colonial invention by the British. For example, shortly after the 2003 war, Toby Dodge suggested that an appropriate historical context for understanding Iraqi politics is the British colonial invention of Iraq and the failure of the British to build a liberal Iraqi state: "If one were to pick up Iraq like a good piece of china and turn it over, it would bear the legend: 'Made in Whitehall, 1920.'" Toby Dodge, *Inventing Iraq: The Failure of Nation Building and a History Denied* (New York: Columbia University Press, 2003), xi.

12. Pursley, "Lines Drawn," 2015a.

13. Pursley, "Lines Drawn," 2015a; "Lines Drawn," 2015b.

14. 'Ali al-Wardi, *Lamahat ijtima'iyya min tarikh al-'iraq al-hadith,* 3 vols. (London: Alwarrak, [1969–1979]) 3: 15–20, 282–83; Farouk-Sluglett and Sluglett, *Iraq Since 1958*, 3.

15. al-Wardi, *Lamahat ijtima'iyya* 3: 15–16.

16. al-Wardi, *Lamahat ijtima'iyya* 3: 15–17.

17. Sarah Abrevaya Stein, "Protected Persons? The Baghdadi Jewish Diaspora, the British State and the Persistence of Empire," *American Historical Review* (2011): 80–108, discusses the legal disputes over the inheritance of Silas Aaron Hardoon—a Baghdadi Jew who worked for David Sassoon and Company in India and died in Shanghai in 1933 with an estate estimated at US$150 million. References in Stein to the Sassoon family trade are in footnote 3.

18. al-Wardi, *Lamahat ijtima'iyya* 3: 17–18.

19. Yitzhak Nakash, *The Shi'is of Iraq* (Princeton, NJ: Princeton University Press, 2003), 169–71.

20. Nakash, *The Shi'is of Iraq*, 106–7; Batatu, *The Old Social Classes*, 32–34.

21. Pete Moore and Christopher Parker, "The War Economy of Iraq," *Middle East Report* 243 (2007): 6–15.

22. Nida Alahmad, "Illuminating a State: State-Building and Electricity in Occupied Iraq," *Humanity: An International Journal of Human Rights, Humanitarianism, and Development* 8 (2017): 335–53.

23. Nida Alahmad, "Rewiring a State: The Techno-Politics of Electricity in the CPA's Iraq," *Middle East Report* 266 (2013).

24. Alahmad, "Illuminating a State."

25. Antina von Schnitzler, "Traveling Technologies: Infrastructure, Ethical Regimes, and the Materiality of Politics in South Africa," *Cultural Anthropology* 23 (2013), 671. Emphasis in original.

26. Joseph Morgan Hodge, "Writing the History of Development (Part 2: Longer, Wider, Deeper)," *Humanity: An International Journal of Human Rights, Humanitarianism, and Development* 7 (2016): 125–74.

27. Hodge, "Writing the History of Development (Part 2)," 137.

28. Joseph Morgan Hodge, "Writing the History of Development (Part 1: The First Wave)," *Humanity: An International Journal of Human Rights, Humanitarianism, and Development* 6 (2015): 446.

29. al-Wardi, *Lamahat ijtima'iyya* 3: 80–83, 301–4; Tripp, *History of Iraq*, 15–18.

30. al-Wardi, *Lamahat ijtima'iyya* 2: 268–9.

31. al-Wardi, *Lamahat ijtima'iyya* 3: 311–12.

32. Orit Bashkin, *New Babylonians: A History of Jews in Modern Iraq* (Stanford, CA: Stanford University Press, 2012), 60.

33. Bashkin, *New Babylonians*, 60.

34. al-Wardi, *Lamahat ijtima'iyya* 3: 311–15.

35. Bashkin, *New Babylonians*, 69.

36. Cited in Delwin A. Roy, "The Educational System of Iraq," *Middle Eastern Studies* 29, no. 2 (1993): 163.

37. Roy, "The Educational System of Iraq," 180.

38. Cited in Roy, "The Educational System of Iraq," 187.

39. Roy, "The Educational System of Iraq," 177, 186.

40. World Bank, "Literacy Rate, Adult Total" chart, https://data.worldbank.org/indicator/SE.ADT.LITR.ZS?end=2013&locations=IQ&start=2000&view=chart.

41. Harling, "Beyond Political Ruptures," 77.

42. Harling, "Beyond Political Ruptures," 82.

43. Harling, "Beyond Political Ruptures," 78–79.

44. Faleh A. Jabar, "Sheikhs and Ideologues: Deconstruction and Reconstruction of Tribes under Patrimonial Totalitarianism in Iraq, 1968–1998," in *Tribes and Power: Nationalism and Ethnicity in the Middle East*, ed. Faleh Abdul-Jabar and Hosham Dawod (London: Saqi, 2003), 73.

45. al-Wardi, *Lamahat ijtima'iyya* 3: 282–83.

46. Batatu, *The Old Social Classes*, 74–75.

47. al-Wardi, *Lamahat ijtima'iyya* 2: 265.

48. al-Wardi, *Lamahat ijtima'iyya* 2: 266.

49. Batatu, *The Old Social Classes*, 74–75.

50. ʻAbbas al-ʻAzzawi, *ʻAshaʼir al-ʻiraq*, vol. 4 (Beirut: Maktabat al-Hadarat, 2010 [1955]), 192–200; al-Wardi, *Lamahat ijtimaʻiyya* 2: 270.

51. Farouk-Sluglett and Sluglett, *Iraq Since 1958*, 4–5.

52. Batatu, *The Old Social Classes*, 63–153.

53. Tripp, *History of Iraq*, 69.

54. Farouk-Sluglett and Sluglett, *Iraq Since 1958*, 31.

55. Batatu, *The Old Social Classes*, 132.

56. Jabar, "Sheikhs and Ideologues," 92–96.

57. Harling, "Beyond Political Ruptures," 68. After 2003 and with the collapse of state institutions, the power and social meaning of a tribe again changed. See for example, Hayder Al-Mohammad, "Relying on One's Tribe: A Snippet of Life in Basra Since the 2003 Invasion," *Anthropology Today* 26, no. 6 (2010).

58. Alissa Walter, "Food as Power: Rations and Local Governance in Baghdad," in "The Baʻth Party in Baghdad: State-Society Relations through Wars, Sanctions, and Authoritarian Rule, 1950–2003" (PhD diss., Georgetown University, 2018), 189.

59. Walter, "Food as Power," 189.

60. Nida Alahmad, "The Politics of Oil and State Survival in Iraq (1991–2003): Beyond the Rentier Thesis," *Constellations* 14 (2007): 586–612.

61. Alahmad, "The Politics of Oil."

62. Timothy Mitchell, *Carbon Democracy: Political Power in the Age of Oil* (London: Verso, 2011).

63. Robert Vitalis, *America's Kingdom: Mythmaking on the Saudi Oil Frontier* (Stanford, CA: Stanford University Press, 2007).

64. Nida Alahmad and Arang Keshavarzian, "A War on Multiple Fronts," *Middle East Report* 257 (2010): 25. Further discussion of how oil was used to finance the war and pursue a dual containment strategy, and how the worry of having an oil production coalition that included Iran and Iraq was a possible reason for the United States and its regional allies to pursue a dual containment strategy in Vitalis, *America's Kingdom*. The Iran-Contra scandal is another example of how, despite the "tilt," the United States did not hesitate to sell weapons to Iran during the early years of the war despite the ban on weapons sales to Iran. See Seymour M. Hersh, "The Iran Pipeline: A Hidden Chapter. A Special Report; U.S. Said to Have Allowed Israel to Sell Arms to Iran," *New York Times*, December 8, 1991.

65. Alahmad, "The Politics of Oil."

66. al-Khafaji, "State Incubation."

67. Batatu, *The Old Social Classes.*

68. Nida Alahmad, "A Perspective from the Middle East: Governance and the Problem of Knowledge," in *Global Governance from Regional Perspectives: A Critical View*, ed. Anna Triandafyllidou (Oxford: Oxford University Press, 2017), 99–118.

69. Special Inspector General for Iraq Reconstruction (SIGIR), *Hard Lessons: The Iraq Reconstruction Experience* (Washington, DC: US Government Printing Office, 2013).

70. Joseph Sassoon, "Iraq's Political Economy Post 2003: From Transition to Corruption," *International Journal of Contemporary Iraqi Studies* 10, no. 1 and 2 (2016): 17–33.

71. International Crisis Group, "Oil and Borders: How to Fix Iraq's Kurdish Crisis," Brussels: Crisis Group Middle East Briefing no. 55 (2017).

CHAPTER 8

1. Samir Saul, *Intérêts économiques français et décolonisation de l'Afrique du Nord (1945–1962)* (Geneva: Droz, 2016), 90; Daniel Lefeuvre, *Chère Algérie: comptes et mécomptes de la tutelle coloniale, 1930–1962*, Bibliothèque d'histoire d'outre-mer (Saint-Denis: Société française d'histoire d'outre-mer, 1997); Hubert Bonin, Catherine Hodeir, and Jean-François Klein, eds., *L'esprit économique impérial 1830–1970: groupes de pression & réseaux du patronat colonial en France & dans l'empire* (Paris: Publications de la Société Française d'Histoire d'Outre-Mer, 2008).

2. Alice Conklin, *A Mission to Civilize: The Republican Idea of Empire in France and West Africa, 1895–1930* (Stanford, CA: Stanford University Press, 1997).

3. Bruce Berman and John Lonsdale, *Unhappy Valley: Conflict in Kenya and Africa*, 2 vols. (Athens: Ohio University Press, 1992); Nicos Poulantzas, *State, Power, Socialism* (London: New Left, 1978).

4. Owen White and Elizabeth Heath, "Introduction: The French Empire and the History of Economic Life," *French Politics, Culture & Society* 35, no. 2 (2017): 76.

5. John Shovlin, *The Political Economy of Virtue* (Ithaca, NY: Cornell University Press, 2006); Charly Coleman, *The Virtues of Abandon: An Anti-Individualist History of the French Enlightenment* (Stanford, CA: Stanford University Press, 2014).

6. For more on this argument see David Todd, "A French Imperial Meridian, 1814–1870," *Past & Present* 201 (2011): 155–86. For the original article see J. Gallagher and R. E. Robinson, "The Imperialism of Free Trade, 1815–1914," *Economic History Review* 6 (1953): 1–15.

7. Frederick Cooper and Jane Burbank, *Empires in World History: Power and the Politics of Difference* (Princeton, NJ: Princeton University Press, 2010), 287.

8. Paul Leroy-Beaulieu, *De la colonisation chez les peuples modernes* (Paris: Cuillaumin, 1874).

9. Sara B. Pritchard, "From Hydroimperialism to Hydrocapitalism: 'French' Hydraulics in France, North Africa, and Beyond," *Social Studies of Science* 42, no. 4 (2012): 591–615; René Arrus, *L'eau en Algérie: de l'impérialisme au développement (1830–1962)* (Grenoble: Presses universitaires de Grenoble, 1985).

10. Luc-André Brunet, *Forging Europe: Industrial Organisation in France, 1940–1952* (London: Palgrave Mcmillan, 2017); Catherine Coquery-Vidrovitch, "Vichy et l'industrialisation aux colonies," *Revue d'histoire de la seconde guerre mondiale* 114 (1979): 69–94; Daniel Lefeuvre, "Vichy et la modernisation de l'Algérie: Intention ou réalité?," *Vingtième Siècle. Revue d'histoire* no. 42 (1994): 7–16.

11. Isabelle Grangaud and M'hamed Oualdi, "Does Colonialism Explain Everything in North Africa? What Historians of the Modern Maghreb Can Bring to the Table," *L'Année du Maghreb* 10 (2014): 233–54.

12. Joshua Schreier, *The Merchants of Oran: A Jewish Port at the Dawn of Empire* (Stanford, CA: Stanford University Press, 2017).

13. Jennifer E. Sessions, *By Sword and Plow, France and the Conquest of Algeria* (Ithaca, NY: Cornell University Press, 2011), 7.

14. Ann Thomson, "Arguments for the Conquest of Algiers in the Late Eighteenth and Early Nineteenth Centuries," *Maghreb Review* 14, no. 1–2 (1989): 108–18.

15. Diana K. Davis, *Resurrecting the Granary of Rome: Environmental History and French Colonial Expansion in North Africa* (Athens: Ohio University Press, 2007).

16. Sessions, *By Sword and Plow,* 183.

17. Edmund Burke, *Prelude to Protectorate in Morocco: Precolonial Protest and Resistance, 1860–1912* (Chicago: University of Chicago Press, 1976).

18. Susan Miller, *A History of Modern Morocco* (New York: Cambridge University Press, 2013), 27.

19. Miller, *A History of Modern Morocco,* 31.

20. Burke, *Prelude to Protectorate in Morocco,* 20.

21. Abdul Azim Islahi, "The Economic Ideas of Two Tunisian Statesmen: Khayr al-Din al-Tunisi and Bayram al-Khamis," in *Economic Thinking of Arab Muslim Writers During the Nineteenth Century* (New York: Palgrave Macmillan, 2015), 78–105; Muhammed As-Saffar, *Disorienting Encounters: Travels of a Moroccan Scholar in*

France 1845–1856, ed. Susan Gilson Miller (Berkeley: University of California Press, 1992).

22. Osama W. Abi-Mershed, *Apostles of Modernity: The Saint-Simonians and the Civilizing Mission in Algeria* (Stanford, CA: Stanford University Press, 2010), 32.

23. Abi-Mershed, *Apostles of Modernity*, 162.

24. Didier Guignard, *L'abus de pouvoir dans l'Algérie coloniale* (Paris: Presses universitaires de Paris Ouest, 2010).

25. John Ruedy, *Modern Algeria: The Origins and Development of a Nation*, 2nd ed. (Bloomington: Indiana University Press, 2005), 97; Micheal Brett, "Legislating for Inequality: The Senatus-Consulte of 14 July 1965," *Bulletin of the School of Oriental and African Studies* 15, no. 3 (1988): 440–61.

26. Quoted in Henry Sivak, "Law, Territory, and the Legal Geography of French Rule in Algeria: The Forestry Domain 1830-1903," (PhD diss., UCLA, 2008), 171.

27. For more on the "Berber myth" see Patricia M. E. Lorcin, *Imperial Identities: Stereotyping, Prejudice and Race in Colonial Algeria* (London: I. B. Tauris 1995). For a history of Algerian immigration and Berber activism in France see Paul A. Silverstein, *Algeria in France: Transpolitics, Race and Nation* (Bloomington: Indiana University Press, 2004).

28. James McDougall, *A History of Algeria* (Cambridge: Cambridge University Press, 2017), 95.

29. Jacques Budin, "La 'reconnaissance' de la propriété rurale dans l'arrondissement de Bône (Annaba) en application des ordonnances des 1er octobre 1844 et 21 juillet 1846," in *Propriété et société en Algérie contemporaine. Quelles approches?*, ed. Didier Guignard (Aix-en-Provence: Institut de recherches et d'études sur le monde arabe et musulman, 2017).

30. The well-known *Jouâd* or *Chôrfa* families, for example, were able to maintain some of their authority by working for the colonial administration. Charles-Robert Ageron, *Histoire de l'Algérie contemporaine, tome II, de l'insurrection de 1871 au déclenchement de la guerre de libération (1954)* (Paris: Presses Universitaires de France, 1979), 222–23.

31. Ageron, *Histoire de l'Algérie contemporaine*, 209.

32. On Saharan economies see Ghislaine Lydon, *On Trans-Saharan Trails: Islamic Law, Trade Networks, and Cross-Cultural Exchange in Nineteenth-Century Western Africa* (New York: Cambridge University Press, 2012); James McDougall and Judith Scheele, *Saharan Frontiers: Space and Mobility in Northwest Africa*, Public Cultures of the Middle East and North Africa (Bloomington: Indiana University Press 2012).

33. Hubert Bonin, *Un outre-mer bancaire méditerranéen: histoire du Crédit foncier d'Algérie et de Tunisie, 1880–1997* (Paris: Société française d'histoire d'outre-mer, 2004).

34. Mohamed Lazhar Gharbi, "Investissements français et déploiement économique en Tunisie (1863–1914): Groupes de pression et esprit impérial," in Bonin, Hodeir, and Klein, *L'esprit économique impérial (1830–1870)*, 581–97.

35. Archives Nationales d'Outre-Mer (ANOM), BIB 20327/1962, "1963: de L'acier à Bône," in *Bulletin de la Caisse d'Équipement pour le Développement de l'Algérie*, no. 3 (February 1961): 5.

36. Daniel Lefeuvre, "Les réactions patronales au Plan de Constantine," *Revue Historique* 276, no. 1 (1986): 167–89.

37. Hildebert Isnard, "Vigne et structures en Algérie," *Diogène* 27 (1959): 77. In Tunisia viticulture was introduced around the same time as Algeria; in Morocco the process began in the first two decades after the proclamation of the protectorate in 1911.

38. Isnard, "Vigne et structures," 77.

39. Algerian wine was considered "medicinal" because it had an extremely high degree of alcohol and was thus often used to cut metropolitan wines. For wine growers in the Midi, it was unthinkable that Algerian wine interests should come into competition with their own properly "French" production.

40. Ahmed Henni, *La colonisation agraire et le sous-développement en Algérie*, Société Nationale d'Édition et de Diffusion (Alger: Ahmed Zabana, 1982); Elizabeth Heath, *Wine, Sugar and the Making of Modern France: Global Economic Crisis and the Racialization of French Citizenship* (Cambridge: Cambridge University Press, 2014); Willy Jansen, "French Bread and Algerian Wine: Conflicting Identities in French Algeria," in *Food, Drink, Identity: Cooking, Eating and Drinking in Europe since the Middle Ages*, ed. Peter Scholliers (Oxford: Berg, 2001), 195–218.

41. Samuel Kalman, *French Colonial Fascism: The Extreme Right in Algeria, 1919–1939* (New York: Palgrave Macmillan 2013), 181.

42. On this term see Richard Grove, "Scotland in South Africa: John Croumbie Brown and the Roots of Settler Environmentalism," in *Ecology and Empire: Environmental History of Settler Societies*, ed. Libby Robin and Tom Robbins (Edinburgh: Keele University Press, 1997), 139–53.

43. *Journal Officiel*, June 8, 1958, 813.

44. Peter Von Sivers, "Rural Uprisings as Political Movements in Colonial Algeria, 1851–1914," in *Islam, Politics, and Social Movements*, ed. Edmund Burke and Ira M, Lapidus (Berkeley: University of California Press 1988), 39–59.

45. Julia A. Clancy-Smith, *Rebel and Saint: Muslim Notables, Populist Protest, Colonial Encounters (Algeria and Tunisia, 1800–1904)* (Berkeley: University of California Press, 1994).

46. Fanny Colonna, "The Nation's 'Unknowning Other:' Three Intellectuals and the Culture(s) of Being Algerian, or the Impossibility of Subaltern Studies in Algeria," *Journal of North African Studies* 8, no. 1 (2003): 155–70.

47. Alain Clément, "L'analyse économique de la question coloniale en France (1870–1914)," *Revue d'économie politique 123* 123, no. 1 (2013): 59.

48. Clément, "L'analyse économique," 59.

49. Raymond F. Betts, *Assimilation and Association in French Colonial Theory, 1890–1914* (New York: Columbia University, 1961).

50. René Galissot, *L'économie de l'Afrique du Nord* (Paris: Presses Universitaire de France (Que sais-je), 1969), 66.

51. Galissot, *L'économie de l'Afrique du Nord*, 66.

52. Clément, "L'analyse économique," 56.

53. Miller, *A History of Modern Morocco*, 113.

54. Jim House, "Shantytowns and Rehousing in Late Colonial Algiers and Casablanca," in *France's Modernizing Mission: Citizenship, Welfare and the End of Empire*, ed. Ed Naylor (London: Palgrave Macmillan, 2018), 133–63.

55. Joel Beinin, *Workers and Thieves: Labor Movements and Popular Uprisings in Tunisia and Egypt* (Stanford, CA: Stanford University Press, 2015). Miller, *A History of Modern Morocco*, 116.

56. Samir Amin, *L'Économie du Maghreb* (Paris: Éditions de Minuit, 1967).

57. Kenneth Perkins, *A History of Modern Tunisia* (Cambridge: Cambridge University Press, 2004), 49.

58. Charles-André Julien, *L'Afrique du Nord en Marche: Algérie-Tunisie-Maroc, 1880–1952* (Paris: Omnibus, 2002), 44–45.

59. Julien, *L'Afrique du Nord en Marche*, 56.

60. Gilbert Meynier, "Algerians and the First World War," *Orient XXI*, May 10, 2016, https://orientxxi.info/l-orient-dans-la-guerre-1914-1918/algerians-and-the-first-world-war,0645,0645.

61. Quoted in Richard S. Fogarty, *Race and War in France: Colonial Subjects in the French Army, 1914–1918* (Baltimore: Johns Hopkins University Press, 2008), 15.

62. Fogarty, *Race and War in France*, 27.

63. Fogarty, *Race and War in France*, 27.

64. Amelia H. Lyons, *The Civilizing Mission in the Metropole: Algerian Families and the French Welfare State during Decolonization* (Stanford, CA: Stanford University Press, 2013).

65. Julien, *L'Afrique du Nord en Marche*, 106.

66. Albert Sarraut, *La mise en valeur des colonies françaises* (Paris: Payot, 1923).

67. Jacques Marseille, *Empire colonial et capitalisme français: Histoire d'un divorce* (Paris: Albin Michel, 1984), 156.

68. Richard S. Fogarty points to a "cultural" belief in the "economic utility of empire" to explain this discrepancy in "The French Empire," in *Empires at War: 1911–1923*, ed. Robert Gerwarth and Erez Manela (Oxford: Oxford University Press, 2014), 119.

69. Antoine Bernard de Raymond, "Une 'Algérie Californienne'? L'économie politique de la standardisation de l'agriculture coloniale (1930–1962)," *Politix*, no. 95 (2011): 23–46; Will D. Swearingen, *Moroccan Mirages: Agrarian Dreams and Deceptions, 1912–1986* (Princeton, NJ: Princeton University Press, 2014).

70. Amin, *L'Économie du Maghreb*, 117.

71. Arrus, *L'eau en Algérie*; Swearingen, *Moroccan Mirages*.

72. Robert Montagne, *Naissance du prolétariat marocain: Enquête collective 1948–1950* (Rabat: Centre Jacques-Berques, 2016 [1951]).

73. Coquery-Vidrovitch, "Vichy et l'industrialisation aux colonies"; Lefeuvre, "Vichy et la modernisation de l'Algérie."

74. Saul, *Intérêts économiques français*, 15.

75. Jeffrey James Byrne, *Mecca of Revolution: Algeria, Decolonization, and the Third World Order* (New York: Oxford University Press, 2016), 125.

76. Daniel Lefeuvre, *Pour en finir avec la repentance coloniale* (Paris: Flammarion, 2006).

CHAPTER 9

I would like to express my appreciation to the editors of this volume for their comments and edits and to Rosie Bsheer and Nadya Sbaiti for their feedback on earlier drafts of this chapter.

1. Samir Khalaf, *Civil and Uncivil Violence in Lebanon: A History of the Internationalization of Communal Conflict* (New York: Columbia University Press, 2002).

2. Nader Hashemi and Danny Postel, eds., *Sectarianization: Mapping the New Politics of the Middle East* (New York: Oxford University Press, 2017), exemplifies the ubiquity of post-2011 comparative studies of sectarianism.

3. Ralph E. Crow, "Confessionalism, Public Administration, and Efficiency in Lebanon," in *Politics in Lebanon*, ed. Leonard Binder (New York: John Wiley & Sons, 1966), 167–86.

4. Khalaf, *Civil and Uncivil Violence*, 151–203.

5. Carolyn Gates, *The Merchant Republic of Lebanon: Rise of an Open Economy* (London: I. B. Tauris, 1998), 6–10.

6. Engin Akarli, *The Long Peace: Ottoman Lebanon, 1861–1920* (Berkeley: University of California Press, 1993), 102–46; Jens Hanssen, *Fin de Siècle Beirut: The Making of an Ottoman Provincial Capital* (Oxford: Oxford University Press, 2005), 55–83, 113–90; Ussama Makdisi, *The Culture of Sectarianism: Community, History, and Violence in Nineteenth-Century Ottoman Lebanon* (Berkeley: University of California Press, 2000), 51–95.

7. Malek Abisaab, *Militant Women of a Fragile Nation* (Syracuse, NY: Syracuse University Press, 2010), 1–16; Hanssen, *Fin de Siècle Beirut*, 84–112; Kristen Alff, "Levantine Joint-Stock Companies, Trans-Mediterranean Partnerships, and Nineteenth-Century Capitalist Development," *Comparative Studies in Society and History* 60, no. 1 (2018): 150–77; Akram Khater, *Inventing Home: Emigration, Gender, and the Middle Class in Lebanon, 1870–1920* (Berkeley: University of California Press, 2001), 19–47.

8. See Kristen Alff's chapter in this volume.

9. Kais Firro, "Silk and Agrarian Changes in Lebanon, 1860–1914," *International Journal of Middle East Studies* 22 (1990): 151–69; Akram Fouad Khater, "'House' to 'Goddess of the House': Gender, Class, and Silk in 19th-Century Mount Lebanon," *International Journal of Middle East Studies* 28 (1996): 325–48; Roger Owen, "The Study of Middle Eastern Industrial History: Notes on the Interrelationship between Factories and Small-Scale Manufacturing with Special References to Lebanese Silk and Egyptian Sugar, 1900–1930," *International Journal of Middle East Studies* 16, no. 4 (1984): 475–87.

10. V. Necla Geyikdagi, *Foreign Investment in the Ottoman Empire: International Trade and Relations, 1854–1914* (London: I. B. Tauris, 2011), 29–73.

11. Hanssen, *Fin de Siècle Beirut*, 84–112.

12. Khater, *Inventing Home*, 48–70; Stacey D. Fahrenthold, *Between the Ottomans and the Entente: The First World War in the Syrian and Lebanese Diaspora, 1908–1925* (Oxford: Oxford University Press, 2019), 14–30. On emigration to other areas, see Andrew Arsan, *Interlopers of Empire: The Lebanese Diaspora in Colonial French West Africa* (New York: Oxford University Press, 2014), 23–39, 47–60.

13. Khater, *Inventing Home*, 108–45.

14. Khater, *Inventing Home*, 108–90.

15. Khater, *Inventing Home*, 179–90; Toufoul Abou-Hodeib, *A Taste for Home: The Modern Middle Class in Ottoman Beirut* (Stanford, CA: Stanford University Press, 2017).

16. Hanssen, *Fin de Siècle Beirut*, 25–54, 87–92; Charles Issawi, "British Trade and the Rise of Beirut, 1830–1860," *International Journal of Middle East Studies* 8, no. 1 (1977): 91–101.

17. The integration of the region into the world economy was one factor. Also important were the lobbying efforts of local politicians, merchants, and landowners and the political pressure of European governments to give Beirut precedence over Acre, which was already an established port. See previously cited sections of Hanssen, *Fin de Siècle Beirut*, as well as Kristen Alff's chapter in this volume.

18. The trope of "entrepreneurial spirt" recurs in several histories of Beirut, Mount Lebanon, or Lebanon. Some who deploy it draw on the theoretical work of Joseph A. Schumpeter. Others echo narratives of Lebanese partisans of laissez-faire policies or the myth of the Phoenician origins of Lebanese national identity: Georges Hakim, "The Economic Basis of Lebanese Policy," in *Politics in Lebanon*, ed. Leonard Binder (New York: John Wiley & Sons, 1966); Yusif A. Sayigh, *Entrepreneurs of Lebanon: The Role of the Business Leader in a Developing Economy* (Cambridge, MA: Harvard University Press, 1962); and Leila Tarazi Fawaz, *Merchants and Migrants in Nineteenth-Century Beirut* (Cambridge, MA: Harvard University Press, 1983).

19. Linda Schilcher, "Famine in Syria, 1915–1918," in *Problems of the Middle East in Historical Perspective. Essays in Honour of Albert Hourani*, edited by John P. Spagnolo and Albert Hourani (Reading, UK: Ithaca, 1996); Melanie S. Tanielian, *The Charity of War: Famine, Humanitarian Aid, and World War I in the Middle East* (Stanford, CA: Stanford University Press, 2018), 51–78; Leila Tarazi Fawaz, *A Land of Aching Hearts: The Middle East in the Great War* (Cambridge, MA: Harvard University Press, 2014), 81–120; Graham Pitts, "Fallow Fields: Famine and the Making of Lebanon" (PhD diss., Georgetown University, 2016).

20. Pitts, "Fallow Fields," 35–45.

21. Abisaab, *Militant Women of a Fragile Nation*, 13.

22. Carole Hakim, *The Origins of the Lebanese National Idea, 1840–1920* (Berkeley: University of California Press, 2013), 231–60; Meir Zamir, *The Formation of Modern Lebanon* (Ithaca, NY: Cornell University Press, 1985), 38–96.

23. Elizabeth Thompson, *Colonial Citizens: Republican Rights, Paternal Privilege, and Gender in French Syria and Lebanon* (New York: Columbia University Press, 2000), 44, 53–55, 66–68.

24. Kais Firro, *Inventing Lebanon: Nationalism and the State under the Mandate* (London: I. B. Tauris, 2003), 71–125; Michael Johnson, *Class & Client in Beirut. The Sunni Muslim Community and the Lebanese State 1840–1985* (London: Ithaca, 1988), 11–96.

25. French colonial officials claimed they were simply continuing Ottoman practices. However, social and cultural historians have shown the complex ways that the post-war personal status system in Lebanon represented a break from both the *millet* system and late Ottoman practices of governance, exemplified by the strict limits the Mandate imposed on the state's power over religious law. The French-established personal status system was linked to a broader structure of sectarian political representation, including official recognition of previously unrecognized sects, establishment of new personal status courts, and new modes of identification with being Lebanese. See Thompson, *Colonial Citizens*, 113–54; Max Weiss, *In the Shadow of Sectarianism: Law, Shi'ism, and the Making of Modern Lebanon* (Cambridge, MA: Harvard University Press, 2010), 92–125.

26. Thompson, *Colonial Citizens*, 94–100, 117–54, 238–43, 272–76.

27. Precise figures on the urban working population are unavailable for the Mandate period. Yet three sets of sources corroborate this conclusion: the annual reports by the French Ministry of Foreign Affairs to the Permanent Mandates Commission of the League of Nations, a series of articles published in *International Labour Review*, and economic and development reports produced in the first decade of independence. See République française, Ministère des affaires étrangères, *Rapport à la Société des Nations sur la situation de la Syrie et du Liban*, 15 vols. (Paris: Imprimerie Nationale, 1925–1939); Fuad Abu-Izziddin and George Hakim, "A Contribution to the Study of Labour Conditions in the Lebanon," *International Labour Review* 28 (1933): 673–82; "Working Conditions in Handicrafts and Modern Industry in Syria," *International Labour Review* 29 (1934): 407–11; "Conditions of Work in Syria and the Lebanon under French Mandate," *International Labour Review* 39 (1939): 513–26; Sir Alexander Gibb & Partners, *Taqrir 'an al-tatawwur al-'iqtisadi fi lubnan* (Beirut: Wizarat al-Iqtisad al-Watani li'l-Jumhuriyya al-Lubnaniyya, 1948).

28. Ilyas al-Bawari, *Tarikh al-haraka al-'ummaliyya wa'l-niqabiyya fi lubnan: 1908–1946* (Beirut: Dar al-Farabi, 1979).

29. The following paragraph synthesizes insights and arguments in Thompson, *Colonial Citizens*, 39–90, and Zamir, *The Formation of Modern Lebanon*, 97–146.

30. Norman Burns, *The Tariff of Syria 1919–1932* (Beirut: American Press, 1933), 12–51; Raymond A. Mallat, *70 Years of Money Muddling in Lebanon 1900–1970: A Guide*

in Monetary Management for Economic Development in Lebanon (Beirut: Aleph, 1973), 99–152.

31. Simon M. W. Jackson, "Mandatory Development: The Political Economy of the French Mandate in Syria and Lebanon, 1915–1939" (PhD diss., New York University, 2009), 200–291.

32. Raja S. Hamideh, *The Fiscal System of Lebanon* (Beirut: Khayyat, 1961); Elias S. Saba, *The Foreign Exchange Systems of Lebanon and Syria 1939–1957* (Beirut: American University of Beirut, 1961).

33. Thompson, *Colonial Citizens*, 155–70, 229–46.

34. Martin W. Wilmington, *The Middle East Supply Centre* (Albany: State University of New York Press, 1971).

35. Sherene Seikaly, *Men of Capital: Scarcity and Economy in Mandate Palestine* (Stanford, CA: Stanford University Press, 2016), 77–126; Robert Vitalis and Steven Heydemann, "War, Keynesianism, and Colonialism: Explaining State-Market Relations in the Postwar Middle East," in *War, Institutions, and Social Change in the Middle East*, ed. Steven Heydemann (Berkeley: University of California Press, 2000), 100–148.

36. Elizabeth Thompson, "The Climax and Crisis of the Colonial Welfare State in Syria and Lebanon during World War II," in *War, Institutions, and Social Change in the Middle East*, ed. Steven Heydemann (Berkeley: University of California Press, 2000), 59–99.

37. For example, Walid Khalidi, *Conflict and Violence in Lebanon: Confrontation in the Middle East* (Cambridge, MA: Harvard Center for International Affairs, 1980).

38. Despite their different theoretical frameworks, Khalaf, Johnson, and Kamal Salibi, *Crossroads to Civil War: Lebanon 1958–1976* (Delmar, NY: Caravan, 1976) concur on this.

39. Michael C. Hudson, *The Precarious Republic: Political Modernization in Lebanon* (New York: Random House, 1968).

40. Youssef Chaitiani, *Post-Colonial Syria and Lebanon: The Decline of Arab Nationalism and the Triumph of the State* (New York: I. B. Tauris, 2007).

41. Hicham Saffieddine, *Banking on the State: The Financial Foundations of Lebanon* (Stanford, CA: Stanford University Press, 2019).

42. Ziad Munif Abu-Rish, "Conflict and Institution Building in Lebanon, 1946–1955" (PhD diss., University of California, Los Angeles, 2014), 58–109.

43. Abu-Rish, "Conflict and Institution Building," 58–109; Iskandar E. Bashir, *Planned Administrative Change in Lebanon* (Beirut: American University of Beirut,

1965); George Grassmuck and Kamal Salibi, *A Manual of Lebanese Administration* (Beirut: Catholic Press, 1955).

44. By 1955, ministries of defense, foreign affairs, information, social affairs, and planning were established. Subsequent cabinets included ministries of housing, industry, water and electric resources, and tourism by 1975.

45. Mallat, *70 Years of Money Muddling in Lebanon*, 71.

46. There were several facets to this qualitative transformation. The first was the incorporation of institutions and functions previously administered by the French High Commission. The second was the expansion of bureaucratic reach in existing realms of state intervention. The third was the creation of new realms of bureaucratic management. See Abu-Rish, "Conflict and Institution Building in Lebanon," 71–90.

47. Abu-Rish and Saffieddine argue this point in different ways.

48. Steven Heydemann, *Authoritarianism in Syria: Institutions and Social Conflict, 1946–1970* (Ithaca, NY: Cornell University Press, 1999), 178–79.

49. Yusuf A. Sayigh, "Economic Implications of UNRWA Operations in Jordan, Syria, and Lebanon" (MA thesis, American University of Beirut, 1952).

50. John Chalcraft, *The Invisible Cage: Syrian Migrant Workers in Lebanon* (Stanford, CA: Stanford University Press, 2009), 53–59.

51. These two dynamics are repeatedly mentioned by most scholars, but neither has yet been the subject of focused study.

52. Toufic K. Gaspard, *A Political Economy of Lebanon, 1948–2002: The Limits of Laissez-Faire* (Leiden: Brill, 2004), 100–186; Roger Owen, "The Economic History of Lebanon 1943–1974: Its Salient Features," in *Toward A Viable Lebanon*, ed. Halim Barakat (Washington, DC: Center for Contemporary Arab Studies, 1988), 27–41; Gates, *The Merchant Republic of Lebanon*, 109–35.

53. Andre Emile Chaib, "The Export Performance of a Small Open Developing Economy: The Lebanese Experience 1951–74" (PhD diss., University of Michigan, 1979), 11.

54. Chaib, "The Export Performance," 43.

55. Chaib, "The Export Performance," 51.

56. Chaib, "The Export Performance," 51.

57. Mona Fawaz, "Strategizing for Housing: An Investigation of the Production and Regulation of Low-Income Housing in the Suburbs of Beirut" (PhD diss., Massachusetts Institute of Technology, 2004); Fuad I. Khuri, *From Village to Suburb: Order and Change in Greater Beirut* (Chicago: University of Chicago Press, 1975).

58. Ilyas al-Bawari, *Tarikh al-haraka al-'ummaliyya wa'l-niqabiyya fi lubnan: 1947–1970* (Beirut: Dar al Farabi, 1980); Rossana Tufaro, "Labor and Conflict in Pre-War Lebanon (1970–1975): A Retrieval of the Political Experience of Factory Committees in the Industrial District of Beirut" (PhD diss., Universita Ca'Forscari Venezia, 2018).

59. Salim Nasr, "Lebanon's War: Is the End in Sight?" *Middle East Report* 162 (January/February 1990): 4–8, 30; Elizabeth Picard, "The Political Economy of Civil War Lebanon," in *War, Institutions, and Social Change in the Middle East*, ed. Steven Heydemann (Berkeley: University of California Press, 2000), 292–324.

60. Picard, "The Political Economy of Civil War Lebanon," 294–96.

61. Picard argues this point well. Jonathan Marshall, *The Lebanese Connection: Corruption, Civil War, and the International Drug Traffic* (Stanford, CA: Stanford University Press, 2012), 75–162, provides a comprehensive analysis of drug production and transportation during the civil war years.

62. Reinoud Leenders, *Spoils of Truce: Corruption and State-Building in Postwar Lebanon* (Ithaca, NY: Cornell University Press, 2012), 122–63. Also see Najib Hourani, "Capitalists in Conflict: The Lebanese Civil War Reconsidered," *Middle East Critique* 24, no. 2 (April 2015): 137–60.

63. There is, as with other eras, a question of periodization. Here, I consider only the dynamics through 2014 because of the as-yet-unfolding processes of infrastructural breakdown, fiscal and foreign currency crises, and political realignments due to the 2015 garbage protests, the 2016 municipal and 2018 parliamentary elections, and the 2019 uprising. These are of course in addition to the local reverberations of regional developments such as the effective defeat of most armed antiregime groups in Syria; popular uprisings in Algeria, Iraq, and Sudan; civil, proxy, and foreign wars in Yemen; and the escalating US-Iran rivalry.

64. Leenders, *Spoils of Truce*, 122–63.

65. Leenders, *Spoils of Truce*, 164–222.

66. Hannes Baumann, *Citizen Hariri: Lebanon's Neo-Liberal Reconstruction* (Oxford: Oxford University Press, 2017); Reinoud Leenders, "Nobody Having Too Much to Answer For: Laissez-Faire, Networks, and Postwar Reconstruction in Lebanon," in *Networks of Privilege in the Middle East: The Politics of Economic Reform Revisited*, ed. Steven Heydemann (New York: Palgrave MacMillan, 2004), 169–200.

67. Nisreen Salti, "No Country for Poor Men: How Lebanon's Debt Has Exacerbated Inequality," September 17, 2019, Diwan: Middle East Insights from Carnegie, https://

carnegie-mec.org/2019/09/17/no-country-for-poor-men-how-lebanon-s-debt-has-exacerbated-inequality-pub-79852.

68. "Central Government Debt, Total (% of GDP)," World Bank Open Data, https://data.worldbank.org/indicator/GC.DOD.TOTL.GD.ZS?most_recent_value_desc=true.

69. Salti, "No Country for Poor Men"; Rouba Chbeir and Marwan Mikhael, *A Historical Analysis of Lebanon's Public Debt* (Beirut: Blominvest Bank, 2019), 4; Jad Chaaban, "I've Got the Power: Mapping Connections between Lebanon's Banking Sector and the Ruling Class" (Working Paper No. 1059, Economic Research Forum, 2016). Local debt accounted for more than 90 percent of gross public debt in 1993, more than 84 percent between 1994 and 1997, and more than 75 percent between 1998 and 1999. Foreign public debt approximated local public debt only during the 2002–8 period when it ranged between a low of 45 percent and a high of 51.2 percent. In 2014 local debt account for more than 60 percent of gross public debt. The figure has continued to rise since then.

70. In December 2014, foreign public debt in Lebanon stood at approximately US$26 billion (as opposed to US$41 billion of domestic public debt), only about 90 percent of which was in the form of bilateral and multilateral loans. See "Public Debt Overview," Republic of Lebanon, Ministry of Finance, http://www.finance.gov.lb/en-us/Finance/PublicDebt/PDTS/.

71. Salti, "No Country for Poor Men." Also see "Commercial Banks—LBP: Term Savings and Deposits," Data Series, Banque du Liban, https://www.bdl.gov.lb/webroot/statistics/table.php?name=t5272–6.

72. Eric Verdeil, "Infrastructure Crises in Beirut and the Struggle to (Not) Reform the Lebanese State," *Arab Studies Journal* 16, no. 1 (Spring 2018): 84–113.

73. Leenders, *Spoils of Truce*, 223–41.

CHAPTER 10

1. Hilton Obenzinger, "In the Shadow of 'God's Sun-Dial': The Construction of American Christian Zionism and the Blackstone Memorial," *Stanford Humanities Review* 5, no. 1 (1995): 62.

2. John B. Judis, *Genesis: Truman, American Jews, and the Origins of the Arab/Israeli Conflict* (New York: Farrar, Straus, and Giroux, 2014).

3. Jefferson Morley, *The Ghost: The Secret Life of CIA Spymaster James Jesus Angleton* (New York: St. Martin's, 2017), 181.

4. Morley, *The Ghost*, 175–78; Roger J. Mattson, "The NUMEC Affair: Did Highly Enriched Uranium from the U.S. Aid Israel's Nuclear Weapons Program?" National Security Archive, https://nsarchive.gwu.edu/briefing-book/nuclear-vault/2016-11-02/numec-affair-did-highly-enriched-uranium-us-aid-israels.

5. Jewish Telegraphic Agency, "Potential Trump Defense Chief Saw 'Military Security Price' for US Support of Israel," November 20, 2016, https://www.jta.org/2016/11/20/news-opinion/politics/possible-trump-pick-for-defense-secretary-said-the-u-s-pays-price-for-israel-support; Statement of General David H. Petraeus Before the Senate Armed Services Committee, March 16, 2010, 12, https://web.archive.org/web/20100331012029/http://armed-services.senate.gov/statemnt/2010/03%20March/Petraeus%2003-16-10.pdf.

6. House Appropriations Subcommittee on Defense hearing, March 2, 2011, C-Span, https://www.c-span.org/video/?298247-1/defense-department-fiscal-year-2012-budget-request, at 2:01.

7. David Tal, "Symbol Not Substance? Israel's Campaign to Acquire Hawk Missiles, 1960–1962," *International History Review* 22, no. 2 (2000): 305.

8. Jeremy Sharp, *U.S. Foreign Aid to Israel* (Washington, DC: Congressional Research Service, 7 August 2019), 2, https://www.everycrsreport.com/files/20190807_RL33222_54f0e84c97f844c91d228835e6cbbd1618f97a2d.pdf.

9. White House, Office of the Press Secretary, "Memorandum of Understanding Reached with Israel," September 14, 2016, https://obamawhitehouse.archives.gov/the-press-office/2016/09/14/fact-sheet-memorandum-understanding-reached-israel.

10. Stephen Snyder, "A Massive US Weapons Deal with Israel Means More Weapons for Its Arab Neighbors, Too," *PRI's The World*, September 22, 2016, https://www.pri.org/stories/2016-09-22/massive-us-weapons-deal-israel-means-more-weapons-its-arab-neighbors-too.

11. Bruce Reidel, "The $110 Billion Arms Deal to Saudi Arabia Is Fake News," Brookings, June 5, 2017, https://www.brookings.edu/blog/markaz/2017/06/05/the-110-billion-arms-deal-to-saudi-arabia-is-fake-news/.

12. William Quandt, *Decade of Decisions: American Policy Toward the Arab-Israeli Conflict, 1967–1976* (Berkeley: University of California Press, 1977), 106.

13. Clyde R. Mark, *Israel: U.S. Foreign Assistance* (Washington, DC: Congressional Research Service, updated April 26, 2005), 13.

14. Ronald Reagan, op-ed, *Washington Post*, August 15, 1979.

15. Mark, *Israel: U.S. Foreign Assistance*, updated May 27 1997, 9.

16. Associated Press, "Congress OKs Watered-down Bill on US-Israel Ties," December 4, 2014, https://www.ynetnews.com/articles/0,7340,L-4599523,00.html.

17. Barbara Opall-Rome, "US, Israel in 'Dress Rehearsal' for Joint Response Against Iran Missile Attack," *Defense News*, March 9, 2018, https://www.defensenews.com/global/mideast-africa/2018/03/08/us-israel-in-dress-rehearsal-for-joint-response-against-iran-missile-attack/.

18. Illy Pe'ery, "What Has the IAF Learned from Defecting Pilots?" Israel Air Force, March 13, 2017, http://www.iaf.org.il/4458-49076-en/IAF.aspx; Jewish Telegraphic Agency, "Syrian Who Defected to Israel Teaches Israelis to Fly Mig Jet," January 31, 1990, https://www.jta.org/1990/01/31/archive/syrian-who-defected-to-israel-teaches-israelis-to-fly-mig-jet.

19. Yoram Gabison, "3 Reasons Why Israel's Largest Privately-Owned Defense Contractor Will Pay $520m for IMI," *Haaretz*, March 12, 2018, https://www.haaretz.com/israel-news/business/three-reasons-why-elbit-is-ready-to-fork-over-520m-for-imi-1.5896205.

20. Yaniv Kubovich, "Israel's Arms Exports Spike, Hitting Record $9 Billion," *Haaretz*, May 2, 2018, https://www.haaretz.com/israel-news/israel-s-defense-export-sales-exceed-record-9-billion-1.6052046.

21. Eytan Halon, "Hi-tech Sector Exceeds 300,000 Workers for First Time," *Jerusalem Post*, August 27, 2019, https://www.jpost.com/Israel-News/Hi-tech-sector-exceeds-300000-workers-for-first-time-599829.

22. Benjamin Beit-Hallahmi, *The Israel Connection: Who Israel Arms and Why* (New York: Pantheon, 1987), 38–75.

23. Beit-Hallahmi, *The Israel Connection*, 132–56; Leonard Weiss, "Flash from the Past: Why an Apparent Israeli Nuclear Test in 1979 Matters Today," *Bulletin of the Atomic Scientists*, September 8, 2015, https://thebulletin.org/flash-past-why-apparent-israeli-nuclear-test-1979-matters-today8734.

24. Beit-Hallahmi, *The Israel Connection*, 85–86.

25. Beit-Hallahmi, *The Israel Connection*, 77.

26. Amir Oren, "The Truth About Israel, Iran and 1980s U.S. Arms Deals," *Haaretz*, November 26, 2010, https://www.haaretz.com/1.5145188.

27. Edo Konrad, "The Story Behind Israel's Shady Military Exports," *+972*, November 22, 2015, https://972mag.com/who-will-stop-the-flow-of-israeli-arms-to-dictatorships/114080/; Alvite Ningthoujam, "Southeast Asia Can't Get Enough of Israel's

Weapons," *National Interest*, June 12, 2016, http://nationalinterest.org/feature/south east-asia-cant-get-enough-israels-weapons-16550.

28. Kubovich, "Israel's Arms Exports Spike."

29. *Haaretz*, "Israel's Largest Arms Clients: India, Azerbaijan and Vietnam," March 15, 2018, https://www.haaretz.com/israel-news/israel-s-largest-arms-clients-india-azerbaijan-and-vietnam-1.5909811.

30. Avner Cohen and William Burr, "What the U.S. Government Really Thought of Israel's Apparent 1979 Nuclear Test," *Politico*, December 8, 2016, https://www.politico.com/magazine/story/2016/12/1979-vela-incident-nuclear-test-israel-south-africa-214507.

31. P. R. Kumaraswamy. "At What Cost Israel-China Ties?" *Middle East Quarterly* 13, no. 2 (2006), https://www.meforum.org/articles/2006/at-what-cost-israel-china-ties.

32. Mark, *Israel: U.S. Foreign Assistance*, updated April 26, 2005, 7–8.

33. William J. Broad, "U.S. and Israel Shelved Laser as a Defense," *New York Times*, July 30, 2006, https://www.nytimes.com/2006/07/30/world/middleeast/30laser.html.

34. Lockheed Martin Israel, https://www.lockheedmartin.com/en-il/index.html.

35. Tyler Rogoway, "New 'Digital Eye Piece' Will Allow U.S. Fighter Pilots to Own the Night Like Never Before," *The Drive*, February 8, 2018, http://www.thedrive.com/the-war-zone/18358/new-digital-eyepiece-will-allow-u-s-fighter-pilots-to-own-the-night-like-never-before.

36. Barbara Opall-Rome, "Lockheed VP: 'There's a Part of Israel in Every F-35,'" *Defense News*, May 4, 2017, https://www.defensenews.com/global/2017/05/04/lockheed-vp-theres-a-part-of-israel-in-every-f-35/.

37. Yuval Azulai and Shmulik Shelach, "Lockheed Martin to Set Up Israeli Development Center," *Globes*, June 4, 2013, http://www.globes.co.il/en/article-1000849860.

38. Tova Cohen, "Lockheed Martin in Research Deal with Israel Tech Company Yissum," *Reuters*, October 6, 2014, https://www.reuters.com/article/us-lockheed-martin-israel-research-idUSKCN0HV0T620141006.

39. Boeing Israel, "Building the Future Together: Boeing in Israel," 2019, https://www.boeing.com/resources/boeingdotcom/company/key_orgs/boeing-international/pdf/israelbackgrounder.pdf.

40. "$37.8M Adds More Israeli Reactive Armor for M2/M3 Bradleys," *Defense Industry Daily*, July 8, 2005, https://www.defenseindustrydaily.com/378m-adds-more-israeli-reactive-armor-for-m2m3-bradleys-0823/.

41. Yaakov Katz, "US Army Using Israeli Surveillance Tech to Protect Troops," *Jerusalem Post*, July 14, 2011, https://www.jpost.com/International/US-Army-using-Israeli-surveillance-tech-to-protect-troops; Yaakov Lappin, "US Army Approves Israeli Surveillance Balloon for Purchase," *Jerusalem Post*, March 19, 2015, https://www.jpost.com/Israel-News/US-Army-approves-Israeli-surveillance-balloon-for-purchase-394405.

42. Yaakov Lappin, "Israel's Elbit to Supply US Marines with Laser System," *Jerusalem Post*, March 22, 2015, https://www.jpost.com/Israel-News/Israels-Elbit-to-supply-US-Marines-with-laser-system-394739.

43. "U.S. Has Chosen Israeli Iron Fist Active Protection System to Secure Armoured Personnel Carrier," *Army Recognition*, June 9, 2016, http://armyrecognition.com/june_2016_global_defense_security_news_industry/u.s._has_chosen_israeli_iron_fist_active_protection_system_to_secure_armoured_personnel_carrier_10906162.html.

44. Jewish Virtual Library, "Israeli Weapons Systems Employed by the U.S.," http://nointervention.com/archive/military/weapons/israelisystems.html.

45. Adam Goldman and Ellen Nakashima, "CIA and Mossad Killed Senior Hezbollah Figure in Car Bombing," *Washington Post*, January 30, 2015, https://www.washingtonpost.com/world/national-security/cia-and-mossad-killed-senior-hezbollah-figure-in-car-bombing/2015/01/30/ebb88682-968a-11e4-8005-1924ede3e54a_story.html; "Was Mughniyeh Hit Really a CIA Op? Israeli Sources Say It Was Mostly Mossad," *Haaretz*, February 16, 2015, https://www.haaretz.com/cia-mossad-bicker-over-credit-for-hit-on-imad-mughniyeh-1.5308266.

46. David E. Sanger, "Obama Order Sped Up Wave of Cyberattacks Against Iran," *New York Times*, June 1, 2012, https://www.nytimes.com/2012/06/01/world/middleeast/obama-ordered-wave-of-cyberattacks-against-iran.html.

47. David E. Sanger and Eric Schmitt, "U.S. Cyberweapons, Used Against Iran and North Korea, Are a Disappointment Against ISIS," *New York Times*, June 12, 2017, https://www.nytimes.com/2017/06/12/world/middleeast/isis-cyber.html.

48. Stephen Graham, *Cities Under Siege: The New Military Urbanism* (London: Verso, 2011); Jeff Halper, *War Against the People: Israel, the Palestinians and Global Pacification* (London: Pluto, 2015).

49. Neve Gordon, "The Political Economy of Israel's Homeland Security/Surveillance Industry," (Queen's University, Kingston, Canada: The New Transpar-

ency Project, Working Paper III, April 28, 2009), 8–9, https://qspace.library.queensu.ca/bitstream/handle/1974/1941/The%2520Political%2520Economy%2520of%2520Israel%25E2%2580%2599s%2520Homeland%2520Security.pdf.

50. The Cirlot Agency, "Elbit Systems of America Peregrine Video," https://www.youtube.com/watch?v=Npu3LeYyRkA.

51. "Hermes 450," http://www.israeli-weapons.com/weapons/aircraft/uav/hermes_450/Hermes_450.html.

52. Kathleen Miller, "Elbit Systems Wins Homeland Security Contract," *Bloomberg*, February 27, 2014, https://www.bloomberg.com/news/articles/2014–02–27/israel-s-elbit-wins-u-s-border-surveillance-contract.

53. Israel Weapons Industries, "IWI US Academy Classes Now Open," January 2017, https://iwi.us/iwi-us-training-division-classes-now-open/.

54. Metropolitan College of New York, "MPA in Emergency and Disaster Management," https://www.mcny.edu/academics/school-public-affairs-administration/mpa-emergency-disaster-management/. An archived reference to the 2005 trip appears at http://www.mcny.edu/publicaffairs/israelgallery.php. The current website does not mention it.

55. IMI Systems, "Training the Key to Success," http://www.imisystems.com/wp-content/uploads/2017/01/IMI-Academy-for-Advanced-HLS-Training.pdf.

56. Georgia State University, "Georgia International Law Enforcement Exchange (GILEE)," http://gilee.gsu.edu/; Anna Simonton, "Inside GILEE, the US-Israel Law Enforcement Training Program Seeking to Redefine Terrorism," *Mondoweiss*, January 5, 2016, http://mondoweiss.net/2016/01/enforcement-training-terrorism/.

57. Simone Wilson, "LAPD Scopes Out Israeli Drones, 'Big Data' Solutions," *Jewish Journal*, February 13, 2014, http://jewishjournal.com/news/nation/126816/.

58. Margaret Hartmann, "NYPD Now Has an Israel Branch," *New York Magazine*, September 6, 2012, http://nymag.com/daily/intelligencer/2012/09/nypd-now-has-an-israel-branch.html.

59. ADL, "Partnering with Law Enforcement," https://www.adl.org/who-we-are/our-organization/signature-programs/partnering-with-law-enforcement.

60. JINSA, http://www.jinsa.org/.

61. Quoted in Jordan Crandall, ed., *Under Fire.1: The Organization and Representation of Violence* (Rotterdam: Witte de With Center for Contemporary Art, 2004), 84.

62. Graham, *Cities Under Siege*, 229.

63. Graham, *Cities Under Siege*, 229; Julian Borger, "Israel Trains US Assassination Squads in Iraq," *The Guardian*, December 8, 2003, https://www.theguardian.com/world/2003/dec/09/iraq.israel.

64. "Daily Alert," Prepared for the Conference of Presidents of Major American Jewish Organizations by the Jerusalem Center for Public Affairs, August 18, 2004, http://www.dailyalert.org/archive/2004-08/2004-08-18.html.

65. Graham, *Cities Under Siege*, 229–30.

66. Graham, *Cities Under Siege*, 194.

67. Dan Williams, "Israel Provides Intelligence on Islamic State—Western Diplomat," *Reuters*, September 8, 2014, https://www.reuters.com/article/mideast-islamicstate-israel/israel-provides-intelligence-on-islamic-state-western-diplomat-idUSL5N0R93CH20140908.

68. Association of America-Israel Chambers of Commerce, http://www.israeltrade.org/.

69. Miriam Pollock, "The Sabras of Silicon Valley," *The Tower* 19 (October 2014), http://www.thetower.org/article/the-sabras-of-silicon-valley/.

70. Leon Lazaroff, "China to Capitalize on Nasdaq Jump with Tech IPOs, BNY Says," *Bloomberg*, May 7, 2012, https://www.bloomberg.com/news/articles/2012-05-07/china-to-take-advantage-of-nasdaq-jump-with-tech-ipos-bny-says.

71. Steven Scheer, "US Intel Plans $5 Bln Investment in Israeli Plant," Reuters, February 21, 2018; Mark Scott, "Intel Buys Mobileye in $15.3 Billion Bid to Lead Self-Driving Car Market," *New York Times*, March 17, 2017, https://www.nytimes.com/2017/03/13/business/dealbook/intel-mobileye-autonomous-cars-israel.html.

72. Investigate, "HP Inc.," http://investigate.afsc.org/company/hp-inc.

73. Who Profits, "Motorola Solutions Israel," https://whoprofits.org/company/motorola-solutions-israel.

74. Yuval Azulai and Tzahi Hoffman, "Motorola Solutions to Provide IDF's Battlefield Smartphone," *Globes*, June 29, 2017, http://www.globes.co.il/en/article-1000906408; Ferry Biedermann, "INVESTING IN: ISRAEL

Microsoft Reportedly Buys Israeli Cybersecurity Firm Hexadite," *CNBC*, May 24, 2017, https://www.cnbc.com/2017/05/24/microsoft-reportedly-buys-israeli-cybersecurity-firm-hexadite.html.

75. Tova Cohen, "PayPal Sets Up Israeli Security Center, Buys CyActive," *Reuters*, March 11, 2015, https://www.reuters.com/article/us-cyactive-m-a-ebay/paypal-sets-up-israeli-security-center-buys-cyactive-idUSKBN0M70VO20150311.

76. Who Profits, "Delta Galil Industries," https://whoprofits.org/company/delta-galil-industries/.

77. Philip Weiss, "'Forward' Columnist and Emily's List Leader Relate 'Gigantic,' 'Shocking' Role of Jewish Democratic Donors," *Mondoweiss*, April 19, 2016, http://mondoweiss.net/2016/04/forward-columnist-and-emilys-list-leader-relate-gigantic-shocking-role-of-jewish-democratic-donors/.

78. Center for Responsive Politics, "2016 Top Donors to Outside Spending Groups," https://www.opensecrets.org/outsidespending/summ.php?cycle=2016&disp=D&type=V&superonly=N. Goldberg spoke of the 50 largest donors; CRP's list now includes the 100 largest donors.

79. Weiss, "'Forward' Columnist and Emily's List Leader Relate"

80. Gil Troy, *The Jewish Vote: Political Power and Identity in US Elections*. Ruderman Program for American Jewish Studies, University of Haifa, 2016, 5, http://rudermanfoundation.org/wp-content/uploads/2017/11/Jewish-Vote-Ruderman-Program.pdf.

81. Center for Responsive Politics, "Top Individual Contributors: All Federal Contributions," https://www.opensecrets.org/overview/topindivs.php?cycle=2016&view=fc.

82. CUFI, homepage, www.cufi.org.

83. Chris Moody, "How Republicans Are Being Taught to Talk about Occupy Wall Street," *The Ticket*, December 1, 2011, https://www.yahoo.com/news/blogs/ticket/republicans-being-taught-talk-occupy-wall-street-133707949.html.

84. Center for Responsive Politics, "Top Individual Contributors: All Federal Contributions."

85. Connie Bruck, "The Influencer," *New Yorker*, May 10, 2010, https://www.newyorker.com/magazine/2010/05/10/the-influencer.

86. Clinton to Saban, July 2, 2015, https://www.documentcloud.org/documents/2158218-hillary-clintons-letter-to-haim-saban-against-bds.html.

87. William Appleman Williams, *Empire as a Way of Life: An Essay on the Causes and Character of America's Present Predicament, Along with a Few Thoughts About an Alternative* (New York: Oxford University Press, 1980).

CHAPTER 11

1. Zachary Lockman, *Comrades and Enemies: Arab and Jewish Workers in Palestine, 1906–1948* (Berkeley: University of California Press, 1996).

2. Sherene Seikaly, *Men of Capital: Scarcity and Economy in Mandate Palestine* (Stanford, CA: Stanford University Press, 2016).

3. Antoine Mansour, "The West Bank Economy: 1948–1984" in *The Palestinian Economy: Studies in Development under Prolonged Occupation*, ed. George T. Abed (London: Routledge, 2015), 71–75.

4. Sara Roy, *The Gaza Strip: The Political Economy of De-development* (Washington, DC: Institute for Palestine Studies, 1995), 76–92.

5. Brian Van Arkadie, *Benefits and Burdens: A Report on the West Bank and Gaza Strip Economies Since 1967* (Washington DC: Carnegie Endowment for International Peace, 1977); S. Dessus and E. Bulmer, "The Choice of Trade Regime Depends on Multiple Other Factors," in *The Economics of Palestine: Economic Policy and Institutional Reform for a Viable Palestinian State*, ed. David Cobhan and Nu'man Kanafani (London: Routledge, 2004), 12–32; World Bank, *Developing the Occupied Territories: An Investment In Peace, vol. 2, The Economy* (Washington, DC: World Bank, 1993).

6. United Nations Conference for Trade and Development, *The Palestinian Economy and Prospects for Regional Cooperation* (Geneva: UNCTAD/GDS/SEU/2, 1998).

7. World Bank, *Developing the Occupied Territories: An Investment in Peace, vol. 4, Agriculture* (Washington, DC: World Bank, 1993).

8. Fadle Naqib, "Economic Aspects of the Palestinian-Israeli Conflict: The Collapse of the Oslo Accord," (World Institute for Development Economics Research/United Nations University Discussion Paper, Series No. 2002/100, 2002).

9. Naqib, "Economic Aspects."

10. Osama Hamed and Radwan Shaban, "One Sided Customs and Monetary Union: The Case of the West Bank and Gaza Strip under Israeli Occupation," in *The Economics of Middle East Peace*, ed. Stanley Fischer, Dani Rodrik, and Elias Tuma (Cambridge, MA: MIT Press, 1993), 117–48.

11. Nu'man Kanafani, *Trade Relations Between Palestine and Israel: Free Trade Area or Customs Union?* (Ramallah: Palestine Economic Policy Research Institute, 1996).

12. German-Arab Chamber of Commerce, *Trade for Peace in the New Middle East* (Cairo: Commission for the European Communities, 1995).

13. World Bank, *Developing the Occupied Territories: An Investment in Peace, vol. 2, The Economy.*

14. At the time of the Israeli occupation in 1967, there were thirty-two bank branches operating in the West Bank, including nine branches in Jerusalem. Six bank branches operated in the Gaza Strip.

15. Osama Hamed, *Palestinian Banking Sector: Statistical Study—Issue 1* (Jerusalem: Palestine Economic Policy Research Institute, 1995).

16. Fadle Naqib, *A Preliminary Evaluation of the Tax System in the West Bank and Gaza Strip* (Ramallah: Palestine Economic Policy Research Institute, 1996).

17. Leila Farsakh, *Palestinian Labour Migration to Israel: Labour, Land Occupation* (London: Routledge, 2005).

18. For the 2019 *Human Development Report* on the State of Palestine see http://hdr.undp.org/sites/all/themes/hdr_theme/country-notes/PSE.pdf.

19. State of Palestine, Human Development Indicators, http://hdr.undp.org/en/countries/profiles/PSE.

20. From 1980 to 1985 the Israeli currency was the shekel (IS). The new Israeli shekel (NIS) was introduced on January 1, 1986, at the rate of NIS 1 = IS 1,000.

21. World Bank, *Developing the Occupied Territories: An Investment in Peace, vol. 2, The Economy.*

22. World Bank, *Developing the Occupied Territories: An Investment in Peace, vol. 2, The Economy.*

23. World Bank, *Developing the Occupied Territories: An Investment in Peace, vol. 2, The Economy.*

24. Arie Arnon, Israel Luski, Avia Spivak, and Jimmy Weinblatt, *The Palestinian Economy: Between Imposed Integration and Voluntary Separation* (Leiden: Brill, 1997).

25. George Abed, "The Palestinian Economy Under Occupation: Introduction and Overview," in *The Palestinian Economy: Studies in Development Under Prolonged Occupation*, ed. George Abed (London: Routledge, 2016), 1–12.

26. United Nations Conference for Trade and Development, *Developments in the Economy of the Occupied Palestinian Territory* (Geneva: UNCTAD/TD/B/40(1)/8), 1993).

27. United Nations Conference for Trade and Development, *Developments in the Economy of the Occupied Palestinian Territory.*

28. United Nations Conference for Trade and Development, *Developments in the Economy of the Occupied Palestinian Territory.*

29. The agreements signed were to cover the transitional period (1994–1998), but they have remained in effect until now. They include the Declaration of Principles (Oslo I) signed in September 1993, the Protocol on Economic Relations (Paris Agreement) signed in April 1994, the Agreement on the Gaza Strip and Jericho Areas (Cairo Agreement) signed in May 1994, and the Israel-Palestinian Interim Agreement on the West Bank and Gaza Strip (Oslo II) signed in September 1995.

30. Amnesty International, *Israel and the Occupied Territories: The Demolition and Dispossession of Palestinian Homes* (Jerusalem: Report No. MDE 15/059/1999, 1999).

31. United Nations Office for the Coordination of Humanitarian Affairs, *The Humanitarian Impact on Palestinians of Israeli Settlements and Other Infrastructure in the West Bank* (Jerusalem, 2007).

32. Sara Roy, "De-development Revisited: Palestinian Economy and Society Since Oslo," *Journal of Palestine Studies* 28, no. 3 (1999): 64–82.

33. As of summer 2010, 520 km of the planned 810 km, or 64 percent, had been completed.

34. Stop the Wall Campaign, "The Wall," 2011, http://www.stopthewall.org/the-wall; B'Tselem, "The Separation Barrier," November 11, 2017, https://www.btselem.org/separation_barrier; UN Office for the Coordination of Humanitarian Affairs, Occupied Palestinian Territory, "The Humanitarian Impact of the Barrier," July 2013, https://www.un.org/unispal/document/auto-insert-200306/.

35. B'Tselem, "13 Feb. 2006: Israel Has De Facto Annexed the Jordan Valley," February 13, 2006, https://www.btselem.org/jordan_valley, and "The Jordan Valley," November 11, 2017, https://www.btselem.org/jordan_valley.

36. Stop the Wall Campaign, "The Wall."

37. Palestinian Authority, *The Palestinian National Early Recovery and Reconstruction Plan for Gaza 2009–2010*. Document presented at the International Conference in Support of the Palestinian Economy for the Reconstruction of Gaza, Sharm El-Sheikh, March, 2, 2009.

38. Aljazeera, "A Guide to the Gaza Strip, From Israel's Occupation to a Decade of Siege, Here Is All You Need to Know about 'the World's Largest Open-Air Prison," (2017), https://www.aljazeera.com/indepth/features/2017/06/guide-gaza-strip-170614124611554.html.

39. Palestinian Central Bureau of Statistics, "PCBS Preliminary Estimates for the Economic Losses in Gaza Strip Caused by Israeli Aggression," 2009. http://www.pcbs.gov.ps/Portals/_pcbs/PressRelease/Gaza_lost_e.pdf.

40. International Monetary Fund, "West Bank and Gaza: Concluding Statement of an IMF Staff Visit," March 18, 2015, https://www.imf.org/en/News/Articles/2015/09/28/04/52/mcs012915; Sophia Jones, "If You Make a Thousand Dollars in Gaza, You'd Make a Million Outside," *Huffington Post*, December 6, 2017, https://www.huffingtonpost.com/2015/05/12/gaza-economy-israel_n_7258154.html.

41. Raja Khalidi and Sobhi Samour, "Neoliberalism as Liberation: The Statehood Program and the Remaking of the Palestinian National Movement," *Journal of Palestine Studies* 40, no. 2 (Winter 2011): 6–25.

42. The BDS movement has three main objectives: ending the occupation of the West Bank and Gaza Strip, equality of Palestinians living inside Israel, and upholding the rights of Palestinian refugees.

43. United Nations Conference for Trade and Development. "Report on UNCTAD Assistance to the Palestinian People: Developments in the Economy of the Occupied Palestinian Territory," (Geneva TD/B/58/4, 2011), http://unctad.org/en/Docs/tdb58d4_en.pdf.

44. Omar Barghouti and Samia Al-Botmeh, *Impact of the BDS Movement on Israel: The Economic Dimension*. Background Paper #3 (Ramallah: Palestine Economic Policy Research Institute, 2014), https://www.mas.ps/files/server/20141911184335-1.pdf.

45. Palestinian Central Bureau of Statistics, *Foreign Trade Statistics* (2010), www.pcbs.gov.ps/Portals/_pcbs/FogreignTrade/countries_e.html.

46. Radwan Shaban, "Worsening Economic Outcomes Since 1994 Despite Elements of Improvement," in *Development Under Adversity: The Palestinian Economy in Transition*, ed. Radwan Shaban and Ishac Diwan (Ramallah: Palestine Economic Policy Research Institute, 1999), 17–32.

47. Palestinian Central Bureau of Statistics, "The Main Indicators of Foreign Trade Observed in Palestine, 2016–2017," http://www.pcbs.gov.ps/Portals/_Rainbow/Documents/Main%20Indicator_A.html.

48. UNCTAD, "The Palestinian Economy: Macroeconomic and Trade Policymaking under Occupation" (Geneva: UNCTAD, 2012).

49. *MAS Economic Monitor* 14 (Ramallah: Palestine Economic Policy Research Institute, 2008).

50. Osama Hamed, *The Banking System: Reality and Potential* (Ramallah: Palestine Economic Policy Research Institute, 1996).

51. Osama Hamed, *Money Supply Estimation, Foreign Exchange Risks and Other Challenges to the Palestinian Economy in the Absence of a National Currency* (Ramallah: Palestine Economic Policy Research Institute, 2015).

52. The Palestine Economic Policy Research Institute, *MAS Economic Monitor—Special Report*. (Ramallah, 2001).

53. World Bank, *Country Economic Memorandum—Growth in West Bank and Gaza: Opportunities and Constraints* I (Washington DC: World Bank, 2006).

54. Israel first refused to transfer revenues to the PA between September 2000 and December 2002. Transfers resumed, but were halted in 2006–7, again, for political reasons.

55. Palestinian Central Bureau of Statistics, "National Accounts Statistics," http://www.pcbs.gov.ps/site/lang__ar/741/default.aspx.

56. Palestinian Central Bureau of Statistics, "National Accounts Statistics."

57. Palestinian Central Bureau of Statistics, "National Accounts Statistics."

58. Shaban, "Worsening Economic Outcomes Since 1994."

59. Paltrade and Palestinian Federation of Industries, *Border Closures: Effect on Private Sector in Gaza*. 2007.

60. Palestinian Authority, *The Palestinian National Early Recovery and Reconstruction Plan for Gaza 2009–2010*. Document presented at the International Conference in Support of the Palestinian Economy for the Reconstruction of Gaza, Sharm El-Sheikh (March, 2, 2009).

61. The Applied Research Institute—Jerusalem, *The Economic Costs of the Israeli Occupation for the Occupied Palestinian Territory* (Jerusalem, 2011, 2015).

62. Radwan Shaban and Samia Al-Botmeh, *Poverty in the West Bank and Gaza Strip* (Ramallah: Economic Policy Research Institute, 1995).

63. Palestinian Central Bureau of Statistics, *Labour Force Survey*. Annual Report (Ramallah, 2009).

64. *Palestine Monitor 2009 Factbook*, www.palestinemonitor.org/spip/IMG/pdf/factbook_Final_online-2.pdf.

65. *Palestine Monitor 2009 Factbook.*

66. Shaban and Al-Botmeh, *Poverty in the West Bank and Gaza Strip.*

67. Palestine Economic Policy Research Institute (MAS), *Economic Monitor* 50 (Ramallah, 2017).

68. Claude Bruderlein, "Human Security Challenges in the Occupied Palestinian Territory," in *Aid, Diplomacy and Facts on the Ground: The Case of Palestine*, ed. M. Keating, A. Le More, and R. Lowe (London: Chatham House, 2005).

69. World Bank, *The Trust Fund for Gaza and the West Bank—Status, Strategy and Request for Replenishment*, Report No: 27094–62 (Washington, DC, 2003).

70. Sahar Taghdisi-Rad, "Political Economy of Aid in Conflict: An Analysis of Pre- and Post-Intifada Donor Behaviour in the Occupied Palestinian Territories," *Stability: International Journal of Security and Development* 4, no. 1 (2015): 1–18, https://www.stabilityjournal.org/articles/10.5334/sta.fl/.

71. UNCTAD, *The Palestinian War-Torn Economy: Aid, Development and State Formation*. Paper No. UNCTAD/GDS/APP/2006/1 (New York: UNCTAD, 2006).

72. Anne Le More, *International Assistance to the Palestinians After Oslo: Political Guilt, Wasted Money* (New York: Routledge, 2008), 148.

73. Palestine Economic Policy Research Institute, *Economic Monitor* 51 (February 2018).

74. Taghdisi-Rad, "Political Economy of Aid in Conflict," 14.

Selected Readings

Full bibliographies for each chapter, as well as other teaching resources are available at the Political Economy Project website, www.politicaleconomyproject.org/book1.

Introduction

Aglietta, Michel. *A Theory of Capitalist Regulation: The US Experience.* London: Verso, 1976.

Amin, Samir. *Accumulation on a World Scale: A Critique of the Theory of Underdevelopment.* New York: Monthly Review, 1974.

Batatu, Hanna. *The Old Social Classes and the Revolutionary Movements of Iraq: A Study of Iraq's Old Landed and Commercial Classes and of its Communists, Ba'thists, and Free Officers.* Princeton, NJ: Princeton University Press, 1978.

Beinin, Joel. *Workers and Peasants in the Modern Middle East.* Cambridge: Cambridge University Press, 2001.

Boyer, Robert. *The Regulation School: A Critical Introduction.* New York: Columbia University Press, 1990.

Chakravarti, Leila Zaki. *Made in Egypt: Gendered Identity and Aspiration on the Globalised Shop Floor.* New York: Berghahn, 2016.

Hammad, Hanan. *Industrial Sexuality: Gender, Urbanization, and Social Transformation in Egypt.* Austin: University of Texas Press, 2016.

Jones, Toby Craig. *Desert Kingdom: How Oil and Water Forged Modern Saudi Arabia.* Cambridge, MA: Harvard University Press, 2010.

Khalili, Laleh. *Sinews of War and Trade: Shipping and Capitalism in the Arabian Peninsula*. London: Verso, 2020.

Khater, Akram. *Inventing Home: Emigration, Gender, and the Middle Class in Lebanon, 1870–1920*. Berkeley: University of California Press, 2001.

Marglin, Stephen, and Juliet Schor, eds. *The Golden Age of Capitalism*. Oxford: Clarendon, 1990.

Owen, Roger. "The Middle East in the Eighteenth Century: An Islamic Society in Decline: A Critique of Gibb and Bowen's *Islamic Society and the West*." *Review of Middle East Studies* 1 (1975): 101–12.

Panitch, Leo, and Sam Gindin. *The Making of Global Capitalism: The Political Economy of American Empire*. London: Verso, 2012.

Pomeranz, Kenneth. *The Great Divergence: China, Europe, and the Making of the Modern World Economy*. Princeton, NJ: Princeton University Press, 2000.

Quataert, Donald. "Labor History in the Ottoman Middle East, 1700–1922," special section of *International Labor and Working-Class History* 60 (October 2001).

Saad, Reem. "State, Landlord, Parliament and Peasant: The Story of the 1992 Tenancy Law in Egypt." In *Agriculture in Egypt: from Pharaonic to Modern Times*, edited by Alan K. Bowman and Eugene Rogan. Oxford: Oxford University Press for the British Academy, 1999.

Thompson, Elizabeth. *Colonial Citizens: Republican Rights, Paternal Privilege, and Gender in French Syria and Lebanon*. New York: Columbia University Press, 2000.

Tucker, Judith E. *Women in Nineteenth Century Egypt*. Cambridge: Cambridge University Press, 1985.

Vitalis, Robert. *America's Kingdom: Mythmaking on the Saudi Oil Frontier*. Stanford, CA: Stanford University Press, 2007.

Vitalis, Robert. *When Capitalists Collide: Business Conflict and the End of Empire in Egypt*. Berkeley: University of California Press, 1995.

Yousfi, Hèla. *L'UGTT, une passion tunisienne: Enquête sur les syndicalistes en révolution 2011–2014*. Tunis: Editions Mohamed Ali / IRMC, 2015.

PART I. CATEGORIES OF ANALYSIS

Chapter 1. Landed Property, Capital Accumulation, and Polymorphous Capitalism: Egypt and the Levant

Akarlı, Engin Deniz. "Gedik: A Bundle of Rights and Obligations for Istanbul Artisansand Traders, 1750–1840." In *Law, Anthropology, and the Construction of the*

Social: Making Persons and Things, edited by Alain Pottage and Martha Mundy, 166–200. Cambridge: Cambridge University Press, 2004.

Alff, Kristen. "The Business of Property: Levantine Joint-Stock Companies, Land, Law, and the Development of Capitalism around the Mediterranean, 1850–1925." PhD diss., Stanford University, 2019.

Alff, Kristen. "Levantine Joint-Stock Companies, Trans-Mediterranean Partnerships, and Nineteenth-Century Capitalist Development." *Comparative Studies in Society and History* 60, no. 1 (2018): 150–77.

Cuno, Kenneth. "Origins of Private Ownership of Land in Egypt." *International Journal of Middle East Studies* 12 (1980): 245–75.

Cuno, Kenneth. *The Pasha's Peasants: Land, Society and Economy in Lower Egypt, 1740–1858*. Cambridge: Cambridge University Press, 1992.

Doumani, Beshara. *Rediscovering Palestine: Merchants and Peasants in Jabal Nablus, 1700–1900*. Berkeley: University of California Press, 1995.

Gottein, S. D. *A Mediterranean Society: The Jewish Communities of the Arab World as Portrayed in the Documents of the Cairo Geniza*. Berkeley: University of California Press, 1978.

Gran, Peter. *Islamic Roots of Capitalism in Egypt, 1760–1840*. Syracuse, NY: Syracuse University Press, 1998.

Löwy, Michael. "Marx and Weber: Critics of Capitalism." *New Politics* XI-2, no. 42 (Winter 2007).

Mikhail, Alan. *Nature and Empire in Ottoman Egypt: An Environmental History*. Cambridge: Cambridge University Press, 2011.

Owen, Roger. *The Middle East in the World Economy, 1800–1914*. London: I. B. Tauris, 2002.

Owen, Roger. "The Study of Middle Eastern Industrial History: Notes on the Interrelationship between Factories and Small-Scale Manufacturing with Special References to Lebanese Silk and Egyptian Sugar, 1900–1930." *International Journal of Middle East Studies* 16, no. 4 (November 1984): 475–87.

Raymond, André. "The Economic Crisis of Egypt in the Eighteenth Century." In *The Islamic Middle East, 700–1900*, edited by Abraham L. Udovitch, 687–707. Princeton, NJ: Darwin, 1981.

Rodinson, Maxime. *Islam and Capitalism*. Translated by Brian Pearce. New York: Pantheon, 1973.

Salzmann, Ariel. "An Ancien Régime Revisited: "Privatization" and Political Economy." *Politics & Society* 21, no. 4 (December 1993): 393–423.

Chapter 2. State, Market, and Class: Egypt, Syria, and Tunisia

Egypt

'Abd al-Fadil, Mahmud. *al-Tahawwulat al-iqtisadiyya fi al-rif al-misri (1952–1970)*. Cairo: al-Hay'a al-Misriyya al-'Amma li'l-Kitab, 1978.

Abul-Magd, Zeinab. *Imagined Empires: A History of Revolt in Egypt*. Berkeley: University of California Press, 2013.

Abul-Magd, Zeinab. *Militarizing the Nation: Army Business and Revolution in Egypt*. New York: Columbia University Press, 2017.

Bier, Laura. "The Family is a Factory: Gender, Citizenship, and the Regulation of Reproduction in Post-War Egypt," *Feminist Studies* 36, no. 2 (Summer 2010): 404–32.

Bush, Ray, ed. *Counter Revolution in Egypt's Countryside*. London: Zed, 2002.

Davis, Eric. *Challenging Colonialism: Bank Misr and Egyptian Industrialization, 1920–1941*. Princeton, NJ: Princeton University Press, 1983.

'Isawi, Ibrahim al-. *Fi islah ma afsadahu al-infitah*. Cairo: Kitab al-Ahali, Jaridat al-Ahali, Hizb al-Tajammu' al-Watani al-Taqaddumi al-Wahdawi, 1984.

Russell, Mona. "Marketing the Modern Egyptian Girl: Whitewashing Soap and Clothes from the Late Nineteenth Century to 1936," *Journal of Middle East Women's Studies* 6, no. 3 (Fall 2010): 19–57.

Vitalis, Robert. *When Capitalists Collide: Business Conflict and the End of Empire in Egypt*. Berkeley: University of California Press, 1995.

Waterbury, John. *The Egypt of Nasser and Sadat: The Political Economy of Two Regimes*. Princeton, NJ: Princeton University Press, 1983.

Syria

Abboud, Samer. *Syria*. Cambridge: Polity Press, 2018.

Batatu, Hanna. *Syria's Peasantry, the Descendants of Its Lesser Rural Notables, and Their Politics*. Princeton, NJ: Princeton University Press, 2012.

Dalila, Arif. "Ajz al-muwazana al-'amma wa-subul mu'alajatuh'" [The general budget: some solutions]. In *Conference Series, Damascus, April 20, 1999*. Damascus: Economic Sciences Association, 1999.

Dalila, Arif. "al-Qita' al-'amm wa-dawruhu fi al-tanmiyya" [The public sector and its role in development]. In *Conference Series, Damascus*. Damascus: Economic Sciences Association, 1986.

Haddad, Bassam. *Business Networks in Syria: The Political Economy of Authoritarian Resilience*. Stanford, CA: Stanford University Press, 2011.

Heydemann, Steven. *Authoritarianism in Syria: Institutions and Social Conflict 1946–1970*. Ithaca, NY: Cornell University Press, 1999.

Hinnebusch, Raymond A. *Authoritarian Power and State Formation in Ba'thist Syria.* Boulder, CO: Westview, 1990.

Hinnebusch, Raymond A. *Syria: Revolution from Above.* London: Routledge, 2001.

Khoury, Philip. *Syria and the French Mandate: The Politics of Arab Nationalism, 1920–1945*. Princeton, NJ: Princeton University Press, 1987.

Kienle, Everhard, ed. *Contemporary Syria: Liberalization between Cold War and Cold Peace*. London: British Academic, 1994.

Longuenesse, Elisabeth. "Labor in Syria." In *The Social History of Labor in the Middle East,* edited by Ellis Jay Goldberg. Boulder, CO: Westview, 1996.

Neep, Daniel. *Occupying Syria under the French Mandate: Insurgency, Space and State Formation*. Cambridge: Cambridge University Press, 2012.

Perthes, Volker. "The Private Sector, Economic Liberalization and the Prospects of Democratization: The Case of Syria and some other Arab Countries." In *Democracy without Democrats? The Renewal of Politics in the Muslim World,* edited by Ghassan Salamé. London: I. B. Tauris, 1994.

Perthes, Volker. *The Political Economy of Syria Under Asad*. London: I. B. Tauris, 1995.

Seale, Patrick. *Asad: The Struggle for the Middle East*. London: I. B. Tauris, 1988.

Waterbury, John. "Twilight of the State Bourgeoisie." *IJMES* 23 (1991).

Tunisia

Attia, Habib. "Les hautes steppes tunisiennes de la société pastorale à la société paysanne." PhD diss., Université Paris Diderot–Paris 7, 1977.

Ayeb, Habib. "Food Issues and Revolution: The Process of Dispossession, Class Solidarity, and Popular Uprising: The Case of Sidi Bouzid in Tunisia." *The Food Question in the Middle East: Cairo Papers in Social Science* 34, no. 4 (2017).

Bellin, Eva Rana. *Stalled Democracy: Capital, Labor, and the Paradox of State-Sponsored Development*. Ithaca, NY: Cornell University Press, 2002.

Duvignaud, Jean. *Change at Shebika: Report from a North African Village*. Austin: University of Texas Press, 1977.

Ferchiou, Sophie. *Les Femmes dans l'agriculture Tunisienne*. Aix-en-Provence: Edisud, 1985.

Lahmar, Mouldi. *Du Mouton à l'olivier: Essai Sur Les Mutations de La Vie Rurale Maghrébine*. Vol. 12. Tunis: Cérès éditions, 1994.

Mahjoub, Azzam. Industrie et accumulation du capital en Tunisie. Centre d'études, de recherches et de publication de la Faculté de droit et des sciences politiques et économiques de Tunis, 1983.

Poncet, Jean. *La colonisation et l'agriculture européennes en Tunisie depuis 1881*. Paris: Impr. Nationale, 1962.

Valensi, Lucette. *Fellahs tunisiens: l'économie rurale et la vie des campagnes aux 18e et 19e siècles*. Paris: Mouton, 1977.

Yousfi, Hèla. *L'UGTT, une passion tunisienne: Enquête sur les syndicalistes en révolution*. Paris: Karthala, 2015.

Chapter 3. Ten Propositions on Oil

Al-Nakib, Farah. *Kuwait Transformed: A History of Oil and Urban Life*. Stanford, CA: Stanford University Press, 2016.

Dietrich, Christopher R. W. *Oil Revolution: Anticolonial Elites, Sovereign Rights, and the Economic Culture of Decolonization*. Cambridge: Cambridge University Press, 2017.

Hanieh, Adam. *Capitalism and Class in the Gulf Arab States*. New York: Palgrave Macmillan, 2011.

Jones, Toby. *Desert Kingdom: How Oil and Water Forged Modern Saudi Arabia*. Cambridge, MA: Harvard University Press, 2010.

Lowi, Miriam. *Oil Wealth and the Poverty of Politics: Algeria Compared*. Cambridge: Cambridge University Press, 2009.

Mahdavy, Hossein. "The Pattern and Problems of Economic Development in Rentier States: The Case of Iran." In *Studies in the Economic History of the Middle East*, edited by M. A. Cook. Oxford: Oxford University Press, 1970.

Mitchell, Timothy. *Carbon Democracy: Political Power in the Age of Oil*. London: Verso, 2012.

Nowell, Gregory. *Mercantile States and the World Oil Cartel, 1900–1939*. Ithaca, NY: Cornell University Press, 1994.

Shafiee, Katayoun. *Machineries of Oil: An Infrastructural History of BP in Iran*. Cambridge, MA.: MIT Press, 2018

Vitalis, Robert. *America's Kingdom: Mythmaking on the Saudi Oil Frontier*. 2nd ed. London: Verso, 2009.

Vitalis, Robert. *Oilcraft: The Myths of Scarcity and Security that Haunt U.S. Energy Policy*. Stanford: Stanford University Press, 2020.

Yergin, Daniel. *The Prize: The Epic Quest for Oil, Money, and Power.* New York: Simon & Schuster, 1991.

Chapter 4. Regional Militaries and the Global Military-Industrial Complex

Adams, Gordon. *The Politics of Defense Contracting: The Iron Triangle.* New Brunswick, NJ: Transaction, 1982.

Akca, Ismet. *Military-Economic Structure in Turkey: Present Situation, Problems and Solutions.* Istanbul: TESEV, 2010.

Bou Nassif, Hicham. "Wedded to Mubarak: The Second Careers and Financial Rewards of Egypt's Military Elite, 1981–2011," *Middle East Journal* 67 no. 4 (Autumn 2013): 509–30.

Brommelhorster, Jorn, and Wolf-Christian Paes, eds. *The Military as an Economic Actor: Soldiers in Business.* New York: Palgrave MacMillan, 2003.

Burrows, Gideon. *The No-Nonsense Guide to the Arms Trade.* London: Verso, 2002.

Droz-Vincent, Philippe. "From Political to Economic Actors: The Changing Role of Middle Eastern Armies." In *Debating Arab Authoritarianism: Dynamics and Durability in Nondemocratic Regimes,* edited by Oliver Schlumberger, 195–211. Stanford, CA: Stanford University Press, 2007.

Grawert, Elke, and Zeinab Abul-Magd, eds. *Businessmen in Arms. How the Military and Other Armed Groups Profit in the MENA Region.* Lanham, MD: Rowman & Littlefield, 2016.

Hartung, William D. *And Weapons for All.* New York: Harper Collins, 1994.

Heydemann, Steven, ed. *War, Institutions, and Social Change in the Middle East.* Berkeley: University of California Press, 2000.

Nitzan, Jonathan, and Shimshon Bichler. "Bringing Capital Accumulation Back In: The Weapondollar-Petrodollar Coalition—Military Contractors, Oil Companies and Middle East 'Energy Conflicts.'" *Review of International Political Economy* 2, no. 3 (Summer 1995): 446–515.

Sayigh, Yezid. "Above the State: The Officers' Republic in Egypt." Carnegie Endowment for International Peace, 2012. https://carnegie-mec.org/2012/08/01/above-state-officers-republic-in-egypt-pub-48972.

Sharabi, Hisham. "Parliamentary Government and Military Autocracy in the Middle East." *Orbis,* no. 4 (1960): 338–55.

Soliman, Samer. *The Autumn of Dictatorship: Fiscal Crisis and Political Change in Egypt Under Mubarak.* Stanford, CA: Stanford University Press, 2011.

Thomas, Martin. *Empires of Intelligence: Security Services and Colonial Disorder After 1914*. Berkeley: University of California Press, 2008.

PART II. COUNTRY/REGIONAL STUDIES

Chapter 5. Rethinking Class and State in the Gulf Cooperation Council States

Al Rasheed, Madawi. *A History of Saudi Arabia*. Cambridge: Cambridge University Press, 2010.

Beblawi, Hazem, and Giacomo Luciani, eds. *The Rentier State: Nation, State and the Integration of the Arab World*. London: Croom Helm, 1987.

Crystal, Jill. *Oil and Politics in the Gulf: Rulers and Merchants in Kuwait and Qatar*. Glasgow: Cambridge University Press, 1995.

Hanieh, Adam. *Money, Markets, and Monarchies: The Gulf Cooperation Council and the Political Economy of the Contemporary Middle East*. Cambridge: Cambridge University Press, 2018.

Hertog, Steffen. *Princes, Brokers and Bureaucrats: Oil and the State in Saudi Arabia*. Ithaca, NY: Cornell University Press, 2011.

Jones, Toby Craig. *Desert Kingdom: How Oil and Water Forged Modern Saudi Arabia*. Cambridge, MA: Harvard University Press, 2010.

Kanna, Ahmad. *Dubai: The City as Corporation*. Minneapolis: University of Minnesota Press, 2011.

Longva, Anh Nga. *Walls Built on Sand: Migration, Exclusion and Society in Kuwait*. Boulder, CO: Westview, 1997.

Mitchell, Timothy. *Carbon Democracy: Political Power in the Age of Oil*. London: Verso, 2011.

Ulrichsen, Kristian Coates. *The Gulf States in International Political Economy*. Basingstoke, UK: Palgrave Macmillan, 2016.

Valeri, Marc. *Oman: Politics and Society in the Qaboos State*. New York: Oxford University Press, 2009.

Vitalis, Robert. *America's Kingdom: Mythmaking on the Saudi Oil Frontier*. Stanford, CA: Stanford University Press, 2007.

Chapter 6. Capitalism in Egypt, Not Egyptian Capitalism

Abbas, Raouf, and Assem El-Dessouky. *The Large Landowning Class and the Peasantry in Egypt, 1837–1952*. Translated by Amer Mohsen and Mona Zikri. 1st ed. Syracuse, NY: Syracuse University Press, 2012.

Bush, Ray. *Economic Crisis and the Politics of Reform in Egypt*. Boulder, CO: Westview, 1999.

Fraser, Nancy. "Behind Marx's Hidden Abode: For an Expanded Conception of Capitalism." *New Left Review*, no. 86 (March–April 2014): 55–72.

Goldberg, Ellis. *Trade, Reputation, and Child Labor in Twentieth-Century Egypt*. New York: Palgrave Macmillan, 2004.

Jakes, Aaron. *Egypt's Occupation: Colonial Economism and the Crises of Capitalism*. Stanford, CA: Stanford University Press, 2020.

Jakes, Aaron, and Ahmad Shokr. "Finding Value in Empire of Cotton." *Critical Historical Studies* 4, no. 1 (Spring 2017): 107–36.

Mitchell, Timothy. *Rule of Experts: Egypt, Techno-Politics, Modernity*. Berkeley: University of California Press, 2002.

Moore, Jason. *Capitalism in the Web of Life: Ecology and the Accumulation of Capital*. New York: Verso, 2015.

Owen, Edward Roger John. *Cotton and the Egyptian Economy, 1820–1914: A Study in Trade and Development*. Oxford: Clarendon, 1969.

Richards, Alan. *Egypt's Agricultural Development, 1800–1980*. Boulder, CO: Westview, 1982.

Shokr, Ahmad. "Beyond the Field: Cotton and the End of Empire in Egypt, 1919–1956." PhD diss., New York University, 2016.

Soliman, Samer. *The Autumn of Dictatorship: Fiscal Crisis and Political Change in Egypt under Mubarak*. Stanford, CA: Stanford University Press, 2011.

Tignor, Robert. *State, Private Enterprise, and Economic Change in Egypt, 1918–1952*. Princeton, NJ: Princeton University Press, 1984.

Vitalis, Robert. *When Capitalists Collide: Business Conflict and the End of Empire in Egypt*. Berkeley: University of California Press, 1995.

Waterbury, John. *The Egypt of Nasser and Sadat: The Political Economy of Two Regimes*. Princeton, NJ: Princeton University Press, 1983.

Chapter 7. State, Oil, and War in the Formation of Iraq

Alahmad, Nida. "The Politics of Oil and State Survival in Iraq (1991–2003): Beyond the Rentier Thesis." *Constellations* 14 (2007): 586–612.

Alahmad, Nida. "Illuminating a State: State-Building and Electricity in Occupied Iraq." *Humanity: An International Journal of Human Rights, Humanitarianism, and Development* 8 (2017a): 335–53.

Alahmad, Nida, and Arang Keshavarzian. "A War on Multiple Fronts." *Middle East Report* 257 (2010): 17–28.

Alnasrawi, Abbas. *The Economy of Iraq: Oil, Wars, Destruction of Development and Prospects, 1950–2010*. Westport, CT: Greenwood, 1994.

Batatu, Hanna. *The Old Social Classes and the Revolutionary Movements of Iraq: A Study of Iraq's Old Landed and Commercial Classes and of Its Communists, Ba'thists and Free Officers*. London: SAQI, 2004 [1978].

Dodge, Toby. *Inventing Iraq: The Failure of Nation Building and a History Denied*. New York: Columbia University Press, 2003.

Farouk-Sluglett, Marion, and Peter Sluglett. "The Historiography of Modern Iraq." *American Historical Review* 29 (1991): 1408–21.

Harling, Peter. "Beyond Political Ruptures: Towards a Historiography of Social Continuity in Iraq." In *Writing the Modern History of Iraq: Historiographical and Political Challenges*, edited by Jordi Tejel, Peter Sluglett, Riccardo Bocco, and Hamit Bozarslan, 61–86. Hackensack, NJ: World Scientific, 2015 [2012].

Jabar, Faleh A. "Sheikhs and Ideologues: Deconstruction and Reconstruction of Tribes under Patrimonial Totalitarianism in Iraq, 1968–1998." In *Tribes and Power: Nationalism and Ethnicity in the Middle East*, edited by Faleh A. Jabar and Hosham Dawod, 69–109. London: SAQI, 2003.

al-Khafaji, Isam. "State Incubation of Iraqi Capitalism." *Middle East Report* 16 (1986).

Makiya, Kanan. *Republic of Fear: The Politics of Modern Iraq*. Berkeley: University of California Press, 1998 [1989].

Moore, Pete, and Christopher Parker. "The War Economy of Iraq." *Middle East Report* 243 (2007): 6–15.

Pursley, Sara. "'Lines Drawn on an Empty Map': Iraq's Borders and the Legend of the Artificial State (Parts 1 & 2)." *Jadaliyya*, June 2 and June 3, 2015. http://www.jadaliyya.com/Details/32140/%60Lines-Drawn-on-an-Empty-Map%60-Iraq's-Borders-and-the-Legend-of-the-Artificial-State-Part-1.

Sassoon, Joseph. "Iraq's Political Economy Post 2003: From Transition to Corruption." *International Journal of Contemporary Iraqi Studies* 10, no. 1&2 (2016): 17–33.

Sassoon, Joseph. *Saddam Hussein's Ba'th Party: Inside an Authoritarian Regime*. New York: Cambridge University Press, 2012.

al-Wardi, 'Ali. *Lamahat ijtima'iyya min tarikh al-'iraq al-hadith*, Vol. 2, *1831–1872*. London: Alwarrak [1969–1979].

al-Wardi, 'Ali. *Lamahat ijtima'iyya min tarikh al-'iraq al-hadith,* Vol. 3, *1876–1914*. London: Alwarrak [1969–1979]

Chapter 8. Colonial Capitalism and Imperial Myth in French North Africa

Amin, Samir. *L'Économie du Maghreb*. Paris: Éditions de Minuit, 1967.

Ageron, Charles-Robert. *Les chemins de la décolonisation de l'empire colonial français*. Paris: L'Institut d'histoire du temps présent, 1986.

Bennoune, Mahfoud. "Primary Capital Accumulation in Colonial Tunisia." *Dialectical Anthropology* 4, no. 3 (1979): 83–100.

Bonin, Hubert. *Un outre-mer bancaire méditerranéen: histoire du Crédit foncier d'Algérie et de Tunisie, 1880–1997*. Paris: Société française d'histoire d'outre-mer, 2004.

Clément, Alain. "L'analyse économique de la question coloniale en France (1870–1914)." *Revue d'économie politique* 123, no. 1 (2013): 51–82.

Davis, Diana K. *Resurrecting the Granary of Rome: Environmental History and French Colonial Expansion in North Africa*. Athens: Ohio University Press, 2007.

Hodeir, Catherine, Hubert Bonin, and Jean-François Klein, eds. *L'esprit économique impérial (1830–1870)*. Paris: Publication de la SFHOM, 2008.

Lefeuvre, Daniel. *Chère Algérie: comptes et mécomptes de la tutelle coloniale, 1930–1962*. Saint-Denis: Société française d'histoire d'outre-mer, 1997.

Marseille, Jacques. *Empire colonial et capitalisme français: Histoire d'un divorce*. Paris: Albin Michel, 1984.

Saul, Samir. *Intérêts économiques français et décolonisation de l'Afrique du Nord (1945–1962)*. Geneva: Droz, 2016.

Swearingen, Will. *Moroccan Mirages: Agrarian Dreams and Deceptions, 1912–1986*. Princeton, NJ: Princeton University Press, 1987.

White, Gregory. *A Comparative Political Economy of Morocco and Tunisia: On the Outside of Europe Looking In*. Albany: State University of New York Press, 2001.

Chapter 9. Lebanon Beyond Exceptionalism

Abissab, Malek. *Militant Women of a Fragile Nation*. Syracuse, NY: Syracuse University Press, 2010.

Baumann, Hannes. *Citizen Hariri: Lebanon's Neo-Liberal Reconstruction*. Oxford: Oxford University Press, 2017.

Couland, Jacques. *Le mouvement syndical au Liban (1919–1946): Son évolution pendant le mandat français de l'occupation à l'évacuation et au Code du travail*. Preface by Jacques Berque. Paris: Editions Sociales, 1970.

Dahir, Masoud. *al-Judhur al-tarikhiyya li'l-mas'ala al-zira'iyya al-lubnaniyya, 1900–1950*. Beirut: Manshurat al-Jami'a al-Lubnaniyya, 1983.

Dubar, Claude, and Salim Nasr. *Les classes sociales au Liban*. Paris: Les Presses de Sciences Po, 1976.

Fawaz, Leila Tarazi. *Merchants and Migrants in Nineteenth-Century Beirut*. Cambridge, MA: Harvard University Press, 1983.

Gaspard, Toufic. *A Political Economy of Lebanon, 1948–2002: The Limits of Laissez Faire*. New York: Brill, 2004.

Gates, Carolyn. *The Merchant Republic of Lebanon: Rise of an Open Economy*. London: I. B. Tauris, 1998.

Gendzier, Irene L. *Notes from the Minefield: United States Intervention in Lebanon and the Middle East, 1945–1958*. New York: Columbia University Press, 2006.

Khater, Akram Fouad. *Inventing Home: Emigration, Gender, and the Middle Class in Lebanon, 1870–1920*. Berkeley: University of California Press, 2001.

Khuri-Makdisi, Ilham. *The Eastern Mediterranean and the Making of Global Radicalism, 1860–1914*. Berkeley: University of California Press, 2010.

Leenders, Reinoud. *Spoils of Truce: Corruption and State-Building in Postwar Lebanon*. Ithaca, NY: Cornell University Press, 2012.

Nucho, Joanne Randa. *Everyday Sectarianism in Urban Lebanon: Infrastructure, Public Services, and Power*. Princeton, NJ: Princeton University Press, 2016.

Picard, Elizabeth. "The Political Economy of Civil War in Lebanon." In *War, Institutions, and Social Change in the Middle East*, edited by Steven Heydemann. Berkeley: University of California Press, 2000.

Safieddine, Hicham. *Banking on the State: The Financial Foundations of Lebanon*. Stanford, CA: Stanford University Press, 2019.

Thompson, Elizabeth. *Colonial Citizens: Republican Rights, Paternal Privilege, and Gender in French Syria and Lebanon*. New York: Columbia University Press, 2000.

Chapter 10. The US-Israeli Alliance

Anziska, Seth. *Preventing Palestine: A Political History from Camp David to Oslo*. Princeton, NJ: Princeton University Press, 2018.

Cohen, Avner, and William Burr. "What the U.S. Government Really Thought of Israel's

Apparent 1979 Nuclear Test," *Politico*, 8 December 2016, https://www.politico.com/magazine/story/2016/12/1979-vela-incident-nuclear-test-israel-south-africa-214507.

Elgindy, Khaled. *Blind Spot: America and the Palestinians, from Balfour to Trump.* Washington DC: Brookings Institution, 2019.

Gendzier, Irene. *Dying to Forget: Oil, Power, Palestine, and the Foundations of U.S. Policy in the Middle East.* New York: Columbia University Press, 2015.

Gordon, Neve. "The Political Economy of Israel's Homeland Security/Surveillance Industry." The New Transparency Project, Queen's University, Kingston, Canada, Working Paper III, April 28, 2009. https://qspace.library.queensu.ca/bitstream/handle/1974/1941/The%2520Political%2520Economy%2520of%2520Israel%25E2%2580%2599s%2520Homeland%2520Security.pdf.

Graham, Stephen. *Cities Under Siege: The New Military Urbanism.* London: Verso, 2011.

Halper, Jeff. *War Against the People: Israel, the Palestinians and Global Pacification.* London: Pluto, 2015.

Jamail, Milton, and Margo Guttierez. *It's No Secret: Israel's Military Involvement in Central America.* Belmont, MA: Association of Arab American University Graduates, 1986.

Judis, John B. *Genesis: Truman, American Jews, and the Origins of the Arab/Israeli Conflict.* New York: Farrar, Straus, and Giroux, 2014.

McAlister, Melani. *Epic Encounters: Culture, Media, and U.S. Interests in the Middle East, 1945–2000.* Berkeley: University of California Press, 2001.

Mearsheimer, John J., and Stephen M. Walt. *The Israel Lobby and U.S. Foreign Policy.* New York: Farrar, Straus and Giroux, 2007.

Obenzinger, Hilton. "In the Shadow of 'God's Sun-Dial': The Construction of American Christian Zionism and the Blackstone Memorial." *Stanford Humanities Review* 5, no. 1 (1995): 60–79.

Ruebner, Josh. *Shattered Hopes: Obama's Failure to Broker Israeli-Palestinian Peace.* London: Verso, 2013.

Sharp, Jeremy. *U.S. Foreign Aid to Israel.* Washington, DC: Congressional Research Service, August 7, 2019.

Thrall, Nathan. *The Only Language They Understand: Forcing Compromise in Israel and Palestine.* New York: Metropolitan Books, 2017.

Zunes, Stephen. "The Israel Lobby: How Powerful is it Really?" *Foreign Policy in Focus*, May 16, 2016.

Chapter 11. Repercussions of Colonialism in the Occupied Palestinian Territories

Abed, George. "The Palestinian Economy Under Occupation: Introduction and Overview." In *The Palestinian Economy: Studies in Development Under Prolonged Occupation*, edited by George Abed, 1–12. London: Routledge, 1988.

Arnon, Arie, Israel Luski, Avia Spivak, and Jimmy Weinblatt. *The Palestinian Economy: Between Imposed Integration and Voluntary Separation*. New York: Brill, 1997.

Farsakh, Leila. *Palestinian Labour Migration to Israel: Labour, Land and Occupation*. London: Routledge, 2005.

Hamed, Osama. *Palestinian Banking Sector: Statistical Study—Issue 1*. Ramallah: Palestine Economic Policy Research Institute, 1995.

Hamed, Osama, and Radwan Shaban. "One Sided Customs and Monetary Union: The Case of the West Bank and Gaza Strip under Israeli Occupation." In *The Economics of Middle East Peace*, edited by Stanley Fischer, Dany Rodrik, and Elias Tuma, 117–48. Cambridge, MA: MIT Press, 1993.

Naqib, Fadle. *Economic Aspects of the Palestinian–Israeli Conflict: The Collapse of the Oslo Accord*. Discussion paper no. 2002/100, United Nations University. Japan: World Institute for Development Economics Research Discussion Paper Series, 2002.

Palestinian Authority. *The Palestinian National Early Recovery and Reconstruction Plan for Gaza 2009–2010*. Presented at the International Conference in Support of the Palestinian Economy for the Reconstruction of Gaza, Sharm El-Sheik, March 2009.

Roy, Sarah. "De-development Revisited: Palestinian Economy and Society Since Oslo." *Journal of Palestine Studies* 28, no. 3 (1999): 64–82.

Seikaly, Sherene. *Men of Capital: Scarcity and Economy in Mandate Palestine*. Stanford, CA: Stanford University Press, 2016.

Shaban, Radwan. "Worsening Economic Outcomes Since 1994 Despite Elements of Improvement." In *Development Under Adversity: The Palestinian Economy in Transition*, edited by Radwan Shaban and Ishaq Diwan, 17–32. Ramallah: Palestine Economic Policy Research Institute, 1999.

United Nations Office for the Coordination of Humanitarian Affairs. *The Humanitarian Impact on Palestinians of Israeli Settlements and Other Infrastructure in the West Bank*. Jerusalem: United Nations Office for the Coordination of Humanitarian Affairs, 2007.

Van Arkadie, Brian. *Benefits and Burdens: A Report on the West Bank and Gaza Strip Economies Since 1967.* Washington, DC: Carnegie Endowment for International Peace, 1977.

World Bank. *Developing the Occupied Territories: An Investment in Peace, vol. 2, The Economy.* Washington, DC: World Bank, 1993.

Index

'Abbud, Ahmad, 18
'Abduh, Muhammad, 12
Abella family, 33
Abu Ghazala, 'Abd al-Halim, 88
Adelson, Sheldon, 210–11, 212, 214
Aflaq, Michel, 47
'Afula, 44
"Agenda for Ottoman History" (Islamoğlu-İnan and Keyder), 17
Agricultural and Manufacturing Council, 36
'Ajlun, 41
Alexandria, 34, 39, 41, 128
Algeria: arms manufacturing in, 97; expansion of European economic power in, 165–66; French conquest of, 164, 166; role of the military in, 86, 88, 90, 92; and the second colonial occupation, 176–77; settler colonialism in, 163, 167–68; wine production in, 163, 169–70, 282n39; in WWI, 174
Ali, Mehmet: and depersonalization of labor, 32; and industrial armaments production, 96; and state centralization, 35, 38, 41, 125–128
American Israel Public Affairs Committee (AIPAC), 210, 211, 212
Amin, Samir, 17
Anatolia, 41
Angleton, James Jesus, 197–98
Anglo-American Middle East Supply Centre, 186
Anglo-Iranian Oil Company, 71, 76
Anglo-Ottoman Convention (1838), 35, 48
Arab-Israeli War of 1967: and the end of developmentalist projects, 46, 53, 55–56, 58, 137–38, 189–90; and the U.S.-Israeli alliance, 196, 198, 199, 200
Arab–Israeli War of 1973, 58, 80, 99, 200, 202
Arab Organization for Industrialization, 96

Arab Socialist Union, 53, 54, 55
Aramco, 9
Asad, Bashar, 65
Asad, Hafiz, 56, 60, 64
Asad, Talal, 16
Aswan High Dam, 2, 53–54, 89, 135

Bahrain. *See* Gulf region
Bank Misr, 18, 49, 54, 132. *See also* Misr Spinning and Weaving
Baring, Evelyn (Lord Cromer), 12, 129
Ba'th Party: of Iraq, 143–44, 150–52, 156; of Syria, 7, 47, 50, 53, 55
Batrun district of Mount Lebanon, 30
Before European Hegemony: The World System A.D. 1250– 1350 (Abu-Lughod), 10
Beirut, 33, 34, 181, 192: 1983 U.S. Embassy bombing in, 200, 201, 206; absentee landowners in, 30; port of, 33, 35, 41, 182, 186, 194, 195, 286n17, 286n18
Ben Ali, Zine al-Abidine, 7, 65
berat, 33. *See also* capitulations
Beyhum family, 34, 37
Blackstone, William, 197
Boeing, 203, 204–5, 206
Bouazizi, Mohammed, 65
bourgeoisie: agrarian segment of, 60, 65; and colonial capitalism, 17; in Egypt, 63; in Syria, 66–67; transnational formations of, 116. *See also* *effendiyya*; military officers, and the political economy of the MENA; national bourgeoisie; *patronat*; state bourgeoisie
Bourguiba, Habib, 7, 48, 50, 52, 56–58, 60, 177
Boycott, Divestment, and Sanctions Movement, 202, 213, 226
Bretton Woods system, 13–15
Britain: attempts by to maintain control over oil production, 76; coal workers in, 74–75; colonial governments of, 44, 47, 128–31, 145, 153–54, 215
BP, 73. *See also* Anglo-Iranian Oil Company
Bush, Laura, 13
Bustrus family, 33

Cairo, 2, 33, 62
capitalism: and colonialism, 51–52, 161–64, 178; emergence and characteristics of, 17, 25–29, 37–38, 44–45; in the Gulf region, 105–07, 111–15, 118–20; and "primitive accumulation," 26–28, 34–35, 124–25; and spatial formations, 123–24, 130, 141–42; in relation to state and social formation, 6–8, 32–34, 110; and the world market, 10, 11, 17, 34, 125. *See also* joint-stock companies; land; national bourgeoise; peasants; state bourgeoise; workers
Capitalism and Underdevelopment in Latin America (Frank), 17
Capitalist Agriculture and the Origins of the European World-Economy in the Sixteenth Century (Wallerstein), 17
capitulations, 33, 165, 166
Carver, Alexander Sidney Henton, 42
CIA, 197, 198, 201, 202, 206

Challenging Colonialism (Davis), 18, 270n50
Chevron, 73
class: in relation to gender and empire, 11–13, 20; in the Gulf region, 105–7; and migration, 182; and social formation, 1–3; and state formation, 110, 114–15, 145, 149–50, 151–52, 158, 180, 183–84; transnational formations of, 115–16, 180. *See also effendiyya*; military officers, and the political economy of the MENA; national bourgeoisie; *patronat*; peasants; state bourgeoisie; workers
Clinton, Hillary, 213
De la colonisation chez les peoples modernes (Leroy-Beaulieu), 162–63, 171
Committee of Union and Progress, 37, 44
Constitutional Bloc, 184, 186
corvée, 27, 28, 31, 38, 126, 128. *See also* capitalism, and "primitive accumulation"
Cotton, 10, 17; *See also* Egypt, cultivation of cotton in; Iraq, cotton trade in; Palestine, cotton trade in; Syria, cotton trade in
Cyclone, 204, 205

Damascus, 34, 39, 181
Dance of the Dialectic (Ollman), 7
Democratic Party, 196, 197, 210–13
development: and the expansion of state power, 148–52; idea and studies of, 8–9, 148; and the second colonial occupation, 176–77. *See also* import-substitution industrialization (ISI); modernization theory
Dinshaway incident, 12

Economic Reform and Structural Adjustment Programs, 89: in Egypt, 62; and the expansion of Gulf capital in MENA, 115; military exceptions to, 89–91; in Tunisia, 65, 225. *See also* international financial institutions; International Monetary Fund; neoliberalism; World Bank
Effendiyya, 3, 149
Egypt: arms manufacturing in, 96; cotton cultivation in, 2, 29, 34–41, 47–48, 53, 124, 126–31, 133, 135, 139; debt and investment in, 127–30, 139–41; economic relations with Gulf countries, 116; effects of the Great Depression in, 133–34; independence movement in, 48–50, 130–34; landlords in, 2, 31, 37, 38, 49, 53, 58, 127, 133–34; 136; role of the military in, 63, 66, 86, 88, 90, 91; shortage of capital in, 124–25, 129; U.S. military aid to, 59, 91, 98, 199. *See also* land; Nasser; national bourgeoise; peasants; Sadat, Anwar; state bourgeoise; workers
Egyptian Labor Corps, 37
Elbit, 201, 204, 205, 206
Elisra Group, 201, 204
Enver Pasha, 37
ExxonMobil, 73

F-35 stealth fighter jet, 204
Fatah, 225

Fayyad family, 33
Fayyad, Salam, 225–26
France: colonial governments of, 48, 161–65, 171–72, 174–75, 183–86, 287n25 (*see also names of specific countries*); coal workers in, 74–75. *See also* French Algeria
Free Officers, 53, 134–35, 135, 154
French Algeria: early development of, 166–67; as an example to other colonies, 171–72; heroes of, 168–69; identity of settlers in, 170; insurrections in, 170–71; and trade with mainland France, 171–72; wine production in, 163, 169–70. *See also* Algeria

Gaza Strip, 224–25, 228, 231
Gemmayzeh neighborhood of Beirut, 33
"Gender: A Useful Category of Historical Analysis" (Scott), 20
genocide, 2, 17, 203
Ghanima, Yusuf, 146
globalization, 15, 86, 131, 175
Globalization and the Politics of Development in the Middle East (Henry and Springborg), 4, 6, 8, 10
grain, 36, 37, 41, 57, 125, 126, 135, 138, 146, 168, 174, 183. *See also* wheat
Gramsci, Antonio, 4, 7
The Great Divergence: China, Europe, and the Making of the Modern World Economy (Pomeranz), 10
Greece, 98
Gulf Cooperation Council, 105
Gulf region: industrial activity in, 111–13; and investments in MENA region, 59, 63, 115–16, 193; migrant workforce in, 116–20, 219–20; and the Nixon Doctrine, 200; patterns of capital ownership and control in, 113–15. *See also* oil; workers, in the Gulf region, in the oil industry, remittances of
Gulf War of 1991, 62, 93, 140, 147, 157, 220

Hadj, Messali, 174
Hama region, 181
Hamas, 225
Harb, Tal'at, 18, 37, 132, 133
al-Hariri, Rafiq, 192
Hawran region, 39, 41, 47, 56, 181
Hollande, François, 13

IMI Systems, 201, 205, 207
Ibrahim Bey, 31, 32
import-substitution industrialization (ISI), 52, 55, 57. *See also* development
Industrial Sexuality (Hammad), 2
infitah, 46, 58, 59, 61, 65, 138, 140
international financial institutions (IFIs), 5, 6, 14–16, 20, 46, 59, 61, 62
International Monetary Fund, 14–16, 89. *See also* Economic Reform and Structural Adjustment Programs; international financial institutions (IFIs)
Iran: and climate change, 84; influence of in Lebanon, 193, 195; and international arms deals, 94–95, 99; oil production in, 15, 75–77, 80–83, 157; Shi'i pilgrims in, 146; and the U.S.-Israeli alliance,

200–1, 206, 211, 213–14; workers in the oil industry of, 74–75
Iran Between Two Revolutions (Abrahamian), 18
Iran-Contra Affair, 202
Iranian Revolution of 1979, 200
Iran-Iraq War: economic effects of, 88, 147, 150, 159, 160; and international arms deals, 98; and oil, 94, 157–58, 159
Iraq: arms manufacturing in, 96; borders of, 145; climate change in, 84; cotton trade in, 146; development projects in, 148–52; education in, 149–51; effect of economic sanctions on, 147, 155; food rationing in, 155; infrastructure in, 145–48; and international arms deals, 94–95, 99; Jewish community of, 146, 149; landlords, 153–55; localization of governance in, 155–56; role of the military in, 86, 88; and oil, 75–77; 147–48, 156–58; U.S. military aid to, 199. *See also* Iran-Iraq war, economic effects of, and oil
Iraq Petroleum Company, 76–77, 157
Iraq War of 2003: and historiography of Iraq, 144–45
Islam and Capitalism (Rodinson), 25–26
The Islamic Roots of Capitalism (Gran), 25
Isma'il Pasha, 36, 38, 44, 48, 128, 132, 133
Israel: arms production in, 201–2; and international arms deals, 98; and military assistance to other countries, 202–3; and policing in the U.S., 206–7; and settler colonialism, 198; strategic importance of to U.S., 200–1. *See also* U.S.-Israeli alliance; Palestine; Palestinian occupied territories
Israel Aerospace Industries (IAI), 201, 204, 205

Jadid, Salah, 55
Jaffa, 35
Jamal Pasha, 37
The Jewish Colonization Association, 36, 42, 44
Jewish National Fund, 36, 42, 44
joint-stock companies, 19, 34: land sales of, 43; and the objectification of labor, 43; vertical integration of, 36–39; and oil, 72–74; women's participation in, 34, 44. *See also* Lebanon, landlords in; Syria, landlords in; peasants, and abstraction of labor, erosion of rights of, efforts to retain usufruct rights by
Jordan: arms manufacturing in, 97; role of the military in, 90, 92, 93; and the occupation of the West Bank, 216
Jubayl district of Mount Lebanon, 30
Jubayli family, 30, 33

Kafr al-Zayyat Cotton Company Ltd, 42
Keynesianism, 13–15, 87, 90
Kisrawan district of Mount Lebanon, 30, 33
Kuwait. *See* Gulf region; Gulf War of 1991; military; military aid; military armaments; military officers

land: efforts to reform ownership of, 53, 134, 136, 149, 152–56; joint-stock purchases of, 38–40; under Ottoman rule, 29–34, 41–42, 152; ownership of in French Tunisia and Morocco, 172–73; regimes of labor on, 28, 41–42; 40–41, 38; and settler colonialism in Algeria, 165, 167–68. *See also* peasants
landlords. *See the names of specific countries*
Lebanon: challenges to the colonial order in, 186; class formation in, 180, 181, 183, 187–88, 189–90; emigration from, 182; European investment capital in, 182; exclusion of in scholarship, 179–80; French colonial policies in, 183–85; industrial activity in, 40–41, 193; landlords in, 39, 183; post–colonial economic development of, 179, 189–92; in regional and world economies, 188–89; republican system of, 184; role of militias in, 190–92; sectarianism in, 179–80; silk production in, 181–83; specificities of neoliberalism in, 193–95; state formation in, 180, 181, 183, 186, 289n48; and WWI, 182–83; workers movement in, 185, 190. *See also* joint-stock companies
Lebanese Civil War, 179, 190–91
Levant. *See* Anatolia; Lebanon; Syria
The Liberation of Women (Amin), 12
Libya. *See* military; military aid; military armaments; military officers; oil
Lockheed Martin, 94, 99, 203–4
Luxemburg, Rosa, 4, 36

Majali family, 93
Makhlouf, Rami, 67
mandate governments, 19, 27, 47, 153–54, 185, 215. *See also* Britain, colonial governments of; France, colonial governments of
Mardam-Beg family, 39
Marseille, Jacques, 161, 175, 177
Marx, Karl, 2, 4, 25, 28, 108, 124
Marxism: and approaches to political economy, 6, 17–18, 19, 25, 27, 107, 177; critiques of, 25
Marxists, 7, 53, 134, 174
Memories of Revolt (Swedenburg), 19
Men of Capital (Seikaly), 19
merchants: in the early modern period, 26–27, 30–34, 146; under Mehmet Ali, 126–27; in the Syrian independence movement, 50. *See also* joint-stock companies
Mersin-Adana (Anatolia), 41, 42
Midhat Pasha, 148–149, 152–53
military: role of in economies of MENA, 87–92, 95–97; role of in politics, 86–87, 93–94
military aid, 59, 91, 98, 198–200
military armaments: and capitalism, 97–98; global industry of, 86; and lobbying, 99–100; and petrodollar recycling, 80–82, 85, 94–95; regional production of, 95–100, 201–2; and the U.S.-Israeli alliance, 196, 198–99, 201, 203

military officers: global networks of, 85, 98–99; 207–08, 258n27; and the political economy of the MENA, 63, 66, 85, 92–93
La mise en valeur des colonies (Sarraut), 175
Misr Spinning and Weaving, 2, 133. *See also* Bank Misr
modernization theory, 9, 16–18, 26, 87. *See also* development, idea and studies of
Morocco: expansion of European economic power in, 165–66; under French rule, 172–73; trade with France, 171–72; in WWI, 174. *See also* France, colonial governments of
Morsi, Muhammad, 91
Mosaddeq, Muhammad, 76
Mubarak, Hosni, 7, 61–63, 88, 91, 101, 140–41
Murad Bey, 31, 32
Musa, Nabawiyya, 12
Muslim Brotherhood, 53, 62, 167, 225

Nabarawi, Ceza, 12
Nasif, Malak Hifni, 12
Nasser, Gamal Abdel: charisma of, 47, 54; policies of, 53–54, 58–59, 88, 134–38
National Bloc, 184, 186
national bourgeoisie, 17–18, 32–33
National Democratic Party, 62, 141
nationalism: economic aspects of, 49, 132–33; and the petroleum industry, 9
Nazareth, 41
Neo-Destour party, 48, 52, 56, 57, 60, 177
neoliberalism, 9, 15, 46: in Egypt, 138–41; in Lebanon, 193–94; and oil, 82; in Palestine, 225–26; in Syria, 64; in Tunisia, 64–65; and the uprisings of 2011, 65–66. *See also* Economic Reform and Structural Adjustment Programs; international financial institutions (IFIs); International Monetary Fund; Sadat, Anwar; Washington Consensus; World Bank
Nixon, Richard, 15, 80, 200, 213
North African Star (Étoile Nord-Africaine, ENA), 174

Obama, Barak, 212, 213
Oil: creating demand for, 71–72; and the Gulf states, 15, 20, 72, 105; and military spending, 80–82; and petrodollar recycling, 80–82, 85, 94–95, 138, 199–200; and the political economy of Iraq, 156–58; price of, 78–80; restricting the supply of, 69–71; and the state, 7, 9, 20; and the study of political economy, 68–69; and war, 157–58; and workers, 74–75, 158; and U.S. empire, 213
oil corporations: and producer states, 72–74, 75–77, 78–80, 157 (*see also* rentier state theory); and U.S. power, 82
oil crisis of 1973, 9, 79–80; 139–40
The Old Social Classes and the Revolutionary Movements of Iraq (Batatu), 18, 143
Oman. *See* Gulf region; military; military aid; military armaments; military officers

Oslo Peace Accords, 222–23, 224, 226–27
Ottoman Empire: rule of in MENA region, 11, 125, 148–50, 152–53; and World-Systems theory, 17. *See also* joint-stock companies, land purchases of; land, under Ottoman rule; peasants
Ottoman Land Code of 1858, 152–53
Over-Stating the Arab State (Ayubi), 6
OPEC, 69, 70, 79
Owen, Roger, 16, 27

Palestine: capital flight from, 188, 216; cotton trade in, 32, 33; entrepreneurs in, 19, settler colonialism in, 42; territories of under Jordanian rule, 216; under the British mandate, 215; underdevelopment of, 215
PLO, 225
Palestinian Authority, 223: neoliberal economic policies of, 225–26
Palestinian Nakba, 188, 213, 215–16
Palestinian occupied territories: and the Apartheid Wall, 224, 226; banking and finance in, 218–19, 227–28; closures in, 223–24, 228; economic dependency of, 222; effect of Israeli customs union on economy of, 218, 227; GDP of, 219–20, 228–29; importance of foreign aid to economy of, 233–34; increasing consumption and declining investment in, 220–21; industrial and service sectors in, 222, 230–31; Israeli administration of, 216–19, 221, 223, 226–27; Israeli companies subcontracting arrangements in, 221, 227; land confiscations in, 217, 223; possible economic effect of BDS for, 226; poverty and inequality in, 233; resistance to Israeli polices in, 226; trade of, 227, 229; unemployment in, 229, 231; workers from, 219–20, 228; 232
The Pasha's Peasants (Cuno), 19, 25–27
The Passing of Traditional Society (Lerner), 9
Patronat, 161, 168–69
peasants: and abstraction of labor, 32–33, 42; and agricultural cooperatives in Tunisia, 57–58; efforts to retain usufruct rights by, 43; erosion of rights of, 38, 154; and European financiers, 129–30; nationalist attempts to reform, 133–34; and settler colonialism in Algeria, 167–68; in Tunisian independence movement, 52; under Gamal Abdel Nasser, 136; under Mehmet Ali, 126. *See also* land
Polanyi, Karl, 4
political economy, 1–4, 8: and climate change, 83–84; Marxist approaches to, 2, 17–19, 25, 28, 107, 108–9, 124, 177; and studies of the Gulf region, 105–6; and studies of Lebanon, 179–80
A Political Economy of the Middle East (Richards and Waterbury), 4–6, 10
Prebisch, Raúl, 17

Qasim, 'Abd al-Karim, 76
Qatar. *See* Gulf region; military; military

aid; military armaments; military officers
Quwwatli family, 39

Rafael Advanced Defense Systems, 201, 204, 206
Rashad, Ibrahim, 133
Reagan, Ronald, 15, 196, 200, 201, 202, 203, 211
Rediscovering Palestine (Doumani), 19, 25–27
Regulation of Peasant Agriculture (1829), 38
Rentier state theory, 7, 77–78, 106–110, 116, 144, 156–58, 160

Sadat, Anwar, 7, 58–59, 62, 88, 96, 138–40
al-Sa'dun, Nasir, 149, 153
Sa'dun tribe, 153
Sa'id Pasha, 48, 127
Saint-Simonians, 165, 166–67
Saudi Arabia: and the U.S., 14, 15, 71, 200. *See also* Gulf region; military; military aid; military armaments; military officers; oil
Schriock, Stephanie, 210
Sha'arawi, Huda, 12
Shari'a courts, 19, 43
Shell, 73, 95
Sidqi, Isma'il, 132, 133
silk, 33–35, 39, 42, 146, 181–83
Singer, Paul, 211
Sisi, Abdel Fattah, 7, 66, 101, 141
slavery, 2, 26, 28, 162, 164, 181. *See also* capitalism, and "primitive accumulation"
Smith, Adam, 4
socialism: in Egypt, 52–56, 138; roll back of, 58–65; in Syria, 52–56; in Tunisia, 56–58
The Stages of Economic Growth (Rostow), 8–9
state: and social formation, 6–7, 107, 110, 114–15; and capital accumulation in Egypt, 124–25; in the historiography of Iraq, 143–44
state bourgeoisie, 6–7, 63–64, 136–37
Structural Adjustment. *See* Economic Reform and Structural Adjustment Programs
Sudan: role of the military in, 86
Suez Canal, 35, 47, 48, 49, 54, 127, 128, 136, 138, 139, 140: effect of on Iraqi economy, 146
Suez War, 136
Sufis, 167–68
Sursuq family, 30, 33, 34, 36, 37, 42
Sursuq, Negib Joseph, 42
Süleymaniye Cami Ve İmaret İnşaat (Barkan), 32
Syria, 47; climate change in, 84; cotton trade in, 39; independence movement in, 50; landlords in, 31, 35, 40, 41, 50–51, 55; role of the military in, 86, 88, 92, 93

Tabat family, 33, 37
Taghdisi-Rad, Sahar, 234
Talaat Pasha, 37

Templers, 36, 37, 42
Thatcher, Margaret, 15
Tlass family, 93
tobacco, 10, 17, 34, 41, 171, 174, 182, 183
Trad family, 33, 37
Treaty of Balta Limanı. *See* Anglo-Ottoman Convention
tribes, 152–155, 160, 173, 278n57
Truman, Harry, 8, 197, 212
Trump, Donald, 100, 198, 199, 211, 212, 213
Tueni family, 33
Tunisia, 47–48: development policies in, 7; expansion of European economic power in, 165–66; independence movement in, 52; landowners in, 52, 58, 60, 65; post-independence period of, 56–58; poverty rate of, 5; trade with France, 171–72; under French rule, 51–52, 172–73; in WWI, 174
Turkey. *See* military; military aid; military armaments; military officers

al-'Umar, Zahir, 33
Union Générale Tunisienne du Travail (UGTT), 48, 52, 56, 61, 64, 67, 173
United Arab Emirates. *See* Gulf region; military; military aid; military officers; military armaments; oil
United Arab Republic (UAR), 50–51, 53–54, 55
United Egyptian Lands Limited, 42
United States: foreign policy toward MENA, 85, 213; post–WWII role of, 13–16; production and consumption of oil in, 70, 71; 72; support of coups in MENA, 76, 82
U.S.-Israel alliance: and arms development, 203–5; constancy of, 196; costs and tensions of, 198, 203; and Holocaust, 196, 197; material and strategic components of, 197, 205–9; and oil, 82; and protestant theology, 196–97; and technology firms, 209; and U.S. empire, 213–14; and U.S. politics, 210–13
USS *Liberty*, 198
Universal Maritime Suez Canal Company, 48
Uprisings of 2011: antecedents to, 63, 65; as evidence of failed economic polices, 20, 47, 64; and state coercion, 6; unresolved causes of, 67
'Urabi, Ahmad, 128

Vitalis, Robert, 18, 270n50

Wafd Party, 48–49
Waghorn, Thomas, 126
Washington Consensus, 15–16, 20, 46, 62, 67, 89, 90, 233
wheat, 33, 36, 37, 39, 125, 135, 169, 175, 183. *See also* grain
women: in the Egyptian labor force, 49; and gendered citizenship, 184; in the Iraqi labor force, 150–51; and joint-stock companies, 34, 44; and labor in Mount Lebanon, 35, 41; representa-

tions of, 13; in the Tunisian labor force, 54; unemployment of in Gaza, 229
Women in Nineteenth-Century Egypt (Tucker), 19–20
workers: in the Gulf region, 107, 116–20, 219–20, 265n38; in Iraq, 150; in the Israeli labor market, 219–20, 228; and labor movements, 63, 66, 185 (*see also* Union Générale Tunisienne du Travail); and the objectification of labor, 43; in the oil industry, 74–75, 77, 158; remittances of, 60, 65, 88, 117, 119, 139, 219, 220, 222; in silk factories, 35, 41; in WWI, 174
World Bank, 5, 8, 14, 177, 193, 233–34. *See also* international financial institutions (IFIs)
World Systems Theory, 17
World War I, 36–37, 42, 48, 130, 132, 174, 182–83

Yemen: climate change in, 84; Egyptian intervention in, 137; role of the military in, 86, 87; Saudi-UAE bombing campaign in, 100

Zaghlul, Sa'd, 48–49
Zionists: lobbying efforts of, 8, 197; settler colonial project of, 19; land purchases by, 36–37, 42–44

Stanford Studies *in* Middle Eastern *and* Islamic Societies *and* Cultures

Joel Beinin and Laleh Khalili, editors

Between Muslims: Religious Difference in Iraqi Kurdistan 2020
ANDREW BUSH

Showpiece City: How Architecture Made Dubai 2020
TODD REISZ

Archive Wars: The Politics of History in Saudi Arabia 2020
ROSIE BSHEER

The Optimist: A Social Biography of Tawfiq Zayyad 2020
TAMIR SOREK

Graveyard of Clerics: Everyday Activism in Saudi Arabia 2020
PASCAL MENORET

Cleft Capitalism: The Social Origins of Failed Market Making in Egypt 2020
AMR ADLY

The Universal Enemy: Jihad, Empire, and the Challenge of Solidarity 2019
DARRYL LI

Waste Siege: The Life of Infrastructure in Palestine 2019
SOPHIA STAMATOPOULOU-ROBBINS

Heritage and the Cultural Struggle for Palestine 2019
CHIARA DE CESARI,

Iran Reframed: Anxieties of Power in the Islamic Republic 2019
NARGES BAJOGHLI

Banking on the State: The Financial Foundations of Lebanon 2019
HICHAM SAFIEDDINE

Familiar Futures: Time, Selfhood, and Sovereignty in Iraq 2019
SARA PURSLEY

Hamas Contained: The Rise and Pacification of Palestinian Resistance 2018
TAREQ BACONI

Hotels and Highways: The Construction of Modernization Theory in Cold War Turkey 2018
BEGÜM ADALET

Bureaucratic Intimacies: Translating Human Rights in Turkey 2017
ELIF M. BABÜL

Impossible Exodus: Iraqi Jews in Israel 2017
ORIT BASHKIN

Brothers Apart: Palestinian Citizens of Israel and the Arab World 2017
MAHA NASSAR

Revolution without Revolutionaries: Making Sense of the Arab Spring 2017
ASEF BAYAT

Soundtrack of the Revolution: The Politics of Music in Iran 2017
NAHID SIAMDOUST

Copts and the Security State: Violence, Coercion, and Sectarianism in Contemporary Egypt 2016
LAURE GUIRGUIS

Circuits of Faith: Migration, Education, and the Wahhabi Mission 2016
MICHAEL FARQUHAR

Morbid Symptoms: Relapse in the Arab Uprising 2016
GILBERT ACHCAR

Imaginative Geographies of Algerian Violence: Conflict Science, Conflict Management, Antipolitics 2015
JACOB MUNDY